I0125846

Board of State Viticultural Commissioners

Directory of the Grape Growers, Wine Makers and Distillers of

California

and of the principal grape growers and wine makers of the eastern states

Board of State Viticultural Commissioners

Directory of the Grape Growers, Wine Makers and Distillers of California
and of the principal grape growers and wine makers of the eastern states

ISBN/EAN: 9783337331627

Printed in Europe, USA, Canada, Australia, Japan

Cover: Foto ©Andreas Hilbeck / pixelio.de

More available books at **www.hansebooks.com**

OF THE

GRAPE GROWERS, WINE MAKERS AND DISTILLERS

OF

CALIFORNIA,

AND OF THE

PRINCIPAL GRAPE GROWERS AND WINE MAKERS OF THE EASTERN STATES.

PUBLISHED BY THE

BOARD OF STATE VITICULTURAL COMMISSIONERS OF CALIFORNIA.

SACRAMENTO:
STATE OFFICE, : : : : : : A. J. JOHNSTON, SUPT. STATE PRINTING.
1891.

OFFICERS AND MEMBERS OF THE BOARD.

J. DeBARTH SHORB, President...............................San Gabriel,
Commissioner for the State at Large.

GEORGE WEST, Vice-President...............................Stockton,
Commissioner for the San Joaquin District.

JOHN T. DOYLE, Treasurer...............................San Francisco,
Commissioner for the State at Large.

1. DeTURK...............................Santa Rosa,
Commissioner for the Sonoma District.

CHARLES BUNDSCHU...............................San Francisco,
Commissioner for the San Francisco District.

R. D. STEPHENS...............................Sacramento,
Commissioner for the Sacramento District.

E. C. PRIBER...............................Napa,
Commissioner for the Napa District.

L. J. ROSE...............................Los Angeles,
Commissioner for the Los Angeles District.

G. G. BLANCHARD...............................Placerville,
Commissioner for the El Dorado District.

WINFIELD SCOTT, Secretary...............................San Francisco.

CLARENCE J. WETMORE...............................Livermore and San Francisco,
Chief Executive Viticultural Officer.

Office of the Board:
317 PINE STREET, SAN FRANCISCO, CAL.

First District—Continued.

No.	NAME OF DISTILLER.	Post Office.
307	Charles Detoy	Mountain View.
308	A. Zicovich	San José.
313	Santa Cruz Mountain Wine Co.	Santa Cruz.
314	Glen Terry Wine Co.	Clayton.
315	Buhach Produce and Manufacturing Co.	Atwater.
318	Theodore Beck	Santa Cruz.
....	E. B. Rodgers	Fresno.

FOURTH DISTRICT.

No.	NAME OF DISTILLER.	Post Office.
7	A. Douet	Amador County.
9	F. Borreo	Napa.
11	S. C. Hastings	Lakeport.
13	James Sweeney	Placerville.
14	J. Kimmer	Green Valley.
20	G. D. Endriss	Coloma.
21	George Hood	Santa Rosa.
22	J. D. Winters	Sonoma County.
24	P. & J. J. Gobbi	Healdsburg.
25	C. J. Dunn	Sonoma County.
26	George Lang	Calistoga.
33	E. C. Priber	Napa.
40	L. Rasmussen	Coloma.
42	Martin Feusier & Co.	Santa Rosa.
43	Henry Mette	Mormon Island.
45	B. Dreyfus & Co.	Sonoma County.
49	Kohler & Van Bergen	Guthrie's Station, Sac'to Co.
53	J. Laurent	St. Helena.
57	M. M. Estee	Napa.
58	E. M. Grimes	Yountville.
73	J. Dowdell	St. Helena.
78	J. Zentgraf	Shingle Springs.
82	Kortum & Fulcher	Calistoga.
84	G. Sieber	Marysville.
85	G. M. Wubbina	Mormon Island.
87	C. P. Adamson	Rutherford.
90	Leland Stanford	Vina.
98	H. Hugot	El Dorado County.
103	California Distillery Co.	St. Helena.
104	J. M. Ramm	Camptonville.
108	Italian-Swiss Agricultural Society	Cloverdale.
113	A. Lancel	Occidental.
122	E. G. Furber	Cloverdale.
129	Kohler & Frohling	Glen Ellen.
131	J. F. Miller	Shasta County.
133	William Hill	Sonoma County.
137	M. J. Azeveda & Co.	Sacramento County.
142	A. B. Driesbach	Grass Valley.
148	A. Isoard	Nevada City.
152	C. Hellwig	Grass Valley.
158	M. S. Nevis	Sacramento.
159	J. Kaiser	Penryn.
161	E. A. Hood	Santa Rosa.
167	G. Engler	Sonoma.
168	Wm. Goldstein	Napa County.
169	Charles Krug	St. Helena.
171	L. Ponlin	Sonoma County.
186	A. Domeniconi	Sonoma.
187	Stamer Bros.	St. Helena.
192	E. W. Davis	Santa Rosa.
193	G. Groezinger	Yountville.
195	Walden & Co.	Geyserville.
196	C. Aguillon	Sonoma.
200	J. Oberti	Cordelia.
202	John Thoman	St. Helena.

FRUIT BRANDY DISTILLERS OF CALIFORNIA.

FOURTH DISTRICT—Continued.

No.	NAME OF DISTILLER.	Post Office.
207	C. Carpy	Napa.
208	J. Chauvet	Glen Ellen.
215	James Finlayson	Sonoma.
216	Joseph Simi	Sonoma County.
219	R. F. Tilveria	Butte County.
221	G. F. Hooper	Sonoma.
222	Natoma Vineyard Company	Natoma.
223	I. DeTurk	Santa Rosa.
224	La Roza & Nevis	Sacramento.
225	J. A. Prien	Napa County.
232	Orleans Distilling Company	Orleans.
234	Beringer Bros.	St. Helena.
235	H. E. Weinberger	St. Helena.
237	J. Lonnibos	Sonoma.
240	C. Gundlach	Sonoma.
243	Bouchou & Batemale	Cordelia.
245	H. Bolle	Sonoma County.
247	G. F. Fisher	Sonoma.
249	J. H. Wheeler	St. Helena.
251	Lay, Clark & Co.	Santa Rosa.
255	F. Sciaroni	St. Helena.
258	A. Korbel	Korbels.
261	P. Bieber	St. Helena.
263	John Benson	Oakville.

DIRECTORY

OF THE

GRAPE GROWERS AND WINE MAKERS OF CALIFORNIA.

Compiled by the Board of State Viticultural Commissioners of California.

2–v

Grape Growers and Wine Makers of California.

ALAMEDA COUNTY.

Name of Owner.	Post Office and Name of Vineyard.	Total Acres in Grapes.	Acres in Bearing.	Acres in Wine Grapes.	Acres in Table Grapes.	Acres in Raisin Grapes.	Wine Maker.	Product in 1889.	Varieties.
Anspacher Bros.	Livermore	25	20	25			No.	12 tons.	Zinfandel, 9; Carignan, 8; Colombar, 8.
Aguillon & Bustelli	Livermore	6	6	6			Yes.	9 tons.	Grosser Blauer, 6.
Agnerbehere, F.	Livermore	15	15	15			No.	12 tons.	Zinfandel, 10.
Altschul, Jos.	Vienna Vineyard, Livermore.	100	85	85	5	10	No.	214 tons.	Zinfandel, 30; Mataro, 30; Carignan, 10; Petite Pinot, 15; Muscat, 10; Table varieties, 5.
Beard, J. L., & Putnam, S. O.	Marciana Vineyard, Warm Springs.	189	180	140	40		Yes.		Zinfandel, Mataro, Charbono, Malvoisie, Malbec, Trousseau, Petite Pinot, Folle Blanche, Petite Bouschet, Golden Chasselas, Muscat, Black Ferrara, Rose Peru, Cornichon, Verdal, Flame Tokay.
Bonner, R.	Niles	6	6	6			No.		Zinfandel, 6.
Bond, Charles	Irvington	35	35	35			Yes.	11,000 gals.	Zinfandel, 21; Cab. Sauvignon, 12; Malvoisie, 2.
Buckley, C. A.	Ravenswood Vineyard, Livermore.	90	90	90			Yes.	120 tons.	Zinfandel, 21; Mataro, 11; Colombar, 20; Petite Pinot, 11; Folle Blanche, 3; Grenache, 3; Chauche Noir, 3; Meunier, 3; Cab. Sauvignon, 3; Sauvignon Blanc, 5; Semillon, 6; Musc. du Bordelais, 1.
Brodt, A. W.	Pleasanton Vineyard.	36	36	36			No.	40 tons.	Gray Riesling, 20; Burger, 10; Zinfandel, 6.
Black, J. F., estate of	Lomitas Vineyard, Livermore.	195	195	195			Yes.	357 tons.	Zinfandel, 50; Cab. Sauvignon, 22; Cab. Franc, 18; Merlot, 15; Sauvignon Blanc, 6; Semillon, 13; Musc. du Bordelais, 2; Folle Blanche, 8; Colombar, 9; Trousseau, 6; Mataro, 3; Carignan, 10; Petite Pinot, 18; Meunier, 3.
Black, Howard	Livermore	20	20	20			No.	19 tons.	Zinfandel, 20.
Blethen, Mrs. A. K. P.	Oakland	9	9	9			No.	9 tons.	Zinfandel, 6; Carignan, 3.
Benjamin, E. H.	Oakland	16	16	16			No.	10 tons.	Zinfandel, 16.

Name	Post Office						Cellar	Product	Varieties
Brecht, August	Livermore	6	6	6			No.		Zinfandel, 6.
Bartlett, W. P.	Livermore	10	10	10	1		No.	9 tons.	Zinfandel, 4; Burger, 3; Golden Chasselas, 2; Mataro, 1.
Bangs, J. L.	Livermore	13	13	5	7		No.		Zinfandel, 5; Black Morocco, 5; Black Hamburg, 2; Muscat, 1.
Crommett, Chas.	Irvington	15	15	15			No.	45 tons.	Zinfandel, 6; Mataro, 1¼; Beclan, 1¼; Cabernet, 1¼; Colombar, 2¼; Orleans Riesling, 2½.
Curtner, Henry	Warm Springs	15	15	12	3		No.	75 tons.	Zinfandel, 12; Muscat, 3.
Clark, Edward	Niles	40	40	20	14	6	No.	100 tons.	Zinfandel, 10; Trousseau, 4; Mataro, 4; Cabernet Sauv., 2; Muscat, 14; Flame Tokay, 6.
Chadbourne, J. A.	Irvington	10	10	10			No.	97 tons.	Zinfandel, 10.
Chickering, W. H.	San Francisco	24	24	16	6	2	No.		Zinfandel, Riesling, Mataro, Grenache, Malvoisie, Charbono, Rose Peru, Muscat.
Concannon, James	Livermore	44	33	44			No.	102 tons.	Zinfandel, 11; Grenache, 10; Mataro, 8; Burger, 8; Carignan, 4; Folle Blanche, 8.
Clay, C. C.	San Francisco	60	60	60			No.	100 tons.	Zinfandel, 39; Mataro, 10; Folle Blanche, 4; Burger, 3; Petite Pinot, 2; Malvoisie, 2.
Callaghan, P.	Livermore	20	20	20			No.	22 tons.	Zinfandel, 20.
Connolly, P.	Livermore	22	22	22			No.	52 tons.	Zinfandel, 11; Mataro, 11.
Cull, L.	Livermore	13	8	8		5	No.	12 tons.	Zinfandel, 7; Riesling, 1; Table varieties, 5.
Crellin Bros.	Ruby Hill Vineyard, Pleasanton.	229	210	229			Yes.	620 tons.	Zinfandel, 70; Mataro, 20; Colombar, 15; Petite Bouschet, 6; Carignan, 5; Riesling, 3; Petite Syrah, 4; Cab. Sauvignon, 15; Cabernet Franc, 15; Merlot, 2; Verdot, 3; Sauvignon Blanc, 12; Semillon, 12; Musc. du Bordelais, 1; Petite Pinot, 8; Burger, 15; Meunier, 5; Mondeuse, 8.
Chauche, A. G.	Mont Rouge Vineyard, Livermore.	63	40	63			Yes.	110 tons.	Zinfandel, 40; Petite Bouschet, 4; Alicante Bouschet, 8; Sauvignon Blanc, Semillon, Muscadelle du Bord., 10; Chablis, 1.
Carpy, C.	San Francisco	7½	7½	7½			No.	18 tons.	Meunier, 1½; Chauche Noir, 2; Zinfandel, 1; Malbec, 3.
Caine, T. W. & Co.	San Francisco	5	5	5			No.	5 tons.	Zinfandel, 5.
Callaghan, Mrs. H.	Livermore	15	15	15			No.	20 tons.	Zinfandel, 15.
Callaghan, John	Livermore	35	35	35			No.	45 tons.	Zinfandel, 35.
Crane, H.	San Leandro	25	25	25			No.	20 tons.	Zinfandel, 7; Mataro, 6; Petite Pinot, 6; Golden Chasselas, 6.
Clay, Meux & Co.	Livermore	35	35	35			No.	60 tons.	Zinfandel, 18; Mataro, 17.
Collins, D. J.	Livermore	8	8	8			No.	6 tons.	Zinfandel, 8.
Chapin, E. W.	San Francisco	20	20	20			No.	19 tons.	Zinfandel, 20.
Davis, Hiram	Irvington	10	10	10			No.	38 tons.	Zinfandel, 10.
Dixon, M. W.	Warm Springs	40	35	40			No.	180 tons.	Johannisberg Riesling, 3; Golden Chasselas, 4; Charbono, 2; Zinfandel, 30; Mission, 1.
De Vaux, Paul	Mission San José	91	79	79	12		Yes.	35,000 gals.	Zinfandel, 50; Cab. Franc, Cab. Sauvignon, Malbec, 18; Mondeuse, 11; Resistant roots, 12.
Dearborn, G. W.	Pleasanton	18	18	18	18		No.	25 tons.	Table varieties, 18.

ALAMEDA COUNTY—Continued.

Name of Owner.	Post Office and Name of Vineyard.	Total Acres in Grapes.	Acres in Bearing.	Acres in Wine Grapes.	Acres in Table Grapes.	Acres in Raisin Grapes.	Wine Maker.	Product in 1889.	Varieties.
Doty, J. M.	Livermore	9	9	9		9	No.	5 tons.	Muscat of Alexandria, 9.
Davis, J. M.	Livermore	47	40	47			No.	90 tons.	Zinfandel, 20; Carignan, 13; Mataro, 3½; Petite Pinot, 2½; Grosser Blauer, 2; Burger, 4; Colombar, 2.
Deneff, John	Livermore	10	10	10			No.	26 tons.	Zinfandel, 10.
Duvall, A.	Bellevue Vineyard, Livermore.	150	120	150			Yes.	300 tons.	Cab. Sauvignon, 10; Malbec, 2; Semillon, 25; Sauvignon Blanc, 2; Musc. du Bord., 6; Sauvignon Vert, 18; Franken Riesling, 5; Chauche Gris, 6; Frontignan, 5; Chanche Noir, 15; Trousseau, 10; Petite Pinot, 6; Charbono, 8; Zinfandel, 15; Mataro, 10; Carignan, 6.
Everson, Wallace	Livermore	85	85	85			Yes.	286 tons.	Zinfandel, 20; Mataro, 20; Colombar, 14; Charbono, 7; Folle Blanche, 10; West's White Prol., 7; Cab. Sauvignon, 4; Cabernet Franc, 2; Petite Syrah, L.
Folger, J. A.	San Francisco	38	38	28	8	2	No.	70 tons.	Zinfandel, 20; Folle Blanche, 6; Malbec, 2; Table varieties, 8; Muscat, 2.
Felton, Chas. N.	Warm Springs	55	55	49	6		No.	275 tons.	Mission, 15; Zinfandel, 34; Rose Peru, 6.
Foster, A.	Mission San José	28	28	28			Yes.	85 tons.	Zinfandel, 15; Petit3 Bouschet, 3; Carignan, 3; Malvoisie, 3; Charbono, 4.
Fowler, F. L.	Dos Mesas Vineyard, Livermore.	60	60	56		4	No.	83 tons.	Cab. Sauvignon, 2; Cab. Franc, 4; Verdot, 2; Petite Syrah, 5; Sauvignon Blanc, 9; Semillon, 16; Mataro, 7; Petite Pinot, 5; Petite Bouschet, 1; Zinfandel, 5; Muscat, 4.
Fink, J. C.	Livermore	50	35	50			No.	16 tons.	Zinfandel, 25; Mataro, 13; Colombar, 12.
Fall, J. H.	Livermore	8	8	8			No.	12 tons.	Petite Pinot, 8; Zinfandel, 4.
Fath, Adam.	Livermore	6	6	5	1		No.	5 tons.	Zinfandel, 3; Colombar, 1; Coloring varieties, 1; Table varieties, 1.
Frasier, Wm.	Oakland	10	--			10	No.	---	Muscat, 10.
Farrelly, R. S.	San Leandro	28	28	26			No.	30 tons.	Zinfandel, 10; Folle Blanche, 5; Cabernet, 4; Burger, 5; Mataro, 2.
Gallagher, James	Livermore	25	15	25			No.	42 tons.	Zinfandel, 10; Mataro, 10; Folle Blanche, 5.
Gregory, Wm.	Livermore	2				2	No.	---	Muscat, 2.
Groth, O. R.	Livermore	22	22	22			No.	56 tons.	Zinfandel, 16; Folle Blanche, 6.

Name	Location	600	600	600	600				Tons	Varieties
Gallegos, Juan	Mission San José	600	600	600	.			Yes.	3,200 tons.	Zinfandel, 459; Mataro, 30; Cabernet Franc, 15; Merlot, 8; Johannisberg Riesling, 15; Trousseau, 5; Tannat, 8; Beclan, 15; Palomino, 20; Cab. Sauvignon, 25.
Grant, Miss A.	San Francisco	18¾	18¾	18¾	18¾			No.	25 tons.	Zinfandel, 8; Mataro, 7; Folle Blanche, 1½; Chauche Noir, 1; Black Ferrara, 1.
Handy, Dr. G. W.	Livermore	7	7	7	7			No.		Zinfandel, 7.
Hanovan, John	Livermore	21	21	20	7	1		No.	35 tons.	Zinfandel, 18; Burger, 2; Table grapes, 1.
Hoyt, John G.	Oakland	13	13		20	11	2	No.	28 tons.	Rose Peru, 4; Verdal, 4; Malvoisie, 3; Muscat, 2.
Hatch, Robertson & Rohrer.	Arlington Vineyard, Livermore.	65	65	65	65			No.	150 tons.	Zinfandel, 30; Mataro, 12; Sauvignon Blanc, 10; Semillon, 10; Musc. du Bord, 3.
Hillebrand, J.	Livermore	15	15	15	15			No.	18 tons.	Zinfandel, 6; Mataro, 4; Gray Riesling, 5.
Healey, B. F.	Livermore	12	12	12	12			No.	46 tons.	Mataro, 7; Zinfandel, 5.
Henderson, A. B.	San Francisco	25	25	25	25			No.	48 tons.	Zinfandel, 5; Mataro, 5; Grenache, 2; Petite Pinot, 5; Sauvignon Blanc, 2; Colombar, 6.
Hawxhurst, Mrs. F. H.	Livermore	4	4	4		3	1	No.	6 tons.	Muscat, Rose Peru, Black Hamburg, 4.
Hayes, Timothy	Livermore	40	37	40	40			No.	100 tons.	Zinfandel, 20; Mataro, 7; Franken Riesling, 3½; Orleans Riesling, 3½; Burger, 2; Malvoisie, 4.
Hall, Harvey	Livermore	10	10	10	10			No.	3 tons.	Zinfandel, 10.
Higuera, Mrs. P. S.	Warm Springs	24	20	21	21			No.	65 tons.	Zinfandel, 21; Muscat, 3.
Hilgard, E. W.	Dos Encinas Vineyard, Mission San José.	33	30½	33	33	3		No.	69½ tons.	Palomino, Clairette Blanche, Cinsaut, Mondeuse, Refosco, Mataro, 4 to 6 acres each; 2 acres Cabernet Franc, Sauvignon, and Verdelho.
Inman, Daniel	Livermore	90	90	90	90			No.	296 tons.	Zinfandel, 70; Mataro, 20.
Jones, J. M.	Livermore	20	20	14	20	6		No.	30 tons.	Zinfandel, 6; Burger, 6; Golden Chasselas, 1; Folle Blanche, 1; Table varieties, 6.
Jordan, Mrs. I.	Livermore	2	2	2	2			No.		Zinfandel, 2.
Jackson, S. E.	Pleasanton	9	9	9	9			No.	13 tons.	Gray Riesling, 5; Zinfandel, 4.
Knox, T. E.	Livermore	22	10	22	22			No.	42½ tons.	Carignan, 5; Mataro, 5; Cab. Sauvignon, 8; Mondeuse, 1; Zinfandel, 3.
Knowles & Handy	Livermore	17	17	17	17			No.	15 tons.	Colombar, 5; Burger, 6; Zinfandel, 6.
Kottinger, J. W.	Pleasanton	12	12	12	12			Yes.	25 tons.	Zinfandel, 12; Folle Blanche, 8; Burger, 7; Mataro, 4.
Koopman, A.	Pleasanton	31	31	31	31			No.	85 tons.	
Lorrain, N.	Livermore	16½	16½	16½	16½			Yes.	25 tons.	Zinfandel, 9; Malvoisie, 3½; Gutedel, 2; Chasselas, 2.
Locke, Prof. E. O.	Evanston, Ill.	39	39	39	39			No.	80 tons.	Zinfandel, 17; Mataro, 7½; Mondeuse, 5; Folle Blanche, 3; Colombar, 6½; Semillon, 1.
Luco, B.	Livermore	16	6	15	15			No.	12 tons.	Zinfandel, 4; Colombar, 4; Mataro, 4; Burger, 3.
Lawlor, Thomas	Livermore	6	12	6	6	1		No.	15 tons.	Zinfandel, 6.
Ladd, Mrs. Sarah	Livermore	12	15	11	11	10		No.	22 tons.	Mission, 11; Table varieties, 1.
Langan, G. W.	Livermore	15	5	5	5		5	No.		Rose Peru, 10; Muscat, 5.
Livermore, Mrs. R.	Livermore	5	5	5	5			No.		Mission, 5.
Lewin, Robert	San Francisco	10	10	10	10			No.	32 tons.	Grenache, 4; Mataro, 6.

ALAMEDA COUNTY—Continued.

Name of Owner.	Post Office and Name of Vineyard.	Total Acres in Grapes.	Acres in Bearing.	Acres in Wine Grapes.	Acres in Table Grapes.	Acres in Raisin Grapes.	Wine Maker.	Product in 1889.	Varieties.
Levy, S.	San Francisco	15	15	14	1		No.	12 tons.	Zinfandel, 7; Malvoisie, 6; Petite Pinot, 1; Black Hamburg, 1.
McIver, C. C.	Mission San José	230	150	270			Yes.	500 tons.	Zinfandel, 100; Mataro, 20; Carignan, 1; Crabb's Black Burgundy, 10; Cab. Sauvignon, 10; Cab. Franc, 10; Merlot, 20; Sauvignon Blanc, 5; Semillon, 5; Musc. du Bordelais, ½; Palomino, 5; Petite Bouschet, 3; Franken Riesling, 4; Johannisberg Riesling, 4; Burger, 25; Folle Blanche, 8; Petite Syrah, 10; Beclan, 20; Mondeuse, 5; resistant roots, 20; experimental, 3.
Morrison, Perry	Niles	3	3	3			No.		Zinfandel, 3.
Mosher, H.	Niles	6	6	6			No.		Zinfandel, 6.
Mayhew, H. A.	Niles	66	66	25	25	16	No.	100 tons.	Muscat, 16; Rose Peru, 10; Zinfandel, 15; Malvoisie, 5; Flame Tokay, 5; Cab. Sauvignon, 5; assorted varieties, 15.
Musser, J. W.	Mission San José	25	25	25			No.		Zinfandel, 10; various varieties, 15.
Meese, G. W.	Pleasanton	13	13	12½		¼	No.	27 tons.	Zinfandel, 9; Johannisberg Riesling, 2; Burger, 1½; Muscat, ½.
May, George	Livermore	4	4		4		No.	38 tons.	Muscat, 10; Black Hamburg, 3; Flame Tokay, 2.
McIver, John	Livermore	15	12		5	10	No.		Muscat.
Munch, C. G.	Livermore	1	1			1	No.		Zinfandel, 13; Burger, 3; Malvoisie, 2; Orleans Riesling, 5; Golden Chasselas, 1.
Merritt, S., estate of.	Oakland	24	24	24			No.	60 tons.	Zinfandel, 24; Burger, 10; Mataro, 6.
McGlashan, R.	Livermore	40	40	40			No.	25 tons.	Mataro, 8.
Mendenhall, M.	Livermore	8	8	8			No.	16 tons.	
Montgomery, A.	Oak Spring Vineyard, San Francisco.	95	95	65	20	10	No.	86 tons.	Zinfandel, 43; Folle Blanche, 4; Malvoisie, 5; Golden Chasselas, 6; Charbono, 3; Colombar, 1; Muscat, 10; Rose Peru, 15; Black Hamburg, 1; Black Morocco, 2; Malaga, 1; Violet Chasselas, 1.
Mel, Louis	Le Bocage Vineyard, Livermore.	29	25	29			No.	60 tons.	Meunier, 8; Verdal, 4; Semillon, 4; Sauvignon B., 2; Musc. du Bordelais, 1; Chauche Noir, 6; Colombar, 2; Folle Blanche, 2.
Matt, Gottleib	Livermore	5		5			No.		Zinfandel, 5.

Name	Post office						Wine made	Product	Varieties
Moreno, Louis	Livermore	28	25	28			Yes.	00 tons.	Zinfandel, 20; Folle Blanche, 8.
Newell, E. C.	Livermore	9	9	9			No.	9 tons.	Colombar, 9.
Neal, J. A., estate of	Pleasanton	2	2	2			No.	5 tons.	Mission.
Osterhout, W. P.	Livermore	31	31	31			No.	63 tons.	Zinfandel, 12; Folle Blanche, 5; Burger, 5; Cabernet, 9.
Power, John	Warm Springs	21	21	20		1	No.	45 tons.	Zinfandel, 19; Mission, 1; Muscat, 1.
Patterson, Mrs. C. O.	Livermore	35	36	35			No.	65 tons.	Zinfandel, 25; Mataro, 7; Petite Pinot, 3.
Paris, Eugene	Livermore	33	27	33			Yes.	75 tons.	Zinfandel, 11; Mataro, 4; Grenache, 4; Petite Pinot, 6; Mondeuse, 2; Folle Blanche, 6.
Riordan, P.	San Francisco	19	19	19			Yes.	275 tons.	Zinfandel, 3; Chasselas, 8; Riesling, 7; Mission, 1.
Rainey, S.	Warm Springs	53½	53½	53½			No.		Zinfandel, 42; Burger, 5; Golden Chasselas, 2; Charbono,2; Riesling,1; Pfefler's Sauvignon,2.
Rea, John	Mission San José	25	18	25			Yes.	75 tons.	Zinfandel, 25.
Robertson, Wm. A.	Mellow Valley Vineyard, Livermore.	20	20	20			No.	28 tons.	Zinfandel, 20.
Rees, Jacob	Livermore	2	2	2	1				Muscat, 1; Rose Peru, 1.
Rose, J. A.	Pleasanton	226	170	222	4	1	No.	725 tons.	Sauvignon Blanc, 13; Semillon, 13; Bouschet, 5; Black Pinot, 10; Zinfandel, 45; Franken Riesling, 15; Gray Riesling, 20; Johannisberg Riesling, 20; Mataro, 10; Burger, 10; Grenache, 3; Carignan, 15; Folle Blanche, 10; Golden Chasselas, 8; Colombar, 15; Cabernet Sauvignon, 10; Table varieties, 4.
Righter, Johnson	Livermore	4	4	4			No.	4 tons.	Zinfandel, 2; Mataro, 2.
Romigair, Mrs. M.	Sunol	30	25	30			Yes.	10,000 gals.	Zinfandel, Chasselas, Riesling, Muscatel, Petite Bouschet, Mataro, Grenache, Carignan.
Stanford, Josiah, est. of	Warm Springs	300	280	270		30	Yes.	200,000 gals.	Zinfandel, 75; Mission, 182; Muscat, 30; Semillon, 2; Cab. Sauvignon, 2; Cab. Franc, 1; Sauvignon Blanc, 2; Merlot, 2; Verdot, 2; Mondeuse, 2.
Salazar, A. J.	Mission San José	115	115	115			Yes.	60,000 gals.	Zinfandel, 60; Mataro, 20; Carignan, 20; Colombar, 7; Mission, 8.
Sigrist, C.	Mission San José	6½	6½	6½			Yes.	4,000 gals.	Riesling, 3; Zinfandel, 3½.
Smith, Julius P.	Olivina Vineyard, Livermore.	661	475	660		1	Yes.	1,300 tons.	Zinfandel, 55; Grenache, 18; Mondeuse, 34; Mataro, 50; Verdot, 9; Cabernet Franc, 90; Cabernet Sauvignon, 5; Carignan, 18; Blaue Elba, 14; Chanche Noir, 10; Petite Syrah, 4; Tannat, 9; Folle Noir, 14; Trousseau, 4; Meunier, 6; Malbec, 20; Petite Bouschet, 11; Petite Pinot, 67; Johannisberg Riesling, 24; Franken Riesling, 18; Orleans Riesling, 5; Gray Riesling, 10; Colombar, 80; Folle Blanche, 50; Chalosse, 5; Burger, 33; Sauvignon Blanc, 24; Golden Chasselas, 17; Boal, 3; Musc. du Bord, 2; Seedless Sultana, 1.

ALAMEDA COUNTY—Continued.

NAME OF OWNER.	Post Office and Name of Vineyard.	Total Acres in Grapes.	Acres in Bearing.	Acres in Wine Grapes.	Acres in Table Grapes.	Acres in Raisin Grapes.	Wine Maker.	Product in 1889.	Varieties.
Stevenson, Mrs. J.	Livermore	22	10	22			No.	23 tons.	Zinfandel,5; Burger,2; Colombar,2; Petite Bouschet, 3; Cab. Sauvignon, 5; Cab. Franc, 5.
Schiejelhie, Wm.	San Francisco	10	10	9	1		No.	18 tons.	Zinfandel, 7; Riesling, 2; Table varieties, 1.
Scoville, J. J.	San Francisco	52½	52½	52½			No.	109 tons.	Folle Blanche, 4; Mataro, 9; Zinfandel,7½; Petite Pinot, 4; Chauche Noir, 2; Colombar, 5; Tannat, 5; Petite Bouschet, 5; Mondeuse, 5; Verdot, 5; Cab. Franc, 3.
Schween, E.	Pleasanton	18	18	18	2		No.	90 tons.	Zinfandel, 6; Riesling, 6; Mataro, 6.
Stover, J. E., estate of.	Pleasanton	60	60	51		7	No.	375 tons.	Zinfandel, 46; Mataro, 5; Muscat, 7; Flame Tokay, 2.
Schlueter, P.	Livermore	17	17	17			No.	45 tons.	Zinfandel, 12; Folle Blanche, 5.
Squires, E. J.	Livermore	21	21			21	No.	36 tons.	Muscat, 21.
Schneider, D.	Livermore	4			4		No.		Table varieties, 4.
Sardella, J.	Mission San José	10	10	10			No.	25 tons.	Carignan, 5; Burger, 5.
Shaffer, S. M.	Livermore	10	10	10			No.	15 tons.	Mataro, 5; Carignan, 5.
Sanford, Mrs. S. C.	Oakland	10	10			10	No.	5 tons.	Muscat, 10.
Schaffer, Louis	Pleasanton	2	2	2			Yes.	40,000 gals.	Mission, 2.
Spotorno, J. B.	Pleasanton	50	50	50			No.	201 tons.	Zinfandel, 37; Colombar, 17; Mataro, 4; Gray Riesling, 2; Burger, 2.
Thonesen, H.	Livermore	62	58	62			No.		Riesling, 2; Burger, 2.
Twohey, Thomas	Livermore	1	1	1			No.	1 ton.	Zinfandel, 1.
True, George.	Livermore	95	90	95			Yes.	200 tons.	Zinfandel, 30; Mataro, 10; Carignan, 10; Petite Pinot, 5; Colombar, 20; Folle Blanche, 20.
Toche, E. C.	Livermore	17	17	17			No.	43 tons.	Mataro, 8½; Zinfandel, 8.
Teeter, D. M.	Livermore	25	25	25			No.	40 tons.	Zinfandel, 15; Mataro, 10.
Twohig, T. I.	Irvington	8	8	8	1		No.	25 tons.	Zinfandel, 8.
Wright, Silas C.	Livermore	37½	37½	31½		5	No.	61 tons.	Zinfandel, 13¼; Malvoisie, 1¼; Burger, 4½; Orleans Riesling, 3; Franken Riesling, 3; Golden Chasselas, 3; Petite Pinot, 1¼; Mataro, 1¼; Muscat, 4½; Malaga, ¾; Table varieties, 1.
Waltenbaugh, P. C.	Livermore	24	24	24			No.	46 tons.	Zinfandel, 6; Folle Blanche, 5; Gray Riesling, 2; Burger, 1; Petite Bouschet, 3; Malbec, 2; Mataro, 2; Mondeuse, 3.

Name	Location							Tons	Varieties
Wheeler, J. H.	Cornelia Vineyard, Livermore.	110	110	98	11	6	Yes.	140 tons.	Seedless Sultana, 6; Petite Pinot, 6; Pinot Blanc, 3; Malbec, 5; Alicante Bouschet, 1; Franken Riesling, 9; Zinfandel, 20; Semillon, 1½; Sauvignon Blanc, 1½; Grosser Blauer, 1; Cab. Sauvignon, 7; Cab. Franc, 6; Trousseau, 4; Mataro, 22; Tokay, 6; Black Ferrara, 5; Chauche Noir, 5; Folle Blanche, 5.
Williams, G. M.	Oakland	37	---	33	4	---	No.	---	Semillon, 18; Sauvignon Blanc, 4; Musc. du Bordelais, 1; Cabernet Franc, 6; Chauche Noir, 4; Table varieties, 4.
Wegener, Mrs. R.	Livermore	55	55	55	---	---	No.	220 tons.	Zinfandel, 23; Golden Chasselas, 6; Charbono, 7; Burger, 8; Malvoisie, 3; Neuchatel Chasselas, 5; Sauvignon Blanc, 1; Verdal, 1; Orleans Riesling, 1; Petite Syrah, 2.
Wilson, A.	Livermore	13	13	10	3	---	No.	68 tons.	Zinfandel, 5; Malvoisie, 3; Burger, 2; Muscat, 3.
Wheeler & Osterhout	Livermore	20	20	16	1	---	No.	20 tons.	Zinfandel, 16; Mataro, 1; Muscat, 3; Rose Peru, 1.
Weller, C.	Warm Springs	31½	31½	29½	2	3	No.	250 tons.	Zinfandel, 14; Cabernet Franc, 1; Trousseau, 1; Mondeuse, 1; Burger, 5; Franken Riesling, 3; Palomino, 2½; Grenache, 1; Charbono, 1; Table varieties, 2.
Wetmore, Charles A.	Cresta Blanca Vineyard, Livermore.	42	42	42	---	---	Yes.	40 tons.	Cabernet Sauvignon, 7½; Cabernet Franc, 4½; Merlot, 1½; Verdot, 1½; Tannat, 3; Pfeffer's Burgundy, 4; Sauvignon Blanc, 6; Semillon, 12; Muscadelle du Bordelaise, 2.
Wente, C. H. & Co.	Bernard Vineyard, Livermore.	49	49	49	---	---	Yes.	152 tons.	Zinfandel, 11; Folle Blanche, 5; Charbono, 3; Mataro, 6; Verdot, 2; Semillon, 4; Burger, 6; Colombar, 8; Sauvignon Blanc, 1½; Musc. du Bord., ½; Tannat, 1; Cab. Franc, 1.
Wetmore, C. J.	Electra Vineyard, Livermore.	40	40	40	---	---	No.	71 tons.	Petite Pinot, 12; Medoc varieties, 6; Sauterne varieties, 9; Lenoir, 2; Mataro, 4; Zinfandel, 4; Charbono, 1; Folle Blanche, 1; Mondeuse, 1.
Weymouth, Almon	Livermore	16	16	14	---	2	No.	17 tons.	Zinfandel, 5; Grenache, 2; Burger, 3; Golden Chasselas, 2; Muscat, 2.
Weymouth, Albert	Livermore	16	16	14	---	2	No.	25 tons.	Zinfandel, 5; Grenache, 2; Burger, 3; Golden Chasselas, 2; Mataro, 2; Muscat, 2.
Weston, F. F.	San Francisco	15	15	15	---	---	No.	15 tons.	Zinfandel, 10; Malvoisie, 3; Petite Pinot, 2.
Wright, W. H.	Livermore	15	15	15	---	---	No.	15 tons.	Zinfandel, 15.
Wood, J. H.	San Francisco	15	15	15	---	---	No.	15 tons.	Zinfandel, 10; Burger, 2; Malvoisie, 3.
Winegar, A. B.	San Francisco	13	13	13	---	---	No.	5 tons.	Zinfandel, 10; Mataro, 3.
	San Francisco	30	30	30	---	---	No.	10 tons.	Zinfandel, 20; Mataro, 5; Folle Blanche, 5.
Zoll, G.	Irvington	15	15	15	---	---	Yes.	33 tons.	Mataro, 5; Zinfandel, 5; Mondeuse, Beclan, Cab. Franc, 5.
Totals for county		6,826	6,060	6,396	236	194			

AMADOR COUNTY.

Name of Owner.	Post Office and Name of Vineyard.	Total Acres in Grapes.	Acres in Bearing.	Acres in Wine Grapes.	Acres in Table Grapes.	Acres in Raisin Grapes.	Wine Maker.	Product in 1889.	Varieties.
Ackley, Walker	Ione								
Baker, Jesse	Ione								
Braddy, Alex.	Ione								
Green, Frank	Ione								
Louis, F.	Ione								
Merkle, E.	Ione								
Newman, G., & Bros.	Ione								
Tubbs, G. L.	Ione								
Woolsey, George	Ione								
Walker, J. C.	Ione								
Batchelder, J.	Jackson								
Caminetti, A.	Jackson								
Froelich, G.	Jackson								
Little, M. J.	Jackson								
Lorteault, E.	Jackson								
Totals for county									

BUTTE COUNTY.

Name of Owner.	Post Office and Name of Vineyard.	Total Acres in Grapes.	Acres in Bearing.	Acres in Wine Grapes.	Acres in Table Grapes.	Acres in Raisin Grapes.	Wine Maker.	Product in 1889.	Varieties.
Baden, Fred.	Bangor	4	4		4				
Clark, L. C.	Bangor	1	1		1				
Connett, M. T.	Bangor	1½	1½			1½			

Gomes, Manuel	Bangor	6	6	6			Yes.		
Mack, D. M.	Bangor	11	11	8	3				
Malcom, D.	Bangor	6	6	3		3			
Miller, Mrs. V.	Bangor	5	5	5			Yes.		
Osgood, Gardner	Bangor	6	6			6			
Rehfness, H.	Bangor	16	16	16			Yes.		
Ringeleben, Albert	Bangor	3	3	3					
Townson, E. M.	Bangor	1	1	1					
Young, Mrs. Elizabeth	Bangor	10	10	10					
Beall, John	Biggs	3	3	3					
Bidwell, John	Chico	500	500			500			
Boness, Wm.	Chico	7	7		7				
Entler, J. F.	Chico	7	7		7				
Hutchins, T. B.	Central House	10	10			10			
Pollock, John	Central House	15	15			15			
Bigelow, M. J.	Gridley	10	10			10			
Richards, V. P.	Gridley	9½	9½		3½	6			
Webber, P. J.	Gridley	20	10			20			
Isenberg, A. J.	John Adams	1½	1½	1½					
Austram, Mrs. A.	Oroville	3½	3½	3½			Yes.		
Gardella, Joe	Oroville	1	1		1				
Leggett, C. H. & J. H.	Oroville	36	36	7	16	13			
Power, Richard	Oroville	26	26	26					
Smith, J. J.	Oroville	7	7	7					
Wheeler, Jas.	Palermo	2½	2½	2½					
Newlen, John	Paradise	3	3			3			
Durban, C. L.	Pentz	17½	17½	2½		15			
Froenfelter, Mrs. H.	Pentz	3½	3½	3½			Yes.		
Munn, Rebecca	Pentz	4½	4½		4	½			
Pence, W. M.	Pentz	18½	18½	2½	16				
Rattrary, John	Wyandotte	2	2			2			
Rutherford, J. T.	Wyandotte	3	3		3				
Totals for county		781	680½	111	65½	604½			

CALAVERAS COUNTY.

Name of Owner.	Post Office and Name of Vineyard.	Total Acres in Grapes.	Acres in Bearing.	Acres in Wine Grapes.	Acres in Table Grapes.	Acres in Raisin Grapes.	Wine Maker.	Product in 1889.	Varieties.
Peters, J. H.	Camanche								
Cutler, Wm.	Milton								
Gregory, M. F.	Milton								
Myers, John	Milton								
Owens, Michael	Milton								
Southwick, J. H.	Milton								
Anne, J.	Mokelumne Hill								
Bandin, L.	Mokelumne Hill								
Canmo, P.	Mokelumne Hill								
Mayer, F.	Mokelumne Hill								
Cavanna, B.	San Andreas	6	6	6			Yes.	18 tons.	
California Company	San Andreas	40	40	40			No.	120 tons.	
Clovece, A.	San Andreas	7	7	7			Yes.	21 tons.	
Covagnaro, A.	San Andreas	25	25	25			Yes.	75 tons.	
Covagnaro & Co.	San Andreas	15	15	15			Yes.	45 tons.	
Costa, Louis	San Andreas	30	30	30			Yes.	90 tons.	
Emerson, Geo.	San Andreas	8	8	8			Yes.	24 tons.	
Erin, Jacob	San Andreas	12	12	12			No.	36 tons.	
Gardella, Chas.	San Andreas	40	40	40			Yes.	120 tons.	
Gennelli, Antone	San Andreas	30	30	30			Yes.	90 tons.	
Glass, James	San Andreas	6	6	6			Yes.	18 tons.	
Guffra & Co.	San Andreas	20	20	20			Yes.	60 tons.	
Guecco, John	San Andreas	10	10	10			Yes.	30 tons.	
Halm, Geo.	San Andreas	15	15	15			No.	46 tons.	
Hemsdorf, John	San Andreas	10	10	10			No.	30 tons.	
Hill, E. A.	San Andreas	10	10	10			No.	30 tons.	
Largomarsino, A.	San Andreas	7	7	7			Yes.	21 tons.	
Lewis, B. F.	San Andreas	8	8	8			No.	24 tons.	
Lofquist, B.	San Andreas	9	9	9			No.	27 tons.	
Mess, A.	San Andreas	8	8	8			No.	24 tons.	
Peirano & Gagleardo	San Andreas	25	25	25			Yes.	75 tons.	
Ricker, B. F.	San Andreas	10	10	10			No.	30 tons.	
Sangumetti, J.	San Andreas	6	6	6			No.	18 tons.	
Sigaluka, A.	San Andreas	20	20	20			Yes.	60 tons.	

Name of Owner	Post Office and Name of Vineyard	Total Acres in Grapes	Acres in Bearing	Acres in Wine Grapes	Acres in Table Grapes	Acres in Raisin Grapes	Wine Maker	Product in 1889	Varieties
Snyder, Peter	San Andreas	10	10	10			No.	30 tons.	
Spencer, W. H.	San Andreas	25	25	25			No.	75 tons.	
Totals for county		404	404	404					

COLUSA COUNTY.

Name of Owner	Post Office and Name of Vineyard	Total Acres in Grapes	Acres in Bearing	Acres in Wine Grapes	Acres in Table Grapes	Acres in Raisin Grapes	Wine Maker	Product in 1889	Varieties
Cain, I. N.	College City	30	20			30	No.		
Calmes, Wm.	College City	30	16			16	No.		
Clarke, W. J.	College City	8	8			8	No.		
Eddy, M.	College City	1½	1½			1½	No.		
Gillaspy, John	College City	6	6			6	No.		
Green, J. C.	College City	30				30	No.		
Reardon, W. H.	College City	10				10	No.		
Watson, John	College City	3	3			3	No.		
Weyand, G.	College City	4	4	4			Yes.		
Cheney, John	Colusa	3	3			3	No.		
Coleman, T. J.	Colusa	16	16		4	12	No.		
De Jarnatt, J. B.	Colusa	25	25			25	No.		
Gray, R. A.	Colusa	12	12			12	No.		
Harris, S.	Colusa	7	5			7	No.		
Herd, W. N.	Colusa	1½	1½			1½	No.		
Hicok, H. H.	Colusa	12	12			12	No.		
Moulton, L. F.	Colusa	46	26		24	22	No.		
Mulligan, J. C.	Colusa	7	7			7	No.		
Pope, J. H.	Colusa	3	3			3	No.		
Totman, J. R.	Colusa	17	3			17	No.		
Fruto Land & Imp. Co.	Elk Creek	65				65	No.		
Weyand, Julius	Little Stony	3½	3½			3½	No.		
Felts, C. C.	Maxwell	20	20	20			No.		
Hudson & Hutchins	Maxwell	40				40	No.		
Hall, A. L.	Orland	4	4			4	No.	12 tons.	Muscat.
Zumwalt, J. O.	Williams	18	18			18	No.		
Totals for county		442½	217½	24	28	370½			

CONTRA COSTA COUNTY.

Name of Owner	Post Office and Name of Vineyard	Total Acres in Grapes	Acres in Bearing	Acres in Wine Grapes	Acres in Table Grapes	Acres in Raisin Grapes	Wine Maker	Product in 1890	Varieties
Beede & Abbott	Antioch	86	50	25	11	50	No.	200 tons.	Zinfandel, Muscat, Tokay.
Bigelow, A. J.	Antioch	50		35			No.		Muscat, Tokay.
Emerson, C. H., & Sons	Antioch	35	5	5	15		No.		Zinfandel.
Flickhamer, Wm.	Antioch	5	3	3			Yes.	L.	Zinfandel.
Pratado, Jos.	Antioch	3		3			No.		Zinfandel.
Jenkins, Thomas	Antioch	15	20	20	15		Yes.		Muscat, Tokay.
Miller, Jos.	Antioch	20	5	5			Yes.		Zinfandel.
Minto, Manuel	Antioch	5	15		15		No.	60 tons.	
Parkinson, M. C.	Antioch	15			5				Muscat, Tokay.
Peters, F. W.	Antioch	5					Yes.		
Prevallo, Jos.	Antioch	4	4	4			Yes.	2,500 guls.	Zinfandel.
Robinson, I. L.	Antioch	30	20	30			No.		Zinfandel.
Ruckslatt, Jos.	Antioch	20		20			Yes.		Muscat, Tokay.
Rouse, Beede & Co.	Antioch	28			28		Yes.		
Vera, I. D.	Antioch	4	4	4			Yes.		Mission, Zinfandel.
Brandt, ----	Brentwood	10	10	10	6		No.		Mission, Zinfandel.
Gibson, Hugh	Brentwood	6	8	6			No.		Wine grapes, mixed.
Humphrey, Misses	Brentwood	13	8	13			No.		Muscat, Tokay.
O'Hara, James	Brentwood	6			4		No.		Muscat, Tokay.
Plaur, Wm.	Brentwood	4					Yes.		Zinfandel.
Wrighton Bros.	Brentwood	10	10	10	10		No.		Muscat.
Plumley, A.	Byron	10	10				No.		Zinfandel, Mataro.
Barber, Truman	Clayton	10		10			No.		Muscat, Tokay.
Benson, W. T.	Clayton	20		20			No.		Zinfandel.
Bigelow, C. P.	Clayton	4			4		No.		Muscat, Tokay.
Blocking, Geo.	Clayton	10	5	10			No.		Zinfandel.
Bollman, D. M.	Clayton	5	3	5			No.		Zinfandel.
Briggs, Elijah	Clayton	3	10	3	3		No.		Mission.
Briggs, H.	Clayton	10	4	7	4		No.		Zinfandel, Muscat.
Brotchie, Geo.	Clayton	4	12				No.		Tokay.
Clymer, Wm.	Clayton	15	3	15			No.		Zinfandel.
Collins, John	Clayton	3	5	3			No.		Zinfandel.
Condie, John	Clayton	5		5			No.		Mission.
De Martini, Paul	Clayton	20		20			Yes.		Zinfandel.

Name	Post Office	(1)	(2)	(3)	(4)	Raisins	Remarks	Varieties
De Martini & Cereghino	Clayton	50	50	50		Yes.		Zinfandel, Mission.
Dominic, Murcheo	Clayton	30		30		No.		Zinfandel.
Glusing, Peter	Clayton	7	2	7		No.		Zinfandel, Mission.
Gunther & Son	Clayton	15	8	10	5	No.		Zinfandel, Muscat.
Hiebice, N.	Clayton	5	8	3		No.		Mixed wine grapes.
Kirkwood, N.	Clayton	5	5	5		No.		Mission.
Lewellyn, John	Clayton	3		10				Zinfandel.
Maguire, Mrs.	Clayton	3	3	3				Zinfandel.
Marsh, Joshua	Clayton	10		10				Zinfandel, Mission.
Mayo, John	Clayton	3½	3½	3½				Mission.
Morgan, Jerry	Clayton	2	2	2				Mission.
Mount Diablo Wine Co.	Clayton	100	100	100		Yes.		Mission, Riesling, Zinfandel, Chasselas.
Norman, Alex.	Clayton	2		2		No.		Mission.
Polly, Henry	Clayton	20	11	15	5	No.	33 tons in '80	Zinfandel, Muscat.
Russellman, T.	Clayton	20	20	20		No.		Zinfandel, Mission.
Rhine, Charles	Clayton	30		30		Yes.		Zinfandel.
Smith, Isaac	Clayton	17	16	16	1	No.	75 tons	Zinfandel, Tokay, Mission.
Terry, R. C.	Glen Terry Wine Co., Clayton.	80	70	60	20	Yes.	226 tons	Zinfandel, Chasselas, Riesling, Mataro, Fontain-ebleau.
Williams, E. W.	Clayton	7		6	1	No.		Muscat, Zinfandel, Black Burgundy.
Avery, H. R.	Concord	5	5	12	5			Muscat.
Babel, Philip	Concord	24			12	No.		Zinfandel, Table.
Ballman, Henry	Concord	4		4		No.		Zinfandel.
Barcullari, Achille	Concord	16		16		No.		Zinfandel.
Bauman, Wm.	Concord	7	7	5	2	No.		Zinfandel, Burger, Table.
Beebe, W. F.	Concord	2	2	4				Mixed.
Billings, W. H.	Concord	8		8	4	No.		Zinfandel.
Bussy, J. T.	Concord	10	3	3	10			Tokay.
Duarte, Frank	Concord	3	8	8		No.		Mission.
Fernandez, Bernardo	Concord (Pinole)	8	5	5		No.		Mission.
Garcia, Juan	Concord	5		6		No.	20 tons	Mission.
Geringer, A.	Concord	6	15	15				
Galindo, John	Concord	15				No.		
Hopkins, Moses	Concord	25		25		No.		Mission.
Kellyon, ——	Concord	32		12	20	No.		Mission.
Langenkamp, Geo. W.	Concord	23	23	8	15	No.		Zinfandel, Mataro, Malvoisie, Burgundy, Black Hamburg.
Lewis, C. Y.	Concord	5	3	3		No.		Zinfandel, mixed table.
McLennan, Charles	Concord	5	5	5		No.		Zinfandel, Mission, Muscat.
Mastrick, George	Concord	4		4		No.		Mission.
Mulligan, John	Concord	40		20		No.		Zinfandel.
Parker, August	Concord	14		14	20	No.		
Peterson, P. M.	Concord	9	9	9		No.		Zinfandel, Mataro.
Pope, Mrs.	Concord	2	2	2		No.		Mission.
Rose, John	Concord	6	3	6		No.		Mission, Zinfandel.

CONTRA COSTA COUNTY—Continued.

Name of Owner	Post Office and Name of Vineyard	Total Acres in Grapes	Acres in Bearing	Acres in Wine Grapes	Acres in Table Grapes	Acres in Raisin Grapes	Wine Maker	Product in 1890	Varieties
Samuels, Asa	Concord	12	12	12			No.	30 tons, '89 / 40 tons, '90	Malvoisie, Zinfandel.
Samuels, John	Concord	2		2			No.		
Solari, H. J.	Concord	16	16	16			No.		Zinfandel.
Stanford, Leland	Gwin Ranch, Concord	25		25			No.		
Thompson, Calvin	Concord	5		5			Yes.		Zinfandel.
Treat, Webster	Concord	50	4	50			No.		Zinfandel, Mission, Mataro.
Tristam, S.	Concord	4	4	4			Yes.		Mission.
Valencia, Henry	Concord	3	3	3			No.		Mission.
Waitman, H. H.	Concord	30		30			No.		
Webb, Barney	Concord	3	3		3			10 tons.	Mixed.
Westcott, Capt. C. W.	Concord	30	3	28	4		No.	60 tons, '89 / 125 tons, '90	Mataro, Carignan, Burger, etc.
Wilhelms, Capt.	Concord	3	3		3		No.		Muscat, Tokay.
Herrick, A. T.	Cornwall	5		4			No.		Mixed wine.
Julian, T. B.	Lafayette	4	4	4					Mixed table.
Whitcomb, C. S.	Lafayette	5	5		5		No.		Mataro, Rose Peru.
Ames, I. P.	Martinez (San Fran.)	30		10	20				Mixed table and wine.
Austin, A. E.	Martinez	3	3		5		No.		Tokay, Muscat.
Baily, James A.	Martinez	5		7	43		No.		Mixed table and Zinfandel.
Barber, M. R.	Martinez	50	30	50			Yes.	100 tons.	Zinfandel.
Bartola, A.	Martinez	3	3	18	22		No.		Tokay, mixed wine, Rose Peru, Black Hamburg.
Bee, F. A.	Martinez	40	40	40			No.		Mission.
Beier, S. A.	Martinez	3	3	3			No.		Zinfandel.
Boss, Alex.	Martinez	60	60	60			No.		Tokay, Zinfandel, Malvoisie, Muscat.
Brann, L.	Hillsdale Vineyard, Martinez (San Fran.)	50		30	20		No.	100 tons.	Tokay, Zinfandel, Muscat.
Bush, David	Martinez	30	22	8	22		No.	22 tons.	
Christian Bros.	Martinez	12	8	12	3		No.		Zinfandel, Malvoisie, Mission.
Christian Bros.	Martinez (San Fran.)	15	12	12	3		No.		Rose Peru, mixed wine, Zinfandel, Mission.
Cluff, William	Martinez (San Fran.)	29	9	4	25		No.		Tokay, Muscat, Rose Peru, Cabernet, Zinfandel.
Daggett, J. R., and Tasheira, George.	Martinez	20	20		20		No.	600 boxes.	Tokay, Muscat, Rose Peru, Black Ferrara.
Dick, Emma.	Martinez (San Fran.)	12		12			No.		Mission, Zinfandel, Chasselas.

Name	Location					Wine	Amount	Varieties
Dukes, William	Martinez	20	8	8	12	No.	24 tons.	Tokay, Zinfandel, Chasselas.
Eggleston, William	Martinez	3	3	3	3	No.		Rose Peru, Zinfandel, Muscat, Chasselas.
Fagan, Mrs. E. A.	Martinez	15	8	12	7	No.		Muscat, Zinfandel, Tokay.
Frazer, George M.	Martinez	15	9	8	8	No.		Muscat, Black Morocco, Tokay.
Gillogily Bros.	Martinez	8	8	8	11	No.		Muscat, Tokay.
Gray, Richard	Martinez (San Fran.)	10		10		No.		
Griffin, Thomas	Martinez	11	1	1	4	No.	7 tons.	Tokay, Rose Peru, Muscat, Chasselas, Malvoisie.
Hardy, H. P.	Martinez	4	4	4	7	No.	24 tons.	Muscat, Rose Peru, Malvoisie.
Hayward, O. H.	Martinez	7	7	7	7	No.	24 tons.	Zinfandel, Tokay, Muscat.
Hoesley, H. P.	Martinez	21	9	14½	6½		14 tons.	Tokay, Muscat, Malvoisie, Chasselas, Zinfandel.
Hogan, T. G.	Martinez (San Fran.)	8	15		7			Muscat.
Ingraham, I. T.	Martinez	27	4	20	8			Tokay, Muscat, Chasselas, Mission, Zinfandel.
Ivey, H. S. & John	Martinez	4		4	7			Muscat.
Jones, J. P.	Martinez							
Joost, Fabian	Martinez	15	15	16	3	Yes.	20,000 gals.	Zinfandel, Muscat.
Kelly, James	Martinez	20	10	17		No.	30 tons.	Zinfandel.
McKenna, James	Martinez	6	6	6		No.		Zinfandel.
Mead, L. G.	Martinez	22			22	No.	16 tons.	Tokay, Muscat, Rose Peru.
Merrill, Dr. C. G.	Martinez (Las Lomas)	80	80	80	80	Yes.	5,000 gals., ['89; 125 tons]	Grenache, Chasselas, Zinfandel, Burgundy.
Messic, I. D.	Martinez	20		5	15	No.		Zinfandel, Rose Peru, Muscat, Tokay.
Muir, John	Martinez (Alhambra)	100	80	30	70	No.		Tokay, Muscat, Zinfandel.
Oldsdoffer, George	Martinez	10		10				Chasselas, Zinfandel.
Overfield, George	Martinez	3		3				
Pasola, ___	Martinez	80	16	10	8	Yes.		Muscat, Tokay, Zinfandel, Chasselas, Mission.
Potter, Samuel	Martinez	68	43	36	7	No.		Twenty varieties, wine and table.
Raap, Henry	Martinez	12		12	35	No.		Zinfandel.
Rogers, E. A.	Martinez	20		20	10	Nc.		Zinfandel.
Rogers, P. F.	Martinez	23	15	15	20	No.		Tokay, Zinfandel, Muscat.
Ryer, F.	Martinez	7			8	No.		Tokay, Muscat.
Smith, N. B.	Martinez (Alhambra)	55	45	10	7	No.		Tokay, Zinfandel, Muscat, Rose Peru, Malaga.
Strentzel, Dr. John	Martinez	110	110	100	35	Yes.		Tokay, Muscat, Chasselas, Mission.
Sturgis & Eddy	HillgirtVyd.,Martinez	70	60	50	10	No.	108 tons.	Muscat, Cabernet, Tokay.
Swett, John.	Martinez	8	8	5	20	No.	75 tons.	Mission.
Tietjen, Mrs. E.	Martinez	5	5	7		No.		Zinfandel, Chasselas, Tokay, Muscat, Rose Peru.
Thomas, D. R.	Martinez	13	13	7	6	No.		Black Burgundy, Zinfandel, Tokay, Muscat.
Thoro, F.	Martinez	10	3	2	3	Yes.		Zinfandel, Tokay, Muscat.
Upham, B. H.	Martinez	8			6	No.		Tokay, Muscat.
Webster, E. A.	Martinez	9			9	No.		Rose Peru, Muscat, Malaga, Ferrara, Emperor, Fontainebleau.
Webster, E. E.	Martinez	35			35	No.		Tokay, Muscat.
Williams, H. W.	Martinez	35	17	10	all	No.	29 tons.	Zinfandel, Tokay, Muscat, Chasselas, Black Hamburg.
Winslow, M.	Martinez					No.		Tokay, Muscat.
Wittenmyer, L. C.	Martinez	20		10	10	No.		Zinfandel, Tokay, Muscat, Chasselas, Black Hamburg.

3-v

CONTRA COSTA COUNTY—Continued.

Name of Owner.	Post Office and Name of Vineyard.	Total Acres in Grapes.	Acres in Bearing.	Acres in Wine Grapes.	Acres in Table Grapes.	Acres in Raisin Grapes.	Wine Maker.	Product in 1890.	Varieties.
Wolford, George	Martinez	7			7				Rose Peru, Tokay, Muscat.
Young, Johnson	Martinez	8	5	4	4		No.		Zinfandel, Muscat.
Minto, William	Orinda Park	5	2	3	2		No.		Zinfandel, Muscat.
Sandow, George	Orinda Park	2			2				Muscat.
Wagner, Theo.	Orinda Park	18	18	14	4		Yes.	5,000 gals.	Zinfandel, Chasselas, Riesling, Mataro, Muscat.
Gambs, John	Pacheco	30	22	30			Yes.	50 tons.	Chasselas, Rose Peru, Zinfandel.
Gregory, A.	Pacheco	10	10	5	5		No.		Table grapes and Zinfandel.
Lamb, E. R.	Pacheco	5		5			No.		Zinfandel.
Lavizola, John	Pacheco	10		10			No.		
Lohse, C. S.	Pacheco	12	1	8	4		No.		Zinfandel, Mission, and Table.
Louchs, F. F.	Pacheco	17	15	17			Yes.	45 tons.	Zinfandel, Mataro, Sauvignon Vert.
Ott, John	Pacheco	10	10	5	5		No.		
O'Kief, John	Pacheco	10		6	4		No.		Zinfandel, Muscat.
Pacheco, Mrs.	Pacheco	6	5	5			No.		Mission.
Russi, George	Pacheco	10	5	10			No.		
Showers, Andrew	Pacheco	40		20	20		No.		Zinfandel, mixed table.
Walker, J. T.	Pacheco	13		10	3		No.		Zinfandel.
Wells, Mrs. Philip	Pacheco	15		15			No.		Muscat, Tokay, Emperor.
Bancroft, H. H.	Pacheco	40			40		No.		Mixed table.
Bent, Henry	Walnut Creek	5			5	1	No.		
Bente, Henry	Walnut Creek	8	8	6½	7		No.	20 tons.	Mission, Tokay, Muscat, Zinfandel, Sweetwater.
Bracket, Mrs.	Walnut Creek	19	12	12			No.		Mission, Muscat.
Geary, L.	Walnut Creek	12	12	12			No.		Zinfandel.
Hazeltine, Chas.	Walnut Creek	8	8	8			No.		Zinfandel, Mission.
Hook, Jas. S.	Walnut Creek	52	52	52			Yes.	230 tons.	Malvoisie, Mission, Rose Peru, Chasselas, mixed wine.
Moore, L.	Walnut Creek	14	8	9	5		No.		Zinfandel, Table.
Moore, L.	Walnut Creek	14		6½	1	6½	No.	15 tons.	Zinfandel, Black Hamburg, Mission, Malvoisie, Muscat.
Napthaly, Jos.	Walnut Creek	80	60	70	10		Yes.		Zinfandel, Chasselas Vert, Riesling, Mataro, and table grapes.
Penniman, W. H.	Walnut Creek	17	17	10	7		No.		Mission, Muscat.
Rosenthal, J.	Walnut Creek								
Shuey, H.	Walnut Creek	2	2	2			No.		Mission.

Name of Owner	Post Office and Name of Vineyard	Total Acres in Grapes	Acres in Bearing	Acres in Wine Grapes	Acres in Table Grapes	Acres in Raisin Grapes	Wine Maker	Product in 1880	Varieties
Smith, Thos.	Walnut Creek	5	5			5			Muscat, Tokay.
Wait, —	Walnut Creek	4	4						Muscat, Tokay.
Weston, C. K.	Walnut Creek	10	10	5	5				Zinfandel, Petite Bouschet, St. Vert, Tokay, Muscat.
Totals for county		3,141½	1,750¾	2,085	975	81½			

EL DORADO COUNTY.

Name of Owner	Post Office and Name of Vineyard	Total Acres in Grapes	Acres in Bearing	Acres in Wine Grapes	Acres in Table Grapes	Acres in Raisin Grapes	Wine Maker	Product in 1880	Varieties
Corson, Geo.	Clarksville	10	10	10			Yes.	15 tons.	
Almstalden, F.	Coloma	30	30		30			90 tons.	
Annable, —	Coloma	10	10		10	10	No.	30 tons.	
Beebe, E.	Coloma	10	10					25 tons.	
Bishop, John	Coloma	15	15		15			45 tons.	
Coloma Vineyard	Coloma	75	75	60	15		Yes.	225 tons.	
Coppleman, J.	Coloma	10	10		10			30 tons.	
Endress, G. D.	Coloma	20	20	20				60 tons.	
Gale, Geo.	Coloma	9	9		9			27 tons.	
Haggart, D.	Coloma	10	10		10			30 tons.	
Hathaway, —	Coloma	2	2		2			6 tons.	
Hooper, W. H.	Coloma	30	30			30	No.	75 tons.	
Hume, R.	Coloma	10	10	10	5	5		25 tons.	
Immer, August	Coloma	30	30	20			No.	75 tons.	
Johnson, C. J.	Coloma	20	20	20	10		No.	50 tons.	
Jones, John	Coloma	10	10		20			30 tons.	
Kane, Patrick	Coloma	20	20					60 tons.	
Keene, James	Coloma	10	10	10	10			25 tons.	
Kesselring, A.	Coloma	10	10			8	No.	30 tons.	
Livingston, Thos.	Coloma	18	18	10	10			45 tons.	
McBeth, R.	Coloma	10	10					30 tons.	
McKay, R.	Coloma	20	20	20			No.	50 tons.	
Mortensen, E.	Coloma	10	10	10			No.	25 tons.	
Moseley, I. I.	Coloma	10	10	10	2			25 tons.	
Meyers, L. I.	Coloma	2	2					6 tons.	
Oterick, W. D.	Coloma	25	25	25				62¼ tons.	

EL DORADO COUNTY—Continued.

NAME OF OWNER.	Post Office and Name of Vineyard.	Total Acres in Grapes.	Acres in Bearing.	Acres in Wine Grapes	Acres in Table Grapes	Acres in Raisin Grapes	Wine Maker	Product in 1889.	Varieties.
Ramsey, Geo. W.	Coloma	10	10	5	10			30 tons.	
Rutherford, J. G.	Coloma	10	10	10	5	5		30 tons.	
Smith, H.	Coloma	20	20		5			60 tons.	
Smith, E. M., and Lamb	Coloma	10	10		10	20		30 tons.	
Valentine, W. H.	Coloma	40	40		20			120 tons.	
Veerkamp, W.	Coloma	5	5		5			15 tons.	
Wagner, Wm.	Coloma	10	10		10			30 tons.	
White, Wm.	Coloma	10	10	5	5		Yes.	25 tons.	
Cramp, P.	Diamond Springs	30	30	30	10			75 tons.	
Dunlop, John	Diamond Springs	20	20	10			No.	60 tons.	
Hickey, Pat.	Diamond Springs	10	10	10			Yes.	25 tons.	
Illson, F.	Diamond Springs	10	10	10				25 tons.	
Koch, Mrs.	Diamond Springs	20	20	20			Yes.	50 tons.	
Miller, Mrs. P.	Diamond Springs	15	15	15			No.	37½ tons.	
Miller, Samuel	Diamond Springs	20	20	20				60 tons.	
Schnider, J.	Diamond Springs	10	10	10				25 tons.	
Wirtz, C.	Diamond Springs	25	25	25			Yes.	62½ tons.	
Zentgroft, Anton	Diamond Springs	5	5	5	2			12½ tons.	
Davis, L. M.	El Dorado	5	5	3			No.	15 tons.	
Forin, C.	El Dorado	10	10	10				30 tons.	
Kinsly, Jacob	El Dorado	5	5	3	2		No.	15 tons.	
McDonald, John	El Dorado	5	5	3	2		No.	15 tons.	
Norton, F.	El Dorado	10	10	10				30 tons.	
Smith, E. H.	El Dorado	10	10		5	5	No.	30 tons.	
Yoble, C.	Frenchtown	20	20	20			Yes.	60 tons.	
Watkins, D.	Granite Hill	10	10		5	5	No.	30 tons.	
Forin, D.	Granite Hill	20	20		10	10	No.	30 tons.	
Veerkamp,	Greenwood	20	20					00 tons.	
Johnson, David	Latrobe	10	10	10			Yes.	30 tons.	
Brandon, T. L.	Latrobe	20	20	20				60 tons.	
Corson, Geo.	Latrobe	10	10	10				50 tons.	
Hitchcock,	Latrobe	10	10	10				2½ tons.	
Kim, J.	Latrobe	20	20	20				60 tons.	
Miller, I. H.	Latrobe	10	10	10				25 tons.	

Name	Location							Tons
Schenck, Chas.	Latrobe	10	10	10				30 tons.
Alden, W. H.	Placerville	10	10	10		No.		30 tons.
Baum, ——	Placerville	25	20	25	10		5	50 tons.
Blanchard, Geo. G.	Placerville	10	25	5	5	No.	5	62½ tons.
Fraser, Thos.	Placerville	10	10	10		No.		30 tons.
Foster, Jas.	Placerville	10	10	10		No.		25 tons.
Hogan, C.	Placerville	30	30	30				25 tons.
Hulburt, B.	Placerville	10	10	10		No.		90 tons.
Kelow, J. W.	Placerville	20	20	30				30 tons.
Maglone, Dr. E. W.	Placerville	5	5		10			60 tons.
Sargent, J.	Placerville	5	5	5	20			15 tons.
Smith, H.	Placerville	20	20	10				15 tons.
Sweeney, James	Placerville	20	20	10	10	No.	5	00 tons.
Tinney, H.	Placerville	10	10		10	No.	5	00 tons.
Weymouth, J. L.	Placerville	10	10					30 tons.
Whitbeck, F. H.	Placerville	5	5	10	5			16 tons.
Witmer, E. W.	Placerville	10	10		5			30 tons.
Zeigler, J.	Placerville	5	5	10	5			30 tons.
Anderson, ——	Pilot Hill	10	10	5	2	No.		12½ tons.
Bailey, A. J.	Pilot Hill	10	10	8				25 tons.
Campbell, G.	Salmon Falls	10	10	10				30 tons.
Foster, J.	Salmon Falls	60	60	60				150 tons.
Hart, Hugo P.	Salmon Falls	40	40	40				120 tons.
Hawkins, J.	Salmon Falls	10	10	10				25 tons.
Iraniss, B.	Salmon Falls	5	5	5				15 tons.
Jackson, M.	Salmon Falls	5	5	5		No.		12½ tons.
Simpson, J.	Salmon Falls	10	10	10				30 tons.
Williams, Arthur	Salmon Falls	5	5	5				15 tons.
Barrett, G.	Shingle Springs	5	5	5				12½ tons.
Bennett, David	Shingle Springs	10	10	10		No.		25 tons.
Davidson, Thomas	Shingle Springs	10	10	10				30 tons.
Dugan, Mrs.	Shingle Springs	5	5	5				12½ tons.
Engesser, F.	Shingle Springs	10	20	9	1			20 tons.
Hall, D. T.	Shingle Springs	40	40	40		Yes.		100 tons.
Hensler, Conrad	Shingle Springs	5	5	3	2	No.		15 tons.
Hoax, John	Shingle Springs	26	28	20	6			52 tons.
Palmer, William	Shingle Springs	5	5	5				12½ tons.
Skinner, George	Shingle Springs	50	50	50				100 tons.
Ulenkamp, ——	Shingle Springs	5	5	5	3			10 tons.
Wolf, H.	Shingle Springs	15	15	12	2			90 tons.
Zentgrof, ——	Shingle Springs	25	25	23				50 tons.
Totals for county		1,512	1,512	1,019	370		123	

FRESNO COUNTY.

Name of Owner	Post Office and Name of Vineyard	Total Acres in Grapes	Total Acres in Wine Grapes	Acres in Wine Grapes not Bearing	Total Acres in Raisin Grapes	Acres in Raisin Grapes Bearing	Acres in Raisin Grapes not Bearing	Acres in Muscats	Acres in Malagas	Acres in Sultanas	Wine Maker
Bain, —— J. E.	Clifton (San Francisco)	25	6		19	9	10	19			No.
Cately, W. L.	Clifton	25			25	25		25			No.
Catley, M. L.	Clifton	13			13	9	4	13			No.
Dean, M. L.	Clifton	40			40		40	40			No.
Fowler, D. T. (Superintendent)	Clifton (Del Rio Rey)	190			190		190	190			No.
Griece, H.	Clifton	15			15	15		15			No.
Hopper, S. D.	Clifton	25			25	15	10	25			No.
Henly, H. W.	Clifton	27			27	27			27		No.
Wilson, R. P.	Clifton	35			35		35	35			No.
Pearson Bros.	Clifton	15			15	15		15			No.
Potter, W. N.	Clifton	25			25		25	15			No.
Rieeley & Williams	Clifton	30			30	5	25	30			No.
Rose, L. A.	Clifton	23			23		23	23			No.
Sanders, W.	Clifton	30			30		30	30			No.
Scott, L. D.	Clifton	80			80	10	70	80			No.
Vance, L. E.	Clifton	20			20		20	20			No.
Wells, B.	Clifton	6			5	5		5			No.
Wilkinson Bros.	Clifton	15			15	4	11	15			No.
Wilson, C.	Clifton	65			65		65	65			No.
Alberg, G. A.	Easton	7			7	4	3	2	5		No.
Almgran, A. P.	Easton	6			6	5	1	6			No.
Anderson, C. F.	Easton	20			20		20	4		16	No.
Atwater, W. B.	Easton	7			7	3	4	7			No.
Beardley, G. E.	Easton	14			14		14	14			No.
Bixby, M. H.	Easton	9			9	9		9			No.
Brooks, Henry	Easton	12			12	6	6	12			No.
Brooks, J. H.	Easton	18			18	10	8	14		4	No.
Carlsen, H.	Easton	5			5	5		5			No.
Chilgren, N.	Easton	20			20	12	8	20			No.
Clark, C. E.	Easton	9			9	9		9			No.
Conlan, William	Easton	30			30		30	30			No.
Dan, John	Easton	10			10		10	10			No.
Davenhill, H.	Easton	6			6	6		5			No.
Davies, John D.	Easton	13			13	13		12		1	No.

Name	No.	No.	No.	No.	No.	No.	No.	No.	No.	P. O.
Dickenson, J. E.			28	22	6	28		2	30	Easton
Dwelle, J. C.			11		11	11		3	14	Easton
Eirickson, C. A.			10		2	10			10	Easton
Ellis, J. R.			60	8	10	50			50	Easton
Ericksen, Hans			6	5		5			5	Easton
Field, A. T.		1	14	8	7	15			15	Easton
Fisher, Jacob			25	5	20	25			25	Easton
Gorden, W. W.			4		4	4			4	Easton
Hansen, Hans		2	3	3		3			3	Easton
Hansen, J.			16		15	15			15	Easton
Hansen, J. S.			9	7	2	9			12	Easton
Hansen, L.		2	7		9	9		3	9	Easton
Hansen, P.		6	10	10		10			10	Easton
Hardwick, E. A.			5	5		5			5	Easton
Hays, N.			5	5		5			5	Easton
Hayse, D. J.			14	4	12	18			16	Easton
Johanson, A.			20	10	18	28			28	Easton
Johnson, J.			5		5	5			5	Easton
Jones, T. B., & Bro.			60		60	60		3	60	Easton
Larsen, H.			27	2	25	27			30	Easton
Larsen, H.			20	20		20			20	Easton
Larsen, Hender			6	6		6		10	6	Easton
Lindrose, J. M.			15	5	10	15			25	Easton
Lindstrom, H.			5		5	5			5	Easton
Lonsdale, F. T.			11		11	11			11	Easton
Lowery, J. T.			30	6	20	30			30	Easton
McCormick, M. E.	1		27	10	28	28		10	28	Easton
McKersie, ——			18		18	18			18	Easton
Madsen, Jans			20	3		20			30	Easton
Madsen, P.			12	10		12			12	Easton
Madsen, Peter			8	12		8			8	Easton
Mooney, P.			12	8		12			12	Easton
Muller, J. P.		2	15	7		15			15	Easton
Nyman, F.			4		5	6		3	9	Easton
O'Donnell, D.	2		6	3	15	6			6	Easton
Palmer, Mrs. C.			9	2	6	8			8	Easton
Peterson, J. H.		2	12	5	3	12			12	Easton
Pickle, J.			15		6	15			15	Easton
Pouton, T.		2	10		7	12			12	Easton
Prather, J. D.			40	4	15	40			40	Easton
Redley, Wm.			10	40	8	10			10	Easton
Rowell, Frank			15	10		15			15	Easton
Rowell, Geo. B.		2	11	15	5	13			11	Easton
Rozey, P.			10	6	13	15		3	16	Easton
Sandstrom, ——		3	15	15		15			15	Easton

FRESNO COUNTY—Continued.

Name of Owner	Post Office and Name of Vineyard	Wine Maker	Acres in Sultanas	Acres in Malagas	Acres in Muscats	Acres in Raisin Grapes not Bearing	Acres in Raisin Grapes Bearing	Total Acres in Raisin Grapes	Acres in Wine Grapes not Bearing	Total Acres in Wine Grapes	Total Acres in Grapes
Sandstrom, F.	Easton	No.	1	5	4		10	10			10
Selden, F. E.	Easton	No.			25	25		25			25
Silver, M. B.	Easton	No.			65		65	65			65
Simpson, J.	Easton	No.			30	30		30			30
Smith, C. C.	Easton	No.			16		16	16			16
Smith, Ed.	Easton	No.		4	30	10	20	30			30
Smith, John.	Easton	No.			6		6	6			6
Snedden, T. B.	Easton	No.		2	41	10	35	45			45
Sorensen, H.	Easton	No.			40	9	31	40			40
Stiles, S. A.	Easton	No.			10	1	11	12			12
Studer, G.	Easton	No.			14		14	14			14
Sudden, James	Easton	No.			10	2	8	10			10
Telin, Chas.	Easton	No.		5	23	9	14	23			23
Thomas, T. B.	Easton	No.		6	6	11		11			11
Tiele, A.	Easton	No.		3	2		8	8			8
Todd, Miss P. P.	Easton	No.		2	17	10	10	20		2	20
Warlow, J. R.	Easton	No.			18		20	20			22
Wass, L.	Easton	No.			18	9	9	18			18
Wescot, W. W.	Easton	No.			12	6	6	12			12
Whitthouse, A. J. F.	Easton	No.			13	13		13			13
Zipperlen, A.	Easton	No.			13	9	4	13			13
Allen, J. E.	Fowler	No.			3	3		3			3
Anderson, J.	Fowler	No.			14	14		14			14
Anthony, W.	Fowler	No.			48	48		48			48
Armstrong, A. B.	Fowler	No.			16		16	16			16
Ash, David	Fowler	No.			40	29	11	40			40
Barling, B. F.	Fowler	No.			25	15	10	25			25
Barnes, W.	Fowler	No.			20	20		20			20
Barnett, Wm.	Fowler	No.			20	18		20			20
Blaquey, O. C.	Fowler	No.			18			18			18
Bomner, John	Fowler	No.			50	10	50	50			50
Bonosil, J. B.	Fowler	No.			50	35	40	50			50
Bunton, W. E.	Fowler	No.			45	5	10	45			45

Name	Location	No.	No.	No.	No.	No.	No.	No.
Burdick, J. P.	Fowler (Oakland)		80	80		80		80
Burton, C. M.	Fowler		15	15	10	15		15
Candis, T.	Fowler		17	7	25	17		17
Cannon, D.	Fowler	2	30	5	5	30		30
Cardwell, W. M.	Fowler		3		22	5		8
Chapman, M.	Fowler		22	20	5	22		22
Clark, M.	Fowler		25		12	25		25
Claughran, J. H.	Fowler		12		10	12		12
Compton, Rev. Mr.	Fowler		10	5	10	10		10
Coolage, F.	Fowler		15	48	12	15		15
Coolage, W. M.	Fowler		60		35	60		60
Cramer, Miss L.	Fowler		35	11	3	35		35
Cuntz, A.	Fowler	1	14	7		14		14
Darling, John	Fowler		7	7		7		7
Darling, L.	Fowler		11	0	5	11		11
Darling, W. G.	Fowler		8		8	8	3	8
Davenport, E.	Fowler		12	9	3	12		12
Davis, F. I.	Fowler		20	20		20		20
Davis, Joe	Fowler		12		12	12		12
Dean, A.	Fowler		11	30		11		11
Docker, S.	Fowler		30		20	30		30
Dodge, G. W.	Fowler		20	15	23	20		20
Edmunds, G. M.	Fowler		23	40		23		23
Elliott, P.	Fowler		15	15		15		15
Ellis, J. R.	Fowler		40	15		40		40
Emmerson, T.	Fowler		15	3		15		15
Extrum, O.	Fowler		3	20	40	3	5	3
Fever,	Fowler		60	5	5	60		60
Foster, Mrs. Mary	Fowler		10	7	7	10		10
Frasier, John	Fowler		14	11	4	14		14
Frolich, Theo.	Fowler		15	4		15		15
Fullerton, G. D.	Fowler		4	28		4		4
Gardner Bros.	Fowler		28		130	28		28
Gautenlaull, A.	Fowler		130			130		130
Gier, C.	Fowler		10	10		10		10
Giffen, Geo. H.	Fowler		16	18		16		16
Gillmore,	Fowler		16		25	16		16
Gilson, J. H.	Fowler		20	20	5	20		20
Goode Bros.	Fowler		45	30	20	45		45
Gower, E.	Fowler		35	10	10	35		35
Gray, A.	Fowler		30	2		30		30
Haber, H. P.	Fowler		18	25	3	18		18
Harris, Amos	Fowler		25	30	56	25		25
Hastie, P. W.	Fowler		33	4	20	33		33
Hathaway, B. H.	Fowler		60	10		60		60

FRESNO COUNTY—Continued.

Name of Owner	Post Office and Name of Vineyard	Total Acres in Grapes	Total Acres in Wine Grapes	Acres in Wine Grapes not Bearing	Total Acres in Raisin Grapes	Acres in Raisin Grapes Bearing	Acres in Raisin Grapes not Bearing	Acres in Muscats	Acres in Malagas	Acres in Sultanas	Wine Maker
Heidrick, A., estate of	Fowler	22			22	7	15	22			No.
Hollingsworth, ___	Fowler	15			15		15	15			No.
Hopkins, L. E.	Fowler	13			13	5	8	13			No.
Hutchinson, B. E.	Fowler	42			42	20	22	42			No.
Jamison, J.	Fowler	50			50	5	45	50			No.
Jett, George	Fowler	35			35	35		35			No.
Johnson, J.	Fowler	35			35	30	5	35			No.
Kennedy, J. F.	Fowler	10			10	3	7	10			No.
Kennedy, J. K.	Fowler	20			20	10	10	20			No.
Kennedy, W. L.	Fowler	6			6		6	6			No.
Kimble, J. C.	Fowler (Oakland)	160			160		160	160	1		Yes.
Kirby, C. K.	Sierra Park Vineyard, Fowler	250	116		134	80	54	131		3	No.
Lamore, J. V.	Fowler	17			17	9	8	17			No.
Leeper, J. W.	Fowler	13			13	4	9	13			No.
Lincoln, G. W.	Fowler	15			15	15		15			No.
Logan, H. E.	Fowler	16			16	16		16			No.
Lyman, F. & C.*	Fowler	15			15	15		15			No.
McFarlane, John	Fowler	22			22	10	12	22			No.
Manley, E.	Fowler	20			20	5	15	20			No.
Manley, W. F.	Fowler	30			30	10	20	30			No.
Martin, ___	Fowler	15			15		15	15			No.
Mason, M. W.	Fowler	3			3		3	3			No.
Maxwell, M. C.	Fowler	16			16		16	16			No.
Melvin, ___	Fowler	20			20		20	20			No.
Merrill, J. M.	Fowler	100			100		100	100			No.
Mitchell, D. F.	Fowler	22			22		22	22			No.
Mitchell, S. H.	Fowler	30			30		30	30			No.
Moore, F. L.	Fowler	20			20	14	6	20			No.
Mullarkay & Bro.	Fowler	60			60	25	35	60			No.
Neuhoefer, C.	Fowler	15			15		15	15			No.
Nock, Thomas	Fowler	14			14		14	14			No.
Norris, C. C.	Fowler	20			20		20	20			No.
Norris, C. H.	Fowler	140			140	40	100	140			No.

*F. & C. Lyman have seventeen acres near Fresno, which see.

Name	No.	No.	No.	No.	No.	No.	Location
Norris, L. H.	35	20	15	35		36	Fowler
Pabon, J.	16	10	6	16	2	18	Fowler
Parkhurst, D. W.	140	100	40	140		140	Fowler
Patten, J. T.	20	20	50	20		70	Fowler
Payton, G.	18	18		18		18	Fowler
Peacock, G.	6		6	6		6	Fowler
Perrin, J. B.	30	25	20	30		30	Fowler
Prather, Joe L.	25			25	10	25	Fowler
Pratt, E. L.	7		7	7		7	Fowler
Prickett, G. W.	31	20	31	31		31	Fowler
Poter Bros.	20	7	8	20		20	Fowler
Reed & Beavan	15	5	5	15		15	Fowler
Rose, M. S.	10	15		10		10	Fowler
Ross, H.	15		10	15		15	Fowler
Rowell, A.	10		3	10		10	Fowler
Runciman, W. H.	6	3		6		6	Fowler
Schaffer, Miss.	40	40	20	40		40	Fowler
Shannon, G. R.	25	5	20	25		25	Fowler
Shannon, W. R.	30	10	8	30		30	Fowler
Shoemaker, A.	20	12	6	20		20	Fowler
Short & Gorden	16	10	14	16		16	Fowler
Simonds, C. G.	35	21	15	35		35	Fowler
Simons, S. H.	20	5	8	21	1	21	Fowler
Stewart, L.	25	17	22	25		25	Fowler
Stone, John.	22		30	22		22	Fowler
Stone, Samuel	30		11	30		30	Fowler
Storie, R. C.	17			17		17	Fowler
Fennan, James	10	6		10		10	Fowler
Thomas, ——	8	10	16	8		8	Fowler
Thompson, ——	15	8		15		15	Fowler
Trobridge, ——	35		30	35		35	Fowler
Uridge, W.	15	35		15		15	Fowler
Vanwormer & Lever	50	15	30	75	25	75	Maud Vineyard, Fowler
Viau, S.	40	20	5	40		40	Fowler
Victor, Frank	70	40	10	70		70	Fowler
Wallace, J. H.	8	40	40	8		8	Fowler
Weinanski, J.	10	3	6	10		10	Fowler
Wetzel, Theo.	40		15	40		40	Fowler
Wilson, H. H. D.	23			23		23	Fowler
Wordsworth, ——	15	17	6	15		15	Fowler
Abby, R. W.	35			35		35	Fresno
Acworth, J. A.	10	35	10	10		10	Fresno
Adelsback, A.	11	4		11		11	Fresno
Alexander, C. M.	10	11	10	10		10	Fresno
Alexander, T. J.	5		5	5		5	Fresno

FRESNO COUNTY—Continued.

Name of Owner	Post Office and Name of Vineyard	Total Acres in Grapes	Total Acres in Wine Grapes	Acres in Wine Grapes not Bearing	Total Acres in Raisin Grapes	Acres in Raisin Grapes Bearing	Acres in Raisin Grapes not Bearing	Acres in Muscats	Acres in Malagas	Acres in Sultanas	Wine Maker
Allen, J.	Fresno	7			7	7		7			No.
Allison, Thomas	Fresno	25			25	10	15	25			No.
Ambrose, John	Fresno	18			18		18	18			Yes.
Anderson, C. G.	Fresno	35	30		5	5			5		No.
Anderson, F.	Fresno	12	9		3	3		2		1	No.
Anderson, Mrs. A. O.	Fresno	30			30		30	30			No.
Anderson, Mrs. M.	Fresno	3			3	2	1	3			No.
Anderson, T. H.	Fresno	12			12	4	8	12			No.
Applegarth, W.	Fresno	80			80	40	40	80			No.
Apply & Co.	Fresno	80			80		80	80			No.
Arakelian, John	Fresno	20	4		16	7	9	10			No.
Ariey, M.	Fresno	15			15	1	14	15			No.
Arekelian, J.	Fresno	10			10		10	10			No.
Armstrong,	Fresno	20	10		10		10	10			No.
Armstrong, W.	Fresno	5			5		5	5			No.
Arty, G. M.	Fresno	16			16	10	6	10			No.
Ashley, John	Fresno	28			28	8	20	28			No.
Austin, J. R.	Fresno	50			50	50		50			No.
Avakian, H.	Fresno	15			15		15	15			No.
Averett & Stephens	Fresno	75			75		75	75			No.
Ayer, Isaac	Fresno	13			13		13	13			No.
Azdarian, A.	Fresno	10			10	5	5	10			No.
Azhderian, H.	Fresno	15			15	10	5	15			No.
Babcock, A. B.	Fresno	25			25	25		15	8	2	No.
Bachant, I.	Fresno	16	14		2	2		2			No.
Bachman, N. L. F.	Fresno	20			20	20		20			No.
Baird Bros.	Fresno	50			50	25	25	48		2	No.
Baird, Mrs. L. B.	Fresno	30			30	30		30			No.
Baker, D.	Fresno	12			12	4	8	12			No.
Baker, L.	Fresno	20	4		16	10	6	16			No.
Baker, W. J., & Co.	Fresno	43	7		36	25	11	36			No.
Balch, George	Fresno	31			31		31	31			No.
Balfour & Fortuno.	Fresno	132			132	15	117	132			No.

Name	Location								No./Yes.
Balfour, Robert, & Fortuno	Fresno		40			40		40	No.
Ball, Frank	Fresno		112		112	112		112	No.
Banister, W. B.	Fresno	6	7	2		7	1	15	No.
Barclay, James	Fresno		15		5	15		15	No.
Barling, A. D.	Fresno		170	20	150	170		170	No.
Barnard, George	Fresno		30	20	10	30		30	No.
Barnwell, W.	Fresno		30	30		30		30	No.
Barr, A.	Fresno		25		25	25		25	No.
Barrett, G. H.	Fresno			35		75		75	Yes.
Barry, John	Fresno		4		25	4		4	No.
Barstow, R. W.	Fresno	1	15		40	16		16	No.
Barton, Robert, estate of	Fresno	100	165	240	4	265	535	800	No.
Bartels, E.	Fresno		8	63	16	8		8	No.
Bates, Dr. C. M.	Fresno		75	22	25	75		75	No.
Beal, G. W.	Fresno		22	52	12	22		22	No.
Beard, John	Fresno		52	52		52		52	No.
Beardslee, C. W.	Fresno		11	8		11	9	11	No.
Beck, R.	Fresno				8			9	No.
Beckwith, R. E.	Fresno		60	20	40	60		60	No.
Beebe, C. A.	Fresno		30	30		30		30	No.
Benenfelt, B.	Fresno		55	10	45	55		55	No.
Bernhauer, W.	Fresno		14	6	8	14		14	No.
Berry, F. G.	Fresno		10		10	10		10	No.
Beverage, J. S.	Fresno		16	4	12	16		16	No.
Bird, R. R. (Superintendent)	Fresno		320	320		320		320	No.
Bislen, P.	Fresno		5	5		5		5	No.
Bissell, H. B.	Fresno		4		4	4		4	No.
Bitner, M.	Fresno		12	2	10	12		12	No.
Blackburn, F. A.	Fresno		48	8	40	48	7	65	No.
Blackwell Bros.	Fresno		12	12		12		12	No.
Blackwell, J.	Fresno		60	35	15	50		50	No.
Blasingame, Lee	Fresno		25	5	20	25	35	60	No.
Boncon, P.	Fresno		5	5		5		5	No.
Bonne, Emma E.	Fresno		40	40		40		40	No.
Boot, Robert	Fresno		14		14	14	2	16	No.
Borrman, J. C.	Fresno		12	12		12		12	No.
Boucher, C. H.	Fresno		10	10		10		10	No.
Bowen,	Fresno		6	8		6		6	No.
Bowen, J. J.	Fresno		20	10	10	20		20	No.
Boyd, George	Fresno		16	18	6	16	7	18	No.
Boyd, Miss Nellie	Fresno	1	9	4		10		10	No.
Bradford, W. R.	Fresno		24	24		24		34	No.
Bradley, J. A.	Fresno (San Francisco)		40	20	20	40		40	No.
Breashear, J. J.	Fresno		20	20		20		20	No.
Bresler, Dr. W. L.	Fresno		5	1	4	5		5	No.

FRESNO COUNTY—Continued.

Wine Maker	Acres in Sultanas	Acres in Malagas	Acres in Muscats	Acres in Raisin Grapes not Bearing	Acres in Raisin Grapes Bearing	Total Acres in Raisin Grapes	Acres in Wine Grapes not Bearing	Total Acres in Wine Grapes	Total Acres in Grapes	Post Office and Name of Vineyard	NAME OF OWNER
No.			40		40	40			40	Fresno	Brisco, W. H.
No.			8		8	8			8	Fresno	Brown, ——
No.			9	9		9			9	Fresno	Brown, Frank
No.			40		40	40			40	Fresno	Brown, J. H.
No.			50		50	50			50	Fresno	Brown, Tom
No.			33	33		33			33	Fresno	Bruce, G.
No.			10	10		10			10	Fresno	Bruce, W.
No.			14		14	14			14	Fresno	Brunum, L.
No.								15	15	Fresno	Buckley, J. R.
No.			35		35	35			35	Fresno	Burgess, T. H.
No.			35		35	35			35	Fresno	Burnam, F.
No.	10		600	55	555	610			610	Fresno	Butler, Alban B.
No.			30		30	30			30	Nestell Vineyard, Fresno	Butler, P. W. (Superintendent)
No.			9		9	9			9	Fresno	Cabott, E. R.
No.		2	5		7	7			7	Fresno	Caffigian, Paul M.
No.			15		15	15			15	Fresno	Cain, C. E.
No.			5		5	5		10	15	Fresno	Cain, Dr.
No.			7		7	7			7	Fresno	Camey, ——
No.			35		35	35			35	Fresno	Campbell, Judge J. B.
No.			38		38	38			38	Fresno	Carey, H.
No.			10		10	10			10	Fresno	Carlson, Gus
No.			5		5	5	5	5	10	Fresno	Carlson, J. M.
No.			3		3	3			3	Fresno	Carrothers, J. A.
No.		8	3		11	11	5	5	16	Fresno	Carter, B. B.
No.		6	54		60	60			60	Fresno	Carter, G. W. T.
No.			35		35	35			35	Fresno	Cartwright, ——
No.			7		7	7			7	Fresno	Cartwright, A.
No.	2		8		8	8			8	Fresno	Cartwright, G. W.
No.			30		30	30			30	Fresno	Cartwright, J. C.
No.			13		13	13			13	Fresno	Cartwright, J. E.
No.			6		6	6			6	Fresno	Cartwright, R. N.
No.			13		13	13			13	Fresno	Castelo, A.
No.		13	35	13	35	35			35	Fresno	Chaddock, E. G.
No.			20	4	16	20			20	Fresno	Childes, O.

Name	Location								
Choice, H. B.	Fresno	No.			17		17	17		20
Church, Firman	Fresno	No.			10		10	10		10
Church, George K.	Fresno	No.			10		10	10		15
Church, George F.	Fresno	No.			20	20		20		20
Church, L. B.	Fresno	No.			100		100	100		100
Clark, C.	Fresno	No.			70	43	27	70		70
Clark, Charles	Fresno	No.	5		60	35	90	65		65
Clark, J.	Fresno	No.	4		3		7	7		7
Clay, Mrs. R. A.	Fresno	No.	1		2	3		3		18
Clifford, V.	Fresno	No.			6	6		6		6
Cogan, Capt. B.	Fresno	No.	10		130	140		140	15	140
Cole, A. R.	Fresno	No.			35	35		35		35
Cole, U.	Fresno	No.	10		4	14		14		14
Collins & Elliott	Fresno	No.			25	10		25		25
Coney, J. F.	Fresno	No.			35		15	3		3
Conger, J. W.	Fresno	No.			25	25	16	25		25
Conlin, C.	Fresno	No.			10		3	10		10
Conn, J.	Fresno	No.			20		10	20		20
Conner, J. C.	Fresno	No.			16		12	16		16
Coley,	Fresno	No.			3		14	3		3
Cook, F. M.	Fresno	No.			30	30	30	30		30
Cornell, C.	Fresno	No.	6		10	4	4	10		10
Cornell, Fred.	Fresno	No.			8	6	8	8		8
Cory, J. M.	Fresno	No.			80		80	80		80
Costagcon, Cohen & Co.	Fresno	No.			10	16		16		16
Coughill, A.	Fresno	No.			15	18	15	15		15
Coughill, C. A.	Fresno	No.			18	30		18		18
Cowen,	Fresno	No.			30	80		30		30
Cowen & Dunlap	Fresno	No.			80	15		80		80
Cowen, W.	Fresno	No.			18			18	11	18
Crane, J.	Fresno	No.	2		1	3	3	3		14
Creelman, J.	Fresno	No.			7	3	7	7		7
Creighton, T. J.	Fresno	No.			35	19	35	35		35
Creighton, T. J.	Fresno	No.	1		6		4	7	4	7
Cropsey, Mrs. E.	Fresno	No.	2		6		8	8	20	8
Cross,	Fresno	No.			7	3	4	7		7
Cross,	Fresno	No.			19	19	8	19		19
Cross, Tom	Fresno	No.			8		8	8		12
Cureton, J. W.	Fresno	No.	5		25	10	20	30		60
Curlen, Mrs.	Fresno	Yes.			3		3	3		3
Curran, Mrs.	Fresno	No.			17	17	7	17	2	17
Curtis, J. L.	Fresno	No.			6	6		6		6
Cutler, C. W.	Fresno	No.			12	5		12		12
Dale, O. R.	Fresno	No.			7	3		7		9
Darling, Fred.	Fresno	No.			130		130	130		130

FRESNO COUNTY—Continued.

Name of Owner	Post Office and Name of Vineyard	Total Acres in Grapes	Total Acres in Wine Grapes	Acres in Wine Grapes not Bearing	Total Acres in Raisin Grapes	Acres in Raisin Grapes Bearing	Acres in Raisin Grapes not Bearing	Acres in Muscats	Acres in Malagas	Acres in Sultanas	Wine Maker
Darnold, J. S.	Fresno	14			14		14	14			No.
Dart Bros.	Fresno	30			30		30	30			No.
Davenhill, William	Fresno	6			6			6			No.
Davis, ____	Fresno	20			20		20	20			No.
Davis, F. A.	Fresno	9			9	9		8	1		No.
Davis, H. E.	Fresno	5			5		5	5			No.
Dean, Miss M.	Fresno	30			30	30		30			No.
Deardoff, Dr. A. G.	Fresno	40			40		40	40			No.
Deering, Henry	Fresno	15			15	15		15			No.
Denicke, M.	Fresno	70	40	10	30	20	10	30			Yes.
Desworth, C. L.	Fresno	5	3		2	2		2			No.
Dickey & Austin	Fresno	15	5		10	5	5	10			No.
Dickey, W. J.	Fresno	35			35	35		35			No.
Dixon, H. S.	Fresno	40			40	40		40			No.
Dodge, Moses	Fresno	15			15	12	3	12	3		No.
Doc, John	Fresno	10			10		10	10			No.
Dumont, W. M.	Fresno	10			10	3	7	10			No.
Doran, J. T.	Fresno	40			40	20	20	40			No.
Dorr, Ben.	Fresno	15			15	15		15			No.
Dorr, John.	Fresno	80			80	70	10	80			No.
Douglass, Frank	Fresno	16	2		14	14		14			No.
Dow, W. H.	Fresno	35			35	20	15	35			No.
Downey, James	Fresno	32			32	21	11	32			No.
Doyle, J.	Fresno	18			18	8	10	18			No.
Drexler, L. P. (Manager Fresno Vineyard Co.)	Fresno (San Francisco)	360	348		12	12		12			Yes.
Dron, Mrs. M. T.	Fresno	15	8		7	5	2	7			No.
Dudley, H.	Fresno	15			15	12	3	15			No.
Dudley, Geo. H.	Fresno	20			20	6	14	20			No.
Duering, H.	Fresno	8			8	8		8			No.
Dunbar, Dr. L. L.	Fresno (San Francisco)	75	5		70	35	35	70			No.
Dunlap, S. F.	Fresno	13			13	8	5	13			No.
Dusenbury, ____	Fresno	10			10	10		10			No.
Eckard, C.	Fresno	7			7		7	7			No.
Eckard, Wm.	Fresno	3			3	3		3			No.

Name	Post Office										
Eckard, W., Jr.	Fresno	4		16		20	20		20		No.
Eden, A. S.	Fresno			35	35		35		35		No.
Edgerly, A. S.	Fresno			65	65	65	65		65		No.
Edwards, E. D.	Fresno			70	5		70	5	75		No.
Eggers & Co.	Eggers Vineyard Co., Fresno			187	120	100	220	420	640		Yes.
Eickhoff, H.	Fresno			18		6	18		30		No.
Eisen, F. T.	Eisen Vineyard Co., Fresno	8	25	15		15	15	285	300		Yes.
Elert, F.	Fresno			15	10	15	15		15		No.
Eliott, Mrs. S.	Fresno			3		3	3		3		No.
Eliott, P.	Fresno			12		12	12		12		No.
Elmore, B. T.	Fresno			10	10		10		10		No.
Elwell, J. J.	Fresno			4		4	4		4		No.
Engebretson, F.	Fresno		5	17	14	3	17		17		No.
Erickson, C.	Fresno			20		20	20		20		No.
Eshleman, Miss M. D.	Fresno			125	70	55	125	25	150		No.
Evans, John	Fresno			16	16	10	16		16		No.
Ewing, Fred.	Fresno			15	5	13	15		15		No.
Fanning, Frank	Fresno			13			13		13		No.
Fanning, Fred.	Fresno			7	7		7		7		Yes.
Fanning, P. R.	Fresno			20		20	20		20		No.
Fawcett, Richard	Fresno			15	15	3	15		15		No.
Fay, E. C.	Fresno			5	2	8	5		5		No.
Fernando, Jim	Fresno			18	10	6	18		18		No.
Fest, O. L.	Fresno			10			16		15		No.
Fisher, S. C.	Fresno			40	40	80	40		40		No.
Fisher, W. A.	Fresno			230	150	10	230		230		No.
Ford, J.	Fresno			15	5	7	15		15		No.
Forsman, M. J.	Fresno	10		7		160	7		7		No.
Forsythe, William	Fresno			150	80	6	160		100		No.
Forsy, W. E. (Superintendent)	La Pasarica Vineyard, Fresno			80		12	80		80		No.
Foster, F.	Fresno	2	1	6		6	6		6		No.
Foster, T. R.	Fresno		2	9	12	12	12		12		Na.
Fowler, D.	Fresno			12		12	12		12		No.
Frasier, S. B.	Fresno			35	35	35	35		35		No.
Freeman, Dr. E.	Fresno			15	15	17	17		17		No.
Freeman, G. N.	Fresno			20	20	20	20		20		No.
Freeman, G. R. & G. E.	Fresno			30	30	20	30		30		No.
Freeman, Rev. G.	Fresno			35	15	8	35		35		No.
Fuller, Geo. W.	Fresno		4	8		8	8		8		No.
Gage, David	Fresno			4	25	8	8		8		No.
Gagliardo & Barileo	Fresno			25	20	25	25	5	30		No.
Gardener, Dr. R. C.	Fresno			20	6	20	20		20		No.
Garrett, J. M.	Fresno			6	8	6	6		6		No.
Gerrebrand, C.	Fresno			16		16	16		16		No.
Ghent, Rev. Mr.	Fresno			50	50	50	50	20	70		No.

4—v

FRESNO COUNTY—Continued.

Name of Owner	Post Office and Name of Vineyard	Total Acres in Grapes	Total Acres in Wine Grapes	Acres in Wine Grapes not Bearing	Total Acres in Raisin Grapes	Acres in Raisin Grapes Bearing	Acres in Raisin Grapes not Bearing	Acres in Muscats	Acres in Malagas	Acres in Sultanas	Wine Maker
Gibbs, T. H. H.	Fresno	12			12	6	6	6	6		No.
Gibson, J. H.	Fresno	40			40	5	35	40			No.
Gipson, Robt.	Fresno	6			6		6		6		No.
Glas, Mrs. K.	Fresno	7			7		7	7			No.
Goldstein, Alex.	Fresno	40			40		40	40			No.
Goodman, J. T.	Fresno	140			140	90	50	130		10	No.
Gordon & Grant	Fresno	145			145	145		145			No.
Gordon Bros.	Fresno	80			80		80	80			No.
Gorham, W. G.	Fresno	6			6	6		6			No.
Gould, E. W.	Fresno	14			14	14		14			No.
Grady, W. D.	Fresno	430			430	200	230	430			No.
Graham, Dr. E.	Fresno	2			2	2		2			No.
Granz, Herman	Fresno	70	55		15	15			20	5	Yes.
Gray, J. D.	Fresno	225	20		205	100	106	180		4	No.
Gray, P.	Fresno	10			10		10	6			No.
Gray, Wm.	Fresno	10			10		10	10			No.
Green & Chace	Fresno	35			35		35	35			No.
Green Bros.	Fresno	60			60		60	60			No.
Green, Frank	Fresno	85			85	25	60	35			No.
Grimstead, A.	Fresno	11			11		11	11			No.
Haber Bros.	Fresno	7	4		3	3		3			No.
Hager, ——	Fresno	15			15	15		15			No.
Hamilton, E.	Fresno	18			18		18	18			No.
Hamilton, J. F.	Fresno	10			10		10	10			No.
Hamilton, Steve.	Fresno	15			15		15	5			No.
Hancock, J. B.	Fresno	5			5		5		15		No.
Handy, Miss	Fresno	20			20	20		20			No.
Hansen, J.	Fresno	24	4		20	20		16			No.
Hansen, Jargen	Fresno	25	5		20		20	19		1	No.
Hansen, M. P.	Fresno	60	4		56		56	44	4		No.
Hansen, Niels	Fresno	18	4		14		14	18			No.
Hansen, N. J.	Fresno	8	4		4		4	4	4		No.
Hansen, N. P.	Fresno	15	2		13		13	13	2		No.

Name	Location	No.	No.	No.	No.	No.	No.	No.	No.	No.
Hanson, H.	Fresno			5		5	5			5
Harbaugh, L. F.	Fresno	1		4		3	6		3	9
Harber, Jos.	Fresno	1		25	3	25	25			25
Harding, J. H.	Fresno			25	25	1	25			25
Hartin, Mrs. M.	Fresno			3			3			3
Harrison, R. J.	Fresno			8	2	8	8			8
Harrub, W. B.	Fresno (Oakland)	1	10	40	40		40			40
Hartley Bros.	Fresno			6		16	16		4	20
Hartley, S. L.	Fresno			75		76	76		5	81
Hartley, Wm.	Fresno			25		25	25			26
Harvey, Wm.	Fresno			32		32	32			32
Hatch, I. H. (Austin estate)	Hedge Row Vineyard, Fresno	3		72		55	75			75
Haven & Laymace	Fresno (Oakland)	1	1	320	320		320			320
Haxkes, H.	Fresno			10		12	12			12
Hays, A. S.	Fresno			30			30		25	30
Hazen,	Fresno (San Francisco)			12	15	12	15			40
Helm, Geo. I.	Fresno				100		100			160
Hender, S. J.	Fresno				9		15			15
Henderson Bros.	Fresno		6			6	30			30
Henderson, E.	Fresno		10			30	12			12
Henningson, A.	Fresno		5			12	6		14	20
Henry, P.	Fresno			5	6	5	10			10
Heringlake, A. C.	Fresno			7	10	7	7			10
Hilberd, E. J.	Fresno			6	5		9			7
Hinsberger, J.	Fresno			30		90	30			14
Hitchings, E. W.	Fresno			13		15	15		5	30
Hoag, B. H.	Fresno	3		40	4		40			40
Hoffman & Anderson	Fresno		2	80	40	80	80		2	80
Hoffman, C.	Fresno			126	50	80	126		10	126
Hogue, S. L.	Fresno			13	46	13	13			13
Hollingworth, S.	Fresno			15			15			15
Hubbard, L. T.	Fresno			250	15	250	250			250
Hudson, D. D.	Fresno			4	4		4			4
Hudson, F.	Fresno			3		3	3			3
Hudson, G.	Fresno			5		8	8			10
Hughes, E. P.	Fresno			40	10		40			60
Hughes, J. F.	Fresno	3		30		90	30			30
Humphrey, E. E.	Fresno			3		30	3			8
Husey, Mrs. A. L.	Fresno			11	11		11			11
Hutchenson, B. E.	Fresno			14	4		14			14
Idle, Thomas	Fresno			20	16		20			20
Inns, C.	Fresno			3		10	3			3
Irwinn, S. J.	Fresno			18		4	18			18
Jackson, Andrew	Fresno			4	8	10	4			6
Jackson, P. C.	Fresno	2			2	4	6			6

FRESNO COUNTY—Continued.

Name of Owner	Post Office and Name of Vineyard	Wine Maker	Acres in Sultanas	Acres in Malagas	Acres in Muscats	Acres in Raisin Grapes not Bearing	Acres in Raisin Grapes Bearing	Total Acres in Raisin Grapes	Acres in Wine Grapes not Bearing	Total Acres in Wine Grapes	Total Acres in Grapes
Jacobson, E.	Fresno	No.			6	6		6			6
Jansen, H.	Fresno	No.		4	24	3	21	24		4	28
Jansen, Hans.	Fresno	No.			12	6	6	12			12
Jargenson, J.	Fresno	No.	1		11	10	5	15			15
Jargger, Wm.	Fresno	No.		2	14	10	7	17			17
Jensen,	Fresno	No.			5		5	5			5
Jensen,	Fresno	No.			11	11		11			11
Jillette,	Fresno	No.			40	40		40			40
Johnson, A.	Fresno	No.			10	10		10			10
Johnson, E.	Fresno	No.			8	5	3	8		2	10
Johnson, G.	Fresno	No.	4	4	5	4	5	9		14	23
Johnson, H.	Fresno	No.			25		25	25		5	30
Johnson, H. P.	Fresno	No.			3		3	3			3
Johnson, J.	Fresno	No.			12	12		12			12
Johnson, J. P.	Fresno	No.		18	2	17	3	20		14	34
Johnson, O.	Fresno	No.			29	13	20	33			33
Johnson, Olf.	Fresno	No.			10	10		10		10	20
Johnson, S.	Fresno	No.			12	4	8	12		2	14
Jorden, A. P.	Fresno	No.			20	8	12	20			20
Kaiser, J.	Fresno	No.			25	15	10	25			25
Kaufman, A.	Fresno	No.			8		8	8		1	8
Kavanaugh, M.	Fresno	No.	2		6	5		5			5
Keizajian, A.	Fresno	No.			14	2	12	14			14
Kelley, J. H.	Fresno	No.			7		9	9		1	10
Kelley, Mike.	Fresno	No.			25	9	16	25			25
Kendel, C. B.	Fresno	No.			14	7	7	14			14
Kenedy, E.	Fresno	No.			15	5	10	15			15
Kenstrup, W.	Fresno	No.			100	1	160	160			160
Keyser Bros.	Fresno	No.			7		6	7		6	13
Kingsberrey, Dr. W.	Freno	No.			60		60	60			60
Kippenberg, John	Fresno	No.			5		5	5			5
Koegel, E.	Fresno	Yes.			14	3	12	16		18	18
Knapp, E.	Fresno	No.		1	9		9	9			9

Name	Location										
Kneedy, M. H.	Fresno	No.			10	10		10			10
Knight, ――	Fresno	No.			20	20		20			20
Kruse, G.	Fresno	Yes.			18	18		18			18
Kruse, H.	Fresno	No.			20	20		20			20
Laird, Miss, estate of	Fresno	No.			10	2	8	10			10
Laird & Woods	Fresno	No.			10	7	3	10			10
Lamkin, J. S.	Fresno	No.			20	20		20			20
Lampe Bros.	Fresno	No.			35	35		35			35
Lamond, G.	Fresno	No.			16	6	16	16			16
Lang, O. O.	Fresno	No.		2	28		24	30			30
Lange, O. O.	Fresno	No.		2	14		16	16			16
Larsen, H. C.	Fresno	No.		1	6		4	7			7
Larsen, Pete	Fresno	No.			12	12		12			12
Lee, J.	Fresno	No.			7	7		7			7
Lee, M. J.	Fresno	No.			10	5	5	10			10
Leonhart Bros.	Fresno	Yes.	1	1	1		3	3		5	8
Levy, H.	Fresno	No.			40	40		40			40
Lewis, D. W.	Fresno	No.			70	15	65	70		80	70
Lind, Mrs. J. S.	Lind Vineyard, Fresno	No.			11		14	17		20	17
Littlefield, S.	Fresno	No.		6	330	3	130	360			380
Logan, F.	Fresno	No.		30	25	290		25			25
Long Bros.	Fresno	No.			10	25		14			14
Loomis, T. L.	Fresno	No.	4		10	6		10			10
Luce, Capt. J. L.	Fresno	Yes.			14			14			14
Lunstrum, J. F.	Fresno	No.			17	17	17	17			17
Lyman, F. & C. P.	Fresno	No.			17		10	17			17
McAllister, Dr. W. B.	Fresno	No.			25	15		25			25
McAninch, H. J.	Fresno	No.			38	36	9	38			38
McCabe, E. B.	Fresno	No.		6	24	15	80	30		6	30
McClean, F.	Fresno	No.			80		20	80			80
McClellen, Rev.	Fresno	No.			20		20	20			20
McConnell & Yergin	Fresno	No.			20	7	3	20			20
McCormick, J. B.	Fresno	No.			17		17	17			17
McDermid Bros.	Fresno	No.			10		10	10			10
McDougall, D. C.	Fresno	No.			10	6		10			10
McDougal, Duncan	Fresno	No.			6			6			6
McFarland, John	Fresno	No.			20		20	20	•		20
McGavitt, Mrs.	Fresno	No.			60	60		60			60
McGeary, ――	Fresno	No.			12	3	12	15			15
McKean, C. W.	Fresno	No.			5	5		5			5
McKey, A. B.	Fresno	No.			15		15	15			15
McKinney, Jane	Fresno	No.	3		14	14		14			14
McLennor, H. M.	Fresno	No.			30	10	20	30			30
McNally, J.	Fresno	No.			10	10		10			10

FRESNO COUNTY—Continued.

Name of Owner	Post Office and Name of Vineyard	Wine Maker	Acres in Sultanas	Acres in Malagas	Acres in Muscats	Acres in Raisin Grapes not Bearing	Acres in Raisin Grapes Bearing	Total Acres in Raisin Grapes	Acres in Wine Grapes not Bearing	Total Acres in Wine Grapes	Total Acres in Grapes
McVey, ——	Fresno	No.			20		20	20			20
McWhirter, George S.	Fresno	No.			5		5	5		9	14
Madson, Hans	Fresno	No.		1	13	8	6	14		2	16
Madven, J.	Fresno	No.			50	20	30	50			50
Maglio, N.	Fresno	No.			15		15	15			15
Malcolmson, W. L.	Fresno	No.			80	80		80			80
Malter, George H.	Fresno	Yes.			40	40	10	50		170	220
Mann, T. N.	Fresno	No.			16	9	7	16			16
Mann, William	Fresno	No.			8		8	8			8
Mannmain, A. K.	Fresno	No.			9	5	5	10			10
Manson, Dr. P.	Fresno	No.		1	70	20	50	70			70
Martin, ——	Fresno	No.			5		5	5			5
Marton, J. M.	Fresno	No.			60		60	60			60
Marton, Robert	Fresno	No.			10		10	10			10
Mason, ——	Fresno	No.			80	80		80			80
Mason, C.	Fresno	No.			21	21		21			21
Maxon, Byron	Fresno	No.			20	20		20			20
Meier, D. W.	Fresno	No.			65	65		65			65
Melvin, ——	Fresno	No.			60	60		60			60
Mendall, Joe	Fresno	No.			18	18		18			18
Merriam, E. D.	Fresno	No.			27	9	18	27			27
Meux, Dr. T. R.	Fresno	No.			12		12	12			12
Meux, J. P.	Fresno	No.			40	40		40			40
Meyers, C. W.	Fresno	No.			30	28	4	30			30
Meyers, D.	Fresno	No.			60	35	15	50			50
Meyers, H.	Fresno	No.			10		10	10			10
Mill, J.	Fresno	No.			25		25	25		50	75
Miller, James A.	Fresno	No.			15		15	15			15
Miller, J. M.	Fresno	No.			20	20		20			20
Mills, John I.	Fresno	No.			30	10	20	30			30
Minnasian, S. M.	Fresno	No.			15		15	15			15
Mitchell, C.	Fresno	No.	2	4	24	20	6	21		3	26
Mitcherson, John	Fresno	No.			8	9	3	12			15

Name	Location	No.	No.	No.	No.	No.	No.	No.	No.	No.
Mock, ——	Fresno			10		10	10			10
Montague, R. E.	Fresno			14		14	14			14
Moon, D.	Fresno			20		20	20			20
Moore, A.	Fresno			8	4	4	8			8
Morris, ——	Fresno			20	10	10	20			20
Morris & Hunt.	Fresno			75	75		75			75
Morrison, A. P.	Fresno			37	37		37			37
Morrison, Sam	Fresno			10		10	10			10
Morse, M. H.	Fresno			50	20	30	50			50
Morton, A. C.	Fresno			10	8	2	10			10
Moulton, J. F.	Fresno		2	60		60	60			60
Mulholland, R. S.	Fresno			14			14			14
Muller, W.	Fresno			6	14	6	8			8
Mulligan, Tom	Fresno			18	2		18			18
Mury & Bowen	Fresno		5	200	18		200			200
Musick, J. D.	Fresno			10	200	10	10			10
Nealson, H.	Fresno		2	30		25	30			30
Nelson Bros.	Fresno			12	5	15	12			12
Nelson, Louis	Fresno		1	15	12	20	15			15
Neuman, J.	Fresno			35		15	40			40
Nickels, Albert	Fresno	2		15	20	20	15		7	15
Nickels, D. E.	Fresno	2		21		15	25	3	3	25
Nicklous, ——	Fresno			15			15			15
North Fork Lumber Co.	Fresno			20	20	8	20			20
Nshikian, G. N.	Fresno			2	5	3	5			12
O'Conner, J.	Fresno			9	3		11			11
Ode, Mrs. J.	Fresno			3			3		30	6
O'Donell, David	Fresno			10	10		10		8	10
Olsen, G.	Fresno			2	2		2			32
Otto, A.	Fresno			14		14	14			22
Ousendorf, B.	Fresno			10	10	30	10		50	10
Pacific Agriculture and Cal. Co.	Fresno			160	120	8	150			200
Packard, A. W.	Fresno			8		7	8			8
Packard, A. W.	Fresno			7			7			7
Pardee, C. A.	Fresno			2	2		2			2
Parish, ——	Fresno		2	200	200		200			200
Fairview Vineyard Co., Fresno				16	16		16			16
Parker, Fred R.	Fresno			30	20	10	30			30
Parker, W. E.	Fresno			50	50	13	50			50
Parkes, B. F.	Fresno			13			13			13
Pason, Capt. Wm.	Fresno			17	17		17			17
Patterson, ——	Fresno			35	35	5	35			35
Patterson, B. P.	Fresno			5		10	5			5
Pattison, J. C.	Fresno			8		21	10			10
Pattison, T. W.	Fresno			21			21			21
Paulsen, C.	Fresno									

FRESNO COUNTY—Continued.

Name of Owner.	Post Office and Name of Vineyard.	Wine Maker.	Acres in Sultanas	Acres in Malagas	Acres in Muscats	Acres in Raisin Grapes not Bearing	Acres in Raisin Grapes Bearing	Total Acres in Raisin Grapes.	Acres in Wine Grapes not Bearing	Total Acres in Wine Grapes	Total Acres in Grapes
Paulsen, C. S.	Fresno	No.		2	17	10	9	19		4	23
Paulsen, M.	Fresno	No.			16		16	16			16
Paulsen, O.	Fresno	No.			10	10		10			10
Paulsen, T.	Fresno	No.			26	28		28			28
Pearson, ——	Fresno	No.			43	35	8	43			43
Pearson, ——	Fresno	No.				5		5			6
Pedro, ——	Fresno	No.			8		8	8			8
Pen, J. N.	Fresno (San Francisco)	No.	15		130	30	115	145			145
Perkins, John	Fresno	No.			35	35		35			35
Pero, H.	Fresno	No.			14	8	6	14			14
Perterc, A.	Fresno	No.	2		20	20		20			20
Peters, A. B.	Fresno	No.			13	2	13	15			15
Pickels, Mrs.	Fresno	No.			20	20		20			20
Polito, L. L.	Fresno	No.	1		6	4	2	6			6
Polkinghorn, E.	Fresno	No.		5	19		25	25			25
Pollard, Ed.	Fresno	No.			18	18		18		4	22
Pool, J. N.	Fresno	No.			60	40	20	60			60
Potter, W. H.	Fresno	No.			20	20		20			20
Pottle, ——	Fresno	No.			20	20		20			20
Prather, Dr.	Fresno	No.			10	10		10			10
Prather, Dr. J. W.	Fresno	No.			25		25	25			25
Prather, S.	Fresno	No.			10		10	10			10
Pratt, D. W.	Fresno	No.			12	10	2	12		3	15
Primo, ——	Fresno	No.			19	19		19			19
Pugh, J. M.	Fresno	No.			35		35	35			35
Pyke, E. A.	Fresno	No.			25	25		25			25
Qualls, N. E.	Fresno	No.			30	30		30			30
Quinlan, M.	Fresno	No.			31	8	23	31			31
Raffin, Mrs. E.	Fresno	No.			35	19	16	35			35
Rankin, J.	Fresno	No.			2		2	2		6	8
Rankin, Mrs. Nellie	Fresno	No.			2		2	2		6	8
Rasmussen, H. C.	Fresno	No.			4		4	4		4	8
Rasmussen, J. N.	Fresno	No.			25	25		25			25
Reder, J.	Fresno	No.	3		8		11	11		10	21

Name	Location								
		Yes.	No.	No.	No.	No.	No.	No.	No.
Reding & Quantz	Fresno						200	200	
Reed, A. W.	Fresno						5	35	
Reed, Miss Jennie	Fresno			30	30	9		40	
Reed, Mrs. J. E.	Fresno			40	40	40		9	
Reed, W. E.	Fresno			9		40		40	
Reese, J. W.	Fresno			40	55	95		95	
Reeves, G. F.	Fresno			95		3		3	
Reily, Dr. J. R.	Fresno			3		32		32	
Reyburn, J. J.	Fresno			32	40	40		40	
Rienhart, A.	Fresno			40	5	5		6	
Ritchards, L. A.	Fresno			5	20	20		20	
Ritchie, Charles	Fresno			20	19	34		34	
Ritchie, John	Fresno			25	3	25		25	
Robb, Francis	Fresno		6	7	11	13		13	
Robinson, C. E.	Fresno		2	8	3	6	5	10	
Robinson, ——	Fresno			20	20	20		20	
Robinson, ——	Fresno		5	5	5	10	1	10	
Robinson, M.	Fresno			6	6	6	32	7	
Roessler, F. M.	Fresno			32		43		75	
Roff, H.	Fresno	4 2	7 2	36	27	13	233	40	233
Rogers, A. M.	Margherita Vineyard, Fresno			30		30		263	
Ronzoni, ——	Fresno			40	20	20	13	20	
Rudy, William	Fresno				10	24		68	
Ryan, Jesse	Fresno			3		3		3	
Sachs, A.	Fresno			40	100	60	10	150	
Sahgeian, H.	Fresno			3		4		16	
Samuelson & Sons	Fresno			150	75			75	
Sanderson, Fred.	Fresno			6		15		15	
Sansted, C. A.	Fresno			75		8		8	
Sarrett, W.	Fresno			15	12	18		30	
Sayer, J. H.	Fresno			8		40		40	
Schell, Mrs. L.	Fresno			30		28		28	
Scoelgens, W.	Fresno (Philadelphia, Penn.)			40		2	46	48	46
Scott, J. W.	Fresno			28		15		15	
Scott, J. W.	Fresno			2		10		14	
Seacropian, S.	Fresno			15	4	4		4	
Seaman, Julia	Fresno			14	20	20		20	
Sebey, Mrs. A. M.	Fresno			4	2	13		15	
Seeberg, L.	Fresno			20	7	18		25	
Sewell, J. H.	Fresno			25		7		7	
Shannon Jeff.	Fresno		8	7		13	17	30	17
Sharer Bros.	Fresno			3	53	53		53	
Shepard, J.	Fresno	2		53		30		30	
Shield, ——	Fresno			30	10	65		75	
Shields, A. J.	Fresno		4	71	40	40		40	

FRESNO COUNTY—Continued.

Name of Owner	Post Office and Name of Vineyard	Total Acres in Grapes	Total Acres in Wine Grapes	Acres in Wine Grapes not Bearing	Total Acres in Raisin Grapes	Acres in Raisin Grapes Bearing	Acres in Raisin Grapes not Bearing	Acres in Muscats	Acres in Malagas	Acres in Sultanas	Wine Maker
Shohamerian, S.	Fresno	5			5		5	4		1	No.
Sinn, Fred.	Fresno	6			6		6	6			No.
Shoegard, N. C.	Fresno	30			30	9	21	30			No.
Sly, Mrs. M.	Fresno	12			12		12	12			No.
Smith, —	Fresno	10			10		10	10			No.
Smith, A. C.	Fresno	12			12	8	4	12			No.
Smith, Alex.	Fresno	8			8		8	8			No.
Smith, Capt. E. E.	Fresno	110			110		110	110			No.
Smith, C.	Fresno	30			30	30		30			No.
Smith, G. A.	Fresno	100			100		100	50	50		No.
Smith, G. W.	Fresno	40			40		40	40			No.
Smith, J. L.	Fresno	30			30		30	30			No.
Smith, L.	Fresno	15	6		9	7	2	7	2		No.
Smith, Robert	Fresno	205			205	60	145	205			No.
Snider, Mrs. M.	Fresno	35	7		28	7	21	8			No.
Snow, W. N.	Fresno	10			10		10	7			No.
Sorensen, N. N.	Fresno	12			12	8	10	10			No.
Southworth, H.	Fresno	32	5		32		4	12			No.
Speake, W. H.	Fresno	16			16		32	32			No.
Spence, A. D.	Fresno	12			12	12	11	11			No.
Stafford, W. —	Fresno	17			17	17		12			No.
Steinwand, Geo. F.	Fresno (Lemoore)	5			5			17			No.
Sterling, G. W.	Fresno	4			4	15		5			No.
Stevens, J. F.	Fresno	30			30	4	5	4			No.
Still, E. N.	Fresno	90			90		4	30			No.
Still & Raynor.	Fresno	8			8	20	15	80			No.
Stone, B. M.	Fresno	5			5		80	8			No.
Stores, O. D.	Fresno	40	20		40		4	5			No.
Storie, F. R.	Fresno	18			18		5	20			No.
Storie, Robert.	Fresno	35			35	20		18			No.
Story Bros.	Fresno	20			20		35	35			No.
Story, W. M., Sr.	Fresno	17			17	17	20	20			No.
Strahl, H. W.	Fresno	17			17			17			No.
Strine, G.	Fresno	32	3		29	29		25		4	No.

Name	Location									
		No.	No.	No.	No.	No.	No.	No.	No.	No.
Studer, George	Fresno			21		21	21			25
Stutzman, Nick	Fresno			13		13	13			13
Sumner, J. M.	Fresno			6		3	6			6
Swagerty, C.	Fresno			12			12			12
Swanson, Mrs.	Fresno		2	4	3	4	4		3	4
Swenson, E.	Fresno	1	1	8	3	7	10			13
Taft, S.	Fresno (San Francisco)			22	4	2)	24	20	130	24
Tarpy, M. F.	Fresno			68	68		68			150
Tayler, G. R.	Fresno	1	6	68	68	20	68			68
Taylor, John	Fresno			36	16	7	38			38
Teague, Wm.	Fresno			6			7			17
Terrill, M.	Fresno		2	15		15	15		10	16
Terry, D. S., estate of	Fresno			60		60	60		16	18
Thomas, John P.	Fresno	1		20	13	7	20		3	60
Thorp, W. H.	Fresno			10	5	6	11			20
Thiesen, M.	Fresno			30	30		30		1	12
Thurman, Mrs. S. J.	Fresno			30	6	30	38			30
Tielman & Paulson	Fresno			16	6	10	16			38
Tilgitt, G. B.	Fresno			8		8	8		4	16
Tolford, William	Fresno	1		10		13	13			8
Tommasini, G.	Fresno			35	10	25	35			17
Townsend, C. M.	Fresno			10		10	10			35
Treadwell, A.	Fresno		14	20		21	21			10
Trezevant, N. M.	Fresno			35	13		34			34
Tripp, I. G.	Fresno			15	35	10	35			35
Truworthy, H. E.	Fresno			8	5	6	15			15
Turnball, G. T.	Fresno			16	3	16	8			8
Tyler, E. P.	Fresno			20			16			16
Tyree, E. P.	Fresno			30	20		20			20
Vanderlip, F. D.	Fresno			15	30	6	30			30
Vandore, Mrs. P.	Fresno			14	9		15			15
Van Vleet, W. B.	Fresno			63	14	22	14		12	14
Vaughn, D. J.	Fresno			55	41	55	63			75
Vial, S. T.	Fresno			35		25	55			55
Vincent, J. P.	Fresno	7	6	18	10	28	35			35
Von Schmidt, A. W.	Fresno			4		18	28		102	130
Voorhees, J.	Fresno			140	4	40	18		12	18
Wahl, L.	Fresno			185	100		4			16
Walker, James	Fresno			15	185	15	140		15	140
Wallace, W. T.	Fresno (San Francisco)			20		20	185			200
Wall, ——	Fresno			21	15	6	15			15
Wallace, H.	Fresno			40		40	20		4	20
Warner & Morse	Fresno			6		6	21			25
Washer, W. A.	Fresno						40			40
Waters, F.	Fresno						6			6

FRESNO COUNTY—Continued.

Name of Owner	Post Office and Name of Vineyard	Total Acres in Grapes	Total Acres in Wine Grapes	Acres in Wine Grapes not Bearing	Total Acres in Raisin Grapes	Acres in Raisin Grapes Bearing	Acres in Raisin Grapes not Bearing	Acres in Muscats	Acres in Malagas	Acres in Sultanas	Wine Maker
Way & Lloyd	Fresno	38			38	35	3	38			No.
Weaver, J. R.	Fresno	15			15		15	15			No.
Weaver, J. W.	Fresno	12			12	12	1	12			No.
Webb, J. W.	Fresno	8			8	7		8			No.
Webster, Dr. L.	Fresno	15	3		12	12		12			No.
Webster,	Fresno	40			40	40		40			No.
Weihe, August	Fresno	85	75		10	10		10			No.
Welchman, Charles	Fresno	40			40	40		40			No.
White, M. H.	Fresno	15			15	15		15	1	1	No.
White, Mrs. M. J.	Fresno	65	2		63	33	30	63	1	1	No.
White, Ray	Fresno	10			10	10		8	10		No.
White, R. A.	Fresno	13	5		8	8		7			No.
White, T. C.	Fresno	10			10	6	4	9			No.
Whitney, W.	Fresno	65			65	65	4	56			No.
Whittaker & Derhart	Fresno	12			12	8	30	12			No.
Whorton, F. A.	Fresno	30			30			30			No.
Whorton, W. W.	Fresno	14			14	14		14			No.
Widber, Jacob	Fresno	15			15	15		15			No.
Wight, Geo. T.	Fresno	30			30	30		30			No.
Wilkenson, Wm.	Fresno	60			60	60		60			No.
Wilkenson, Wm.	Fresno	40			40	40		40			No.
Wilcox, O.	Fresno	5			5	5		5			No.
Williams, A. C.	Fresno	4			4	4		4			No.
Williams, F.	Fresno	60			60		60	60			No.
Williams, R.	Fresno	15			15	6	9	15			No.
Williams, J. W.	Fresno	30	15		30	15	15	30			No.
Williams, W. M.	Fresno	84			19	12	7	19	1		No.
Williamson, C.	Fresno	80			80		30	80			No.
Williamson, David	Fresno (Nevada Vista)	12			12	9	3	11			No.
Wilson, G. A.	Fresno	14			14		14	14			No.
Wilson, H. P.	Fresno	120	5		120		120	120			No.
Wilson, L. T.	Fresno	11			6	4	2	6		1	No.
Wilson, Mrs. H. B.	Fresno	5			5		5	5			No.
	Fresno	10			10	10		9			No.

Name	Location	No.	No.	No.	No.	No.	No.
Wilson, Mrs. I.	Fresno			8		9	9
Wilson, W. B.	Fresno	1		11	2	9	11
Wimbland, J.	Fresno			4	4	14	4
Wimple, H. A.	Fresno			14		5	14
Wing, Miss M. A.	Fresno			5		30	5
Wing, R. W.	Fresno			147	117		147
Wolf, C.	Fresno			15	15		15
Woodworth, Major B. J. R.	Fresno (Las Palmas)			70	40	30	70
Woolfolk, C. E.	Fresno			5		5	5
Wright, ___	Fresno			40	30	40	40
Wylie, G. W.	Fresno			35	152	5	35
Wyott & Samuels	Fresno	3	7	152	11		152
Young, W. More	Fresno			26	40	25	38
Youngberg, J. E.	Fresno (Alameda)			40			40
Zigler, J. T.	Fresno			12		12	12
Zimmerman, F. & B.	Fresno			45	15	45	45
___	Fresno (Paragon)			15			15
Anderson, A. N.	Kingsburg			80	80		80
Anderson, John	Kingsburg			18		18	18
Anderson, Nels.	Kingsburg			3		3	8
Arling, E. C.	Kingsburg			14		14	14
Bare, H. W.	Kingsburg			5			5
Borg, Olaf	Kingsburg			25	5		5
Borg, P. A.	Kingsburg			18	25		25
Burns, Dr. J. F.	Kingsburg			20	18		18
Cameron, Miss J.	Kingsburg			20	20		20
Carlson, ___	Kingsburg			3	20		20
Carlson, C. O.	Kingsburg			10	3		3
Cellander, C.	Kingsburg			5	10		10
Champers, C.	Kingsburg			20	5		5
Clark, J. P.	Kingsburg			10	20		20
Cline, S.	Kingsburg			135	10		10
Creason, C.	Kingsburg			10	135		135
Crocker, Jim	Kingsburg			40	10		10
Danielson, J.	Kingsburg			15	40	3	40
Davis, J. P.	Kingsburg			26	12	3	15
Davis, S. & Co.	Kingsburg			63	23		26
Draper, E.	Kingsburg			4	63	4	63
Dustin, C.	Kingsburg			5			4
Elder, John	Kingsburg			20	5		5
Endicott, Charles	Kingsburg			32	20		20
Erickson, Pete.	Kingsburg			15	32		32
Erickson, N. G.	Kingsburg			13	15		15

FRESNO COUNTY—Continued.

Name of Owner.	Post Office and Name of Vineyard.	Total Acres in Grapes	Total Acres in Wine Grapes	Acres in Wine Grapes not Bearing	Total Acres in Raisin Grapes	Acres in Raisin Grapes Bearing	Acres in Raisin Grapes not Bearing	Acres in Muscats	Acres in Malagas	Acres in Sultanas	Wine Maker.
Fisher, E. A.	Kingsburg	25			25		25	25			No.
Forney, J. F.	Kingsburg	5			5		5	5			No.
Fulgham, G. S.	Kingsburg	22			22	3	22	22			No.
Garner, F. B.	Kingsburg	5			5		2	5			No.
Golding, W. H.	Kingsburg	8			8	7	8	8			No.
Hannick, A. A.	Kingsburg	12			12		10	12			No.
Hanson, F.	Kingsburg	18			18		18	18			No.
Hatch, C. M.	Kingsburg	15			15		15	15			No.
Hegberg, —	Kingsburg	10			10		10	10			No.
Johnson, A.	Kingsburg	12			12		12	12			No.
Johnson, J.	Kingsburg	3			3	3		3			No.
Johnson, O.	Kingsburg	10			10		10	10			No.
Johnson, Peter A.	Kingsburg	25			25		25	25			No.
Johnson, S. G.	Kingsburg	12			12		12	12			No.
Layton & Roe.	Kingsburg	16			16	10	6	16			No.
Lind, A.	Kingsburg	8			8		8	8			No.
Linquist, J. W.	Kingsburg	12			12		12	12			No.
Livermore, Mrs. H. G.	Kingsburg	12			12		12	12			No.
Lund, A.	Kingsburg	7			7		7	7			No.
Martin, J.	Kingsburg	9			9		9	9			No.
Martin, T.	Kingsburg	10			10		10	10			No.
Martin, W. T.	Kingsburg	8			8	8		8			No.
Maxwell, Z. T.	Kingsburg	15			15	6	9	15			No.
Morrison, E. D.	Kingsburg	20			20		20	20			No.
Nelson, C. O.	Kingsburg	13			13		13	13			No.
Nelson, T.	Kingsburg	10			10		10	10			No.
Nord, P.	Kingsburg	5			5		5	5			No.
Olsen, J.	Kingsburg	15			15		15	15			No.
Pearson, J.	Kingsburg	12			12		12	12			No.
Peterson, E.	Kingsburg	12			12	12		12			No.
Peterson, J.	Kingsburg	25			25		25	25			No.
Peterson, J.	Kingsburg	6			6		6	6			No.
Poulson, Wm.	Kingsburg	20			20		20	20			No.
Purves, J.	Kingsburg	10			10		10	10			No.

Name	Location	No.	No.	No.	No.
Rosendahl, A. G.	Kingsburg	15	15	—	15
Rosendahl, F. D.	Kingsburg	100	40	60	100
Ross, Samuel	Kingsburg	10	10	—	10
Rowell, Frank	Kingsburg	25	25	—	25
Rycen, Paul S.	Kingsburg	10	10	—	10
Shannon, C.	Kingsburg	10	10	—	10
Shannon, Mrs. M.	Kingsburg	25	20	5	25
Sharp, E. A.	Kingsburg	8	8	—	8
Smith, A. P.	Kingsburg	10	10	—	10
Sonderlund, Z.	Kingsburg	15	—	15	15
Sonderlund, Z. N.	Kingsburg	40	—	40	40
Stid, E.	Kingsburg	10	10	—	10
Suenberg, H.	Kingsburg	10	10	—	10
Swanson, C.	Kingsburg	8	8	—	8
Weisler, J.	Kingsburg	12	8	4	12
Woodard, Henry T.	Kingsburg	40	40	—	40
Youngren, Capt. F.	Kingsburg	8	8	20	8
Anderson, A. G., estate of	Kings River	20	—	—	20
Benadom, ——	Kings River	5	5	5	5
Benadom, W. O.	Kings River	15	15	30	15
Brown, Wm.	Kings River	20	15	5	20
Caldwell Estate	Kings River	30	—	—	30
Douglas, T. C.	Kings River	5	10	—	5
Frankwod Farm	Kings River	10	30	—	10
Hazelton, Wm.	Kings River	30	40	—	30
Hume, ——	Kings River	40	5	—	40
Mitchill, Mrs. E. A.	Kings River	5	10	—	5
Mt. Campbell Vineyard	Kings River	10	70	25	10
Powers, A. H.	Kings River	70	80	—	70
Small, G.	Kings River	80	55	—	80
Wilson, Jim	Kings River	15	15	—	15
Wood, Robert	Kings River	5	5	—	5
Anthony, S. J.	Madera	40	40	—	40
Arnold, J.	Madera	5	5	—	5
Atkinson, E. R.	Madera	40	40	—	40
Avey, G. B.	Madera	5	5	—	5
Baber, E. J.	Madera	10	10	—	10
Badders, Harvey	Madera	20	20	—	20
Bennett, Ed. A.	Madera	10	10	—	10
Bitherson, James	Madera	5	5	—	5
Blackman, Winfred	Madera	10	10	—	10
Black, W. L.	Madera	5	5	—	5
Borden Farm	Madera	10	10	3	10
Borden, Rhodes	Madera	3	10	10	3

FRESNO COUNTY—Continued.

Name of Owner	Post Office and Name of Vineyard	Wine Maker	Acres in Sultanas	Acres in Malagas	Acres in Muscats	Acres in Raisin Grapes not Bearing	Acres in Raisin Grapes Bearing	Total Acres in Raisin Grapes	Acres in Wine Grapes not Bearing	Total Acres in Wine Grapes	Total Acres in Grapes
Borden, Ruffin	Madera	No.			5		5	5			5
Boust, E. J.	Madera	No.			12	12		12			12
Boust, W. W.	Madera	No.			35	35		35			35
Brisco, M. C.	Madera	No.			20	20		20			20
Brisco, S. M.	Madera	No.			40	40		40			40
Bristol, W. E.	Madera	No.			10	10		10			10
Brown, L. S.	Madera	No.			5	5		5			5
Brown, John	Madera	No.			140	140		140			140
Brusie, Thomas	Madera	No.			111	75	36	111		2	113
Buttrick, Chas.	Madera	No.			10	10		10			10
Campwell, Mrs.	Madera	No.			5	5		5			5
Carroll, Charles	Madera	No.			5	5		5			5
Cason, J. J.	Madera	No.			17	17		17			17
Challenger, Wm.	Madera	No.			10	10		10			10
Childs, R. W.	Madera	No.			12	12		12			12
Collier, Ida B.	Madera	No.			5	5		5			5
Connolly, Ed. R.	Madera	No.			5	5		5			5
Copage, Mrs. Tom	Madera	No.									
Covill, L. B.	Madera	No.			10	10		10			10
Cox, E. H.	Madera	No.			100	100		100			100
Cummings, P. J.	Madera	No.			5	5		5			5
Cunningham, J. C.	Madera	No.			2		2	2			2
Curron, T. A.	Madera	No.			10	10		10			10
Cutts, J. O.	Madera	No.			10	10		10			10
Danphing, E.	Madera	No.			10	10		10			10
Danphing, G. A.	Madera	No.			10	10		10			10
Danphing, W. G.	Madera	No.			10	10		10			10
Davis, Mary A.	Madera	No.			10	10		10			10
Davis, T. P.	Madera	No.			5	5		5			5
De Kress, Margaret	Madera	No.			5	5		5			5
De Mill, H. E.	Madera	No.			20		20	20		50	70
Doyle Vineyard	Madera	No.									
Dunham, F. A.	Madera	No.			5	5		5			5
Egelston, F. E.	Madera	No.			5	5		5			5

Name	No.	No.	No.	No.	No.	County
Eves, C. M.		5	5	5	5	Madera
Fay, R. C.		10	10	10	10	Madera
Fellows, Mrs. E. B.		5	5	5	5	Madera
Fellows, J. B.		5	5	5	5	Madera
Fletcher, J. C.		10	10	10	10	Madera
Frame, Arthur		5	5	5	5	Madera
Glass, Frank A., Sr.		18	18	18	18	Madera
Glass, Frank A., Jr.		18	18	18	18	Madera
Gorden, James		21	21	21	21	Madera
Graham, William		15	15	15	15	Madera
Hall, Charles A.		10	10	10	10	Madera
Hamilton, John		10	10	10	10	Madera
Hanward, E. P.		10	10	10	10	Madera
Harris, D. B.		40	40	40	40	Madera
Harris, W. C.		10	10	10	10	Madera
Herington, T. E.		4	4	4	4	Madera
Hill, Thomas	10	10	10	10	10	Madera
Hill, William T.		10	10	10	10	Madera
Hitchler, B. C.		5	5	5	5	Madera
Hoffman, L. C.		5	5	5	5	Madera
Hughes, John J.		5	5	5	5	Madera
Jeune, Charles					15	Madera
Johnson, A. C.		10	10	10	25	Madera
Jones, Ben W.		5	5	5	5	Madera
Jones, D. L.		10	10	10	10	Madera
Jones, E. M.		5	5	5	5	Madera
Jones, F. J.		5	5	5	5	Madera
Jones, G. E.		10	10	10	10	Madera
Jones, Reese W.		5	5	5	5	Madera
Jones, Rev. H. L.		10	10	10	10	Madera
Jones, R. H.		5	5	5	5	Madera
Jones, Thomas A.		5	5	5	5	Madera
Jones, Thomas G.		10	10	10	10	Madera
Jones, Wm. L.		10	10	10	10	Madera
Jones, W. M.		5	5	5	5	Madera
Keller, J. H.		5	5	5	5	Madera
Kessler, H. B.		20	20	20	20	Madera
Kirkham, F. M.		10	10	10	10	Madera
Knoll, F. M.		10	10	10	10	Madera
Kregi, Henry		5	5	5	5	Madera
Kuhn, Wm. D.		5	5	5	5	Madera
Lamb, W. N.		5	5	5	5	Madera
Lloyd, David		15	15	15	15	Madera
Lloyd, Thomas		10	10	10	10	Madera
Long, J. H.		5	5	5	5	Madera
		20	20	20	20	Madera

5–v

Fresno County—Continued.

Name of Owner	Post Office and Name of Vineyard	Wine Maker	Acres in Sultanas	Acres in Malagas	Acres in Muscats	Acres in Raisin Grapes not Bearing	Acres in Raisin Grapes Bearing	Total Acres in Raisin Grapes	Acres in Wine Grapes not Bearing	Total Acres in Wine Grapes	Total Acres in Grapes
McCann, J. T.	Madera	No.			40	40		40			40
McCann, S. E.	Madera	No.			40	40		40			40
McKendrick, James	Madera	No.			5	5		5			5
Madera Improvement Co.	Madera	No.			80	80		80			80
Madera Vineyard Co.	Madera	Yes.		5	30		35	35		120	155
Malikowski, John	Madera	No.	5		5	5		5			5
Martindale, H. A.	Madera	No.			10	10		10			10
Meyers, Jim	Madera	No.			6		11	11			11
Miles, W. F.	Madera	No.			10	10		10			10
Miller, C. B.	Madera	No.			5	5		5			5
Montague, J. W.	Madera	No.			20	20		20			20
Moore, E.	Madera	No.			11	2	8	11			11
Morgan, Eben	Madera	No.			5	5		5			5
Neisen, Jas.	Madera	No.			5	5		5			5
Newman, V. B.	Madera	No.			10	10		10			10
Nickelson, Mrs. E. C.	Madera	No.			18		18	18		2	20
Noble, W. H.	Madera	No.			5	5		5			5
Penfield, C. L.	Madera	No.			5	5		5			5
Perry, O. D.	Madera	No.			5	5		5			5
Phillips, H. J.	Madera	No.			5	5		5			5
Pope, Fred. J.	Madera	No.			10		10	10			10
Poppvich, I.	Madera	No.			10	10		10			10
Powell, Wm.	Madera	No.			40	40		40			40
Quants,	Madera	No.			5	5		5			5
Ray, R. H.	Madera	No.			10	10		10			10
Reese, M. J.	Madera	No.			5	5		5			5
Reynolds, F. R.	Madera	No.			10	10		10			10
Rhoades, J. R.	Madera	No.			5	5		5			5
Ritter, Josiah	Madera	No.			60	60		60			60
Roberts, R.	Madera	No.			10	10		10			10
Rush, Z. C.	Madera	No.		25	150	75	100	175		50	225
Say, A. L.	Madera	No.			6	6		6			6
Scurman, M. H.	Madera	No.			5	5		5			5
Sharp, L. O.	Madera	No.			2		2	2			2

Name	Location	No.	No.	No.	No.	No.	No.
Sledge, L. A.	Madera	4			4		10
Smith, B. K.	Madera	20	20		20		20
Smith, F. E.	Madera	10	10		10		10
Smith, Robt.	Madera	5	5		5		5
Stockton, M. H., estate of	Madera	18		18	18	50	68
Squarrey, W. H.	Madera	20	20		20		20
Thomas, L. B.	Madera	5	5		5		5
Thompson, James H.	Madera	5	7	7	5		5
Tozer, J. E.	Madera	14	10		14		14
Turner, G. A.	Madera	10	5		10		10
Turner, W. W.	Madera	5	5		5		5
Van Antwerp, S. C.	Madera	5	15		5		5
Ware, S. C.	Madera	15	5		15		15
Wassen, Robt.	Madera	5	20		5		5
Watkins, J. W.	Madera	20	5		20		20
Weaver, James	Madera	5	5		5		5
West, L. C.	Madera	5	10		5		5
Williams, E. D.	Madera	10	5		10		10
Williams, H. M.	Madera	5	15		5		5
Williams, J. H.	Madera	15	60		15		15
Williams, M. K.	Madera	60	5		60		60
Wilson, Milo W.	Madera	5	5		5		5
Wing, Charles	Madera	5	5		5		5
Wolfe, E. J.	Madera	5	10		5		5
Wolfe, W. E.	Madera	10	5		10		10
Wood, C. E.	Madera	5		16	5		5
Baker, W. B.	Malaga	16	13	27	16		16
Barr, T. A.	Malaga	40		8	40		40
Birkett, Geo. B.	Malaga	8	5	30	8		8
Brisco, J. W.	Malaga	35	10	25	35		35
Brisco, R. W.	Malaga	35	2	32	35		35
Burnham, L.	Malaga	34	9	9	34		34
Butfish,	Malaga	18	2	38	18		18
Carver, H. M.	Malaga	40	43	15	40		40
Chenowith, J.	Malaga	58		15	58		58
Cribb, C. D.	Malaga	15		36	15		15
Cribb, E. C.	Malaga	36	30		36		36
Darling, A. P. & E. M.	Malaga	30		12	30		30
Densimore, E.	Malaga	12			12		12
Dicks, D.	Malaga	8	8	85	8		8
Dunn, Thomas	Malaga	75	40	5	76		75
Eddie, E. E.	Malaga	20	15	110	20		20
Gould, E. H.	Malaga	110	1	15	110		110
Gould, L.	Malaga	16	10	25	16		16
Harlem, George	Malaga	35			35		35

FRESNO COUNTY—Continued.

Wine Maker	Acres in Sultanas	Acres in Malagas	Acres in Muscats	Acres in Raisin Grapes not Bearing	Acres in Raisin Grapes Bearing	Total Acres in Raisin Grapes	Acres in Wine Grapes not Bearing	Total Acres in Wine Grapes	Total Acres in Grapes	Post Office and Name of Vineyard	Name of Owner
No.			23	15	8	23			23	Malaga	Harlem, M. R.
No.			40	15	25	40			40	Malaga	Haycroft, E. R.
No.			40		40	40			40	Malaga	Haycroft, L. M.
No.			5		5	5			5	Malaga	Haycroft, R. D.
No.			20	15	5	20			20	Malaga	Hintmann, John
No.			75	10	65	75			75	Malaga	Howlen & Smith
No.			18		18	18			18	Malaga	Iverson, C.
No.			50		50	50			50	Malaga	La Rue, E. H.
No.			75		75	75			75	Malaga	La Rue, H. W.
No.			35		35	35			35	Malaga	La Rue, J. H.
No.			60		60	60			60	Malaga	La Rue, S. R.
No.			80	80		80			80	Malaga	Mattio, A.
No.			80		80	80			80	Malaga	Mott, F. M.
No.			15		15	15			15	Malaga	Munger, T.
No.			16		16	16			16	Malaga	Nelson, J. Y.
No.			30	10	20	30			30	Malaga	Ord, John
No.			17	17		17			17	Malaga	Oliver, R. E.
No.			6	6		6			6	Malaga	Scott, Miss E.
No.			28		28	28			28	Malaga	Slater, J. I.
No.			36	36		36			36	Malaga	St. John, E. F.
No.			15	15		15			15	Malaga	Van Keuren, G.
No.			170	10	160	170			170	Malaga	Viau, N.
No.			80		80	80			80	Malaga	Woodward, A. B.
Yes.			60		60	60	20	280	340	Minturn Vineyard, Minturn	Minturn, James W.
Yes.			40		40	40		660	700	Sierra Vista Vineyard, Minturn	Minturn, Thomas R.
No.			49		49	49		30	79	Minturn	Wallace, J. H. & W. G.
Yes.								230	230	Sunset Vineyard, Minturn	Webster & Sargent
No.			30		30	30			30	Oleander	Akin, A. G.
No.			28	20	8	28			28	Oleander	Ashley, J. L.
No.			23	11	12	23			23	Oleander	Balch, A.
No.			9		9	9			9	Oleander	Balding, H.
No.			14	2	12	14			14	Oleander	Baldwin, M. M.
No.			16	10		16			16	Oleander	Bejardin, ——
No.			16	16		16			16	Oleander	Briggs, Mrs. J.

Name	Post Office	No.	No.	No.	No.	No.	No.	No.
Brooks, W.			12		12	12		12
Bryan, S. A.			13		13	13		13
Bucklan, A. C.			9		9	9		9
Calder, G. W.			15		15	15		15
Chappell, F. H.			13	4	9	13		13
Chase, P. V.			8	8		8		8
Clark, C. R.			15		15	15		15
Clark, P.			15		15	15		15
Cook, H. E.			60		60	60		60
Cook, W. H.			30	7	23	30		30
Curtis Fruit Company			107		107	107		107
Davis, C. H. A.			33	20	13	33		33
Dogan, T.		3	10	13		13		13
Earl, E. T.			20		20	20		20
Elliott, George	Oleander	1	55	50	5	55		55
Eshleman, L. E.	Keystone Vineyard, Oleander		32		32	32		32
Eskelsen, K.	Oleander		8	2	7	9		9
Estes, F.	Oleander		17	3	14	17		17
Fernold, Capt. J. P.	Oleander		27	4	23	27		27
Forseman, Hugh	Oleander		7		7	7		7
Fowels, A. W.	Oleander		7		7	7		7
Galloway, J. D.	Oleander		15	2	13	15		15
Griffin, A.	Oleander		24	5	19	24		24
Grover, P. H.	Oleander		7		7	7		7
Hall, W.	Oleander		40		40	40		40
Hall, Wm. E.	Montecito Vineyard, Oleander		120	20	100	120		120
Hallock, D. S.	Oleander		6			5		5
Hambley, F.	Oleander		17	5	12	17		17
Hansen, C.	Oleander		7		7	7		7
Hansen, N. P.	Oleander		12		12	12		12
Hardie, Wm.	Oleander		14		14	14		14
Harris, L.	Oleander		23		23	23		23
Hardigan, Mrs. N.	Oleander		10		10	10		10
Hatch, Mrs. D. P.	Oleander		12		12	12		12
Hawke, H. A.	Oleander		34		34	34		34
Hopkins, F. B.	Oleander		23	23		23		23
Hutchinson, —	Oleander		30	30		30		30
James, M.	Oleander		3	3		3		3
Jansen, G. B.	Oleander		5	5		5		5
Kiast, J.	Oleander		15		15	15		15
Kohler, P.	Oleander		30		30	30		30
Kroge, M. N.	Oleander		12	4	8	12		12
Landon, E. T.	Oleander		21		21	21		21
Landon, G., Jr.	Oleander		18		18	18		18
Larsen, H.	Oleander		17	3	14	17		17

FRESNO COUNTY—Continued.

Name of Owner	Post Office and Name of Vineyard	Wine Maker	Acres in Sultanas	Acres in Malagas	Acres in Muscats	Acres in Raisin Grapes not Bearing	Acres in Raisin Grapes Bearing	Total Acres in Raisin Grapes	Acres in Wine Grapes not Bearing	Total Acres in Wine Grapes	Total Acres in Grapes
Larsen, R.	Oleander	No.			10	10		10			10
Libby, C. A.	Oleander	No.			12	3	9	12			12
McLaughlin, Capt. D.	Oleander	No.			35		35	35			35
Martin, E. H.	Oleander	No.			17	5	12	17			17
Mathews, J. M.	Oleander	No.			18	4	14	18			18
Mawstlian, G.	Oleander	No.			25	25		25			25
Maxon, Dr. W.	Oleander	No.			12		12	12			12
Mitchell, Wm.	Oleander	No.			13		13	13			13
Montgomery, W. E.	Oleander	No.			35	10	25	35			35
Moore, Charles	Oleander	No.			15		15	15			15
Moore, A.	Oleander	No.			12		12	12			12
Morrison, R.	Oleander	No.			16	10	6	16			16
Mott, W. L.	Oleander	No.			10		10	10			10
Nason, E. H.	Oleander	No.			23	15	8	23			23
Nelson, N. B.	Oleander	No.			3		3	3			3
Nelson, N. P.	Oleander	No.			15	5	10	15			15
Nelson, P. T.	Oleander	No.			15	2	13	15			15
Nelson, S.	Oleander	No.			14	4	10	14			14
Nickelson, W. J.	Oleander	No.			5		5	5		3	8
Nielsen, B.	Oleander	No.			15		15	15			15
Nielsen, Peter	Oleander	No.			10		10	10			10
North, Charlie	Oleander	No.			25		25	25			25
North, J. W., estate of	Oleander	No.			35		35	35			35
Nudd, H. I.	Oleander	No.			125		125	125			125
Nudd, H. L.	Oleander	No.			130	7	123	130			130
Nye, A. B.	Oleander (Oakland)	No.			35		35	35			35
Nye, A. B.	Oleander	No.			20		20	20			20
Page, Dan.	Oleander	No.			20		20	20			20
Peterson, C. D.	Oleander	No.			12	2	10	12		4	16
Pilegard, George	Oleander	No.			20	10	10	20			20
Roach, Ed.	Oleander	No.			8		8	8			8
Roberts, John	Oleander	No.		5	10		10	10			15

Name	Location	No.	No.	No.	No.	No.	No.
Robertson, F.	Oleander	15	3	12	15		15
Rodda & Nobman	Maple Park Vineyard, Oleander	100	20	80	100		100
Seelhorn & Hamilton	Oleander	25	25		25		25
Simmons, W. M.	Oleander	12	5	7	12		12
Stiles, F. A.	Oleander	14		14	14		14
Twogood, S. H.	Oleander	37		37	37		37
Whorton, R. C.	Oleander	3		3	3		3
Wilson, Bud	Oleander	30	40	30	30		30
Wristen, W. D.	Oleander	90		60	90		90
Henry, Olive	Porterville	5		5	5		5
McDonald, O. E.	Porterville	40	40		40		40
McDonald, R. H.	Pioneer Raisin Co., Porterville	200	200		200		200
Ayers, E. L.	Reedly	5	6		5		5
Bander, T. J.	Reedly	30	30		30		30
California Fruit, Wine, and Land Co.	Reedly	250	125	125	250		250
Curtis, D. T.	Reedly	20	20		20		20
Day, B. F.	Reedly	8	8		8		8
Fairwether, F.	Reedly	15	15		15		15
Garner, C.	Reedly	3	3		3		3
Gregg, R.	Reedly	5	5		5		5
Gregg, S. A.	Reedly	10	10		10		10
Hirchfield, A.	Reedly	10	10		10		10
Holcomb, I.	Reedly	25	25		25		25
Holmes, E. W.	Reedly	5	5		5		5
Johnson, —	Reedly	20	20		20		20
Kanur, F.	Reedly	5	5		5		5
Lyon, J. P.	Reedly	25	25		25		25
McKeal, D.	Reedly	4	4		4		4
Manterbaugh, —	Reedly	5	5		5		5
Marrett, Frank	Reedly	5	5		5		5
Nance, C.	Reedly	15	15		15		15
Nance, George	Reedly	12	12		12		12
Neil, W. B.	Reedly	4	4		4		4
Reed, J. R.	Reedly	25	25		25		25
Reed, S. L.	Reedly	22	22		22		22
Reed, T. L.	Reedly	3	3		3		3
Simpson, A. T.	Reedly	4	4		4		4
Smith, A. N.	Reedly	5	5		5		5
Stoll, Fred	Reedly	15	15		15		15
Williams, A. J.	Reedly	5	5		5		5
Wimus, H.	Reedly	5	5		5		5
Wright, J. G.	Reedly	80	80	80	80		80
Colwell, W.	Sanders	8		8	8		8
Davies, W.	Sanders						
Duddy, M. H.	Sanders	12	12		12		12

FRESNO COUNTY—Continued.

Name of Owner	Post Office and Name of Vineyard	Wine Maker	Acres in Sultanas	Acres in Malagas	Acres in Muscats	Acres in Raisin Grapes not Bearing	Acres in Raisin Grapes Bearing	Total Acres in Raisin Grapes	Acres in Wine Grapes not Bearing	Total Acres in Wine Grapes	Total Acres in Grapes
Jack, Bob	Sanders	No.			15	5	10	15			15
Laird, L. N.	Sanders	No.			14	6	8	14			14
Love, C. O.	Sanders	No.			16	13	3	16			16
Love, William	Sanders	No.			10	4	6	10			10
McCrear, A.	Sanders	No.			20	20		20			20
Marshall, J. M.	Sanders	No.			20	5	15	20			20
Mason, ___	Sanders	No.			25	20	5	25			25
Miller, M.	Sanders	No.		5	60		65	65			65
Parlier, I. N.	Sanders	No.			83	80	3	83			83
Sanders, W. A.	Sanders	No.			6		6	6			6
Smith, A. D.	Sanders	No.			5	2	3	5			5
True, J.	Sanger	No.			15	7	8	15			15
Bullis, Tom	Sanger	No.			5	5		5			5
Cody, T. B.	Sanger	No.			14	14		14			14
Coldren, O.	Sanger	No.			3	3		3			3
Day, Milt.	Sanger	No.			3	3		3			3
Dean, M. L.	Sanger	No.			47	47		47			47
Edwards, C. H.	Sanger	No.			20	20		20			20
Furgerson, J. W.	Sanger	No.			10	10		10			10
Giles, F. E.	Sanger	No.			5	5		5			5
Giles, T. A.	Sanger	No.			3	3		3			3
Heckle, John	Sanger	No.			5	5		5			5
Hydrith, Mrs.	Sanger	No.			3	3		3			3
Langles, Joe	Sanger	No.			10	10		10			10
McDowell, G. W.	Sanger	No.								10	10
Meyers, C.	Sanger	No.			45	10	35	45			45
Meyers, Geo.	Sanger	No.			55	25	30	55			55
Paden, R. G.	Sanger	No.			10	10		10			10
Remsbottom, J.	Sanger	No.			10	10		10			10
St. Louis, Geo.	Sanger	No.			20	20		20			20
Smith, Asa.	Sanger	No.			4	4		4			4
Stewart, J. C.	Sanger	No.			5	5		5			5
Stump, J. P.	Sanger	No.			20	17	3	20			20
Underwood, J. G.	Sanger	No.			30		30	30			30

Name	Place	No.	No.	No.	No.	No.
Walton Bros.	Sanger	15	15		15	15
Walton, Dr. J. A.	Sanger	5	5		5	5
Walton, Joe	Sanger	10	10		10	10
Winkeman, J. P.	Sanger	5	5		5	5
Abbott, A.	Selma	35		35	35	35
Allen, M.	Selma	3	3		3	3
Allen, P.	Selma	35	35		35	35
All, John	Selma	5	5		5	6
Appling, E. K.	Selma	12	10	2	12	12
Baird, Miss	Selma	20	20		20	20
Barieau, A.	Selma	5		5	5	5
Barnes, F. G.	Selma	10	10		10	10
Bell, J. R.	Selma	25	25		25	25
Berry, William	Selma	5		5	5	5
Bevins, A.	Selma	40	30	10	40	40
Bewley, James	Selma	10	5	5	10	10
Bond, Mrs. L. I.	Selma (Stockton)	7		7	7	7
Bonds, G. W.	Selma	35	35		35	35
Booth, S. C.	Selma	6		6	6	6
Bowman, —	Selma	40	40		40	40
Boyd, T. M.	Selma	20	18	2	20	20
Branch, J. S.	Selma	20	20		20	20
Brewer, Miss Mollie	Selma	20	20		20	20
Brewer, T. E.	Selma	20	20		20	20
Brown, Frank	Selma	16	14	2	16	16
Brown, John	Selma	20	20		20	20
Brown, W.	Selma	7	7		7	7
Burton, Frank	Selma	30	30		30	30
Calhoun, Wm.	Selma	10	10		10	10
Carrington, M. B.	Selma	20	20		20	20
Carsburg, H. M. H.	Selma	46	46		46	46
Carter, Miss	Selma	6		6	6	6
Cauch, —	Selma	10	10		10	10
Chandler, W.	Selma (Alameda)	95	75	20	95	95
Chappell, S. R.	Selma	12	12		12	12
Christison, —	Selma	2		2	2	2
Clark, —	Selma	15	15		15	15
Clark, J. R.	Selma	15	15		15	15
Cline, J. J.	Selma	60	60		60	60
Cline, L. J.	Selma	30	30		30	30
Cline, S. J.	Selma	30	30		30	30
Cline, William	Selma	10	10		10	10
Coats, L. A.	Selma	4		4	4	9
Cobb, G. A.	Selma	15		15	15	15
Cohen, Mrs.	Selma	20	20		20	20

FRESNO COUNTY—Continued.

Wine Maker	Acres in Sultanas	Acres in Malagas	Acres in Muscats	Acres in Raisin Grapes not Bearing	Acres in Raisin Grapes Bearing	Total Acres in Raisin Grapes	Acres in Wine Grapes not Bearing	Total Acres in Wine Grapes	Total Acres in Grapes	Post Office and Name of Vineyard	Name of Owner
No.			10	10		10			10	Selma.	Cohen, Mrs.
No.			10		10	10			10	Selma.	Cook, L. D.
No.			8		8	8			8	Selma.	Cook, Mrs. L.
No.			20	20		20			20	Selma.	Cooper, J.
No.			14	14		14			14	Selma.	Cooper, Robert
No.			25	25		25			25	Selma.	Cox, W. T.
No.			23	20	3	23			23	Selma.	Cutler, H. C.
No.			20	20		20			20	Selma.	Dale, M. E.
No.			17	17		17			17	Selma.	Davis, E.
No.			4	4		4			4	Selma.	De Munbrum, W. L.
No.			20	20		20			20	Selma.	De Witt, O.
No.			75	65	10	75			75	Selma.	De Witt, T. B.
No.			12	8	4	12			12	Selma.	Drew, G. F.
No.			15	15		15			15	Selma.	Dudley, E.
No.			100	100		100			100	Selma.	Duke, T. L.
No.			15	15		15			15	Selma.	Duns, L. C.
No.			75	75		75			75	Selma.	Dusy, Frank
No.			5	5		5			5	Selma.	Dye, J. A.
No.			10		10	10			10	Selma.	Elhart, Lee
No.			8	8		8			8	Selma.	Erickson, G.
No.			8	8		8			8	Selma.	Erickson, J.
No.			40	40		40			40	Selma.	Estell, F. S.
No.			8	8		8			8	Selma.	Evens, W. M.
No.			5		5	5			5	Selma.	Fanning, —
No.			25	25		25			25	Selma.	Fautz, J. L.
No.			8	8		8			8	Selma.	Fisher, J. K.
No.			2		2	2			2	Selma.	Fowler, J. B.
No.			25	21	4	25			25	Selma.	Fuller, Geo. A.
No.			20	20		20			20	Selma.	Gaither, I. A.
No.			20	20		20			20	Selma.	Gilberg, J.
No.			30	30		30			30	Selma.	Gilbert, J. L.
No.			7	7		7			7	Selma.	Gorden, S. T.
No.			25		25	25			25	Selma.	Graham, J.
No.			25	6	20	25			25	Selma.	Graham, Wm.

Name	Location	No.	No.	No.	No.	No.	No.
Graper, H. C.	Selma.		12	12		12	12
Green, J.	Selma.		12	12		12	12
Gross, H. G.		8	8	16		16	16
Hampson,	Selma.		20	20		20	20
Hampson, L. J.	Selma.		8	8		8	8
Harnsburger, L. J.	Selma.		60	60		60	60
Hanson, H. P.	Selma.		5	5		5	5
Harbinson, James	Selma.		10	10		10	10
Hardwick, C. S.	Selma.		16	16		16	16
Hermberg,	Selma.		8	8		8	8
Hillgrove, C.	Selma.		10	10		10	10
Hillsman,	Selma.		20	20		20	20
Hinds, G. D.	Selma.		6		6	6	6
Holton, S. B.	Selma.		100	65	35	100	100
Holvers,	Selma.	5	10	10		10	10
Hulbert, H. S.	Selma.		40		40	40	40
Ingles, Mrs. W.	Selma.		13	3	10	13	13
Ingram, H. P.	Selma.		10	10		10	10
Jacobson, E.	Selma.		50	50		50	50
Jenkins, Sam	Selma.		6	6		6	6
Johnson, E.	Selma.		5	3	2	5	5
Johnson, J.	Selma.		40		40	40	40
Jones, A. D.	Selma.		50	38	12	50	50
Jones, Nelson	Selma.		5	5		5	5
Jones, T. B.	Selma.		160	100	60	160	160
Jones, T. L.	Selma.		5	5		5	5
Joseph, Antone	Selma.		30	30		30	30
Kin Lee Tin	Selma.		17	3	14	17	17
King, S. M.	Selma.		50	50		50	50
Kerick, Miss G.	Selma.		20	20		20	20
La Grange, Wm.	Selma.		10	10		10	10
Lake, J. S.	Selma.		13	16		13	13
Lang, N.	Selma.		8	5		8	8
Lewis, M.	Selma.		50	8	8	50	50
Ludington, J.	Selma.		12	5	45	12	12
McClelland, Dr. J. L.	Selma.		30	12		30	30
McClelland, H. R.	Selma.		70	30		70	70
McClelland, John S.	Selma.			70			
McLaughlin, Mrs. B. A.	Selma.		25	5	30	25	25
McMullen, A.	Selma.		60	25		60	60
Magee, Mrs. R.	Selma.		10	30	30	10	10
Manlove,	Selma.		95	10	6	95	95
Marsh, C. A.	Selma.		14	65	8	14	14
Martin, J.	Selma.		20	8		20	20
Martin, T.	Selma.		5	12		5	5

FRESNO COUNTY—Continued.

Name of Owner	Post Office and Name of Vineyard	Wine Maker	Acres in Sultanas	Acres in Malagas	Acres in Muscats	Acres in Raisin Grapes not Bearing	Acres in Raisin Grapes Bearing	Total Acres in Raisin Grapes	Acres in Wine Grapes not Bearing	Total Acres in Wine Grapes	Total Acres in Grapes
Martin, Thomas	Selma	No.			20	20		20			20
Mathews, T. B.	Selma	No.			60	30	30	60			60
Maxwell, W.	Selma	No.			5	5		5			5
Mooney,	Selma	No.			10	5	5	10			10
Mosberry, A.	Selma	No.			5		5	5			5
Nevins, E. M.	Selma	No.			60	60		60			60
Newell, Thomas	Selma	No.			60	60		60			60
Olsen, J.	Selma	No.			15	15		15			15
Olsen, O.	Selma	No.			20		20	20			20
Otis, Geo. B.	Selma	No.			20		20	20			20
Palmer, Dr. G. H.	Selma	No.		5	70	75		75			75
Payne, J. C.	Selma	No.			14		14	14			14
Perry, D. G.	Selma	No.			45	10	35	45			45
Peters, F. H.	Selma	No.			13	8	5	13			13
Potts, John	Selma	No.			8	8		8			8
Peters, Mrs. M.	Selma	No.			15	15		15			15
Peterson,	Selma	No.			10		10	10			10
Proctor, A.	Selma	No.			16	16		16			16
Rankin, D. W.	Selma	No.			20	16	4	20			20
Rhodes, H. G.	Selma	No.			30	30		30			30
Rice, J. W.	Selma	No.			20	20		20			20
Roadhouse, J.	Selma	No.			10	10		10			10
Robinson, Mrs. M.	Selma	No.			30	30		30			30
Ross, Mrs.	Selma	No.			3		3	3			3
Russell, E. M.	Selma	No.			45	45		45			45
Sanstrom, E. R.	Selma	No.			10	10		10			10
Sarringhausen, F.	Selma	No.			8	8		8			8
Say, H.	Selma	No.			40	40		40			40
Say, J. H.	Selma	No.			35	20	15	35			35
Scott, T. C.	Selma	No.			7	7		7			7
Shaw, H. R.	Selma	No.			40	40		40			40
Sheard, B.	Selma	No.			20	20		20			20
Sheets, J. B.	Selma	No.			10	10		10			10
Sherman, M. B.	Selma	No.			9	9		9			9

Name	No.	No.	No.	No.	No.	Location
Sherman, T. S.	9	9		9	9	Selma
Sides, M.	80	80	60	80	80	Selma
Smith, A. B.	20	20	8	20	20	Selma
Smith, L.	15	7	2	15	15	Selma
Smith, T. & N. G.	11	9	3	11	15	Selma
Smith, W. T.	5	2	30	5	5	Selma
Snodgrass, D. S.	40	10		40	40	Selma
Spivey, W. A.	12	12		12	12	Selma
Staley, R. D.	25	26	2	25	25	Selma
Staley, Wm.	2		60	2	2	Selma
Stevens, E. M.	100	50		100	100	Selma
Stroud, J. A.	100	180		190	180	Selma
Sweeney, Joseph	5	5	16	6	6	Selma
Teil, H. M.	40	24		40	40	Selma
Tellier, P.	15	15		15	15	Selma
Terrey, William	10	10	8	10	10	Selma
Thomas, J. H.	15	7	5	15	15	Selma
Tilley, J. W.	5		2	5	5	Selma
Traber, Mrs. M. E.	5	6		5	6	Selma
Unger, F.	2			2	2	Selma
Vanderberg, B. D.	90	90	2	90	90	Selma
Vanderberg, C. M.	18	18		18	18	Selma
Vanderberg, P. A.	5	5		5	5	Selma
Van Emmons, W. E.	5	3		5	6	Selma
Van Emmons, W. S.	12	12		12	12	Selma
Venosel, F.	27	27	3	27	27	Selma
Walker, C. F.	3		40	3	3	Selma
Walker, John	40	8	14	40	40	Selma
Walkers, O. A.	22	10		22	22	Selma
Warner, W. C.	10	20		10	10	Selma
Watkins, James	20	25		20	20	Selma
Williams, B. C.	25	2		25	25	Selma
Williams, J. C.	7	18	5	7	7	Selma
Williams, W. W.	16	11		16	16	Selma
Wilson, E. G.	11	7		11	11	Selma
Woodruff, —	7	7		7	7	Selma
Woods, C.	5	5		5	5	Selma
Yergin, Rev.	6		6	6	6	Selma
Yost, W. A.	20	20		20	20	Selma
Ziediker, J. W.	9	6	3	9	9	Selma
Zimmerman, R. E.	10	8	2	10	10	Selma
Beazy, C.	17	12	5	17	17	Selma
Burnett, J. G.	40	40		40	43	Wildflower
Carrington, N.	2		2	2	2	Wildflower

FRESNO COUNTY—Continued.

Name of Owner	Post Office and Name of Vineyard	Wine Maker	Acres in Sultanas	Acres in Malagas	Acres in Muscats	Acres in Raisin Grapes not Bearing	Acres in Raisin Grapes Bearing	Total Acres in Raisin Grapes	Acres in Wine Grapes not Bearing	Total Acres in Wine Grapes	Total Acres in Grapes
Crawford, John	Wildflower	No.			20	20		20		1	21
Elfers, —	Wildflower	No.			6		6	6			6
Elliott, I. H.	Wildflower	No.			15	12	3	15			15
Hager, J. F.	Wildflower	No.			30	20	10	30			30
Hansberger, H.	Wildflower	No.			60	60		60			60
Heilbron, A.	Wildflower	No.			80	80		80			80
Holton, R. E.	Wildflower	No.			100	50	50	100			100
Jones, P. D.	Wildflower	No.	2		30	32		32			32
Joplin, C.	Wildflower	No.			10	10		10			10
Marshall, H. O.	Wildflower	No.			5		5	5			5
Pyott, J. W.	Wildflower	No.			8	8		8			8
Rice, A. C.	Wildflower	No.			40	40		40			40
Walker, J. H.	Wildflower	No.			12	12		12			12
Wood, J.	Wildflower	No.			55	55		55			55
Totals for county			190	826	42,910	26,176	17,750	43,928	73	5,574	49,500

FRESNO COUNTY. (Vineyards in Tulare County.)

Name of Owner	Post Office and Name of Vineyard	Wine Maker	Acres in Sultanas	Acres in Malagas	Acres in Muscats	Acres in Raisin Grapes not Bearing	Acres in Raisin Grapes Bearing	Total Acres in Raisin Grapes	Acres in Wine Grapes not Bearing	Total Acres in Wine Grapes	Total Acres in Grapes
Anderson, L.	Kingsburg	No.			15	7	8	15			15
Anderson, Samuel	Kingsburg	No.			15	15		15			15
Booth, Robert	Kingsburg	No.			30	30		30			30
Carlson, A. P.	Kingsburg	No.			16	16		16			16
Carlson, C.	Kingsburg	No.			10	10		10			10
Carlson, J. M.	Kingsburg	No.			15	15		15			15
Carlson, Miss Lena	Kingsburg	No.			38	38		38			38
Cole, J.	Kingsburg	No.			18		18	18			18
Dahlgren, L.	Kingsburg	No.			17	17		17			17
Fanholm, F.	Kingsburg	No.			10	10		10			10
Hammer, C.	Kingsburg	No.			10	3	7	10			10
Hanson, Nels	Kingsburg	No.			10	10		10			10
Harp, L.	Kingsburg	No.			30		30	30			30
Hedberg, E.	Kingsburg	No.			20	5	15	20			20
Johnson, C. A.	Kingsburg	No.			16	6	10	16			16
Johnson, J. A.	Kingsburg	No.			16	16		16			16
Johnson, O. S.	Kingsburg	No.			6	6		6			6
Johnson, S. M.	Kingsburg	No.			20	20		20			20
Johnson, W.	Kingsburg	No.			25	5	20	25			25
Kanutz, Ed.	Kingsburg	No.			25	25		25			25
Larson, H. L.	Kingsburg	No.			6	6		6			6
Larson, W.	Kingsburg	No.			8		8	8			8
Lindquist, P.	Kingsburg	No.			35	35		35			35
Lindquist, P. O.	Kingsburg	No.			15	15		15			15
Nelson, C. S.	Kingsburg	No.			8	8		8			8
Oldham, S. C.	Kingsburg	No.			40	16	24	40			40
Olsen, L.	Kingsburg	No.			85	85		85		15	100
Peterson, N.	Kingsburg	No.			28		28	28			28
Swanson, N.	Kingsburg	No.			5	5		5			5
Wittgren, P. A.	Kingsburg	No.			13	13		13			13

INYO COUNTY.

Name of Owner.	Post Office and Name of Vineyard.	Total Acres in Grapes.	Acres in Bearing.	Acres in Wine Grapes.	Acres in Table Grapes.	Acres in Raisin Grapes.	Wine Maker.	Product in 1884.	Varieties.
Baker, Mrs. Fannie	Big Pine	1	1		1		No.	3 tons.	
Bell, Mrs. S. A.	Big Pine	2	2		2		No.	6 tons.	
McAfee, Mrs. A. C.	Big Pine	2	2		2			6 tons.	
Bulfritt, William	Bishop	1	1		1			2½ tons.	
Collins, A. O.	Bishop	10	10	5		5		3 tons.	
King, Mrs. Sarah	Bishop	1	1		1			30 tons.	
McfEe, J. S.	Bishop	1	1		1			3 tons.	
Watson, W. G.	Bishop	1	1		1			3 tons.	
Albers, Theo.	Independence	2	2		2			2½ tons.	
Hunter, W. S.	Independence	1	1		1			5 tons.	
Kispert, John	Independence	2	2		2			2½ tons.	
McAver, Finlay	Independence	4	2		2	2		10 tons.	
Robinson, H. J.	Independence	2	2		2			5 tons.	
Robinson, E.	Independence	2	2		2			5 tons.	
Schabbled, Fred.	Independence	1	1		1			2½ tons.	
Shepherd, John	Independence	1	1		1			5 tons.	
Stromeyer, Fred.	Independence	7	5		5	2		17½ tons.	
Symms, J. W.	Independence	2	2	2				5 tons.	
Vagt, Jacob	Independence	1	1		1			2½ tons.	
Walters, C. A.	Independence	1	1		1			2½ tons.	
Dias, R., estate of	Lone Pine	4	4	4				6 tons.	
Lucas, John	Lone Pine	1½	1½	1½				3¾ tons.	
Van Dyke, R.	Lone Pine	1	1		1			2½ tons.	
Zann, S.	Lone Pine	1	1		1			2½ tons.	
Totals for county		52½	48½	12½	31	9			

KERN COUNTY.

Name of Owner.	Post Office and Name of Vineyard.	Total Acres in Grapes	Total Acres in Wine Grapes.	Acres in Wine Grapes not Bearing	Total Acres in Raisin Grapes.	Acres in Raisin Grapes Bearing	Acres in Raisin Grapes not Bearing	Acres in Muscats	Acres in Malagas	Acres in Sultanas	Wine Maker.
Andrew, H. W.	Bakersfield	10			10		10	10			No.
Briscoe & Delessus	Bakersfield	18			18		18	18			No.
Brower, C.	Bakersfield	30			30		30	30			No.
Brown, J. D.	Bakersfield	20			20		20	20			No.
Burnett, J.	Bakersfield	30			30		30	30			No.
Burton, J. D.	Bakersfield	20			20		20	20			No.
Cross, C. W.	Bakersfield	20			20		20	20			No.
Croll, John	Bakersfield	10			10		10	10			No.
Demon, J. & W.	Bakersfield	20			20		20	20			No.
Densmore, E. A.	Bakersfield	20			20		20	20			No.
Densmore, F. A.	Bakersfield	20			20		20	20			No.
Fry, J. A.	Bakersfield	30			30		30	30			No.
Galtes, Paul	Bakersfield	20			20		20	20			No.
Herman, H. M.	Bakersfield	10			10		10	10			No.
Kelley, W.	Bakersfield	160			160		160	160			No.
La Corona Vineyard	Bakersfield	5			5		5	5			No.
Legress, J. M.	Bakersfield	10			10		10	10			No.
Menser, G.	Bakersfield	20			20		20	20			No.
Monyhan & Crowley	Bakersfield	20			20		20	20			No.
Morrison, M. E.	Bakersfield	8			8		8	8			No.
Pierce, C. C.	Bakersfield	80			80		80	80			No.
Rio Bravo Vineyard Company	Bakersfield	18			18		18	18			No.
Robinson, G. C.	Bakersfield	20			20		20	20			No.
Ross, L. R.	Bakersfield	320			320		320	320			No.
Rosedale Vineyard Company	Bakersfield	15			15		15	15			No.
Storms, A. W.	Bakersfield	20			20		20	20			No.
Slavan, A. E.	Bakersfield	30			30		30	30			No.
Smith, J. E.	Bakersfield	20			20		20	20			No.
Sturges, S.	Bakersfield	40			40		40	40			No.
Stump, L. C.	Bakersfield	15			15		15	15			No.
Swain, A. H.	Bakersfield	10			10		10	10			No.
Thorp, Capt. J.	Bakersfield	10			10		10	10			No.
Theisen, Peter	Bakersfield	15			15		15	15			No.
Underwood, W. E.	Bakersfield										No.

KERN COUNTY—Continued.

Name of Owner.	Post Office and Name of Vineyard.	Total Acres in Grapes.	Total Acres in Wine Grapes.	Acres in Wine Grapes not Bearing.	Total Acres in Raisin Grapes.	Acres in Raisin Grapes Bearing.	Acres in Raisin Grapes not Bearing.	Acres in Muscats.	Acres in Malagas.	Acres in Sultanas.	Wine Maker.
Waters, W.	Bakersfield	10			10		10	10			No.
Wright, G. M.	Bakersfield	10			10		10	10			No.
Wright, T. E.	Bakersfield	10			10		18	10			No.
Wolf, Mrs. J. W.	Bakersfield	18			18		8	18			No.
Wolter, Jake	Bakersfield	8			8		30	8			No.
Wells, A. A.	Bakersfield	30			30			30			No.
Totals for county		1,200			1,200		1,200	1,200			

LAKE COUNTY.

Name of Owner.	Post Office and Name of Vineyard.	Total Acres in Grapes.	Acres in Bearing.	Acres in Wine Grapes.	Acres in Table Grapes.	Acres in Raisin Grapes.	Wine Maker.	Product in 1889.	Varieties.
Buckingham, Geo. A.	Kelseyville	45	45	35	10		Yes.	75 tons.	Zinfandel, Muscat.
Hastings, I. N.	Kelseyville	5	5	5			No.	10 tons.	Mixed varieties.
Berger, L. P.	Lakeport	7	7	7			No.	15 tons.	Varieties.
Boggs, L. C.	Lakeport	5	5	5			No.	10 tons.	Varieties, Mission.
Lyon, Mrs.	Lakeport	12	12	12			No.	20 tons.	Varieties.
Mayer, George	Lakeport	35	10	35			No.	20 tons.	Varieties.
Thorington, George	Lakeport	5	5	5			No.	10 tons.	Mission, mixed.
Barry, Claude	Lower Lake	8	8	8			No.	20 tons.	Zinfandel, Chasselas.
Billesback, T.	Lower Lake	8	8	8			No.	20 tons.	Zinfandel, Chasselas.
Bluth Bros.	Lower Lake	20	20	20			Yes.	40 tons.	Zinfandel.
Cummings, C.	Lower Lake	6	6	5			No.	10 tons.	Mission.
Delucchi, Peter	Lower Lake	20	20	20			No.	50 tons.	Zinfandel, Chasselas.

KERN COUNTY—ADDITIONAL.

The following list of vine growers in Kern County was received too late for insertion in its proper place:

NAME.	Post Office.	Acres in Grapes.
Adams, W. B.	Bakersfield	4
Bacon, G. W.	Bakersfield	4
Batty, A. W.	Bakersfield	10
Barker, J. W.	Bakersfield	6
Bacon, J. K.	Bakersfield	15
Beck, A. J.	Bakersfield	10
Beck, E. F.	Bakersfield	8
Brough, Amelia	Bakersfield	10
Butler, A. J.	Bakersfield	7
Carr, John	Bakersfield	25
Close, W. J.	Bakersfield	14
Davis, J. F.	Bakersfield	20
Demaine, W. & G.	Bakersfield	10
Duvall, J. W.	Bakersfield	17
Duvall, Mrs. J. W.	Bakersfield	5
Elliot, E. E.	Bakersfield	20
Ferguson, J. W.	Bakersfield	20
Garry, W. H.	Bakersfield	10
Gibson, G. H.	Bakersfield	10
Harmon, ——	Bakersfield	30
Hawkyard, G.	Bakersfield	10
Henry, Rev.	Bakersfield	5
Huff, P. J.	Bakersfield	5
Hunt, W. C.	Bakersfield	40
Hunt, Richard	Bakersfield	18
Isbester, W. E.	Bakersfield	14
Jones, J. H.	Bakersfield	15
Knowles, C. G.	Bakersfield	20
Lane, William	Bakersfield	30
Loveland, E. H.	Bakersfield	35
Lowe, F. D.	Bakersfield	18
McLean, W. C.	Bakersfield	9
Merritt, ——	Bakersfield	5
Morrah, J. W.	Bakersfield	10
Ogelvie, H. T.	Bakersfield	15
Palmer, L. B.	Bakersfield	25
Pearson, ——	Bakersfield	20
Pierce, ——	Bakersfield	30
Pike, E. I.	Bakersfield	10
Randall, William	Bakersfield	10
Randall, G. W.	Bakersfield	10
Revill, ——	Bakersfield	20
Riddell, W. L.	Bakersfield	20
Robertson, G. W.	Bakersfield	6
Robinson, F. W.	Bakersfield	6
Rockwell, E. P.	Bakersfield	40
Rudd, R.	Bakersfield	20
Russell, J.	Bakersfield	30
Segress, J. A.	Bakersfield	30
Sensen, G. W.	Bakersfield	10
Shepherd, W. R.	Bakersfield	10
Shortemuier, H. E.	Bakersfield	20
Strobel, J. B.	Bakersfield	5
Thiesen, P. O.	Bakersfield	30
Thompson, J. W.	Bakersfield	15
Thompson, G. H.	Bakersfield	16
Tupman, E.	Bakersfield	5
Tupman, R.	Bakersfield	20
Tupman, H. T.	Bakersfield	5
Upton, William	Bakersfield	4
Uren, ——	Bakersfield	10
Waters, 1.	Bakersfield	9
Winters, H. S.	Bakersfield	7
White, Ray	Bakersfield	14
Young, E.	Bakersfield	12

All of the above are Muscat vineyards, and from one to two years old.

Name	Location						Product	Varieties
Getz, Joseph	Lower Lake	25	25	25		No.	60 tons.	Zinfandel, Chasselas.
Hanson, D.	Lower Lake	8	8	8		No.	16 tons.	Chasselas.
Harris, James	Lower Lake	15	15	15		No.	35 tons.	Zinfandel.
Jones, Dan	Lower Lake	5			5	Yes.	Not bearing.	Seedless Sultana.
Keatinge, M.	Lower Lake	100	80	100		Yes.	40,000 gals. / 160 tons.	Zinfandel, Chasselas.
Kugelman, L.	Lower Lake	25	25	23		No.	75 tons.	Zinfandel.
Kunish, J.	Lower Lake	14	14	14		No.	80 tons.	Riesling.
Nagle, John	Lower Lake	15	15	16		No.	40 tons.	Varieties.
Nicolai, J. G.	Lower Lake	8	8	8		No.	20 tons.	Burger.
Priest, Thomas	Lower Lake	10	10	10		No.	20 tons.	Mission, Malvoisie.
Schnell, H.	Lower Lake	5	5	5		No.	10 tons.	Varieties.
Schweiss, A.	Lower Lake	5	5	5		No.	20 tons.	Zinfandel.
Specht, Wm.	Lower Lake	8	8	8		No.	20 tons.	Chasselas, Burger.
Tennyson, J. A.	Lower Lake	10	10	10		No.	20 tons.	Varieties.
Voight,	Lower Lake	16	18	16		Yes.	35 tons.	Zinfandel.
Water Company	Lower Lake	300	300	300		No.	600 tons.	Burger, Zinfandel, Chasselas.
Bradford Bros.	Middletown	20	20	20		No.	40 tons.	Zinfandel, Malvoisie.
Cassady, Ed.	Middletown	12	12	12		No.	30 tons.	Zinfandel, Chasselas.
Coates, J. R.	Middletown	30	30	30		No.	75 tons.	Malvoisie, mixed.
Cottrell, Silas.	Middletown	6	6	6		No.	12 tons.	Zinfandel.
Fox, John.	Middletown	6	6	6		No.	10 tons	Riesling.
Gunning, F.	Middletown	10	10	10		No.	25 tons.	Zinfandel.
Hibbard, Chas.	Middletown	5	5	5		No.	10 tons.	Zinfandel.
Howard, C. L.	Middletown	5	5	5		No.	10 tons.	Zinfandel.
Langtry, Mrs.	Middletown	20	20	20		Yes.	50 tons.	Burgundy.
Lolree, Dr.	Middletown	35	35	35		Yes.	75 tons.	Burgundy, Chasselas.
McKinley, Geo. A.	Middletown	15	15	15		No.	60 tons.	Zinfandel.
Mootier, C.	Middletown	8	8	8		No.	15 tons.	Varieties.
Norton, A. E.	Middletown	5	5	5		No.	10 tons.	Chasselas, Riesling.
Schnelle, Chas.	Middletown	5	5	5		No.	10 tons.	Zinfandel.
Schwartz, John	Middletown	12	12	12		No.	25 tons.	Zinfandel.
Short, J. C.	Middletown	8	8	8		No.	20 tons.	Zinfandel.
Valentine & Rocco	Middletown	20	20	20		No.	50 tons.	Zinfandel, Riesling.
Hammond Bros.	Upper Lake	30	30	30		No.	50 tons.	Zinfandel.
Hastings, S. C.	Upper Lake	60	60	60		Yes.	120 tons.	Zinfandel.
Morrison, S.	Upper Lake	5	5	5		No.	10 tons.	Zinfandel, Mission.
Totals for county		1,061	1,008	1,046	15			

LOS ANGELES COUNTY.

Name of Owner.	Post Office and Name of Vineyard.	Total Acres in Grapes.	Acres in Bearing.	Acres in Wine Grapes.	Acres in Table Grapes.	Acres in Raisin Grapes.	Wine Maker.	Product in 1889.	Varieties.
Brown, Cyrus	Downey						No.		
Curtis, B. M.	Downey						No.		
O'Connor, Pat.	Downey						No.		
Quill, Jas.	Downey						No.		
Van Ness, F.	Downey						Yes.		Tokay.
Weiss, F.	Downey						No.		
Batcheller, J. W.	Fruitland						No.		Muscat.
Bell, J. G.	Fruitland						No.		Muscat, Zinfandel.
Moscatti,	Fruitland						No.		Muscat.
Brown, H.	Glendale	25	25	25					Trousseau, Mission, Burger.
Gibbs, P. L.	Glendale						No.		Zinfandel.
Glassel, H.	Glendale	40	40	40					Zinfandel, Trousseau,
Riggin, E.	Glendale						No.		Burger, Zinfandel, Blaue Elba.
Sampson, M. L.	Glendale						No.		Zinfandel, Muscat.
Smith, A. M.	Glendale						No.		Pisco.
Squire, F. M.	Glendale						No.		Mission.
Stratton, G. S.	Glendale						No.		Blaue Elba.
Taylor, D. W.	Glendale						No.		Mission.
Verdi,	Glendale						No.		Zinfandel.
Chamberlain, W. H.	La Cañada	13	13	13			No.		Muscat, Sultana.
Dunks, Mrs.	La Cañada	4	4	4			No.		Zinfandel.
Hall, T. S.	La Cañada	10	10	10			Yes.		Zinfandel, Burger.
Knight, Jesse	La Cañada	6	6	6			No.		Zinfandel.
Lanterman, J. F.	La Cañada	15	15	15			No.		Muscat, Sultana.
Spofforth & Bainbridge	La Cañada	5	5	5			No.		Mataro.
Veiler, O. A.	La Cañada						No.		
Williams, A. W.	La Cañada	7	7	7			No.		Zinfandel.
Allen, A. E., estate of	Mountain Wine Co., Lamanda Park	350	350	350			Yes.		
Bonine, A. E.	Lamanda Park	5	5	5			No.		
Brigden, A.	Lamanda Park	75	75	75			Yes.		
Butler, J. H.	Lamanda Park	10	10	10			No.		
Cogswell, W. C.	Lamanda Park	5	5	5			No.		
Craig, James	Lamanda Park	60	60	60			No.		

Name	Post Office						Varieties
Crank, J. F.	Lamanda Park	250	250	250	Yes.		
Crisp, J.	Lamanda Park	50	50	50	No.		
Engel, P.	Lamanda Park	15	15	15	No.		
Hastings Estate	Lamanda Park	350	350	350	No.		
Hugus, J. W.	Lamanda Park	100	100	100	No.		
Johnson, Capt.	Lamanda Park	6	6	6	No.		
Kinney, Abbot	Lamanda Park	15	15	15	No.		
Koontz, J. D.	Lamanda Park	10	10	10	No.		
Pealerbough,	Lamanda Park	20	20	20	No.		
Reid, P. T.	Lamanda Park	35	35	35	No.		
Ruddy,	Lamanda Park	15	15	15	No.		
Sierra Madre Vintage Company.	Lamanda Park	20	20	20	Yes.		
Toler,	Lamanda Park	50	50	50	No.		
Vosburg, J. C.	Lamanda Park	30	30	30	No.		
Williams, Jas	Lamanda Park	5	5	5	Yes.		
Dillon & Kenealy.	Los Angeles	200	200	200	Yes.		Zinfandel, Trousseau, Mataro, Riesling, Burger.
Stern, Chas., & Sons	Los Angeles						Zinfandel, Trousseau.
Glassel, A.	Los Angeles	35	35	35			Blaue Elba, Burger.
Wack, Paul	Los Angeles				Yes.		
Andrews, J.	Norwalk	10					
Dollard, John	Norwalk	5					
Heberle, Geo.	Norwalk	55					
Johnson, D. D.	Norwalk	50					
Leeper, Mrs.	Norwalk	12					
Pendleton, W.	Norwalk	40					
Smith, George	Norwalk	20					
Surbeck, H.	Norwalk	25					
Todhunter, Alfred	Norwalk	25					
Scattered vines	Norwalk	60					
Becker, A. B.	Pasadena						
Branburg, J.	Pasadena						
Brown, C. C.	Pasadena						
Hugus, J.	Pasadena						
Jacobs, A.	Pasadena						
Oak Knoll	Pasadena						
Pasadena Improv't Co.	Pasadena						
Pierce, M. H.	North Pasadena						
Raymond Improv't Co.	Pasadena						
Woodbury, J. P.	Pasadena						
Andrews, S. N. ⎱ Dole, W. B. ⎰ Dole, J.	Pomona	10	10	5	No.	5	Zinfandel, Sultana.
Belderain, J. A.	Pomona	10	10	10	No.		Zanfandel.
Bolt, Rev. J.	Pomona (San Gabriel)	10	10	10	No.		Mission.

LOS ANGELES COUNTY—Continued.

Name of Owner	Post Office and Name of Vineyard	Total Acres in Grapes	Acres in Bearing	Acres in Wine Grapes	Acres in Table Grapes	Acres in Raisin Grapes	Wine Maker	Product in 1889	Varieties
Currier, A. D.	Pomona	10	10			10	No.		Muscat.
Dalton, W.	Pomona	2	2	2			No.		Burger.
Disnerat, J.	Pomona	10	10	10					Burger.
Ford, S.	Pomona	10	10	10					Zinfandel.
Fryer, H. F.	Pomona	10	10	10					Zinfandel.
Harvey, James	Pomona	5	5	5					Mission.
Hillman, I.	Pomona	20	20	20					Zinfandel.
Hoops, Peter	Pomona	20	20	20					Zinfandel, Burger.
Keller, E. W.	Pomona	60	60	60					Zinfandel, Trousseau.
McClary, G. W.	Pomona	2	2	2					Burger, Zinfandel, Trousseau.
McClintock, A.	Pomona	4	4	4					Mission.
Martin, P. S.	Pomona	2	2	2					Zinfandel.
Mell, D. A.	Pomona	20	20	20					Muscat.
Mirande, G.	Pomona	50	50	50		2	Yes.		Zinfandel, Trousseau, Mission.
Packard, J. A.	Pomona	5	5	5			No.		Zinfandel, Mataro, Burger.
Palomares, Mrs.	Pomona	30	30	30			No.		Mission.
Park & Oldham	Pomona	6	6			6	No.		Mataro, Zinfandel.
Parsons, E.	Pomona	3	3	3			No.		Muscat.
Pomona L'd & Water Co.	Pomona	10	10	10			No.		Mission.
Sanders, H.	Pomona	35	35	35			No.		Zinfandel.
Seaver, C.	Pomona	17	17	17			Yes.		Mataro, Zinfandel, Trousseau.
Smith, A. H.	Pomona	70	70	70			No.		Mission.
Smith, F. J.	Pomona	5	5	5			No.		Zinfandel, Mataro.
Vejar, R.	Pomona	8	8	8			No.		Mission.
Walz, J. A.	Pomona	5	5	5			No.		Zinfandel, Burger.
Vacque, E. W.	Puente	10	10	10			No.		Mission.
Pine, S.	Rincon						Yes.		Mission, Zinfandel.
Baldwin, E. J.	Santa Anita	300	300	300			No.		Zinfandel, Burger, Mataro.
Bishop, T. B.	San Gabriel	75	75	75			No.		Tokay, Emperor.
Chapman, A. B.	San Gabriel	50	50	10	40		No.		Blaue Elba.
Cooper, Mrs. M. C.	San Gabriel	22	22	22			No.		Blaue Elba, Trousseau.
Fargo, C. F.	San Gabriel	35	35	35			No.		Blaue Elba.
McDonald, H. D.	San Gabriel	6	6	6			No.		Blaue Elba.
McDonald, J. A.	San Gabriel	2	2	2			No.		Blaue Elba.

Name of Owner	Post Office and Name of Vineyard	Total Acres in Grapes	Acres in Bearing	Acres in Wine Grapes	Acres in Table Grapes	Acres in Raisin Grapes	Wine Maker	Product in 1889.	Varieties.
Mayberry, E. T.	San Gabriel	200	200	200			No.		Muscat, Trousseau, Mataro, Zinfandel, Malvoisie.
Patton, G.	San Gabriel	50	50	50			No.		Sultana, Trousseau, Burger.
Purcell, Gervaise	San Gabriel	40	40	40			No.		Zinfandel, Golden Chasselas, Blaue Elba.
Rose, L. J., & Co. (Limited.)	San Gabriel (Sunny Slope).	640	640	640			Yes.	860 tons.	Twelve varieties.
San Gabriel Wine Co.	San Gabriel (Ramona)	390	390	390			Yes.		Eleven varieties.
Shorb, J. DeBarth.	San Gabriel	160	160	160			Yes.		Zinfandel, Grenache.
Fryer, J. M.	Spadra	10	10	10			No.		Zinfandel.
Ling, M.	Spadra	10	10	10			No.		Zinfandel, Trousseau.
Oddus, J.	Spadra								
Sippi, ——	Spadra	10	10	10			No.		Mataro.
Devine, Robert	Tropico	18	18	18			No.		Burger, Blaue Elba.
Mitchell, H. M. (estate)	Tropico	35	35	35					Burger, Zinfandel.
Total acreage*		4,096	4,363	4,632	40	23			

*Partial.

MARIN COUNTY.

Name of Owner	Post Office and Name of Vineyard	Total Acres in Grapes	Acres in Bearing.	Acres in Wine Grapes	Acres in Table Grapes	Acres in Raisin Grapes	Wine Maker	Product in 1889.	Varieties.
Pixley, F. M.	Corte Madera (San F.)	5	5	5			No.	5 tons.	Varieties.
Miller, B. T.	Nicasio	5	5	5			No.	10 tons.	Zinfandel.
Burdell, Dr. G.	Novato	100	100	100			No.	125 tons.	Zinfandel.
De Long, Frank C.	Novato	200	150	200			No.	200 tons.	Zinfandel, Mission.
Devoto, L. A.	Novato	6		6				Not bearing.	Zinfandel.
Scone, A. G.	Novato	10	10	10			Yes.	5 tons.	Zinfandel, Mission.
Escalle, J.	San Rafael	25	25	25			Yes.	40 tons.	Zinfandel, varieties.
Grosjean, C.	San Rafael	28	28	28			No.	20 tons.	Zinfandel.
Kent, A. E.	San Rafael (San Fran.)	5	5		5		No.	10 tons.	Muscat, Tokay.
McAllister, Hall	San Rafael	40	40	20	20		No.	60 tons.	Zinfandel, Tokay, Muscat.
Miller, James	San Rafael	25	25	25			No.	50 tons.	Zinfandel.
Mund, T.	San Rafael	5		5				Not bearing.	Varieties.
Nevada Bank	San Rafael (San Fran.)	40	40	40			No.	90 tons.	Zinfandel.
Scholnman, F.	San Rafael	5	5	5			No.	12 tons.	Zinfandel.
Short, J. O'B.	San Rafael	5	5	5			No.	10 tons.	Zinfandel.
Totals for county		502	441	477	25				

MENDOCINO COUNTY.

NAME OF OWNER.	Post Office and Name of Vineyard.	Total Acres in Grapes.	Acres in Bearing.	Acres in Wine Grapes.	Acres in Table Grapes.	Acres in Raisin Grapes.	Wine Maker.	Product in 1889.	Varieties
Cook, ——	Boonville	5	5		5		No.	10 tons.	Muscat.
Orr, Sam	Calpella	5	5	5			No.	10 tons.	Mission.
Peters, F.	Calpella	20	20	20			Yes.	20 tons.	Zinfandel.
Cochrane, T.	Cloverdale	8	8	8			No.	15 tons.	Zinfandel.
Crohn, Christ	Cloverdale	12	6	10	2		No.	10 tons.	Zinfandel, Muscat.
Edwards, John	Cloverdale	20	20	20			No.	50 tons.	Zinfandel, Mission.
Lambert, William	Cloverdale	20	20	20			No.	50 tons.	Zinfandel, Mission.
Dooley, E. H.	Hopland	5	5	5			No.	10 tons.	Zinfandel, varieties.
Foster, H. W.	Hopland	10	10	10			No.	30 tons.	Zinfandel.
Howell, Orrin	Hopland	10	10	10			No.	5 tons.	Zinfandel.
Loretz, Christ	Hopland	5	5	5			No.	5 tons.	Zinfandel.
Meyers Bros.	Hopland	5	5	5				Not bearing.	Zinfandel.
Demeke, John	Ukiah	5		5	7		Yes.	Not bearing.	Zinfandel.
Gobbi, Dan.	Ukiah	17	17	10			No.	60 tons.	Zinfandel, Tokay, Catawba.
Gobbi, L.	Ukiah	8	8	8			No.	20 tons.	Zinfandel.
McClure, J. B.	Ukiah	12	12	12			No.	12 tons.	Zinfandel.
O'Shay, D.	Ukiah	8	8	8			No.	16 tons.	Mission.
Seward, A. J.	Ukiah	17	17	17			No.	50 tons.	Mixed varieties.
Wheeler, E. D.	Ukiah	7	7	7			No.	10 tons.	Varieties.
Wilcox, ——	Ukiah	5	5	5			No.	10 tons.	Mission.
Totals for county		204	183	190	14				

MERCED COUNTY.

Name of Owner	Post Office and Name of Vineyard	Total Acres in Grapes	Total Acres in Wine Grapes	Acres in Wine Grapes not Bearing	Total Acres in Raisin Grapes	Acres in Raisin Grapes Bearing	Acres in Raisin Grapes not Bearing	Acres in Muscats	Acres in Malagas	Acres in Sultanas	Wine Maker
Ashe, R. Porter	Atwater	10			10	10		10			No.
Buhach P. & M. Co.	Atwater	130	122		8	8		8			No.
Mitchell, J. W.	Atwater	300			300		300	60	240		No.
Mitchell, W. D.	Atwater	35			35		35	23	12		No.
Smith, Z. T.	Atwater	10			10		10		10		No.
Bendt, John	Ingomar	30			30	30		30			No.
Clark, D. P.	Ingomar	5			5	5		5			No.
Drummond, J. Q.	Ingomar	20			20		20	20			No.
Edwards, J. H.	Livingston	15	5		10	10		10			No.
Stevenson, J. J.	Livingston	10	10								No.
Turner, W. C.	Livingston	10	10								No.
Miller, Henry	Los Baños	60	20		40		40	40			No.
Akin, W. B.	Merced	12	6		6		6	4	2		No.
Atwater, —	Merced	2	2	2							No.
Bay, —	Merced	10			10		10	10			No.
Bell, Wm.	Merced	7			7		7	7			No.
Canne, C. D.	Merced	10			10		10	10			No.
Clarke, W. F.	Merced	5	5								No.
Dean & Son	Merced	90			90		90	90			No.
Elliott, W. E.	Merced	8			8	8		8			No.
Galland, J. B.	Merced	80			80	80		80			No.
Goldman, M.	Merced	31	28		3	3		2			No.
Henderson, C.	Merced	4	4								No.
Hooper, C. W.	Merced	110	10		100		100	100		1	No.
Howell Bros.	Merced	15			15		15	15			No.
Huffman, C. H.	Merced	100			100		100	100			No.
James, G.	Merced	10			10		10	10			No.
Landrim & Baker	Merced	20			20		20	5	15		No.
Landrum, C.	Merced	16			16		16	16			No.
Lukwin, —	Merced	20			20		20	20			No.
Lyons, G. W.	Merced	20			20		20	20			No.
McSwain, J. F.	Merced	10			10		10	10			No.
Mejan, —	Merced	5			5		5	5			No.
Merced Land and Fruit Co.	Merced	180			180		180	180			No.

MERCED COUNTY—Continued.

Name of Owner	Post Office and Name of Vineyard	Total Acres in Grapes	Total Acres in Wine Grapes	Acres in Wine Grapes not Bearing	Total Acres in Raisin Grapes	Acres in Raisin Grapes Bearing	Acres in Raisin Grapes not Bearing	Acres in Muscats	Acres in Malagas	Acres in Sultanas	Wine Maker
Olds, Ed.	Merced	40			40		40	3¾	2		No.
Peterson & Peobley	Merced	15			15		15		15		No.
Plengans,	Merced	5			5		5	5			No.
Rotterdam Syndicate	Merced	30			30		30	30			No.
Sanders, J. J.	Merced	3	3								No.
Thieme Bros.	Merced	10			10		10	10			No.
Tother,	Merced	7			7		7	7			No.
Tzerny, J.	Merced	10			10		10	10			No.
Van De Hoope, A.	Merced	10			10		10	10			No.
Warfield & Goldman	Merced	20			20		20		20		No.
Wilson & Nordway	Merced	40			40	10	30	30	10		No.
Newman, S.	Newman	15	15								No.
Buckley, R. H.	Snelling	10	10								No.
Coconor, J. B.	Snelling	13	7		6	6		6			No.
Fee, Mrs. P.	Snelling	3	3								No.
Felthouse, John	Snelling	8	8								No.
Fisher, A.	Snelling	25	25								No.
Fitzhugh, E. C.	Snelling	5	5								No.
Grimes, I.	Snelling	20	20								No.
Hains, I.	Snelling	4	4								No.
Halstead, G. W.	Snelling	9	9								No.
Ivett, John	Snelling	2	2								No.
Jacobs & Co.	Snelling	30	30								No.
Largomarsini, A.	Snelling	5	2		3	3		3			No.
Montgomery, J. A.	Snelling	25	25								No.
Minges, J. W.	Snelling	8	8								No.
Robinson, J. H.	Snelling	10	10								No.
Spears, S. K.	Snelling	4	4								No.
Vachard, Mrs. M.	Snelling	10	5		5	5		5			No.
Bunker, N. E.	Sturgeon	4	4								No.
Guiseppi & Co.	Volta	50	20		30	30		30			No.
Totals for county		1,846	425	2	1,419	212	1,207	1,092	326	1	

MONTEREY COUNTY.

Name of Owner.	Post Office and Name of Vineyard.	Total Acres in Grapes.	Acres in Bearing.	Acres in Wine Grapes.	Acres in Table Grapes.	Acres in Raisin Grapes.	Wine Maker.	Product in 1889.	Varieties.
Alvarado, H.	Bradley								
Kernelli & Co.	Gonzales								
Pugh,	Gonzales								
Marsillot, M. G.	Parkfield								
Carter, Michel	Salinas								
Hebert, L.	Salinas								
Hebborn, J. R.	Salinas								
With, Jos.	Salinas								
Garrissere, F.	San Ardo								
Witman, J.	San Lucas								

NAPA COUNTY.

Name of Owner.	Post Office and Name of Vineyard.	Total Acres in Grapes.	Acres in Bearing.	Acres in Wine Grapes.	Acres in Table Grapes.	Acres in Raisin Grapes.	Wine Maker.	Product in 1890.	Varieties.
Angwin, E.	Angwin	5	5	5			No.	14 tons.	Malvoisie, Zinfandel.
Austin, Robt.	Angwin	30	30	30			Yes.	55 tons.	Riesling, Zinfandel.
Baskerville, S.	Angwin	10	10	10			No.	24 tons.	Riesling, Chasselas, Zinfandel.
Hastings, Judge	Angwin	100	100	100			Yes.	365 tons.	Burger, Zinfandel.
Keyes, W. S.	Angwin	100	100	100			Yes.	370 tons.	Burger, Chasselas, Zinfandel.
Martinelli, J.	Angwin	8	4	8			Yes.	100 gals.	Zinfandel.
Murry Bros.	Angwin	15	10	15			No.	46 tons.	Zinfandel.
Beaumont, Mrs.	Calistoga	25	25	25			No.	60 tons.	Zinfandel, Riesling.
Bennett Bros.	Calistoga	20	20	20			No.	60 tons.	Zinfandel, Chasselas.
Bennett, J. L.	Calistoga	8	8	8			No.	48 tons.	Zinfandel, Burger.

NAPA COUNTY—Continued.

Name of Owner.	Post Office and Name of Vineyard.	Total Acres in Grapes.	Acres in Bearing.	Acres in Wine Grapes.	Acres in Table Grapes.	Acres in Raisin Grapes.	Wine Maker.	Product in 1890.	Varieties.
Bingham Bros.	Calistoga	30	30	30			No.	85 tons.	Zinfandel, Burger.
Borchett, J.	Calistoga	20	20	20			No.	80 tons.	Zinfandel, Burger.
Borchett, M. L.	Calistoga	40	40	40			No.	120 tons.	Zinfandel, Malvoisie.
Bonnsall, Mrs. P. D.	Calistoga	36	36	36			No.	146 tons.	Zinfandel, Chasselas, Malvoisie.
Brown, E.	Calistoga	18	18	18			No.	80 tons.	Zinfandel, Chasselas.
Butler, Mrs.	Calistoga	12	12	12			No.	45 tons.	Zinfandel, Riesling.
Basely, B.	Calistoga	10	10	10			No.	30 tons.	Zinfandel, Riesling.
Clots, —	Calistoga	10	10	10			No.	35 tons.	Zinfandel, Burger.
Cole, R. B.	Calistoga	10	10	10			No.	25 tons.	Zinfandel, Burger.
Cole, W.	Calistoga	20	20	20			No.	100 tons.	Mission.
Connor, G. J.	Calistoga	7	7	7			No.	18 tons.	Zinfandel, Malvoisie.
Crouch, F. A.	Calistoga	19	19	19			No.	80 tons.	Chasselas, Malvoisie.
Culver, J. V.	Calistoga	10	10	10			No.	30 tons.	Zinfandel, Riesling.
Dexter, H. S.	Calistoga	45	18	45			No.	16 tons.	Zinfandel, Sauvignon Vert, Riesling.
Dormay, F.	Calistoga	35	35	35			No.	75 tons.	Cabernet, Sauvignon Vert, Mataro, Riesling.
Eberling, W.	Calistoga	8	8	8			No.	30 tons.	Malvoisie, Mataro, Sauvignon Vert.
Farron & Clydesdale	Calistoga	10	10	10			No.	60 tons.	Zinfandel, Burger.
Fellows, —	Calistoga	10	10	10			No.	45 tons.	Zinfandel, Chasselas.
Furness, Mrs. S. C.	Calistoga	45	45	45			No.	125 tons.	Burger, Zinfandel, Sauvignon Vert, Chasselas.
Garnett, A. G.	Calistoga	50	50	50			No.	100 tons.	Mission.
Garnett, J. K.	Calistoga	30	30	30			Yes.	120 tons.	Zinfandel, Riesling.
Grimm, A. & C.	Calistoga	40	40	40			Yes.	150 tons.	Burger, Zinfandel, Sauvignon Vert, Reisling, Pinot.
Haley, Mrs. M.	Calistoga	8	8	8			No.	12 tons.	Zinfandel, Golden Chasselas.
Hansen, L. M.	Calistoga	10	10	10			No.	25 tons.	Zinfandel, Riesling.
Hansen, W.	Calistoga	5	5	5			No.	16 tons.	Zinfandel, Riesling.
Hintze, Joseph	Calistoga	25	25	25			No.	64 tons.	Zinfandel, Riesling.
Hittel, C.	Calistoga	13	13	13			Yes.	50 tons.	Zinfandel, Chasselas, Sauvignon Vert.
Hoover, A.	Calistoga	10	10	10			No.	30 tons.	Zinfandel, Burger, Chasselas.
Kellett, S.	Calistoga	60	60	60			No.	200 tons.	Zinfandel, Riesling, Mataro, Sauvignon Vert.
Lang, George	Calistoga	40	40	40			Yes.	70 tons.	Zinfandel, Riesling.
Lang, J.	Calistoga	18	18	18			No.	55 tons.	Zinfandel, Riesling.
Light Bros.	Calistoga	30	30	30			Yes.	125 tons.	Zinfandel, Chasselas.
Light, E.	Calistoga	30	30	30			No.	120 tons.	Zinfandel, Mataro, Chasselas.

Name	Post Office						Tons		Varieties
Lillie, C. H.	Calistoga	10	10	10		No.	44 tons.		Sauvignon Vert, Riesling, Chasselas.
McMerritt,	Calistoga	15	15	15		No.	50 tons.		Zinfandel, Riesling, Chasselas.
Manuel, David	Calistoga	19	19	19		No.	70 tons.		Zinfandel, Mission, Malvoisie.
Markhoff, H.	Calistoga	8	8	8		Yes.	25 tons.		Zinfandel, Riesling.
Mathewson, W.	Calistoga	15	15	15		No.	60 tons.		Zinfandel, Riesling.
Monk,	Calistoga	10	10	10		No.	30 tons.		Zinfandel, Riesling.
Moore, C. J. B.	Calistoga	7	7	7		Yes.	28 tons.		Zinfandel, Riesling.
Murphy, B.	Calistoga	5	5	5		No.	12 tons.		Zinfandel.
Osborn,	Calistoga	30	30	30		No.	90 tons.		Zinfandel, Burgundy.
Peterson,	Calistoga	30	30	30		No.	70 tons.		Zinfandel, Burger, Riesling.
Phillips, W. L.	Calistoga	30	30	30		Yes.	175 tons.		Zinfandel, Riesling.
Pickett, C. N.	Calistoga	25	18	25		No.	70 tons.		Zinfandel, Riesling.
Randall, J. G.	Calistoga	10	10	10		No.	20 tons.		Zinfandel, Riesling.
Ribbon, A.	Calistoga	5	6	5		No.	15 tons.		Zinfandel, Burger.
Roberts, J.	Calistoga	10	10	10		No.	90 tons.		Zinfandel, Riesling.
Rutherford, J.	Calistoga	20	20	20		No.	115 tons.		Zinfandel, Burger, Riesling.
Schmidt, P. R.	Calistoga	25	25	25		No.	87 tons.		Sauvignon Vert, Mataro, Riesling.
Schnitzer,	Calistoga	40	40	40		No.	120 tons.		Zinfandel, Mataro.
Simmons, A.	Calistoga	8	8	8		No.	20 tons.		Zinfandel, Malvoisie.
Smith, Mrs. J. H.	Calistoga	14	14	14		No.	60 tons.		Riesling.
Smith, R. P.	Calistoga	20	20	20		No.	60 tons.		Zinfandel, Riesling, Golden Chasselas.
Snyder, H.	Calistoga	16	16	16		No.	20 tons.		Zinfandel, Riesling.
Snyder,	Calistoga	30	30	30		No.	100 tons.		Zinfandel, Riesling.
Spiers, W.	Calistoga	15	15	15		No.	44 tons.		Chasselas, Riesling.
Sullivan, J. J.	Calistoga	6	6	6		No.	35 tons.		Zinfandel, Riesling.
Teale, J. A.	Calistoga	12	12	12		No.	40 tons.		Zinfandel, Riesling.
Teale, P.	Calistoga	5	5	5		No.	20 tons.		Zinfandel, Riesling.
Tubbs, A. L.	Calistoga	110	110	110		Yes.	420 tons.		Zinfandel, Cavernet, Mataro, Burger, Sauvignon Vert.
Tucker, J. W.	Calistoga	8	8	8		No.	40 tons.		Zinfandel, Riesling.
Veal, T. F.	Calistoga	10	10	10		No.	62 tons.		Mataro, Sauvignon Vert.
Walsh, Thos.	Calistoga	30	30	30		Yes.	100 tons.		Zinfandel, Burger.
Way, S. C.	Calistoga	16	16	16		No.	88 tons.		Zinfandel, Chasselas, Riesling.
Williams, J.	Calistoga	14	14	14		No.	40 tons.		Zinfandel, Riesling.
Yangle, H.	Calistoga	8	8	8		No.	35 tons.		Zinfandel, Sauvignon Vert.
York, J. W.	Calistoga	20	20	20		Yes.	90 tons.		Zinfandel, Riesling.
York, W.	Calistoga	20	20	20		Yes.	100 tons.		Zinfandel, Burger.
Zoeller, A.	Calistoga	20	20	20		Yes.	50 tons.		Zinfandel, Riesling, Burger.
Boothe, J.	Childs	6	6	6		No.	17 tons.		Zinfandel, Riesling.
Brownlee, Mrs.	Childs	20	20	20		Yes.	60 tons.		Zinfandel, Chasselas.
Eubanks, R. G.	Childs	28	28	28		No.	170 tons.		Zinfandel, Riesling.
Gladon,	Childs	23	23	23		No.	65 tons.		Zinfandel, Riesling.
Pellett, A.	Childs	12	12	12		No.	30 tons.		Zinfandel, Malvoisie, Chasselas.
Priest, J. J.	Childs	10	10	10		No.	25 tons.		Zinfandel, Chasselas.
Rutherford, R.	Childs	10	10	10		No.	20 tons.		Zinfandel, Riesling.

NAPA COUNTY—Continued.

Name of Owner.	Post Office and Name of Vineyard.	Total Acres in Grapes.	Acres in Bearing.	Acres in Wine Grapes.	Acres in Table Grapes.	Acres in Raisin Grapes.	Wine Maker.	Product in 1890.	Varieties.
Sievers, F.	Childs	13	13	13			No.	40 tons.	Zinfandel, Riesling.
Taylor, J.	Childs	20	20	20			No.	100 tons.	Zinfandel, Burger, Chasselas.
Brownlee, Robt.	Creston Station	50	50	50			No.	120 tons.	Zinfandel, Burger, Chasselas.
Barnett, E. J.	Lidell	5	5	5			No.	15 tons.	Mission.
Duvall, J. B.	Lidell	5	5	5			No.	14 tons.	Zinfandel.
Lidell, W. H.	Lidell	15	15	15			No.	27 tons.	Zinfandel, Riesling.
Workover, Thomas	Lidell	15	15	15			No.	35 tons.	Mission, Riesling.
Allen, C. H.	Lidell	12	12	12			No.	25 tons.	Zinfandel.
Bachman, Charles	Napa	8	8	8			No.	20 tons.	Chasselas, Cabernet, Mataro.
Banchero, L.	Napa	25	20	25			Yes.	30 tons.	Zinfandel, Malvoisie, Burgundy.
Bank of Napa	Occidental Vyd., Napa	80	80	80			Yes.	248 tons.	Chasselas, Malvoisie, Zinfandel, Burger.
Bauer, ——	Napa	12	7	7			Yes.	4,000 gals.	Zinfandel, Gutedel Vert.
Bauer Estate	Napa	50	50	50			Yes.	100 tons.	Chasselas, Riesling, Burgundy.
Bengles, W. H.	Napa	10	10	10			No.	20 tons.	Zinfandel.
Behrns, W. F.	Napa	8	8	8			No.	20 tons.	Zinfandel.
Buetto, B.	Napa	12	12	12			Yes.	45 tons.	Chasselas, Zinfandel, Riesling.
Borreo, T.	Napa	60	60	60			Yes.	125 tons.	Zinfandel.
Bridgman, ——	Napa	20	20	20			No.	37 tons.	Zinfandel.
Carbone, Antonio	Napa	40	40	40			Yes.	125 tons.	Burger, Zinfandel, Mataro, Burgundy.
Chapman, Henry	Napa	17	17	11	6		No.	20 tons.	Burger, Chasselas, Zinfandel.
Crouch, Robt.	Napa	12	12	12			No.	50 tons.	Burger, Zinfandel.
Crowey, Mrs. J.	Napa	20	20	20			No.	40 tons.	Zinfandel.
Daniels, J. O.	Napa	4	4	4			No.	10 tons.	Malvoisie.
Dell, C.	Napa	20		20			Yes.	9,000 gals.	Zinfandel, Black Burgundy.
Domergue, A. S.	Napa	15	15	15				30 tons.	Zinfandel, Black Burgundy.
Dulhig, Jas.	Napa	60	60	60			No.	150 tons.	Zinfandel, Burger, Malvoisie.
Estee, M. M.	Hedge Side, Napa	400	350	400			Yes.	100,000 gals.	Zinfandel, Cabernet, and many others.
Fay, Jos.	Napa	10	10	10			No.	25 tons.	Zinfandel.
Flannigan, P.	Napa	25	25	25			No.	65 tons.	Burger.
Forbes, A. B.	Napa	35	35	35			No.	90 tons.	Zinfandel, Malvoisie, Burger.
France & Cotorelli	Napa	30	30	30			No.	70 tons.	Zinfandel, Riesling.
Garfield, L. W.	Napa	30	30	30			No.	50 tons.	Zinfandel, Malvoisie, Riesling, Chasselas.
Garrabrant, A.	Napa	5	5	5			No.	20 tons.	Zinfandel, Burger.
Garvin, Daniel	Napa	12	12	12			No.	30 tons.	Zinfandel, Burger.

Name	County					Wine made	Product	Varieties
Geddes, C. E.	Napa	7	7	7		No.	15 tons.	Zinfandel, Chasselas, Lenoir.
Gelpe, Mrs.	Napa	6	6	6		No.	20 tons.	Zinfandel.
Gildersleeve, G. W.	Napa	15	15	15		No.	22 tons.	Muscat, Zinfandel, Malvoisie.
Gnepper, E.	Napa	20	20	20		No.	45 tons.	Zinfandel, Burger.
Goldstein, E. L.	Napa	60	60	60		Yes.	120 tons.	Zinfandel, Riesling, Sauvignon Vert, Burger.
Goodman, J. H., & Co.	Napa	200	200	200		Yes.	600 tons.	Chasselas, Cabernet Vert, Burger, Zinfandel, and twenty others.
Grant, J. P.	Napa	15	15	15		No.	40 tons.	Zinfandel, Mission.
Green, A. J.	Napa	7	7	7		No.	33 tons.	Zinfandel.
Grossman, A. H.	Napa	80	20	80		Yes.	60 tons.	Zinfandel, Riesling.
Gyle, Jos.	Napa	17	12	17		No.	12 tons.	Burgundy, Zinfandel, Malvoisie.
Haake, John	Napa	5	5	5		No.	74 tons.	Cabernet, Malvoisie.
Hanon, Mrs. M. E.	Napa	35	35	35		No.	90 tons.	Cabernet, Zinfandel.
Hardman, L. W.	Napa	70	70	70		No.	25 tons.	Malvoisie, Chasselas, Zinfandel.
Harden, John	Napa	5	5	5		No.	70 tons.	Chasselas.
Harker Bros.	Napa	35	35	31	4	No.	40 tons.	Rose Peru, Riesling, Zinfandel, Chasselas.
Harris, J. R.	Napa	15	15	12	3	No.	75 tons.	Muscat, Zinfandel, Malvoisie, Chasselas.
Hazen, H.	Cedar Knoll, Napa	50	25	25		Yes.	40 tons.	Zinfandel, Riesling, Chasselas.
Heidoff, H.	Napa	5	5	5		No.	40 tons.	Zinfandel.
Hein, John	Napa	18	12	18		Yes.	100 tons.	Zinfandel.
Heinricks, Geo.	Napa	20	20	20		No.	50 tons.	Zinfandel.
Heinricks, Peter	Napa	20	20	20		No.	35 tons.	Zinfandel.
Hewlitt, P. B.	Napa	49	49	49		No.	40 tons.	Zinfandel, Malvoisie.
Johnson, ___.	Napa	25	25	25		No.	10 tons.	Zinfandel, Riesling.
Jordan, R.	Napa	36	36	36		No.	30 tons.	Zinfandel, Malvoisie, Chasselas, Burgundy.
Klam, J.	Napa	18	18	18		No.	60 tons.	Zinfandel, Malvoisie, Chasselas, Burger.
Klarn, J. A.	Napa	20	20	20		No.	13 tons.	Zinfandel, Malvoisie.
Kneif, J. F.	Napa	2	2	2		Yes.	60 tons.	Zinfandel.
Koster, John	Napa	19	19	19	8	No.	10 tons.	Zinfandel.
Lange, N.___	Napa	25	25	25		No.	70 tons.	Burger, Riesling.
Lochibaum, Mrs.	Napa	6	6	6		No.	82 tons.	Burger, Riesling.
McClelland & Co.	Napa	18	18	18		No.	100 tons.	Zinfandel.
McGreer, R.	Napa	4	4	4		No.	2,000 gals.	Zinfandel, Burger, Burgundy.
McFarland, A. M.	Napa	24	24	24		Yes.	9 tons.	Zinfandel, Burger, Riesling.
Mangini, G.	Napa	35	35	35		No.	50 tons.	Zinfandel, Chasselas.
Mansfield, J. M.	Napa	85	85	85		Yes.	200 tons.	Zinfandel, Mission, Malvoisie.
Marks, F. F.	Napa	5	5	5		No.	40 tons.	Riesling, Black Pinot, Burger.
Martin, W. H.	Napa	23	23	23		No.	30 tons.	Zinfandel.
May, G. W.	Oak Knoll Vyd, Napa	70	70	70		Yes.	30 tons.	Burger.
Melone, Drury.	Napa	18	16	18		No.		Zinfandel, Malvoisie, Burgundy, Sauvignon.
Meredith Estate	Napa	20	20	20		No.		Chasselas, Malvoisie, Burgundy.
Meyer, P.	Napa	90	90	90		Yes.		Zinfandel.
Miller, Mrs. John	La Vergne Vyd, Napa	16	16	16		No.	30 tons.	Zinfandel, Malvoisie, Burgundy, Burgundy.
Mosher, C.	Napa	25	25	25		No.		Chasselas, Malvoisie, Burgundy.
Parker, Mrs. E.	Napa	75	75	75		No.	120 tons.	Chasselas, Zinfandel, Burger, Burgundy.

NAPA COUNTY—Continued.

Name of Owner.	Post Office and Name of Vineyard.	Total Acres in Grapes.	Acres in Bearing.	Acres in Wine Grapes.	Acres in Table Grapes.	Acres in Raisin Grapes.	Wine Maker.	Product in 1890.	Varieties.
Penny, Mrs.	Napa	15	15	15			No.	35 tons.	Zinfandel, Riesling.
Pettingell, J. A.	White Rock Vd., Napa.	5	5	5			Yes.	12 tons.	Zinfandel.
Prentis, A. T.	Napa	25	25	25			No.	69 tons.	Zinfandel, Chasselas.
Priet, P.	DeOret Viney'd, Napa	90	90	90			Yes.	75 tons.	Zinfandel, Riesling, Burger.
Quirk, Timothy	Napa	41	10	41			No.	70 tons.	Zinfandel.
Robinson, C.	Napa	40	25	40			Yes.	95 tons.	Zinfandel, Riesling.
Rose, Mrs. M. J.	Napa	17	17	17			No.	55 tons.	Zinfandel, Mission.
Rheddy, Mr.	Napa	35	35	35			Yes.	84 tons.	Zinfandel, Burger, Riesling.
Sackett, Kirk	Napa	12	12	12			No.	12 tons.	Burgundy.
Salmina, Frank	Napa	10	5	10			Yes.	18 tons.	Burgundy.
Sawyer, E. D.	Napa	7	7	7			No.	20 tons.	Zinfandel.
Scilligo, A.	Napa	20	20	20			Yes.	45 tons.	Zinfandel, Riesling.
Simonton Estate	Tulveay Viney'd, Napa	200	60	200			No.	100 tons.	Chasselas, Zinfandel, Riesling.
Smith, B. B.	Napa	30	30	30			No.	74 tons.	Zinfandel, Burger.
Smith, J. F.	Napa	10	10	10			No.	18 tons.	Zinfandel, Riesling.
Smith, Mrs. L. R.	Napa	5	5	5			No.	25 tons.	Zinfandel, Malvoisie.
Sneed, W. T.	Napa	8	8	8			No.	20 tons.	Zinfandel, Malvoisie, Chasselas, Burgundy.
Somers, E. R.	Napa	16	16	16			No.	42 tons.	Zinfandel, Gray Riesling, Malvoisie.
Stanley, J. A.	Napa	100	50	100			Yes.	175 tons.	Zinfandel, Cabernet, Mataro, Burgundy, Burger Vert, Lenoir, Sauvignon Vert.
Starkweather, L. S.	Napa	30	30	30			No.	70 tons.	Riesling, Burgundy, Burger.
Streich, E.	Napa	8	6	8			Yes.	10 tons.	Zinfandel, Burgundy.
Stromberg, B. F.	Napa	15	15	15			No.	8 tons.	Zinfandel, Riesling, Golden Chasselas, Malvoisie.
Sullivan, J. C.	Napa	10	8	10			No.	20 tons.	Zinfandel, Riesling.
Switzer, Geo.	Napa	7	7	7			No.	15 tons.	Zinfandel, Riesling.
Tascho, Harry	Napa	8	8	8			No.	15 tons.	Zinfandel, Burger.
Thompson, Chas.	Napa	250	250	250			Yes.	860 tons.	Zinfandel, Burger, Riesling, Chasselas, Burgundy.
Thompson, John	Napa	20	20	20			No.	43 tons.	Zinfandel, Burger, Malvoisie, Chasselas.
Tourner, J.	Napa	25	25	25			Yes.	150 tons.	Zinfandel, Burgundy, Mataro, Malvoisie.
Tracy, Thos.	Napa	15	15	15			No.	25 tons.	Zinfandel.
Trubody, W. A.	Napa	10	10	10			No.	25 tons.	Mission, Malvoisie.
Trueb, H.	Napa	15	15	15			No.	54 tons.	Zinfandel, Chasselas, Malvoisie.
True, J. R.	Napa	23	23	18	5		No.	40 tons.	Zinfandel, Muscat, Tokay.

Name	Location						Tons	Varieties
Verroni, Frank	Napa	15	15	15		No.	35 tons.	Zinfandel, Burger.
Walker, J. T.	Napa	5	5	5		No.	15 tons.	Zinfandel.
Ward, J. H.	Napa	40	40	40		No.	118 tons.	Zinfandel, Burger, Riesling.
Wilcox, J. H.	Napa	6	1½	6	10	No.	4 tons.	Cabernet, Sauvignon.
Wilson, Joseph	Napa	15	15	15		No.	42 tons.	Zinfandel, Muscat, Tokay.
Wybaillie, Frank	Napa	5	5	5		Yes.	12 tons.	Zinfandel, Burger, Riesling.
Young, Mrs. E. G.	Napa	50	50	50		No.	150 tons.	Zinfandel, Riesling.
Benson, J.	Oakville	60	60	60		Yes.	250 tons.	Zinfandel, Chasselas, Burgundy, Sauvignon Vert.
Claix, Bruno	Oakville	210	210	210		Yes.	1,000 tons.	Zinfandel, Riesling, Mataro, S. Vert, Burgundy.
Crabb, H. W.	Oakville	200	125	200		Yes.	375 tons.	Zinfandel, Riesling, Cabernet, Sauvignon Vert.
Creely, J.	Oakville	10	10	10		No.	35 tons.	Zinfandel, Riesling.
Davis, J. C.	Oakville	70	60	70		Yes.	175 tons.	Zinfandel, Riesling, Sauvignon Vert.
Delmont, Dr. F.	Oakville	18	18	18		No.	16 tons.	Zinfandel, Burger.
Dietrich Bros.	Oakville	30	18	30		No.	50 tons.	Zinfandel, Riesling.
Dwyer, Thomas	Oakville	10	30	10		No.	94 tons.	Zinfandel, Chasselas, Riesling.
Fealy, M.	Oakville	5	10	5		No.	35 tons.	Zinfandel, Burger, Burgundy, Riesling.
Forrester, John	Oakville	17	12	17		No.	13 tons.	Zinfandel, Chasselas.
Gibbs, Mrs.	Riverside Vineyard, Oakville.	30	25	30*		No.	40 tons.	Zinfandel, Riesling,
Godert, Philip						No.	140 tons.	Zinfandel, Malvoisie.
Gray, J.	Oakville	15	15	15		No.	50 tons.	Riesling, Sauvignon Vert, Carignan.
Hansen, A.	Oakville	17	17	17		No.	40 tons.	Zinfandel, Chasselas.
Hottle, P. G.	Oakville	30	20	30		No.	79 tons.	Zinfandel, Riesling, Chasselas.
Howard, J. C.	Oakville	10	10	10		No.	42 tons.	Zinfandel, Riesling.
Jeaumonod, A.	Oakville	20	20	20		Yes.	50 tons.	Zinfandel, Riesling.
Kenny, G. L.	Oakville	15	15	15		No.	48 tons.	Riesling.
Locker, W.	Oakville	30	30	30		Yes.	49 tons.	Riesling, Zinfandel, Malvoisie.
Montgomery, Alex.	Oakville	70	70	70		No.	200 tons.	Riesling, Chasselas.
Pierce, D.	Onkville	20	20	20		No.	20 tons.	Zinfandel.
Robson, R. L.	Oakville	50	50	50		No.	65 tons.	Zinfandel, Riesling.
Sellinger, J. C.	Oakville	15	15	15		No.	40 tons.	Zinfandel, Chasselas.
Steckler, J.	Oakville	30	30	30		No.	88 tons.	Riesling, Zinfandel, Chasselas.
Walters, Mrs. C.	Oakville	35	35	35		No.	110 tons.	Riesling, Zinfandel, Chasselas.
Walters, J.	Oakville	40	40	40		No.	200 tons.	Riesling, Zinfandel.
Whitton, G.	Oakville	30	30	30		No.	35 tons.	Zinfandel, Malvoisie.
Clark Bros.	Pope Valley	3	3	3		No.	4 tons.	Mission.
Ellis, C.	Pope Valley	16	16	16		No.	30 tons.	Zinfandel, Chasselas.
Fitch, C.	Pope Valley	5	5	5		No.	18 tons.	Zinfandel.
Hans, Ed.	Pope Valley	5	5	5		No.	20 tons.	Zinfandel.
Hoffman, C.	Pope Valley	7	6	7		No.	4 tons.	Zinfandel.
Howy, G.	Pope Valley	20	20	20		Yes.	40 tons.	Malvoisie, Riesling.
Lawley Ranch	Pope Valley	10	10	10	5	No.	25 tons.	Malvoisie, Muscat, Tokay.
Mitchell, A. J.	Pope Valley	2	2	2		No.	7 tons.	Muscat.
Richard Bros.	Pope Valley	8	8	8		No.	15 tons.	Zinfandel.
Samuels, N.	Pope Valley	5	5	5		No.	10 tons.	Zinfandel, Malvoisie.

NAPA COUNTY—Continued.

Name of Owner	Post Office and Name of Vineyard	Total Acres in Grapes	Acres in Bearing	Acres in Wine Grapes	Acres in Table Grapes	Acres in Raisin Grapes	Wine Maker	Product in 1890	Varieties
Schaffer, C.	Pope Valley	3	3	2	1		No.	6 tons.	Zinfandel.
Silsbaugh, N.	Pope Valley	5	5	5			No.	12 tons.	Zinfandel.
Stafford & Son	Pope Valley	45	46	45			No.	180 tons.	Zinfandel, Chasselas.
Wardner, S.	Pope Valley	6	6	6			No.	29 tons.	Zinfandel.
Woodworth, Wm.	Pope Valley	13	13	13			No.	25 tons.	Zinfandel, Mission.
Adamson, C. P.	Rutherford	25	25	25			No.	60 tons.	Riesling, Muscat, Malvoisie.
Atkinson, J. B.	Rutherford	150	150	150			Yes.	800 tons.	Zinfandel, Riesling, Mataro.
Beerstecher, C. J.	Rutherford	115	115	115			Yes.	650 tons.	Zinfandel, St. Vert, Riesling, Burgundy.
Bond, Mrs.	Rutherford	100	100	100			No.	30,000 gals.	Zinfandel, Chasselas, Riesling.
Bottomwar, J.	Rutherford	10	10	10			Yes.	24 tons.	Zinfandel, Riesling.
Bradley, W. T.	Rutherford	20	20	20			No.	60 tons.	Zinfandel, Chasselas, Riesling.
Bruan, G. S.	Rutherford	20	20	20			No.	100 tons.	Zinfandel, Chasselas, Riesling.
Cregler, W.	Rutherford	18	18	18			No.	57 tons.	Zinfandel, Sauvignon Vert.
Debaune, L.	Rutherford	60	60	60			Yes.	180 tons.	Zinfandel.
Dent, J.	Rutherford	7	7	7			No.	20 tons.	Zinfandel, Burger, Riesling.
Dertrich, H. C.	Rutherford	30	30	30			No.	400 tons.	Zinfandel, Burger.
Doak, D.	Rutherford	10	10	10*			No.	35 tons.	Zinfandel, Riesling.
Downey, D.	Rutherford	10	10	10			No.	38 tons.	Zinfandel, Riesling, Chasselas, Pinot.
Ewer & Atkinson	Rutherford	40	40	40			Yes.	180 tons.	Zinfandel, Riesling, Chasselas.
Ewer, S.	Rutherford	7	7	7			Yes.	100,000 gals.	Zinfandel, Mataro, Riesling, Chasselas.
Fojada, P.	Rutherford	80	80	80			Yes.	225 tons.	Zinfandel, Riesling.
Fouche, ——	Rutherford	10	10	10			Yes.	30 tons.	Zinfandel, Riesling.
Fouchetti, ——	Rutherford	13	13	13			Yes.	40 tons.	Zinfandel, Chasselas.
Greer Bros.	Rutherford	27	27	27			Yes.	90 tons.	Zinfandel, Chasselas.
Hannahan, Mrs.	Rutherford	45	45	45			No.	250 tons.	Zinfandel, Chasselas, Burger.
Hastings, S. C.	Rutherford	40	40	40			No.	110 tons.	Zinfandel, Chasselas, Riesling.
Hoffman, ——	Rutherford	20	20	20			No.	40 tons.	Zinfandel, Riesling.
Huesman, Prof.	Oak Glen Vineyard, Rutherford.	50	50	50			Yes.	100 tons.	Zinfandel, Chasselas, Riesling.
	Rutherford	35	23	35			Yes.	60 tons.	Zinfandel, Chasselas, Riesling.
Lange, Henry	Rutherford	17	17	17			Yes.	60 tons.	Zinfandel, Mataro, Carignan.
McCombs, A. E.	Rutherford	15	15	15			No.	40 tons.	Zinfandel, Chasselas, Riesling.
McIntyre, J. J.	Rutherford	20	15	15	5		No.	70 tons.	Zinfandel, Chasselas.
McPike, A. J.	Rutherford	10	10	10			No.	22 tons.	Zinfandel, Riesling.

Name	Post Office					Wine	Tons	Varieties
Mayfield, J. M.	Rutherford	91	91	91		Yes.	250 tons.	Zinfandel, Burgundy.
Menniger, Charles	Rutherford	10	10	10		No.	25 tons.	Zinfandel, Riesling.
Merley, W.	Rutherford	14	14	14		No.	40 tons.	Zinfandel, Riesling.
Morton, J. M.	Rutherford	20	20	20		No.	50 tons.	Zinfandel, Riesling, Mataro.
Newkirk, J. J.	Rutherford	36	38	36		Yes.	100 tons.	Zinfandel, Riesling.
Nieubaum, Capt. G.	Rutherford	280	175	260		No.	25 tons.	Zinfandel.
Parkman, Mrs.	Avondale Vineyard, Rutherford.	10	10	10		No.		Zinfandel, Burgundy, Burger.
Porter, William	Rutherford.	60	60	60		No.	180 tons.	
Pritchard, L.	Rutherford	20	20	20		No.	48 tons.	Zinfandel, Mission, Malvoisie.
Pritchard, Mrs.	Rutherford	6	4	6		No.	5 tons.	Zinfandel.
Pritchard, T. C.	Rutherford	19	19	19		No.	55 tons.	Zinfandel, Grenache.
Quilman, Capt.	Rutherford	8	8	8		No.	22 tons.	Zinfandel, Riesling.
Rutherford, T. L.	Rutherford	60	60	60		Yes.	250 tons.	Zinfandel, Chasselas.
Sawyer, N.	Rutherford	30	30	30		Yes.	160 tons.	Burgundy, Riesling, Sauvignon Vert.
Scheggia, C.	Rutherford	50	44	50		No.	100 tons.	Zinfandel, Riesling.
Seidenburg, Geo.	Rutherford	25	25	25		No.	50 tons.	Zinfandel, Riesling.
Shaw, S.	Rutherford	25	25	25		Yes.	100 tons.	Zinfandel, Riesling, Chasselas.
Smith, A. J.	Rutherford	25	25	25		Yes.	80 tons.	Zinfandel, Riesling, Chasselas.
Smith, C. E.	Rutherford	9	9	9		No.	20 tons.	Zinfandel, Riesling.
Smith, C. P.	Rutherford	20	20	20		No.	60 tons.	Zinfandel, Riesling, Malvoisie, Chasselas, Burgundy.
Snowball, ——	Rutherford	75	75	75		Yes.	300 tons.	Zinfandel, Riesling, Chasselas.
Stammer, C.	Rutherford	10	10	10		Yes.		Zinfandel, Riesling.
Steckter, J.	Rutherford	30	30	30		No.	30 tons.	Zinfandel, Riesling.
Stice, D. C.	Rutherford	15	15	15		No.	42 tons.	Zinfandel, Chasselas.
Stice, Moses	Rutherford	15	15	15		No.	125 tons.	Zinfandel.
Trefethen, E. A.	Rutherford	25	25	25		No.	250 tons.	Zinfandel, Riesling, Mataro.
Thompson, Chas.	Rutherford	40	40	40		Yes.	40 tons.	Zinfandel, Chasselas, Malvoisie, Burger.
Vann, Thos.	Rutherford	64	64	64		No.	110 tons.	Zinfandel, Chasselas, Riesling, Burgundy.
Van Vleet, E. J.	Rutherford	30	30	40	10	No.	125 tons.	Zinfandel, Tokay, Malaga.
Wakefield, H. K.	Rutherford	40	40	40		Yes.	70 tons.	Zinfandel, Riesling.
Weeks, W. P.	Rutherford	21	21	21		Yes.	260 tons.	Zinfandel, Riesling.
Wheeler, C. & J. H.	Rutherford	86	86	88		Yes.	115 tons.	Zinfandel, Riesling, Burger.
Wheeler, J.	Rutherford	35	35	35		Yes.	148 tons.	Zinfandel, Riesling, Chasselas.
Wherle, ——	Rutherford	50	50	50		Yes.	50 tons.	Zinfandel, Riesling.
Willey, F.	Rutherford	20	20	20		No.	240 tons.	Zinfandel, Riesling, Chasselas.
Wood, R. E.	Rutherford	40	40	40		No.	27 tons.	Zinfandel, Burger.
Adkins, S.	St. Helena	15	15	15		No.	200 tons.	Zinfandel, Sauvignon Vert, Chasselas.
Aiker, W.	St. Helena	30	30	80		No.	44 tons.	Zinfandel, Burger, Chasselas.
Allison, J. H.	St. Helena	17	17	17		No.	120 tons.	Zinfandel, Sauvignon Vert, Chasselas.
Al-ip, A. B.	St. Helena	50	45	50		Yes.	150 tons.	Zinfandel, Mataro, Burgundy, Chasselas, Burger.
Amsbury, T.	St. Helena	30	30	30		Yes.	80 tons.	Zinfandel, Burgundy, Riesling.
Ashton, F.	St. Helena	25	25	25		Yes.	80 tons.	Zinfandel, Mataro, Riesling.
Baile, M. G.	St. Helena	20	20	20		Yes.		Chasselas, Riesling, Burger.

NAPA COUNTY—Continued.

NAME OF OWNER.	Post Office and Name of Vineyard.	Total Acres in Grapes.	Acres in Bearing.	Acres in Wine Grapes.	Acres in Table Grapes.	Acres in Raisin Grapes.	Wine Maker.	Product in 1890.	Varieties.
Bartoli, A.	St. Helena	20	20	20			No.	40 tons.	Zinfandel, Malvoisie.
Beardsley, G. R.	St. Helena	12	12	12			No.	40 tons.	Zinfandel, Riesling.
Beers, Dr. H. W.	St. Helena	30	30	30			No.	60 tons.	Zinfandel, Sauvignon Vert, Riesling.
Behnike, F.	St. Helena	10	10	10			No.	35 tons.	Zinfandel, Sauvignon Vert, Pinot Bosche.
Behringer Bros.	St. Helena	155	155	165			Yes.	690 tons.	Zinfandel, Chasselas, Riesling, Mataro, Carignan, Burger.
Benner, G. L.	St. Helena	16	14	16			No.	75 tons.	Burgundy, Chasselas, Riesling.
Berry, T.	St. Helena	10	10	10			No.	28 tons.	Zinfandel, Chasselas.
Bianchi, A.	St. Helena	50	50	50			No.	80 tons.	Zinfandel, Burger.
Bieber, Paul	St. Helena	25	25	25			Yes.	45 tons.	Riesling, Zinfandel.
Blackman, O. S.	St. Helena	20	20	20			No.	60 tons.	Riesling, Zinfandel.
Blunt, J. H.	St. Helena	5	5	5			No.	14 tons.	Riesling, Zinfandel.
Booker, J. W.	St. Helena	9	9	9			No.	35 tons.	Malvoisie, Zinfandel.
Bopp, Mrs.	St. Helena	6	6	6			No.	18 tons.	Burger, Zinfandel.
Bourne, W. D.	St. Helena	120	120	120			Yes.	400 tons.	Zinfandel, Burgundy, Riesling, Mataro.
Bourne, W. B.	St. Helena	600	600	600			Yes.	1,750 tons.	Zinfandel, Burger, Riesling,
Breitenbucher, Geo.	St. Helena	12	12	12			Yes.	50 tons.	Zinfandel, Chasselas.
Brockhoff, C. H.	St. Helena	23	23	23			No.	70 tons.	
Brown, Jos.	St. Helena	14	14	14			No.	30 tons.	Zinfandel, Riesling.
Bruch, Mrs.	St. Helena	20	20	20			No.	60 tons.	Zinfandel, Riesling.
Burgess, C. M.	St. Helena	55	55	55			Yes.	220 tons.	Zinfandel, Burger, Carignan, Mataro.
Burke, W. H.	St. Helena	40	40	40			No.	120 tons.	Zinfandel, Chasselas, Riesling.
Calvery, O.	St. Helena	5	5	5			No.	7 tons.	Zinfandel, Riesling.
Carr, B. O.	St. Helena	25	25	25			No.	50 tons.	Chasselas, Mission, Sauvignon Vert.
Carter, S. A.	St. Helena	11	11	11			No.	84 tons.	Chasselas, Zinfandel, Burger.
Carver, D. B.	St. Helena	16	16	16			No.	40 tons.	Zinfandel, Riesling.
Carver, D. B.	St. Helena	78	78	78			No.	300 tons.	Zinfandel, Riesling.
Ca-tner, W. H., Jr.	St. Helena	30	30	30			No.	125 tons.	Cabernet, Zinfandel, Riesling.
Castner, W. H., Jr.	St. Helena	30	30	30			Yes.	125 tons.	Burgundy, Zinfandel, Riesling.
Chabot, Mrs. R.	St. Helena	32	32	32			Yes.	100 tons.	Sauvignon Vert, Zinfandel, Riesling.
Christie, M.	St. Helena	15	15	15			No.	35 tons.	Zinfandel, Riesling.
Church, M.	St. Helena	15	15	15			No.	42 tons.	Chasselas, Zinfandel.
Coit, Mrs. L.	St. Helena	130	130	130			No.	250 tons.	Zinfandel, Burger, Malvoisie.
Cole, D.	St. Helena	20	20	20			No.	150 tons.	Zinfandel, Riesling.

GRAPE GROWERS AND WINE MAKERS OF CALIFORNIA.

Name	Location					Tons	Varieties
Conn, C.	St. Helena	50	50	50	Yes.	142 tons.	Cabernet, Burgundy, Chasselas.
Cook, M. C.	St. Helena	7	7	7	No.	39 tons.	Zinfandel, Riesling, Chasselas.
Corthay Estate	St. Helena	40	40	40	Yes.	80 tons.	Zinfandel, Riesling.
Crane, Dr. G. B.	St. Helena	125	125	125	Yes.	275 tons.	Zinfandel, Riesling, Burgundy.
Cregan, Mrs.	St. Helena	18	18	18	No.	65 tons.	Zinfandel, Chasselas.
Cruey, J.	St. Helena	34	34	34	No.	100 tons.	Zinfandel, Burgundy, Burger, Mataro.
Cullem, H.	St. Helena	3	3	3	No.	8 tons.	Riesling.
Dinning, Mrs. P.	St. Helena	50	50	50	No.	75 tons.	Zinfandel, Burger, Malvoisie.
Dixon, Miss A.	St. Helena	25	20	25	Yes.	30 tons.	Zinfandel, Chasselas.
Dowdell, J.	St. Helena	17	17	17	Yes.	100 tons.	Zinfandel, Riesling.
Edge Hill Vineyard Co.	St. Helena	200	200	200	No.	400 tons.	Chasselas, Riesling, S. Vert, Carignan, Mataro.
Ellis, B.	St. Helena	15	15	15	No.	30 tons.	Zinfandel, Riesling.
Farmer, —	St. Helena	28	28	28	Yes.	100 tons.	Chasselas, Chasselas.
Fountain, G. C.	St. Helena	33	30	33	No.	60 tons.	Zinfandel, Riesling, Chasselas.
Fountain, M.	St. Helena	20	20	20	No.	100 tons.	Zinfandel, Riesling.
Fountain, Mr.	St. Helena	72	72	72	Yes.	64 tons.	Chasselas, Burger, Riesling.
Fountain, Sarah.	St. Helena	12	12	12	No.	250 tons.	Zinfandel, Riesling.
Fradet, F.	St. Helena	10	6	10	No.	40 tons.	Zinfandel.
Frentani, Mrs.	St. Helena	20	20	20	No.	20 tons.	Zinfandel, Riesling.
Fulton, Mrs.	St. Helena	10	10	10	Yes.	81 tons.	Zinfandel, Riesling.
Gendotti Bros.	St. Helena	15	15	15	No.	15 tons.	Zinfandel.
Gibson, Mr.	St. Helena	14	14	14	Yes.	50 tons.	Zinfandel.
Glandon, L.	St. Helena	15	15	15	No.	40 tons.	Zinfandel, Chasselas.
Glugus, Mrs.	St. Helena	10	10	10	No.	60 tons.	Zinfandel, Riesling.
Graham, J. M.	St. Helena	22	22	22	Yes.	25 tons.	Burger, Muscatel, Golden Chasselas.
Gratton, W. H.	St. Helena	70	70	70	No.	50 tons.	Zinfandel, Burger, Malvoisie.
Gratton, W. H.	St. Helena	60	65	60	Yes.	180 tons.	Zinfandel, Burger, Burgundy, Chasselas.
Greer, Thomas	St. Helena	12	10	12	No.	150 tons.	Zinfandel, Burgundy, Sauvignon Vert.
Griffith, C. C.	St. Helena	8	8	8	Yes.	15 tons.	Zinfandel, Chasselas.
Gussot, A.	St. Helena	15	15	15	No.	35 tons.	Zinfandel, Chasselas.
Hackney, —	St. Helena	5	5	5	Yes.	6 tons.	Zinfandel, Burgundy.
Hall, E. M.	St. Helena	100	100	100	No.	400 tons.	Zinfandel, Chasselas, Pinot.
Hall, J. K.	St. Helena	20	20	20	No.	75 tons.	Zinfandel, Riesling.
Hannah, J. A.	St. Helena	16	16	16	No.	68 tons.	Zinfandel, Riesling, Burgundy, Malvoisie.
Hasenminer, F.	St. Helena	10	10	10	No.	33 tons.	Zinfandel, Burgundy, Reisling.
Hastie, Mrs. L. E.	St. Helena	7	7	7	Yes.	15 tons.	Zinfandel, Riesling.
Helms, H. W.	St. Helena	23	23	23	No.	70 tons.	Zinfandel, Chasselas.
Heyman, E.	St. Helena	24	24	24	Yes.	110 tons.	Zinfandel, Chasselas, Riesling, Burger.
Hirsch, J.	St. Helena	30	30	30	No.	75 tons.	Zinfandel.
Hogrist, M.	St. Helena	12	9	12	No.	20 tons.	Zinfandel, Riesling.
Hudson, M.	St. Helena	8	8	9	No.	22 tons.	Zinfandel, Riesling.
Hudson, P.	St. Helena	8	8	8	No.	20 tons.	Zinfandel, Malvoisie.
Hughes, F. D.	St. Helena	9	9	9	No.	40 tons.	Zinfandel, Burger, Malvoisie.
Hunt, D.	St. Helena	16	16	16	No.	50 tons.	Zinfandel, Burger, Riesling.
Jaumer, Louis	St. Helena	44	44	44	Yes.	128 tons.	Zinfandel, Chasselas, Riesling, Burger.

NAPA COUNTY—Continued.

Name of Owner.	Post Office and Name of Vineyard.	Total Acres in Grapes.	Acres in Bearing.	Acres in Wine Grapes.	Acres in Table Grapes.	Acres in Raisin Grapes.	Wine Maker.	Product in 1890.	Varieties.
Ink, T. H.	St. Helena	116	115	115			Yes.	300 tons.	Zinfandel, Riesling.
Inman, M. F.	St. Helena	17	17	17			No.	90 tons.	Chasselas, Malvoisie, Burger.
Jones, Owen.	St. Helena	40	36	40			Yes.	60 tons.	Riesling, Mataro, Carignan.
Julien, H.	St. Helena	30	30	30			Yes.	87 tons.	Riesling, Zinfandel.
Kellett, S.	St. Helena	60	60	60			No.	200 tons.	Mataro, Zinfandel, Franken, S. Vert, Carignan.
Kemper, M.	St. Helena	60	40	60			No.	75 tons.	Malvoisie, Zinfandel, Chasselas.
Kief, F.	St. Helena	25	25	25			No.	40 tons.	Zinfandel, Riesling.
Kildorf, M.	St. Helena	30	30	30			No.	75 tons.	Zinfandel, Riesling.
Kinkle Bros.	St. Helena	30	25	25			Yes.	40 tons.	Zinfandel, Chasselas.
Kraft, F.	St. Helena	23	23	23			No.	125 tons.	Zinfandel, Malvoisie.
Kroeber, F. W.	St. Helena	12	12	12			No.	50 tons.	Zinfandel, Riesling.
Krug, C.	St. Helena	125	125	125			Yes.	470 tons.	Zinfandel, Muscatel, Carignan, Mataro, Chasselas, Burger.
Lament Estate	St. Helena	60	50	60			Yes.	112 tons.	Zinfandel, Riesling.
Largay, A.	St. Helena	15	15	15			No.	40 tons.	Zinfandel, Riesling.
Lazarus, M.	St. Helena	9	9	9			Yes.	64 tons.	Zinfandel, Riesling.
Lemme, R.	St. Helena	80	80	80			Yes.	300 tons.	Zinfandel, Chasselas, Riesling.
Lenthold, H. J.	St. Helena	13	13	13			Yes.	50 tons.	Zinfandel.
Lewelling, H. J.	St. Helena	150	150	150			No.	300 tons.	Zinfandel, Mataro, Burgundy.
Lille, A.	St. Helena	10	10	10			Yes.	35 tons.	Zinfandel, Burgundy.
Locher, F. W.	St. Helena	8	8	8			No.	35 tons.	Zinfandel, Riesling, Carignan.
Lockwood, F. E.	St. Helena	10	10	10			No.	30 tons.	Zinfandel.
Loyd, Mrs. M. P.	St. Helena	30	30	30			No.	60 tons.	Zinfandel, Burger, Chasselas.
Lyman, W. W.	St. Helena	75	75	75			No.	250 tons.	Riesling, Burger.
McCord, J. H.	St. Helena	50	40	50			Yes.	150 tons.	Riesling, Zinfandel, Burger.
McCully & Arnold	Arbutus Villa, St. Helena.	20	20	20			No.	00 tons.	Riesling, Zinfandel, Malvoisie.
McEachran, Mrs. C. T.	St. Helena	40	40	40			No.	115 tons.	Riesling, Zinfandel, Burger.
McFarland, A.	St. Helena	35	35	35			Yes.	114 tons.	Zinfandel, Chasselas.
McFarland Bros.	St. Helena	30	30	30			Yes.	160 tons.	Riesling, Zinfandel.
McGuire, J. A. K.	St. Helena	75	75	75			Yes.	240 tons.	Riesling, Zinfandel.
McPike, J.	St. Helena	90	90	90			Yes.	360 tons.	Zinfandel, Chasselas.
Meacham, H. M.	St. Helena	11	11	11			No.	47 tons.	Burgundy, Pinot, Chasselas.
Mee, Geo.	St. Helena	40	40	40			Yes.	110 tons.	Zinfandel, Mataro, Riesling.

Name	Location						Tons	Varieties
Meredith, G.	St. Helena	12	12	12		Yes.	30 tons.	Malvoisie, Mataro, Carignan.
Merriam Bros.	St. Helena	25	25	25		Yes.	100 tons.	Zinfandel, Riesling, Carignan.
Metzner & Co.	St. Helena	90	90	90		Yes.	270 tons.	Zinfandel, Riesling, Burgundy.
Miley, J.	St. Helena	34	34	34		Yes.	100 tons.	Zinfandel, Chasselas, Riesling, Malvoisie.
Mills, ——	St. Helena	8	8	8		No.	24 tons.	Zinfandel, Riesling.
Mitchell, E.	St. Helena	3	3	3		No.	12 tons.	Riesling, Chasselas.
Mixon, J.	St. Helena	10	10	10		No.	35 tons.	Riesling, Zinfandel.
Morley, A.	St. Helena	6	6	6		No.	40 tons.	Chasselas, Malvoisie.
Mosley, C. J.	St. Helena	15	15	15		No.	95 tons.	Chasselas, Zinfandel, Burger.
Mulwyer, ——	St. Helena	30	30	30		No.	60 tons.	Chasselas, Zinfandel.
Munske, H.	St. Helena	13	13	13		No.	25 tons.	Chasselas, Zinfandel, Mataro.
Musgrove, E.	St. Helena	31	31	31		No.	60 tons.	Riesling, Chasselas, Malvoisie.
Myers, Geo.	St. Helena	100	100	100		Yes.	360 tons.	Riesling, Zinfandel.
Norton, J. G.	St. Helena	50	50	50		Yes.	150 tons.	Riesling, Zinfandel.
Palmer, E. P.	St. Helena	40	40	40		No.	115 tons.	Riesling, Zinfandel.
Parkham, Mrs.	St. Helena	15	15	15		Yes.	48 tons.	Chasselas, Riesling.
Parrot, T.	St. Helena	80	80	110		Yes.	250 tons.	Cabernet.
Payne, M.	St. Helena	22	22	22		No.	90 tons.	Chasselas, Zinfandel.
Pearson, Alice.	St. Helena	60	60	60		No.	175 tons.	Chasselas, Riesling, Zinfandel.
Pellet, H. A.	St. Helena	40	40	40		Yes.	175 tons.	Burger, Riesling, Chasselas, Mataro, Muscatel, Carignan.
Peterson, J.	St. Helena	48	48	48		Yes.	180 tons.	Zinfandel, Chasselas, Burgundy.
Pfister, W.	St. Helena	14	14	14		Yes.	60 tons.	Zinfandel, Burger.
Phillips, W. L.	St. Helena	60	60	60		No.	140 tons.	Zinfandel, Riesling.
Pond, Dr. M. B.	St. Helena	12	12	12		No.	30 tons.	Zinfandel, Chasselas.
Pope, Mrs. A. J.	St. Helena	12	12	12		No.	43 tons.	Muscatel, Chasselas.
Potterton, A.	St. Helena	17	17	17		No.	40 tons.	Zinfandel, Chasselas, Riesling.
Potterton, A.	St. Helena	25	25	25		No.	50 tons.	Burger, Chasselas, Riesling.
Pratt, Geo.	St. Helena	40	40	40		No.	150 tons.	Malvoisie, Le Noir, Sauvignon Vert.
Pratt, R. H.	St. Helena	20	20	20		No.	90 tons.	Zinfandel, Mataro, Riesling.
Pritchard, Chas.	St. Helena	32	32	32		No.	100 tons.	Zinfandel, Riesling.
Rampendahl, A.	St. Helena	18	18	18		No.	80 tons.	Zinfandel, Chasselas, Riesling.
Rampendahl, H.	St. Helena	9	9	9		No.	40 tons.	Zinfandel, Riesling.
Rawley, C. J.	St. Helena	55	55	55		No.	115 tons.	Zinfandel, Riesling.
Reiman, H.	St. Helena	23	23	23		Yes.	50 tons.	Zinfandel, Burgundy, Riesling.
Rennie Bros.	St. Helena	40	35	40		No.	160 tons.	Zinfandel, Malvoisie.
Rohlwing, Mrs.	St. Helena	9	9	9		No.	14 tons.	Zinfandel, Malvoisie.
Rose, D.	St. Helena	50	50	50		No.	85 tons.	Zinfandel, Riesling.
Rosenbaum	St. Helena	15	15	15		No.	10 tons.	Zinfandel, Riesling.
Rossi, A.	St. Helena	45	45	45		Yes.	100 tons.	Zinfandel, Mataro.
Rossi, ——	St. Helena	20	20	20			45 tons.	Zinfandel, Riesling.
Roulett, Mr.	St. Helena	8	8	8		No.	20 tons.	Zinfandel, Malvoisie.
Sawyer, N.	St. Helena	28	28	30		Yes	100 tons.	Zinfandel, Riesling.
Schonewald, G.	St. Helena	15	15	15		No.	50 tons.	Zinfandel, Burgundy.
Schram, J.	St. Helena	100	100	100		Yes.	270 tons.	Zinfandel, Sauvignon Vert, Burgundy.

NAPA COUNTY—Continued.

Name of Owner.	Post Office and Name of Vineyard.	Total Acres in Grapes.	Acres in Bearing.	Acres in Wine Grapes.	Acres in Table Grapes.	Acres in Raisin Grapes.	Wine Maker.	Product in 1890.	Varieties.
Schwepfer, A., estate of	St. Helena	15	15	15			No.	50 tons.	Zinfandel, Riesling.
Sender, L.	St. Helena	50	50	50			Yes.	200 tons.	Zinfandel, Riesling, Burgundy, Carignan.
Senekler, H.	St. Helena	130	90	130			No.	360 tons.	Zinfandel, Burger, Burgundy.
Shamp, Mrs. P. K.	St. Helena	15	15	15			No.	50 tons.	Zinfandel, Riesling.
Shepherdson, L. B.	St. Helena	16	13	16			No.	35 tons.	Mataro, Carignan, Chasselas.
Shepherdson, M.	St. Helena	15	15	15			No.	70 tons.	Zinfandel, Riesling.
Sigelman, C.	St. Helena	15	8	15			No.	15 tons.	Zinfandel, Riesling.
Simmons, H.	St. Helena	12	12	12			No.	39 tons.	Zinfandel, Riesing.
Starr, H. D.	St. Helena	46	46	46			No.	120 tons.	Zinfandel, Riesling.
Steel, Thos. H.	St. Helena	21	15	21			No.	70 tons.	Zinfandel, Burger.
Tainter, Mrs.	St. Helena	16	16	16			Yes.	65 tons.	Zinfandel, Chasselas, Carignan.
Thomann, J.	St. Helena	40	40	40			Yes.	120 tons.	Zinfandel, Burgundy.
Trainor, L.	St. Helena	30	30	40			No.	90 tons.	Zinfandel, Riesling.
Tychson, Mrs.	St. Helena	65	65	65			Yes.	110 tons.	Zinfandel, Riesling, Burgundy.
Unknown	St. Helena	130	130	130			Yes.	300 tons.	
Van Doren, ——	St. Helena	17	17	17			No.	75 tons.	Zinfandel, Riesling.
Walter, E.	St. Helena	25	20	25			Yes.	37 tons.	Zinfandel, Chasselas, Riesling.
Weaks, W. P.	St. Helena	18	18	18			Yes.	65 tons.	Zinfandel, Chasselas, Riesling.
Weinberger, Mrs. H.	St. Helena	60	60	60			Yes.	200 tons.	
Weiser, Ernest	St. Helena	17	10	17			Yes.	25 tons.	Zinfandel, Mataro, Chasselas.
Weitcher, George	St. Helena	10	10	10			Yes.	37 tons.	Zinfandel, Riesling.
Wells, Fargo & Co.	St. Helena	46	46	46			No.	150 tons.	Zinfandel, Riesling, Cabernet.
Wentzner, Mr.	St. Helena	65	66	65			Yes.	280 tons.	Zinfandel, Riesling, Chasselas.
West, W.	St. Helena	23	23	23			Yes.	75 tons.	Zinfandel, Chasselas, Burgundy, Burger.
Western Bros.	St. Helena	20	12	20			No.	24 tons.	Zinfandel, Burgundy, Riesling.
Weston, Frank	St. Helena	12	12	12			No.	40 tons.	Pinot, Riesling.
White, H.	St. Helena	16	16	16			No.	05 tons.	Zinfandel, Riesling.
White, Henry	St. Helena	12	12	12			Yes.	39 tons.	Zinfandel, Riesling.
Williams, A. L.	St. Helena	30	30	30			Yes.	75 tons.	Zinfandel, Burger, Ricsling.
Woost, F.	St. Helena	25	25	25			No.	75 tons.	Zinfandel, Chasselas, Riesling.
Worrell, G. B.	St. Helena	18	18	18			No.	54 tons.	Zinfandel, Chasselas, Riesling.
Worrell & Ward	St. Helena	28	28	28			Yes.	80 tons.	Zinfandel, Mission, Malvoisie.
York, E. M.	St. Helena	25	25	25			Yes.	165 tons.	Zinfandel, Burger, Bosche.
York, J.	St. Helena	35	35	35			No.	100 tons.	Zinfandel, Burgundy, Sauvignon Vert.

Name	Location		Y/N					Tons	Varieties
York, W. E	St. Helena	---	No	---	25	25	25	100 tons	Zinfandel, Chasselas.
Zange, E.	St. Helena	---	Yes	---	30	30	30	175 tons	Zinfandel, Chasselas, Riesling, Sauvignon Vert.
Zeernigble, L.	St. Helena	---	No	---	50	50	50	200 tons	Zinfandel, Burger, Riesling.
Attinger, D.	Yountville	---	Yes	---	24	24	24	90 tons	Chasselas, Burgrundy, Riesling.
Bailey, A.	Yountville	---	No	---	40	40	40	10 tons	Zinfandel, Riesling.
Bradshaw, B.	Yountville	---	No	---	20	20	20	40 tons	Zinfandel.
Bressart, Emil	Yountville	---	Yes	---	20	20	20	120 tons	Zinfandel, Chasselas, Burger.
Carter, ———	Yountville	---	No	---	33	33	33	40 tons	Zinfandel, Riesling.
Carter, S.	Yountville	---	No	---	25	25	25	85 tons	Zinfandel, Chasselas, Burger.
Darms, B.	Yountville	---	No	---	12	12	12	110 tons	Zinfandel, Malvoisie.
Davis, J., & Son	Yountville	---	No	---	36	36	36	125 tons	Zinfandel, Chasselas, Riesling.
Downey, P.	Yountville	---	No	---	60	55	60	24 tons	Zinfandel, Chasselas.
Drew, Mrs. C. C.	Yountville	---	No	---	12	12	12	17 tons	Zinfandel.
Ellis, F. W.	Yountville	---	No	---	5	5	5	165 tons	Chasselas, Riesling.
Fajiani Bros.	Yountville	---	No	---	37	25	37	75 tons	Zinfandel, Burger.
Fawver, Thomas	Yountville	---	Yes	---	50	50	50	260 tons	Zinfandel, Riesling, Chasselas.
Frash, F.	Yountville	---	No	---	60	60	60	50 tons	Zinfandel, Sauvignon Vert, Chasselas.
Frye, Col. J. D.	Yountville	---	Yes	---	15	15	15	282 tons	Zinfandel, Burger, Cabernet, Mataro, Sauvignon Vert.
George, Levi P.	Yountville	---	No	---	120	120	120	180 tons	Burger, Zinfandel, Malvoisie.
Gibbs, Mrs. W. H.	Yountville	---	No	---	20	20	20	200 tons	Zinfandel, Riesling.
Graves, W. B.	Yountville	---	No	---	100	100	100	100 tons	Zinfandel, Riesling.
Groezinger, G.	Yountville	---	Yes	---	15	15	15	500 tons	Zinfandel, Madeira, Sauvignon Vert, Hungarian, Bouschet.
Hahn, J.	Yountville	---	No	---	200	200	200	193 tons	Zinfandel, Burger, Riesling.
Holland, W. H.	Yountville	---	No	---	90	90	90	50 tons	Zinfandel.
Johnson, William	Yountville	---	No	---	15	15	15	63 tons	Zinfandel, Malvoisie, Mission.
Kelly, Mr.	Yountville	---	No	---	15	15	15	40 tons	Zinfandel, Malvoisie.
La Rue, H. M.	Yountville	---	No	---	80	80	80	350 tons	Zinfandel, Mataro, Sauvignon Vert.
Long, R.	Yountville	---	No	---	45	45	45	39 tons	Zinfandel, Riesling, Burger.
Lycan, M. C.	Yountville	---	No	---	12	12	12	75 tons	Zinfandel, Chasselas, Burger, Malvoisie.
McCord, N.	Yountville	---	No	---	10	10	10	27 tons	Zinfandel, Malvoisie, Chasselas.
Morris, Frank	Yountville	---	No	---	12	12	12	20 tons	Zinfandel, Burger, Chasselas.
Nauer Bros.	Yountville	---	Yes	---	25	25	25	100 tons	Zinfandel, Burger, Chasselas.
Old, Jacob	Yountville	---	No	---	60	60	60	75 tons	Zinfandel, Malvoisie.
Osborn, Geo	Yountville	---	No	---	20	20	20	17 tons	Zinfandel, Chasselas.
Pedlar, J. R.	Yountville	---	No	---	10	10	10	18 tons	Zinfandel, Mataro.
Pedro, M.	Yountville	---	No	---	18	18	18	45 tons	Zinfandel, Chasselas.
Roberts, ———	Yountville	---	No	---	48	48	48	110 tons	Zinfandel, Riesling, Burger.
Robertson, R.	Yountville	---	No	---	16	16	16	83 tons	Zinfandel, Burgrundy, Burger, Chasselas, S. Vert.
Ross, W. T.	Yountville	---	No	---	30	30	30	30 tons	Zinfandel, Malvoisie.
Safford, R. B.	Yountville	---	No	---	30	30	30	50 tons	Zinfandel, Burger, Malvoisie.
Salmina, Jas.	Yountville	---	No	---	15	15	15	25 tons	Zinfandel, Burger.
Schofield. Mrs. B. M.	Yountville	---	No	---	12	12	12	45 tons	Zinfandel, Burger.
Squire, H. P.	Yountville	---	No	---	16	16	16	45 tons	Zinfandel, Riesling.

NAPA COUNTY—Continued.

NAME OF OWNER.	Post Office and Name of Vineyard.	Total Acres in Grapes.	Acres in Bearing.	Acres in Wine Grapes.	Acres in Table Grapes.	Acres in Raisin Grapes.	Wine Maker.	Product in 1890.	Varieties.
Stefel, Mr.	Yountville	15	10	15			No.	50 tons.	Zinfandel, Malvoisie, Riesling.
Tidermann, H.	Yountville	15	15	15			No.	35 tons.	Zinfandel, Golden Chasselas.
Tonachs, J.	Yountville	8	8	8			No.	15 tons.	Zinfandel, Riesling.
Van Winkle, Mrs.	Yountville	23	23	23			No.	50 tons.	Zinfandel, Riesling.
Veterans' Home	Yountville	46	46	46			No.	150 tons.	Zinfandel, Riesling.
Voltz, Mrs.	Yountville	30	20	30			Yes.	40 tons.	Zinfandel, Malvoisie.
Wetz, J.	Yountville	18	18	18			No.	115 tons.	Zinfandel, Riesling, Burgundy.
Whitton, G.	Yountville	30	30	30			Yes.	35 tons.	Zinfandel, Malvoisie.
Whitton, M. S.	Yountville	16	16	16			Yes.	60 tons.	Riesling, Chasselas.
Totals for county		18,229	17,003	18,177	52				

NEVADA COUNTY.

NAME OF OWNER.	Post Office and Name of Vineyard.	Total Acres in Grapes.	Acres in Bearing.	Acres in Wine Grapes.	Acres in Table Grapes.	Acres in Raisin Grapes.	Wine Maker.	Product in 1889.	Varieties.
Combie, C.	Colfax	10	10	10			Yes.	30 tons.	
Driesbach, A. B.	Grass Valley	50	50	30	20		Yes.	150 tons.	
Hepler, Charles	Grass Valley	5	5	5			Yes.	15 tons.	
Helwig, _____	Grass Valley	8	8	8			Yes.	24 tons.	
Hughes, Thomas	Grass Valley	6	8	8			Yes.	18 tons.	
Lehman, _____	Grass Valley	40	40	40			Yes.	120 tons.	
Lontzemheiser, Wm.	Grass Valley	5	5	5			Yes.	15 tons.	
Nichols, Henry	Grass Valley	4	4	4			Yes.	12 tons.	
Payne, Thomas N.	Grass Valley	30	30	20	10		Yes.	90 tons.	

NAME OF OWNER.	Post Office and Name of Vineyard.	Total Acres in Grapes.	Acres in Bearing.	Acres in Wine Grapes.	Acres in Table Grapes.	Acres in Raisin Grapes.	Wine Maker.	Product in 1889.	Varieties.
Perrin, A. F.	Grass Valley	12	12	12				36 tons.	
Petitjean, J.	Grass Valley	6	6	6			Yes.	18 tons.	
Pettyjohn, Theo.	Grass Valley	5	5	5				15 tons.	
Hartwig, A.	Nevada City	5	5	5				15 tons.	
Lutey, Mrs. M.	Nevada City							15 tons.	
Monroe, W. A.	Nevada City	20	20	20			Yes.	60 tons.	
Nevada Co. Winery	Nevada City							8,000 gals.	
Orzalli, A.	Nevada City	6	6	8				18 tons.	
Ott, J. J.	Nevada City	3	3	3				9 tons.	
Totals for county		220	220	190	30				

ORANGE COUNTY.

NAME OF OWNER.	Post Office and Name of Vineyard.	Total Acres in Grapes.	Acres in Bearing.	Acres in Wine Grapes.	Acres in Table Grapes.	Acres in Raisin Grapes.	Wine Maker.	Product in 1889.	Varieties.
Langenberger, A.	Anaheim	6	6	6			Yes.		Carignan.
Wehmeyer, Henry	Anaheim	8		8			Yes.		Mission, Muscat.
Hager & Co.	Orange	70	70	70			No.		
Hellman, I. C.	} Orange	56	46	56			No.		Muscat.
Goodwin, L. C.									
Handy, O. (agent)	Orange	4	4			4	No.		Muscat.
Gerkin, Fred.									
Rohrs, Fred.	Santa Anita								
Totals for county		144	126	140		4			

PLACER COUNTY.

Name of Owner.	Post Office and Name of Vineyard.	Total Acres in Grapes.	Acres in Bearing.	Acres in Wine Grapes.	Acres in Table Grapes.	Acres in Raisin Grapes.	Wine Maker.	Product in 1889.	Varieties.
Agard, M.	Auburn								
Bernhard, B.	Auburn								
Bowman, H. H.	Auburn	20	20		20		No.	50 tons.	
Chapin, F. C.	Auburn								
Closs, Fred.	Auburn								
Curtis, W. H.	Auburn	30	30		30				
Deetkin, G. F.	Auburn								
Gould, L. A.	Auburn								
Nickerson, J. R.	Auburn								
Seaver, Charles A.	Auburn	20	20		20		No.	50 tons.	
Snooks Bros.	Auburn	40	40		40		No.	100 tons.	
Wilcoxson, J.	Auburn	80	80		80		No.	75 tons.	
Baker, George G.	Auburn	10	10		10		No.	25 tons.	
Bennett, R. W.	Colfax	20	20		20		No.	50 tons.	
Bell, A. G.	Colfax	5	5	5			No.	12½ tons.	
Bryant, H. S.	Colfax	60	60		60		No.	150 tons.	
Cape Horn Vineyard	Colfax								
Dawson, J. E.	Colfax								
Edinger, F. S.	Colfax								
Hanson, Charles	Colfax								
Harkness, Edson	Colfax								
Hayford, G. O.	Colfax	5	5		5		No.	12½ tons.	
Hayford, William	Colfax	40	40		40		No.	100 tons.	
Irving, F. G.	Colfax								
Irving, William	Colfax								
Kingston, Thomas	Colfax								
Lobner, M.	Colfax								
Moore, E. W.	Colfax								
Rowland, K. A.	Colfax								
Stevert, A. H.	Colfax								
Spencer, W. D.	Colfax	5	5		5		No.	12½ tons.	
Ware, W. H.	Colfax	20	20		20		No.	50 tons.	
Whitcomb, J. B.	Colfax								
Holly, W.	Doty's Flat								

Name	Location							Product
Stinger, Mrs.								
Tancred, G.	Doty's Flat							
Baker, W. M.	Doty's Flat							
Dawson, John E.	Lander							
Arndt, F.	Lincoln	20	20			20	No.	50 tons.
Barrett, Mrs.	Lincoln	40	40				Yes.	100 tons.
Camn, W. H.	Lincoln	5	5		10	10	No.	12½ tons.
Cartright, A. D.	Lincoln	30	30	30	10	5	No.	90 tons.
Cartright, H. M.	Lincoln	15	15		15	5	No.	37½ tons.
Cary, L. A.	Lincoln	20	20		20	10	No.	50 tons.
Crosby, J. C.	Lincoln	25	25		25		No.	62½ tons.
Dodd, I.	Lincoln							
Drummond, M.	Lincoln							
East, J. W.	Lincoln							
Fagg, Belle	Lincoln							
Fagg, Mrs. Geo.	Lincoln							
Foster, Wm.	Lincoln	40	40		40	20	No.	100 tons.
Fowler, Larkin	Lincoln	20	20		20		No.	60 tons.
Gage, L. C.	Lincoln	40	40	30	10		No.	100 tons.
Gladding, Chas.	Lincoln	60	60	30	30		No.	150 tons.
Hall, Mrs. John	Lincoln							
Manser, John	Lincoln	200	100		100	100	No.	600 tons.
Marison, Dr. A	Lincoln							
Mayer, W. J.	Lincoln							
Miller, J. B.	Lincoln	10	10		10		No.	25 tons.
Nelson, N.	Lincoln	15	15		15			
Pendleton, Dr. P. F.	Lincoln	25	25		25	5	No.	37½ tons.
Shillingburg, —	Lincoln	5	5		5	15	No.	62½ tons.
Skinner, D. W.	Lincoln	15	15		15		No.	15 tons.
Skinner, M. D.	Lincoln	40	20		20		No.	37½ tons.
Sprague, C. G.	Lincoln	4	4		4		No.	120 tons.
Wells, —	Michigan Bluff						No.	12 tons.
Adams, C. T.	Newcastle	20	20		20			
Barkhouse, H. W.	Newcastle	40	40		40			
Bernhard, B.	Newcastle	70	70		70		No.	60 tons.
Boggs, J.	Newcastle	5	5		5		No.	120 tons.
Crook, A. B.	Newcastle						No.	210 tons.
Fagg, A. M.	Newcastle						No.	15 tons.
Gester, W. B.	Newcastle							
Gould, C.	Newcastle							
Madden, J. F.	Newcastle							
Maslin, S. P.	Newcastle	40	40		40		No.	120 tons.
Morrison, J. J.	Newcastle	40	40		40		No.	120 tons.
Rider, Andrew	Newcastle	40	40		40		No.	120 tons.
Sherman, R. B.	Newcastle							

PLACER COUNTY—Continued.

Name of Owner.	Post Office and Name of Vineyard.	Total Acres in Grapes.	Acres in Bearing.	Acres in Wine Grapes.	Acres in Table Grapes.	Acres in Raisin Grapes.	Wine Maker.	Product in 1889.	Varieties.
Wood, A. S.	Newcastle	40	40		40		No.	120 tons.	
Bowman, M.	Ophir								
Bromley, J.	Ophir								
Geraldson, Mrs.	Ophir								
Peck, N. R.	Ophir								
Allen, H.	Penryn	100	100		50	50	No.	300 tons.	
Bannon, E.	Penryn	40	40	30	10		No.	100 tons.	
Hawk, G. J.	Penryn	160	160		80	80	Yes.	480 tons.	
Keiser, John.	Penryn	40	40	40			No.	100 tons.	
Marquart,	Penryn	80	80		40	40	No.	240 tons.	
Mazal, J. C.	Pino	20	20	10	10		No.	50 tons.	
Barrett, C. H.	Rocklin								
Brown, Otis	Rocklin	100	100		60	40	No.	250 tons.	
California Raisin Co.	Rocklin	100	100				No.	250 tons.	
Crocker, L. L.	Rocklin	40	40				Yes.	100 tons.	
Hines Estate	Rocklin	100	100	75			No.		
Hoyt, I.	Rocklin								
Spring Valley Vineyard	Rocklin								
Westcott, C. P.	Rocklin								
Wood, W.	Rocklin								
Alvord, W.	Roseville	20	20	5	10	5	No.	40 tons.	
Berdika, Mrs.	Roseville	20	20		10	10	No.	60 tons.	
Booth, E.	Roseville	50	50	20	15	15	Yes.	150 tons.	
Forsyth, P.	Roseville	20	20	5	10	5	No.	40 tons.	
Geisendoffer, G.	Roseville	15	15	15			Yes.	37½ tons.	
Harris, J. J.	Roseville	80	80	35	30	15	No.	160 tons.	
Herbert,	Roseville	25	25	5	10	10	No.	50 tons.	
Lawson, C.	Roseville	50	50	20	5	6	No.	75 tons.	
McClung,	Roseville	50	50	10	10	20	Yes.	100 tons.	
Perry, Mrs.	Roseville	10	10	10			No.	25 tons.	
Rogers, Joseph	Roseville	30	30	5	10	5	No.	60 tons.	
Russell, J. H.	Roseville	20	20	5	10	5	No.	40 tons.	
Shilhouse, Mrs.	Roseville	6	6		6		No.	12 tons.	
Totals for county		2,285	2,169	354	1,431	500			

SACRAMENTO COUNTY.

Name of Owner.	Post Office and Name of Vineyard.	Total Acres in Grapes.	Acres in Bearing.	Acres in Wine Grapes.	Acres in Table Grapes.	Acres in Raisin Grapes.	Wine Maker.	Product in 1889.	Varieties.
Ebel & Stehr	American River	5	5		5				
Davis, Mrs. R. F.	Andrus Island	6	2	5		2			
Cross, J. F.	Antelope	2			5				
Driver, E. S.	Antelope	10	10	10					
McBride, J. A.	Brighton	10	7	7		½			
Parsons, Jno.	Center Township	7	1½						
Bolton, C.	Clay	1½	1½	1½	1				
Steele, Thos.	Clay	1½			2½				
Hagel, Jno.	Conley	1	1	2½	3				
Rieff, J. L.	Conley	5	5						
Whitney, J. W.	Conley	3	3						
Crofton, Jno.	Conley								
Green, Jos.	Courtland		6	6					
Hollister, D.	Courtland								
Hall, G.	Courtland								
Painter, Levi	Courtland								
Runyon, Wm. N.	Courtland								
Runyon, Sol.	Courtland								
Runyon, O. R.	Courtland								
Talmadge, C. V.	Courtland								
West, C. W.	Elliott	6	6						
Allen, Rich. estate of.	Elk Grove	1	1	1					
Aldrich, L. M.	Elk Grove	8	8	6					
Bradford, J. B.	Elk Grove	10	10	10					
Bradford, F. W.	Elk Grove	40	36	21	15				
Beans, B. F.	Elk Grove	30	30	10	20				
Boder, W. J.	Elk Grove	2½	2½		2½				
Bond, A. E.	Elk Grove	1	1		1				
Carr, George T.	Elk Grove	10	3		3				
Clinton, A.	Elk Grove								
Coffman, A.	Elk Grove	7	7						
Colton, B. F.	Elk Grove	7½	2½	7					
Coons, David	Elk Grove	¼	¼	2½	¾				
Cox, E. W.	Elk Grove	8	8	5	3				

Sacramento County—Continued.

Name of Owner	Post Office and Name of Vineyard	Total Acres in Grapes	Acres in Bearing	Acres in Wine Grapes	Acres in Table Grapes	Acres in Raisin Grapes	Wine Maker	Product in 1889	Varieties
Craddock, John	Elk Grove	8¾	4½	4	8¾				
Dart, L. S.	Elk Grove	4	4	4					
Dixon, Mrs. E.	Elk Grove	4⅔	4⅔		1				
Duffy, John	Elk Grove	3	3	2	1				
Eschinger, M., estate of	Elk Grove	1	1		3				
Etling, Charles C.	Elk Grove	3	3		8				
Foulks, George	Elk Grove	8	50	31					
Fox, J. A.	Elk Grove	50	50		8	11			
Freeman, I. F.	Elk Grove	16	16	10	5				
Gage, F. P.	Elk Grove	1	1	1	6				
Garrett, Samuel	Elk Grove	1	1	1	1				
Hunt, George L.	Elk Grove	5	5	5					
Hutchinsen, Mrs. H. A.	Elk Grove	5	5	2					
Jackson, Mrs. C. A.	Elk Grove	2	2	8					
Johnson, T. W.	Elk Grove	25	8	13	12				
Kerby, C.	Elk Grove	3	3	1	2				
Kerr, George H.	Elk Grove	50	50	20	10	20			
Kerr, J. H.	Elk Grove	10	10	10					
Leavitt, M.	Elk Grove	1	1	1					
Le Boyde, John	Elk Grove	1	1						
Lee, John	Elk Grove	2	2	10					
Lee, Laura	Elk Grove	3	3	2					
Lewis, Ed., Jr.	Elk Grove	1½	1½		1½				
Loll, Aug.	Elk Grove	3	3	3					
Lowry, Henry	Elk Grove	5	5	5					
Macy, Seth	Elk Grove	1	1		1				
Maholm, Mrs. J. B.	Elk Grove	1	1		1				
McConnell, Thos.	Elk Grove	2	2		2				
Meinardi & Bro.	Elk Grove	10	10	8	2				
Nelmes, W. H.	Elk Grove	1	1	1					
Nesche, Geo.	Elk Grove	4	4	4					
Opley, A.	Elk Grove	6	3	6					
Ottman, G.	Elk Grove	1	1	1					
Parker, Mary	Elk Grove	4	4	4					

Name	Location				
Polhemus, C.B., est. of	Elk Grove		1	1	1
Rhoa es, I. R.	Elk Grove		3	3	3
Schirner, Annie B.	Elk Grove		3	3	3
Scholl, John	Elk Grove		1½	1½	1½
Shepherd, J. E.	Elk Grove	3	2	2	2
Sherwood, D. H.	Elk Grove	1	3	3	3
Silleck, Chas.	Elk Grove		1	1	1
Spring, Mrs. F. C.	Elk Grove	3	1½	1½	1½
Stetter, F.	Elk Grove	3	2	5	5
Steuart, N. I.	Elk Grove		4	4	4
Sehlmyer, J. F.	Elk Grove		2	2	2
Theobald, Elizabeth	Elk Grove	3	1	1½	1½
Thompson, Mrs. A. M.	Elk Grove	1	6	6	6
Treat, Mrs. C. M.	Elk Grove		7	7	7
Thompson, T. J.	Elk Grove	1	3	3	3
Upton, David	Elk Grove		1	1	1
Winklemun, P., est. of	Elk Grove	2½	2½	5	5
Williamson, George S.	Elk Grove	8	8	8	8
Brown, J. P.	Florin		1	1	1
Buell, C. L.	Florin	2½	2½	2½	4½
Buell, D. H.	Florin	10	10	10	15
Carlisle, G. W.	Florin	1		1	3
Culverson, J. P.	Florin	5		5	5
Coulson, John	Florin		3	8	8
Davis, James	Florin	2½	2½	2½	2½
Davenport, R.	Florin	3½	1¾	5	5
Ditson, M. S.	Florin	2	8	10	10
Enos, Jas., estate of	Florin		13	13	13
Fassett, L. H., estate of	Florin	12	13	25	25
Finch, D.	Florin	7	8	15	15
French, C. F.	Florin	7	7	7	8
Gardner, Esau	Florin	25	70	85	95
Hoey, T.	Florin		1	1	1
Howell, R.	Florin	1	1	2	2
Jackson, J. E.	Florin	1	2	2	2
Jenkins, M.	Florin	10	4	12	14
Johnson, C. F.	Florin	9		9	9
Kramer, Peter	Florin	7		7	7
Kennedy, S. W.	Florin		5	5	5
Lea, Charles	Florin	5	1	1	1
Lewis, Ann	Florin	1		1½	1½
Marrett, Miss S.	Florin	1½	1	1	1
Maxfield, R. G. & G. W.	Florin	1			3½

8-v

SACRAMENTO COUNTY—Continued.

Name of Owner.	Post Office and Name of Vineyard.	Total Acres in Grapes.	Acres in Bearing.	Acres in Wine Grapes.	Acres in Table Grapes.	Acres in Raisin Grapes.	Wine Maker.	Product in 1889.	Varieties.
Menzel, H.	Florin	5½	5½	2	3½				
McLaughlin, John	Florin	9	9	9					
McNie, John	Florin	5	5		5				
Mische, G.	Florin								
Murphy, Sarah G.	Florin	12	12	12					
Neely, William F.	Florin	15	15	10	5				
Patton, C. S.	Florin	12	8	4	8				
Patton, F.	Florin	7	7	3	4				
Perez, F.	Florin	30	30	15	15				
Reese, David	Florin	30	30	20	10				
Reese, E., estate of.	Florin	5	5	5					
Reese, John	Florin	5	5	3	2				
Reid, Mrs. A. M.	Florin	4	4	2	2				
Rodrigus, John S.	Florin	12	12	9	3				
Renwick, T.	Florin	22	15	15	10				
Robinson, W. H.	Florin	13	13	3	10				
Rutter, James	Florin	70	70	35	35				
Sanders, Mrs. N. T.	Florin	11	11		11				
Scholefield, J. L.	Florin	8	8	6	2				
Scholefield, W.	Florin	5	5	3	2				
Simons, J. A.	Florin	5	5	5					
Slawson, B. G.	Florin	2½	2½	2	2¾				
Smith, Miss F. E.	Florin	5	3	3	3				
Smith, F. M., estate of	Florin	6	6	5	3				
Smith, W. C., & Son	Florin	1½	1½		1¾				
Steward, L. C.	Florin	12	12		12				
Tabor, W. J.	Florin	8	6	1½	8				
Taylor, Thomas	Florin	2	2		2				
Troutman, A.	Florin	2½	2½		2				
Tootell, James	Florin	15	15	7	8				
Towle, C.	Florin	15	15		15				
Walton, R.	Florin	11	6	2	4				
Whitman, Mrs. M. A.	Florin	7½	2		2				
Williams, M.	Florin	6½	2	2½	3				

Wilson, Leaner	Florin	5	5	3	2				
Nuttall, Chas.	Folsom	30	30	30					
Benedix, C.	Franklin	3	3		1	2			
Bradford, J. B.	Franklin								
Core, A. F.	Franklin	2½	2½	2½					
Derr, Henry	Franklin	1	1	1					
Ehrhardt, John	Franklin	6	6	6					
Keema, H.	Franklin	3	3	3					
McLanahan, D.	Franklin	1	1		1				
Olsen, Ole	Franklin	½	½		½				
Schmidt, John	Franklin	1½	1½	1½					
Strong, P. A.	Franklin	2½	2	2½					
Hite, J. G.	Freeport	3	3	2	1				
Moore, Mrs. J. W.	Freeport	2		2					
Baggiano, G.	Galt	1½	1½	1½					
Bisanio, A.	Galt	1½	1½	1½					
Bock, William	Galt	½	½		½				
Bryant, A. B.	Galt	½	½			½			
Chase, Hiram	Galt	4	2	3		1			
Gage, J. P.	Galt	81	81			81			
Haller, William	Galt	½	½	½					
Harvey, Obed	Galt	1¾	1¾		1¾				
Hauschildt, H.	Galt	1	1	1					
Kreeger, S.	Galt	½	½		½				
Makel, Geo. N.	Galt	6	6	6			Yes.		
Marengo, A.	Galt	2½		2½					
Montague, Alex.	Galt	8				8			
McFarland, John	Galt	1½	1½	1½					
Pohn, S. W.	Galt	1	1		1				
Quiggle, V. S.	Galt	3				3			
Roy, Don	Galt	2	1		2				
Whitaker, A.	Galt	½	½			½			
Young, Elizabeth	Galt	2½	2½	2½					
Kohler & Van Bergen	Guthries	4	4	4			Yes.		
Herbert, L.	Hicksville	½	½	½					
Hoffknecht, F.	Hicksville	200	200	200					
Howard, H. C.	Hicksville	30	30	30					
Mahim, Jane	Hicksville	2	2	2					
Valensin, Alice M.	Hicksville	3	3	3					
Miller, Peter	Lake House	16	16	16					
Jeans, Adolph	Mayhews	20	20		20				
Stephens, R. D.	Mayhews	20	20		20				
Wells, Eli	Mayhews	32	32	25	7				
Colbaker, A.	Mississippi Township	2	2		2				
Hancock, John	Mormon Island	5	5	3	2			10 tons.	

SACRAMENTO COUNTY—Continued.

Name of Owner.	Post Office and Name of Vineyard.	Total Acres in Grapes.	Acres in Bearing.	Acres in Wine Grapes.	Acres in Table Grapes.	Acres in Raisin Grapes.	Wine Maker.	Product in 1889.	Varieties.
Hart, Ed.	Mormon Island	40	40	40				100 tons.	
Hart, Powell	Mormon Island	15	15	15				37½ tons.	
Hawk, John.	Mormon Island	40	40	28	12			80 tons.	
Hoke, James H.	Mormon Island	6	6			6	Yes.		
L pes, J hn	Mormon Island	12	12	10	2			24 tons.	
Mette, Henry	Mormon Island	80	80	70	5	5	Yes.	200 tons.	
Minck, Gerhard	Mormon Island	10	10	8	2			20 tons.	
Mutual Life Ins. Co.	Mormon Island	80	80	70	5	5	Yes.	200 tons.	
Pellikin, Geo.	Mormon Island	20	20	15	5			40 tons.	
Slackerman, H.	Mormon Island	5	5	4	1			10 tons.	
Stroup, Mrs.	Mormon Island	30	30	25	5		Yes.	75 tons.	
Verbena, H.	Mormon Island	30	30	20	10		Yes.	60 tons.	
Natoma Vineyard Co.	Natoma	1,500	1,250	1,300	200				
Barnby, Mrs. R.	Perkins	15	15	11	4				
Bennett, Jno.	Perkins	5	5	1	4				
Bidwell, H. G.	Perkins	4	4	4					
Brown, Ront.	Perkins	4	3	1	3				
Bundock, H.	Perkins	2	2		2				
Davis, A. B.	Perkins	5½	6½	1½	5				
Davis, Owen T.	Perkins	11	11		11				
Davis, W. O.	Perkins	3	3		3				
Ferguson, R. J.	Perkins	3	3		3				
Foster, S. G.	Perkins	1	1		1				
Hall, Alex.	Perkins	7	7	7					
Harlow, Geo. W.	Perkins	9	9	8	1				
Harlow, J. M.	Perkins	4½	4½	2½	4½				
Horotman, C.	Perkins	2½	2½	2		2			
Jackman, S. H.	Perkins	3	3	3	3				
Lea, Isaac	Perkins	6	6		7				
Lowe, Asa, estate of	Perkins	7	7		7				
Manlove, W. S.	Perkins	90	40	40	50				
Miller, W. A.	Perkins	30	15	27	3				
Murphy, P. H.	Perkins	9	6		9				
Perkins, T. C.	Perkins	2	2	2					

Name	District				
Russell, P.	Perkins		7	7½	7½
Tackney, John	Perkins		1¼	1½	1½
Boye, C. M.	Routiers		7	7	10¾
Boyde, Mrs. I.	Routiers				2
Briggs, G. G., heirs of	Routiers	150	150	150	150
Carroll, Pat.	Routiers		2	2	2
Espie, Alex.	Routiers		13	13	13
Hoey, Peter	Routiers	66	56	56	56
Kelley, Ed.	Routiers		3	3	3
McDonald, Geo. A.	Routiers	1½	1½	1½	6½
Nuttall, Isaac	Routiers		35	35	35
Quoil, Stephen	Routiers		5	5	5
Rodman, L. G.	Routiers	2	16	16	16
Routier, Jos.	Routiers		23	25	25
Shields, Peter	Routiers		18	18	18
Studerus, John, Sr.	Routiers		14	14	14
Taylor, J. B., estate of	Routiers		15	15	15
Williams, Ellen	Routiers		4	10	20
Baker, Geo. B.	Russell			7	7
Beaudry, J. C.	Russell		8	22	22
Brooks, William	Russell			6	6
Chapin, F. F.	Russell		1	2	2
Hunphrey, A. B.	Russell		8	45	95
Stoner, Mrs. B.	Russell		11	11	11
Booth, Newton	Sacramento			4	4
Brockway, C. Z.	Sacramento	2		1	1
Burns, A. B.	Sacramento		10	5	5
Casselli, V.	Sacramento			16	16
Clark, N.	Sacramento			25	25
Curtis, William	Sacramento		10	20	20
Duden, Geo.	Sacramento			1	1
Easton, R. A.	Sacramento		7	8	1
Eldred, I. P.	Sacramento			3¾	3¾
Fawcett, J. H.	Sacramento			10	10
Greer, E.	Sacramento		2	16	20
Guista, F.	Sacramento			7	5
Hack, Geo. W.	Sacramento			1	1
Hoppe, Julia	Sacramento			2	10
Howrigan, Thos.	Sacramento		3	5	5
Keefe, Wm.	Sacramento			3	3
Kendall, W. S.	Sacramento		60	20	90
McNair, W.	Sacramento	10		2	2
Palmer, Emily J.	Sacramento		12	12	12
Pimentell, F.	Sacramento		2¼	2¼	2¼
Pool, S. W.	Sacramento		4	4	4

SACRAMENTO COUNTY—Continued.

Name of Owner.	Post Office and Name of Vineyard.	Total Acres in Grapes.	Acres in Bearing.	Acres in Wine Grapes.	Acres in Table Grapes.	Acres in Raisin Grapes.	Wine Maker.	Product in 1889.	Varieties.
Stillson, Geo. S.	Sacramento	15	10	15					
Strauch, D.	Sacramento	1½	1½		1½				
Stubbs, John L.	Sacramento	2			2	3			
Welty, J. B.	Sacramento	25	23	20					
Holmes, H.	Union House	7	7	7					
Mack, Charles E.	Union House	8	5	4	4				
Sims, Joseph	Union House	25	15	25					
Wightman, Mark	Union House	1½	1½	1½					
Green, L. D.	Walnut Grove	2	2		2				
Branscomb, S. A.	Walsh Station	1	1	1					
Ellis, W. H.	Walsh Station	8	8	8					
Lee, Annie R.	Walsh Station	6	6		6				
Manley, W. C. & J. A.	Walsh Station	15	6	3					
McManus, A. G., Sr.	Walsh Station	2	3	2					
Miller, A. D.	Walsh Station	4	4	4	¾				
Schulze, John, est. of	Walsh Station	4	4	4					
Sherwood, J. O.	Walsh Station	2	2		2				
Totals for county		4,630	4,028	3,131	1,164	335			

SAN BENITO COUNTY.

NAME OF OWNER.	Post Office and Name of Vineyard.	Total Acres in Grapes.	Acres in Bearing.	Acres in Wine Grapes.	Acres in Table Grapes.	Acres in Raisin Grapes.	Wine Maker.	Product in 1889.	Varieties.
Bolado, Joaq	Tres Pinos	30	30	30			Yes.	1,000 gals.	Imported varieties.
Flint, Thos.	San Juan	25	25		25		No.		Imported varieties.
Palmtag, Wm.	Hollister	120	80	110	10		Yes.	42,000 gals.	Imported varieties.
Totals for county		175	135	140	35				

SAN BERNARDINO COUNTY.

NAME OF OWNER.	Post Office and Name of Vineyard.	Total Acres in Grapes.	Acres in Bearing.	Acres in Wine Grapes.	Acres in Table Grapes.	Acres in Raisin Grapes.	Wine Maker.	Product in 1889.	Varieties.
Anderson, John	Colton	89	89	89					
Bean, Chas.	Colton	5	5	5					
Belarde, Q.	Colton	3	3	3					
Downie & Mirandette	Colton	84	84	84					
Ralph, M.	Colton	8	8	8					
Stockman & Burns	Colton	40	40			40	No.		Muscat.
Benson, A. N.	Crafton	22	22			22	No.		Muscat.
Burton, G. H.	Crafton	12	12			12	No.		Muscat.
Byrns, M.	Crafton	12	12			12	No.		Muscat.
Cave, P. & B.	Crafton	11	11			11	No.		Muscat.
Covington, P.	Crafton	3	3			3	No.		Muscat.
Crafts, G. H.	Crafton	15	15			15	No.		Muscat.
Crafts, H. G.	Crafton	14	14			14	No.		Muscat.
Crafts, Mrs. R.	Crafton	14	14			14	No.		Muscat.
Craig, William	Crafton	11	11			11	No.		Muscat.

SAN BERNARDINO COUNTY—Continued.

Name of Owner.	Post Office and Name of Vineyard.	Total Acres in Grapes.	Acres in Bearing.	Acres in Wine Grapes.	Acres in Table Grapes.	Acres in Raisin Grapes.	Wine Maker.	Product in 1889.	Varieties.
Eason, Abner	Crafton	12	12			12	No.		Muscat.
Gowers, ——	Crafton	6	6			6	No.		Muscat.
McGinness, R. E.	Crafton	5	5			5	No.		Muscat.
Paine, C. R.	Crafton	10	10			10	No.		Muscat.
Anderson, J. J.	Cucamonga	5	5			5	No.		Muscat.
Beldon, W. C.	Cucamonga	3	3			3	No.		Muscat.
Brown, C. T.	Cucamonga	5	5			5	No.		Sultana.
Corsen, Charles	Cucamonga	5	5			5	No.		Muscat.
Cucamonga Wine Co.	Cucamonga	400	400	400			Yes.		
Done, Volney	Cucamonga	3	3			3	No.		Muscat.
Guptal, A.	Cucamonga	6	6			6	No.		Muscat.
Hague, William F.	Cucamonga	10	10			10	No.		Muscat.
Haven, George	Cucamonga	120	120	100		20	No.		
Henderson, E. F.	Cucamonga	28	28	2		26	No.		Muscat, Sultana.
Kincaid, N. M.	Cucamonga	10	10			10	No.		Muscat.
Lord, G. W.	Cucamonga	5	5			5	No.		Muscat.
Madix, John	Cucamonga	6	6			6	No.		Muscat.
Manchester, C. D.	Cucamonga	3	3			3	No.		Sultana.
Milliken, D. B.	Cucamonga, North	120	120	100		20	No.		Muscat.
Ogden, William	Cucamonga	10	10			10	No.		
Orchard, ——	Cucamonga	20	20			18	No.		Sultana.
Petsch, J. A. P.	Cucamonga	16	16	2		16	No.		
Ray, Captain A.	Cucamonga	5	5			5	No.		Muscat.
Read, Dr. E. W.	Cucamonga	5	5	6		5	No.		Muscat.
Riggins, C. H.	Cucamonga	15	15	15			No.		
Rundle, George	Cucamonga	18	18			18	No.		Muscat, Sultana.
Smith, F. G.	Cucamonga	6	6				No.		
Smith, John	Cucamonga	21	21	6		18	No.		Muscat, Sultana.
Smith, Lewis	Cucamonga	6	6	3			No.		
Sontag, H.	Cucamonga	8	8	6		8	No.		Muscat.
Southworth, Dr.	Cucamonga, North	8	8			8	No.		Muscat.
Stevens, D.	Cucamonga, North	6	6			6	No.		Muscat.
Stinchfield, A.	Cucamonga	6	6			6	No.		Muscat.
Thayer, Geo.	Cucamonga	6	6			6	No.		Muscat.

Name	Location	No.			Variety
Whitfield, Wm.	Cucamonga	5	5	5	Muscat, Sultana.
Wilkins,	Cucamonga	20	20	20	Muscat, Sultana.
Bean,	Dry Branch	120	120	120	Muscat.
Bright,	Dry Branch	13	13	13	Muscat.
Church,	Dry Branch	10	10	10	Muscat.
Collins, G. S.	Dry Branch	30	30	30	Muscat.
Collins,	Dry Branch	5	5	5	Muscat.
Ganur,	Dry Branch	4	4	4	Muscat.
Hamilton,	Dry Branch	12	12	12	Muscat.
Horswill,	Dry Branch	12	12	12	Muscat.
Ingram,	Dry Branch	13	13	13	Muscat.
Landsdall,	Dry Branch	12	12	12	Muscat.
Roach,	Dry Branch	4	4	4	Muscat.
Wall,	Dry Branch	7	7	7	Muscat.
Burgess, Mrs.	Etiwanda	6	6	6	Muscat.
Coffeen, A.	Etiwanda	5	5	5	Muscat.
Crandall, G.	Etiwanda	15	15	15	Muscat.
Donnelly, Mrs.	Etiwanda	12	12	12	Muscat.
Dugdale, H. W.	Etiwanda	6	6	6	Muscat.
Fox, A. H.	Etiwanda	10	10	10	Muscat.
Gilbert, W. H.	Etiwanda	6	6	6	Muscat.
Gildersleeve, J.	Etiwanda	15	15	15	Muscat.
Gurley, H. B.	Etiwanda	20	20	20	Muscat.
Hattersley, H.	Etiwanda	35	35	35	Muscat.
Hazlett, Dr.	Etiwanda	7	7	7	Muscat.
Hibbard, S.	Etiwanda	20	20	20	Muscat.
Hollis, C.	Etiwanda	15	15	15	Muscat.
Johnson, G. F.	Etiwanda	20	20	20	Muscat.
Johnson, Jas.	Etiwanda	16	16	16	Muscat.
Jones, R. J.	Etiwanda	30	30	30	Muscat.
Kemp, S. C.	Etiwanda	13	13	13	Muscat.
Kumler, A.	Etiwanda	35	35	35	Muscat.
Langham	Etiwanda	10	10	10	Muscat.
Leslie, J. F.	Etiwanda	15	15	15	Muscat.
Linville, J.	Etiwanda	15	15	15	Muscat.
Love, W. K.	Etiwanda	20	20	20	Muscat.
Louthian, R. L.	Etiwanda	65	65	65	Muscat.
McBain, W.	Etiwanda	15	15	15	Muscat.
McCall, J. C.	Etiwanda	10	10	10	Muscat.
Miller,	Etiwanda	18	18	18	Muscat.
Olney, P.	Etiwanda	15	15	15	Muscat.
Perrine, C. O.	Etiwanda	40	40	40	Muscat.
Ross, C. N.	Etiwanda	40	40	40	Muscat.
Scott, J. H.	Etiwanda	15	15	15	Muscat.
Seymour, P. C.	Etiwanda	25	25	25	Muscat.

San Bernardino County—Continued.

Name of Owner.	Post Office and Name of Vineyard.	Total Acres in Grapes.	Acres in Bearing.	Acres in Wine Grapes.	Acres in Table Grapes.	Acres in Raisin Grapes.	Wine Maker.	Product in 1889.	Varieties.
Sheppard, A. L.	Etiwanda	15	15			15	No.		Muscat.
Steiner, A.	Etiwanda	10	10			10	No.		Muscat.
Taylor, P.	Etiwanda	17	17			17	No.		Muscat.
Tregear, J.	Etiwanda	10	10			10	No.		Muscat.
Wilkinson, C.	Etiwanda	10	10			10	No.		Muscat.
Winstanley, F.	Etiwanda	35	35			35	No.		Muscat.
Baldridge, B. L.	Highlands	4	4			4	No.		Muscat.
Beattie, J. W.	Highlands	6	6			6	No.		Muscat.
Barley & Colvin	Highlands	6	6			6	No.		Muscat.
Clemmans, Dr. C. P.	Highlands	6	6			6	No.		Muscat.
Cook, T. T.	Highlands	4	4			4	No.		Muscat.
Corwin, W. S.	Highlands	4	4			4	No.		Muscat.
Cram, L. F.	Highlands	6	6			6	No.		Muscat.
Cunningham & Stone	Highlands	22	22			22	No.		Muscat.
Curtis, J. W.	Highlands	15	15			15	No.		Muscat.
Ely, Ed.	Highlands	13	13			13	No.		Muscat.
Foster, A. T.	Highlands	10	10			10	No.		Muscat.
Gill & Fording	Highlands	5	5			5	No.		Muscat.
Glass, W. H.	Highlands	16	16			16	No.		Muscat.
Grove, L. L.	Highlands	4	4			4	No.		Muscat.
Grow, W. F.	Highlands	4	4			4	No.		Muscat.
Haven, Geo.	Highlands	8	8			8	No.		Muscat.
Henderson, E. R.	Highlands	5	5			5	No.		Muscat.
Henderson, R. W.	Highlands	10	10			10	No.		Muscat.
Henderson, W. T.	Highlands	4	4			4	No.		Muscat.
Hidden, Chas., Sr.	Highlands	7	7			7	No.		Muscat.
Longmire, R.	Highlands	3	3			3	No.		Muscat.
Noyes, W. T.	Highlands	4	4			4	No.		Muscat.
Parker, E. H.	Highlands	5	5			5	No.		Muscat.
Rogers, W. P.	Highlands	4	4			4	No.		Muscat.
Wallace Bros.	Highlands	6	6			6	No.		Muscat.
Watson Bros.	Highlands	2	2			2	No.		Muscat.
Baldridge, Rev.	Messina								Muscat.
Barrett, S. H.	Messina								Muscat.

Name	Variety	Type		No.			
Cunningham, R. F.	Messina						
Foster, A. T.	Messina						
Fowler, B.	Messina						
Glass, W. H.	Messina						
Hoven, G. W.	Messina						
Henderson, R. W.	Messina						
Henderson, W. T.	Messina						
Hidden, Chas.	Messina						
Noyes, W. T.	Messina						
Parker, H. E.	Messina						
Quinman, H. J.	Messina						
Rogers, W. P.	Messina						
Stevens, W.	Messina						
Wallace, S. S.	Messina						
Willard, —	Messina						
Allan, —	Ontario	Muscat.	No.	10		10	10
Allen, A.	Ontario	Muscat.	No.	4		4	4
Baits, —	Ontario	Muscat.	No.	8		8	8
Barrett, G. S.	Ontario	Muscat.	No.	6		6	6
Borthwick, —	Ontario	Muscat.	No.	3		3	3
Cocke, J. H.	Ontario	Muscat.	No.	7		7	7
Darling, —	Ontario	Muscat.	No.	15		15	15
Dearden, W.	Ontario	Muscat.	No.	10		10	10
Dyer, P. M.	Ontario	Muscat.	No.	2		2	2
Eldridge, C. W.	Ontario (New York)	Muscat.	No.	4		4	4
Frankish, —	Ontario	Muscat.	No.	5		5	5
Garcia, J. S.	Ontario	Muscat.	No.	5		5	5
Gargan, P.	Ontario	Muscat.	No.	2		2	2
Gullock, —	Ontario	Muscat.	No.	6		6	6
Harper, —	Ontario	Muscat.	No.	6		6	6
Hatch, E. M.	Ontario	Muscat.	No.	4		4	4
Holmes, J.	Ontario	Muscat.	No.	2		2	2
Holmes, T.	Ontario	Muscat.	No.	8		8	8
Hyer, Dr. G.	Ontario	Muscat.	No.	10		10	10
Jackson, H. W.	Ontario	Muscat.	No.	2		2	2
Joliffe, E. H.	Ontario	Muscat.	No.	20		20	20
McFatridge, P. W.	Ontario	Muscat.	No.	18	8	18	18
McIntyre, G.	Ontario	Muscat and wine varieties.	No.	3	9	9	9
May, W. H.	Ontario	Wine varieties.	No.	10		10	10
Merriman, —	Ontario	Muscat.	No.	5		5	5
Morgan, H. H.	Ontario	Muscat.	No.	5		5	5
Morgan, M. M.	Ontario	Muscat.	No.	7		7	7
Nicol, D.	Ontario	Muscat.	No.	3		3	3
Nugent, M.	Ontario	Muscat.	No.	6		6	6
Platner, —	Ontario	Muscat.	No.	20		20	20

SAN BERNARDINO COUNTY—Continued.

Name of Owner.	Post Office and Name of Vineyard.	Total Acres in Grapes.	Acres in Bearing.	Acres in Wine Grapes.	Acres in Table Grapes.	Acres in Raisin Grapes.	Wine Maker.	Product in 1889.	Varieties.
Rosenfeldt, Mrs.	Ontario	10	10			10	No.	--	Muscat.
Sowerwine, C.	Ontario	4	4			4	No.	--	Muscat.
Sykes, Dr.	Ontario	19	19			19	No.	--	Muscat.
Tays, J. B.	Ontario	20	20	10		10	No.	--	Muscat and wine varieties.
Van Wise, —	Ontario	3	3			3	No.	--	Muscat.
Whittock, —	Ontario	7	7			7	No.	--	Muscat.
Biggin, Henry	Redlands	--	--	--	--	--	No.	--	Muscat.
Branch, H.	Redlands	--	--	--	--	--	No.	--	Muscat.
Brown, T. W.	Redlands (San Fran.)	--	--	--	--	--	No.	--	Muscat.
Burton, Col. G. H.	Redlands	--	--	--	--	--	No.	--	Muscat.
Cook, Simeon	Redlands (Riverside)	--	--	--	--	--	No.	--	Muscat.
Crafts, Geo. H.	Redlands	--	--	--	--	--	No.	--	Muscat.
Craig, Dr. W.	Redlands	--	--	--	--	--	No.	--	Muscat.
Cutts, E. B.	Redlands	--	--	--	--	--	No.	--	Muscat.
Dean, C. T.	Redlands	--	--	--	--	--	No.	--	Muscat.
Diffinbacker, —	Redlands	--	--	--	--	--	No.	--	Muscat.
Fussil, P. B.	Redlands	--	--	--	--	--	No.	--	Muscat.
Gaylord, Cass	Redlands	--	--	--	--	--	No.	--	Muscat.
Haight, Ira C.	Redlands	--	--	--	--	--	No.	--	Muscat.
Harris, O. W.	Redlands	--	--	--	--	--	No.	--	Muscat.
Hayes, S. J.	Redlands	--	--	--	--	--	No.	--	Muscat.
Hewett, I. I.	Redlands	--	--	--	--	--	No.	--	Muscat.
Higby, H. E.	Redlands	--	--	--	--	--	No.	--	Muscat.
Holliday, W. T.	Redlands	--	--	--	--	--	No.	--	Muscat.
Hosking, John	Redlands	--	--	--	--	--	No.	--	Muscat.
Hornbeck, E.	Redlands	--	--	--	--	--	No.	--	Muscat.
Ladd, T. W.	Redlands	--	--	--	--	--	No.	--	Muscat.
Lindenburg, Wm.	Redlands	--	--	--	--	--	No.	--	Muscat.
Lowrie, Walter	Redlands	--	--	--	--	--	No.	--	Muscat.
McGinnis, R. E.	Redlands	--	--	--	--	--	No.	--	Muscat.
Marshall, Hugh	Redlands	--	--	--	--	--	No.	--	Muscat.
Meacham, David	Redlands	--	--	--	--	--	No.	--	Muscat.
Morrison, F. P.	Redlands	--	--	--	--	--	No.	--	Muscat.

Name	Location				No.	Variety
Paine, C. R.	Redlands					Muscat.
Rowe, Charles	Redlands					Muscat.
Saunders, A. G.	Redlands					Muscat.
Waite, E. J.	Redlands					Muscat.
Wilson, J. S.	Redlands					Muscat.
Wiemar, Wm.	Redlands (San Bernardino).					Muscat.
Worthing, —	Redlands	20	20	20	No.	Muscat.
Burdick, J.	Rialto	10	10	10	No.	Muscat.
Cowan, —	Rialto	5	5	5	No.	Muscat.
Fountain, J. H	Rialto				No.	Muscat.
McCracken, J.	Rialto				No.	Muscat.
Merrill, Governor	Rialto	40	40	40	No.	Muscat.
Milligan, J. H.	Rialto	5	5	5	No.	Muscat.
Ralston, J. H.	Rialto	5	5	5	No.	Muscat.
Rogers, —	Rialto	10	10	10	No.	Muscat.
St. John, —	Rialto	5	5	5	No.	Muscat.
Sweesy, J.	Rialto	5	5	5	No.	Muscat.
Sweesy, V. M.	Rialto	5	5	5	No.	Muscat.
Turner, G. N.	Rialto	10	10	10	No.	Muscat.
Wright, J.	Rialto	18	18	18	No.	Muscat.
Benedict, H. J.	Riverside	5	5	5	No.	Muscat.
Benson, Ralph	Riverside	10	10	10	No.	Muscat.
Bliss, S. P.	Riverside	10	10	10	No.	Muscat.
Boyd, Jas.	Riverside	3	3	3	No.	Muscat.
Brethours, J. H.	Riverside, South	5	5	5	No.	Muscat.
Brown, A. H.	Riverside	2	2	2	No.	Muscat.
Hutton, Rev.	Riverside	2	2	2	No.	Muscat.
Chamblin, T. H. B.	Riverside	10	10	10	No.	Muscat.
Clark, Henry	Riverside, South	10	10	10	No.	Muscat.
Craw, J. W.	Riverside	2	2	2	No.	Muscat.
Crittenden, J. W.	Riverside	12	12	12	No.	Muscat.
Cr-sby, C. A.	Riverside	6	6	6	No.	Muscat.
Culpepper, —	Riverside	10	10	10	No.	Muscat.
Ellfott, Wm.	Riverside	10	10	10	No.	Muscat.
Failes, E. W.	Riverside, South	10	10	10	No.	Muscat.
Finch, Wm.	Riverside	12	12	12	No.	Muscat.
Fountain, Jas.	Riverside, South	5	5	5	No.	Muscat.
Fowler, H.	Riverside	40	40	40	No.	Muscat.
Gill & Dyer	Riverside, South	6	6	6	No.	Muscat.
Grant, Alec	Riverside	5	5	5	No.	Muscat.
Guffin, G.	Riverside	6	6	6	No.	Muscat.
Hall, P.	Riverside, South	22	22	22	No.	Muscat.
Harrington, —	Riverside, South	13	13	13	No.	Muscat.
Haynes, Mrs.	Riverside				No.	Muscat.

San Bernardino County—Continued.

Name of Owner.	Post Office and Name of Vineyard.	Total Acres in Grapes.	Acres in Bearing.	Acres in Wine Grapes.	Acres in Table Grapes.	Acres in Raisin Grapes.	Wine Maker.	Product in 1889.	Varieties.
Hewitt, J. J.	Riverside	14	14			14	No.		Muscat.
Higgins, Wm.	Riverside, West.	10	10			10	No.		Muscat.
Holden, Wm.	Riverside	7	7			7	No.		Muscat.
Holmes, E. W.	Riverside	2	2			2	No.		Muscat.
Holt, L. M.	Riverside, South.	10	10			10	No.		Muscat.
Hotson, ——	Riverside	10	10			10	No.		Muscat.
Hubbard, Miss Z. S.	Riverside, West.	5	5			5	No.		Muscat.
Huberty, John	Riverside	10	10			10	No.		Muscat.
Hurd, Chas.	Riverside	4	4			4	No.		Muscat.
Jansen, José	Riverside, West.	30	30			30	No.		Muscat.
Jarvis, Dr.	Riverside	12	12			12	No.		Muscat.
Jenkins, Dr.	Riverside	10	10			10	No.		Muscat.
Johnson, A. P.	Riverside, South.	7	7			7	No.		Muscat.
Jones, H. P.	Riverside	5	5			5	No.		Muscat.
Lett, W. P.	Riverside	30	30			30	No.		Muscat.
Lockwood, H. P.	Riverside	18	18			18	No.		Muscat.
Love, James	Riverside, West.	4	4			4	No.		Muscat.
McCoy, Sam	Riverside	20	20			20	No.		Muscat.
McFarland, John	Riverside	7	7			7	No.		Muscat.
Newlands, J. L.	Riverside						No.		Muscat.
North, J. G.	Riverside, West.	10	10			10	No.		Muscat.
Parkes, Judge	Riverside	5	5			5	No.		Muscat.
Patton, Dr.	Riverside	6	6			6	No.		Muscat.
Patton, S. S.	Riverside	20	20			20	No.		Muscat.
Pulse, H.	Riverside	23	23			23	No.		Muscat, Sultana.
Richards, J. S.	Riverside, South.	4	4			4	No.		Muscat.
Rolph, J.	Riverside, West.	4	4			4	No.		Muscat.
Rusell, W.	Riverside	20	20			20	No.		Muscat.
Schell, S. D.	Riverside, West.	27	27			27	No.		Muscat.
Smith, Ben	Riverside	10	10			10	No.		Muscat.
Streeter, Hon. H. N.	Riverside	10	10			10	No.		Muscat.
Strong, D. S.	Riverside	4	4			4	No.		Muscat.
Walter, Mrs., estate of.	Riverside	4	4			4	No.		Muscat.
Waring, L. G.	Riverside	2	2			2	No.		Muscat.

Name of Owner	Post Office and Name of Vineyard	Total Acres in Grapes	Acres in Bearing	Acres in Wine Grapes	Acres in Table Grapes	Acres in Raisin Grapes	Wine Maker	Product in 1889	Varieties
Wilbur, J.	Riverside	5	5			5	No.		Muscat.
Wilbur, J. W.	Riverside	8	8			8	No.		Muscat.
Wright, Miss F. M.	Riverside	5	5			5	No.		Muscat.
Wright, Mrs.	Riverside	4	4			4	No.		Muscat.
Wood, A.	Riverside, South	10	10			10	No.		Muscat.
Anderson, John	San Bernardino	80	80	80					Zinfandel, Mission.
Cram, L. F.	San Bernardino								Muscat.
Davidson, Capt. A. S.	San Bernardino	80	80	80					Muscat.
Douring, J. P.	San Bernardino								Zinfandel, Riesling, Mission, Burger.
Drew, H. L.	San Bernardino	12	12	10		2			
Haight, J. B.	San Bernardino								Muscat.
Harmon, S. W.	San Bernardino								
Hicks, Mrs.	San Bernardino								
Kene, Dr.	San Bernardino								Muscat.
Palmer, S. E. A.	San Bernardino								
Schimp, Adolph	San Bernardino								
Sommers, ——	San Bernardino								Muscat.
Waterman, Governor.	San Bernardino								Muscat.
Weis, ——	San Bernardino								
Whitney, J. J.	San Bernardino								Muscat.
Totals for county		3,615	3,615	1,024		2,691			

SAN DIEGO COUNTY.

Name of Owner	Post Office and Name of Vineyard	Total Acres in Grapes	Acres in Bearing	Acres in Wine Grapes	Acres in Table Grapes	Acres in Raisin Grapes	Wine Maker	Product in 1889	Varieties
Campbell, E. L.	Alpine	10	10			10	No.		Muscat.
Hereford, Dr.	Alpine	10	10			10	No.		Muscat.
High Bros.	Alpine	12	12			12	No.		Muscat.
Michler, Dr.	Alpine	6	5			6	No.		Muscat.
Nugent, Dr.	Alpine	17	17	7		10	No.		Muscat, Zinfandel.
Pontius, Dr.	Alpine	8	8			8	No.		Muscat.
Snow, ——	Alpine	4	4			4	No.		Muscat.
Wood, C. M.	Alpine								Muscat.
Sikes, H. A.	Bernardo	8	8			8	No.		Muscat.

SAN DIEGO COUNTY—Continued.

Name of Owner	Post Office and Name of Vineyard	Total Acres in Grapes	Acres in Bearing	Acres in Wine Grapes	Acres in Table Grapes	Acres in Raisin Grapes	Wine Maker	Product in 1889	Varieties
Brower, H.	Dehesia	6				6	No.		Muscat.
Davis, E.	Dehesia	10	5			10	No.		Muscat.
Greg Bros.	Dehesia	4	4			4	No.		Muscat.
Hartley, M. D. L.	Dehesia	8	8			8	No.		Muscat.
McFarlan, J. R.	Dehesia	28	28		6	22	No.		Muscat.
Sheldon, D. S.	Dehesia	25	25			25	No.		Muscat.
Starr, W. E.	Dehesia	10	10			10	No.		Muscat.
Sykes, G. W.	Dehesia	17	17			14	No.		Muscat.
Tuttle, Amos	Dehesia	10	10		3	10	No.		Muscat, Black Morocco.
Weed, H. N.	Dehesia	8	8			8	No.		Muscat.
Achard, P.	El Cajon	7	7			7	No.		Muscat.
Allen, R. C.	El Cajon	30	30			30	No.		Muscat.
Allingham, Wm	El Cajon	30	30			30	No.		Muscat.
Asher, J. M.	El Cajon	9	9			9	No.		Muscat.
Avery, E.	El Cajon	35	35			35	No.		Muscat.
Banett, S. W.	El Cajon	25	25			25	No.		Muscat.
Bowers, G.	El Cajon	55	55	5		55	No.		Sultana, Zinfandel.
Brayton,	El Cajon	25	25			20	No.		Muscat, Zinfandel.
Chase, Major L.	El Cajon (San Diego)	70	70		15	55	No.		Muscat, Rose Peru, Tokay, Black Hamburg, Sultana.
Christian, H. D.	El Cajon	15	15			15	No.		Muscat.
Cogswell, Dr. Thos. A.	El Cajon	3	3			3	No.		Muscat.
Conklin, N. H.	El Cajon	12	12			12	No.		Muscat.
Covert, Miss.	El Cajon	18	18			18	No.		Muscat.
Cowles Estate	El Cajon	210	210			210	No.		Muscat.
Cox, S. J.	El Cajon	12	12			12	No.		Muscat.
Crosby & Souther	Boston R'nch, El Cajon	586	586			586	No.		Muscat.
Crosby, W. S.	El Cajon (Boston)	60	60			60	No.		Muscat.
Culbertson, H.	El Cajon	12	12			12	No.		Muscat.
Dabney, H.	El Cajon	52	52			52	No.		Muscat.
Davis, E. P.	El Cajon (Boston)	30	30			80	No.		Muscat.
Drullard, H. K.	El Cajon (Boston)	120	120			120	No.		Muscat.
Dunham, H. W.	El Cajon (Boston)	10	10			10	No.		Muscat.
Ferguson, —	El Cajon	4	4			4	No.		Muscat.

Name	Location				(Zinf.)	No.	Variety
Folsom, Dr.	El Cajon (Boston)	50	50	50		No.	Muscat.
Folsom, Miss A.	El Cajon (Boston)	20	20	20		No.	Muscat.
Folsom, Miss E.	El Cajon (Boston)	20	20	20		No.	Muscat.
Folsom, Miss P.	El Cajon (Boston)	10	10	10		No.	Muscat.
Folsom, Mrs.	El Cajon (Boston)	20	20	20		No.	Muscat.
Gilbert, A. W.	El Cajon	40	40	40		No.	Muscat.
Goetze, Wm.	El Cajon	10	10	10		No.	Muscat.
Gordon, J. F.	El Cajon	125	125	125		No.	Muscat.
Gray, Mrs. J. S.	El Cajon (Boston)	6	6	6		No.	Muscat.
Guy, W. R.	El Cajon	20	20	20		No.	Muscat.
Hale, F. W.	El Cajon (Boston)	50	50	50		No.	Muscat.
Hall, J. P.	El Cajon (Boston)	40	40	40		No.	Muscat.
Hancock, Nelson	El Cajon	10	10	10		No.	Muscat.
Harbaugh, A. G.	El Cajon (Boston)	35	35	35		No.	Muscat.
Hawley, A. W.	El Cajon	35	35	35		No.	Muscat.
Hawley, G. M.	El Cajon	18	18	18		No.	Muscat.
Hawley, Guy	El Cajon	10	10	10		No.	Muscat.
Hawley, W. D.	El Cajon	10	10	10		No.	Muscat.
Hill, Uri	El Cajon (Boston)	15	15	15	5	No.	Muscat, Zinfandel.
Hoffman, Dr.	El Cajon	5	5	5		No.	Muscat.
Holt, G. H.	El Cajon	175	175	175		No.	Muscat.
Hovey, Mrs. M.	El Cajon (Boston)	90	90	90		No.	Muscat.
Johnson, C. M.	El Cajon	125	125	125		No.	Muscat.
Lewis, Dr.	El Cajon	10	10	10		No.	Muscat.
McFadden, D. B.	El Cajon	7	7	7	10	No.	Muscat, Zinfandel.
McKoon, B. P.	El Cajon	30	30	30		No.	Muscat.
McKoon, M. P.	El Cajon (Boston)	3	3	3		No.	Muscat.
Mansfield, Miss S.	El Cajon	10	10	10		No.	Muscat.
Marshall, S. M.	El Cajon	125	125	125		No.	Muscat.
Martin, Jas.	El Cajon	6	6	6		No.	Muscat.
Mason, J.	El Cajon	15	15	15		No.	Muscat.
Millar, T. F.	El Cajon	10	10	10		No.	Muscat.
Moody,	El Cajon	5	5	5		No.	Muscat.
Murdock,	El Cajon	7	7	7		No.	Muscat.
Nichols, F. L.	El Cajon	20	20	20		No.	Muscat.
Ogden, D.	El Cajon	20	20	20		No.	Zinfandel.
Overmeyer, N.	El Cajon	100	100	100		No.	Muscat.
Peel, W. C.	El Cajon	50	50	50		No.	Muscat.
Pennell, Mrs.	El Cajon	40	40	40		No.	Muscat.
Puttenhan,	El Cajon (Boston)	10	10	10	9	No.	Muscat, Zinfandel.
Richards, C. S.	El Cajon	200	200	200		No.	Muscat.
Richards, Kimball & Stewart	El Cajon	6	15	15		No.	Muscat, Zinfandel.
Scott, W. W.	El Cajon	80	80	80		No.	Muscat.
Shepard, Mrs.	El Cajon	30	30	30		No.	Muscat.

9—v

San Diego County—Continued.

Name of Owner.	Post Office and Name of Vineyard.	Total Acres in Grapes.	Acres in Bearing.	Acres in Wine Grapes.	Acres in Table Grapes.	Acres in Raisin Grapes.	Wine Maker.	Product in 1889.	Varieties.
Somers, W. H.	El Cajon	11	11			11	No.		Muscat.
Steele, Mrs. E. B.	El Cajon (Elmira, N.Y)	20	20			20	No.		Muscat.
Stevens, W. J.	El Cajon	6	6			6	No.		Muscat.
Walker, A.	El Cajon	7	7			7	No.		Muscat.
Walker, Theo.	El Cajon	7	7			7	No.		Muscat.
Weddle, M. P.	El Cajon	40	40		10	30	No.		Mataro, Muscat, Trousseau.
Weston, S. C.	El Cajon	8	8			8	No.		Muscat.
Worcester, Dr.	El Cajon	10	10			10	Yes.		Muscat, Carignan.
Abrams, J.	Escondido	6	8	2		4	No.		Muscat.
Calloway, C.	Escondido	8	8			8	No.		Muscat.
Collins, Mrs. C.	Escondido	8	8			8	No.		Muscat.
Dickson, J. C.	Escondido	10	10			10	No.		Muscat.
Escondido Town and Land Company	Escondido	70	70			70	No.		Muscat.
Heffelman, S. E.	Escondido	18	18			18	No.		Muscat.
Keniston, D.	Escondido	14	14	2		12	No.		Muscat.
Merriam, Ed. A.	Escondido	40	40			40	No.		
Oaks, O.	Escondido	12	12			12	No.		Muscat.
Shutt, P. M.	Escondido	10	10			10	No.		Muscat.
Thomas, R. A.	Escondido	3	3		1	2	No.		Table grapes.
Walsh, William	Escondido	16	16	6		10	Yes.		
Walker, J. W., for Haegler	Escondido	22	22	4	2	16	No.		Six or seven varieties.
Withington, D. L.	Escondido	5	5		1	5	No.		Muscat.
Wooldredge, Wm. D.	Escondido	20	20			19	No.		Eight varieties table grapes.
Barrett, W. H.	Jamul	10	10			10	No.		Table grapes.
Ferguson, W. D.	Jamul	10	10			10	No.		Table grapes.
Hernon, B.	Jamul	5	5			5	No.		Eight varieties table grapes.
Maxfield, D. C.	Jamul	5	5			5	No.		Table grapes.
Maxfield, G. L.	Jamul	8	8			8	No.		Table grapes.
Page, W.	Jamul	4	4			4	No.		Table grapes.
Saxton, W. R.	Jamul	6	6			6	No.		Table grapes.
Ferry, W. H.	Lakeside	40	40			40	No.		Table grapes.
Francisco, C. F.	Lakeside	20	20			20	No.		Table grapes.

Name	Location	Acres in vines	Acres bearing	Acres not bearing	Wine made	Varieties
Hill, B.	Lakeside	30	15	15	Yes.	Zinfandel, Muscat, Mataro.
Winchester, J.	Lakeside	10	10		No.	Muscat.
Frisbie, J. C.	Mission Valley	6	6		No.	Muscat.
Jacques, ——	Mission Valley	20	20		No.	Muscat.
Schorlenberg, F. S.	Mission Valley	20	20		No.	Muscat.
Tomlins, M.	Moosa	12	12		No.	Muscat.
Clark, S. W.	Otay	4	4		No.	Muscat.
Perry, S. D.	Otay	10	10		No.	Muscat.
Wolsey, ——	Otay	5	5		No.	Muscat.
Chilson, Miss Ella	Palm Valley	10	10		No.	Muscat.
Hawley & Wheaton	Palm Valley	15	15		No.	Muscat.
Hawley, C. E.	Palm Valley	10	10		No.	Muscat.
McCullum, J. G.	Palm Valley	15	15		No.	Muscat.
Palmdale Land Co.	Palm Valley	110	110		No.	Muscat.
Twogood, A. J.	Palm Valley	16	16		No.	Muscat.
Twogood & Cutter	Palm Valley	10	10		No.	Muscat.
Nance, J. W.	Perris	4	4		No.	Muscat.
Ryder, B. H.	Perris	10	10		No.	Muscat.
Whiting, J.	Perris	6	6		No.	Muscat.
Bowron, S.	Poway	2	2		No.	Muscat.
Campbell, J. C.	Poway	10	10		No.	Muscat.
Cambron, T. G.	Poway	10	10			Muscat.
Dearboon, Mrs. L. G.	Poway	8	8			Muscat.
Fikas, L.	Poway	5	5		No.	Muscat.
Gilbert, C. G.	Poway	6	6		No.	Muscat.
Hartzell, T. B.	Poway	3	3		No.	Muscat.
Havermale, S. G.	Poway	6	6		No.	Muscat.
Hilleray, Dr. L. N.	Poway	40	40		No.	Muscat.
Hilleray, Wm.	Poway	2	2		No.	Muscat.
Kent, Horace	Poway	20	20		No.	Muscat.
Leicester, Mrs.	Poway	10	10		No.	Muscat.
Lynch, Captain L.	Poway	20	20		No.	Muscat.
Mayhew, T.	Poway	6	6		No.	Muscat.
Nelson, Niles	Poway	6	6		No.	Muscat.
Parnell, G. W.	Poway	2	2			Muscat.
Rickey, J. H.	Poway	3	3		No.	Muscat.
Savage, C. C.	Poway	12	12		No.	Muscat.
Sikes, H.	Poway	15	15		No.	Muscat.
Watson. C. C.	Poway	20	20		No.	Muscat.
Camp, Wm. B.	San Marcos	8	8		Yes.	Four varieties wine grapes.
Carpenter, Alex.	San Marcos	14	14		No.	Muscat.
Crawford, T. R.	San Pasqual	12	12		No.	Muscat.
Johnson, L. O.	San Pasqual	18	13	5	No.	Muscat.
Olds Bros.	San Pasqual	13	13		Yes.	Mission, Sweetwater.
Storm, F. R.	San Pasqual	30	28	1	No.	Muscat.

San Diego County—Continued.

Name of Owner.	Post Office and Name of Vineyard.	Total Acres in Grapes.	Acres in Bearing.	Acres in Wine Grapes.	Acres in Table Grapes.	Acres in Raisin Grapes.	Wine Maker.	Product in 1889.	Varieties.
Thompson, W. F.	San Pasqual	12	12	...	...	12	No.	...	Muscat.
Winn, Wm.	San Pasqual	12	12	...	...	12	No.	...	Muscat.
Wolfe, Geo. W., Jr.	San Pasqual	20	20	...	...	20	No.	...	Muscat.
Cochrans, P.	Twin Oaks	6	6	...	...	6	No.	...	Muscat.
Harrison, Jno. V.	Twin Oaks	12	12	...	...	12	No.	...	Muscat.
Kuchel Bros.	Twin Oaks	28	28	16	...	12	Yes.	...	Muscat, Grenache, Mataro.
McDougall, C. A.	Twin Oaks	18	18	...	...	18	Yes.	...	
Merriam, G. F.	Twin Oaks	65	65	45	1	19	Yes.	...	Forty-five varieties.
Richards, E. L.	Twin Oaks	4	4	...	...	4	No.	...	Muscat.
Wheland, J.	Twin Oaks	8	8	...	...	8	No.	...	Muscat.
Wilcox, J.	Twin Oaks	4	4	...	...	4	No.	...	Muscat.
Fraser, James	Valley Center	15	15	...	...	15	No.	...	Muscat.
Huckaby, D.	Valley Center	14	14	...	...	14	No.	...	Muscat.
Moore, John W.	Valley Center	5	5	...	...	5	No.	...	Muscat.
Totals for county		4,627	4,423	132	40	4,445			

San Joaquin County.

Name of Owner.	Post Office and Name of Vineyard.	Total Acres in Grapes.	Acres in Bearing.	Acres in Wine Grapes.	Acres in Table Grapes.	Acres in Raisin Grapes.	Wine Maker.	Product in 1889.	Varieties.
Hammond, R. G.	Lockeford	5	5	5	...	...	...	...	...
Beckman, H. F.	Lodi	5	5	5	...	...	...	...	...
Beckman, William	Lodi	5	5	5	...	...	...	...	...
Bishofberger, J.	Lodi	5	5	5	...	...	...	...	...

Name	Post Office					Remarks
Franklin, Mrs. E.	Lodi		80	80	80	Yes.
Langford, B. F.	Lodi		5	5	5	
Lawrence, Q.	Lodi		2	2	2	
Mowry, L.	Lodi	10	5	5	5	
Shindy, M. W.	Lodi	5	5	5	5	
Smart, D. M.	Lodi		5	5	5	
Alling, N. E.	Stockton		20	20	20	
Anderson, C. M.	Stockton	40	5	5	5	
Archer, John	Stockton		5	40	40	
Armbrust, Henry	Stockton		5	5	5	
Barynan, A. G.	Stockton		10	5	5	
Beer, John	Stockton	5	20	20	20	
Bidwell, C. W.	Stockton		5	5	5	
Bishop, H. B.	Stockton	5	10	10	10	
Bonham, A. L.	Stockton		10	10	10	
Brown, B. H.	Stockton	40	5	5	5	
Campodonica, G.	Stockton		40	40	40	
Clowes, E. C.	Stockton	5	5	5	5	
Cobb, Chas.	Stockton	40	10	10	10	
Corcoran, F. J.	Stockton		13	13	13	
Corella, G.	Stockton		10	10	10	
Fiske, Ezra	Stockton	10	28	28	28	
Fitch, H. B.	Stockton		10	10	10	
Fitzgerald, P.	Stockton		25	25	25	Yes.
Fopiano, G.	Stockton		5	5	5	
Gale, J. D.	Stockton	5	5	5	5	
Galgaini, V.	Stockton		20	20	20	
Gambetta, J.	Stockton	10	10	10	10	
Gerlach, L.	Stockton		8	8	8	
Haas, Chas.	Stockton		10	10	10	
Hammond, A.	Stockton		5	5	5	
Hewlett, Samuel	Stockton		13	13	13	
Hollenstein, J.	Stockton	10	10	10	10	
Keiver, D. W.	Stockton		10	10	10	
Klipple, G. W.	Stockton		10	10	10	
Klipple, J.	Stockton	10	20	20	20	Yes.
Ladd, G. S.	Stockton	4	4	8	8	
Lagario, D., D., & Co.	Stockton		5	5	5	
Lang, John	Stockton	8	2	10	10	
Learned, Dr. A.	Stockton	8		8	8	
Leffler, R. G.	Stockton		5	5	5	
Lewis, J.	Stockton		5	5	5	
Long, C. C.	Stockton	5	5	5	5	
Looper, W. C.	Stockton		5	·		
Loveland, D. W.	Stockton		5	5	5	

SAN JOAQUIN COUNTY—Continued.

Name of Owner.	Post Office and Name of Vineyard.	Total Acres in Grapes.	Acres in Bearing.	Acres in Wine Grapes.	Acres in Table Grapes.	Acres in Raisin Grapes.	Wine Maker.	Product in 1889.	Varieties
McIntosh, E. J.	Stockton	5	5	5					
Marks, H.	Stockton	27	27	27					
Marks, M.	Stockton	27	27	27					
Meyers, Mrs. Samuel	Stockton	6	6	4	2				
Moore, John E.	Stockton	70	70	50	20				
Moore, S.	Stockton	5	5		5				
Musto, P.	Stockton						Yes.		
Norton, C. W.	Stockton	10	10		10				
Overheiser, W. I.	Stockton	8	8	4	4				
Peccardio, G.	Stockton	20	20	15	5				
Podesta, G.	Stockton	7	7		5				
Prato, D.	Stockton	10	10		10				
Root, N. T.	Stockton						Yes.		
Rothenbusch, D.	Stockton	20	20	20					
Salbach, E.	Stockton	50	50	30	20				
Sanguinetti, S.	Stockton	10	10	10					
Smith, J. C.	Stockton	10	10	10					
Smith, R. R.	Stockton	5	5		5				
Sperry, G. B.	Stockton	5	5		5				
Siagnaro, A.	Stockton	15	15	15					
Stephens, T. J.	Stockton	7	7	7					
Strait, S. Y.	Stockton	5	5	5					
Thomas, A. C.	Stockton	5	5		5				
Tull, T. C.	Stockton	55	55	55					
Von Detten, C.	Stockton	5	5		5		Yes.		
Ward, W. R.	Stockton								
West, Frank A.	Stockton	100	100	80	20				
West, Geo.	Stockton	70	70	50	20		Yes.		
West, W. B.	Stockton	6	6	5			Yes.		
Young, Mrs.	Stockton	30	30	15	15				
Zingrego, J. C.	Stockton	9	9	9					
Zingrego, M.	Stockton	8	8	8					
Aldrich, J.	Woodbridge	7	7	7					
Fowler, J. M.	Woodbridge								

		Total Acres in Grapes	Acres in Bearing	Acres in Wine Grapes	Acres in Table Grapes	Acres in Raisin Grapes	Wine Maker	Product in 1889	Varieties
Franklin, Chris. C.	Woodbridge	10	10	10					
Gillingham,	Woodbridge	5	5	5					
Parrott Bros.	Woodbridge	20	20	15	5				
Shattuck, H. C.	Woodbridge	3	8	8					
Thompson, John	Woodbridge	10	10	5	5				
Totals for county		1,246	1,146	900	346				

SAN LUIS OBISPO COUNTY.

NAME OF OWNER.	Post Office and Name of Vineyard	Total Acres in Grapes	Acres in Bearing	Acres in Wine Grapes	Acres in Table Grapes	Acres in Raisin Grapes	Wine Maker	Product in 1889	Varieties
Ernst, John	Creston	22	10	8	14		Yes.		Zinfandel.
Ernst, William	Creston	15	12	14	1		Yes.	800 tons.	Mataro, Carignan.
Ernst Bros.	Creston	20	10	5	-15				Zinfandel, Muscat.
Webster, J. V.	Creston								
Other smaller vineyards	Creston								
Black, John	Huasna								
De Neergard, Louis	La Panza	40	40	40			No.		
Hasbrouck, A. B.	Musick								
Meachum, J.	Musick								
Andrews, J. P.	San Luis Obispo	10	10	10			No.		
Correa, Mrs. F.	San Luis Obispo	3	3	3			No.		
Castro, Mrs. R.	San Luis Obispo	2	2	2			No.		
Cervantes, Mrs.	San Luis Obispo	2	2	2			No.		
Corbutt, J.	San Luis Obispo	14	14	11	3		No.		
Dallidet, H. P.	San Luis Obispo	90	90	90			Yes.		
Goldtree Bros.	San Luis Obispo	4		4			Yes.	4,000 gals.	Zinfandel, Riesling.
Guillemin, F.	San Luis Obispo	1	1			1	Yes.		
Hampton, Geo. W.	San Luis Obispo						Yes.		
Harloe, Capt.	San Luis Obispo	80	65	15			Yes.		
Hays, W. W.	San Luis Obispo						Yes.		Muscat, Mataro, Black Morocco, Zinfandel, Chasselas. Mission.
Hollister, J. H., & Co.	San Luis Obispo	14	14	14			No.		
Johnson, Chas. H.	San Luis Obispo	3					No.		
Johnson, J. J.	San Luis Obispo	3							

SAN LUIS OBISPO COUNTY—Continued.

NAME OF OWNER.	Post Office and Name of Vineyard.	Total Acres in Grapes.	Acres in Bearing.	Acres in Wine Grapes.	Acres in Table Grapes.	Acres in Raisin Grapes.	Wine Maker.	Product in 1889.	Varieties.
Kurtz, A. M.	San Luis Obispo	8	8	8			No.		
McCoppin, Frank	San Luis Obispo	40	40	40			No.		
Maxwell, L.	San Luis Obispo	10	10	10					
Minoli, L.	San Luis Obispo	2					No.		
Quintana, P.	San Luis Obispo	4					No.		
Steele, George	San Luis Obispo	10							
Anderson, J. R.	Templeton	12	12	12			Yes.		Zinfandel, Burger.
Mathews, D. J.	Templeton	5	5	5			No.		Zinfandel, Burger.
Palmer, S. G.	Templeton	15	15	15			No.	50 tons.	Zinfandel, Burger.
York, A.	Templeton	40	30	40			Yes.	60 tons.	Zinfandel, Burger.
Totals for county		471	421	437	38	1			

There are also about twelve acres additional in Templeton, in small lots of from one quarter of an acre to one acre.

SAN MATEO COUNTY.

NAME OF OWNER.	Post Office and Name of Vineyard.	Total Acres in Grapes.	Acres in Bearing.	Acres in Wine Grapes.	Acres in Table Grapes.	Acres in Raisin Grapes.	Wine Maker.	Product in 1889.	Varieties.
Bruno, Owen	Belmont (San Fran.)	20	20	20			No.		Zinfandel.
Cerasco, B.	Belmont (San Fran.)	35	35	35			No.		Zinfandel.
Frapoli, B., estate of	Belmont (San Fran.)	30	30	30			Yes.		Zinfandel.
Mezes, S. M., estate of	Belmont	4	4		4		No.		Mixed.
Scalmanini, C., est. of	Belmont (San Fran.)	82	82	82			Yes.		Zinfandel, Burgundy, Malvoisie.
Kibler, John	Coast Range	1½			1½				Mixed, mostly Muscat.

Name	Location						Resistant	Varieties.
Munro & Peters	Buckhorn Farm, Coast Range.	6			5	1		Zinfandel, Sweetwater, Muscat.
Nahmens, N. C.	Coast Range	2	2	2			No.	Zinfandel, Pinot.
Doyle, John T.	Menlo Park	36	36	36¼			Yes.	Mission.
Finger, A., estate of	Redwood City	2½		1			No.	Mixed, mostly Mission.
Hargan, ———	Redwood City	2	2	2				California stock grafted.
Smith, Andrew	Redwood City	12	12	12	1	1	No.	Zinfandel, Sultana, Black Hamburg, Muscat.
Titus, John	Redwood City	16	16	15			No.	Mission.
Barroilhet, H., estate of	San Mateo	4	4	3	1	1	No.	Mission.
Mahe, Gustave, est. of	San Mateo	55	55	55			No.	Mixed varieties.
Alexander, John K.	Searsville	4	4	4			No.	Mataro.
Allen, J. M.	Searsville (San Fran.)	7	7	7			No.	Mixed varieties.
Doyle, Morris	Searsville (San Fran.)	6	6	6			No.	Mixed varieties.
Hooper, J. A.	Searsville (San Fran.)	30	30	20	10		Yes.	Zinfandel and mixed wine and table varieties.
Jones, S. L., estate of	Searsville (San Fran.)	100	100	85		15	No.	Muscat and mixed varieties.
Kelley, Hugh	Searsville	8	8	8			Yes.	Zinfandel.
Lawler, Davis	Searsville	19	19	10			No.	Burgundy, Mataro, Zinfandel.
Martinez, Antonio	Searsville	13	13	13			No.	Malvoisie, Chasselas, Zinfandel.
Preston, E. F.	Searsville (San Fran.)	80	80	80			Yes.	Mataro, Riesling, Zinfandel, and others.
Rix, E. A.	Searsville (San Fran.)	20	20	17	3		No.	Seventeen acres in resistant stock and grafted, three in mixed.
Spring V. Water Co.	Searsville	5	5	3	2		No.	Mixed wine and table varieties.
Lane, ———	Woodside	20	20	18	2		Yes.	Zinfandel, Chasselas, Muscat, Malvoisie.
Rixford, E. H.	La Questa Vineyard, Woodside	5	5	5				Zinfandel.
Sickert & Billings	Woodside	160	Few.	160				Resistant grafted varieties.
Tripp, R. O.	Woodside	5¾	5½	5	2		Yes.	Chauche Noir, Muscat.
Totals for county		788½	604	142½	26	15		

SANTA BARBARA COUNTY.

Name of Owner.	Post Office and Name of Vineyard.	Total Acres in Grapes.	Acres in Bearing.	Acres in Wine Grapes.	Acres in Table Grapes.	Acres in Raisin Grapes.	Wine Maker.	Product in 1889.	Varieties.
Blood, ——	Carpenteria	4	4	4			No.		Mission.
Flood, ——	Carpenteria	2	2	2			No.		
Knapp, E. J.	Carpenteria						No.		Mission.
Sexton, Joseph	Goleta	4	4	4			No.		Mission.
Broughton, R. J.	Las Cruces						No.		Mission.
McLean, Hon. Alex.	Lompoc						No.		
Caire, Justinian	Santa Cruz Island (San Francisco).	60	60	60			Yes.		Zinfandel; other varieties as an experiment.
Arroqui, John	Santa Barbara	5	5	5			Yes.		Mission.
Archer, ——	Santa Barbara	2	2	2			No.		Mission.
Blake, F. A.	Santa Barbara	6	6		6		No.		Muscat, Olivet.
Byrister, ——	Santa Barbara	4	4	4			Yes.		Mission.
Caballeri, Nicholas	Santa Barbara	6	6	6			Yes.		Mission.
Charity, Sisters of.	Santa Barbara	2	2	2			No.		Mission.
Dreyfuss, I.	Santa Barbara	10	10	10			No.		Zinfandel.
Everett, ——	Santa Barbara	5	5	5			Yes.		Mission, Zinfandel.
Faber, George	Santa Barbara	2	2	2			No.		Mission.
Finch, Dr.	Santa Barbara	2	2	2			No.		Mission.
Franklin, ——	Santa Barbara	5	5	5			Yes.		Mission.
Grondona, D.	Santa Barbara	1	1	1			Yes.		Mission.
Garitson, G. M.	Santa Barbara						Yes.		
Gooduluch & Johnson	Santa Barbara						No.		
Goux, J. E.	Santa Barbara						No.		
Holden, Oscar	Santa Barbara	6	6	6			No.		Mission.
Hiller, J. N.	Santa Barbara	10	10	10			No.		Zinfandel.
Kincade, J. H.	Santa Barbara	5	5	5			No.		Mission.
Lavees, Wm.	Santa Barbara						Yes.		
Leet, Charles	Santa Barbara	3	3	3			Yes.		Mission.
Maguire, H.	Santa Barbara	5	5	5			No.		Mission.
McCaffrey, James	Santa Barbara						Yes.		
Miller, ——	Santa Barbara	5	5	5			No.		Mission.
Orata, G., estate of.	Santa Barbara						Yes.		
Owens, Wm.	Santa Barbara								Mission.
Packard, A.	Santa Barbara	40	40	40			Yes.		Mission.

Name of Owner	Post Office	Total Acres in Grapes	Acres in Bearing	Acres in Wine Grapes	Acres in Table Grapes	Acres in Raisin Grapes	Wine Maker	Product	Varieties
Pendola, G., estate of	Santa Barbara	5	5	5			Yes.		Mission.
Parma, G. B.	Santa Barbara	25	12	8	4		Yes.		Mission, Zinfandel, Tokay, Muscat, Black Hamburg, Black Morocco, Black Prince.
Botiller, P.	Santa Barbara	2	2	2			Yes.		Mission.
Sullivan,	Santa Barbara	2	2	2			No.		Mission, and many others.
Scull, ——	Santa Barbara	5	5	5			No.		Mission.
Santa Barbara Mission	Santa Barbara	4	4	4			No.		Mission.
Tucker, Dr.	Santa Barbara	1	1	1			No.		Mission.
Van Grasvold, F. J.	Santa Barbara						No.		
Williams, George	Santa Ynez	5	5	5			Yes.		Mission.
Birabent, J. M.	Santa Ynez	5	5	5			Yes.		Mission.
Junin, Louis	Santa Ynez	20	20	20			No.		Mission.
Moore, Thomas	Santa Ynez	4	4	4					
Totals for county		270	197	260	10				

SANTA CLARA COUNTY.

Name of Owner	Post Office and Name of Vineyard.	Total Acres in Grapes	Acres in Bearing	Acres in Wine Grapes	Acres in Table Grapes	Acres in Raisin Grapes	Wine Maker	Product	Varieties
Agnew, A.	Agnews	4	4	4			No.	11 tons, '90	
Bissell, Mrs. V.	Alma	5	5	3	2		No.	5 tons, '90	
Bishop, W. A.	Alma	40	30		40				
Carella, John	Alma	4	4	4			No.	12 tons, '89	
Chellman & Wilson	Alma	3½	3½	2	1½			12 tons, '89	
Frank, C. A.	Alma	2	2	2	2			7 tons, '89	
Grundell, Mrs. J. E.	Alma	4	4				No.		
Guidici, S. E.	Alma	5	5	3	2		Yes.	24 tons, '89	
Koppitts, John	Alma	4	2		4		No.		
Lane, Van	Alma	2		1	1		No.		
Loenn, J. S. & A. P.	Alma (San José)		38				Yes.	6 tons, '89	
McKiernan, Chas.	Alma	50		60			Yes.	26,000 gals.	Charbono, 20; Mataro, 5; Sauvignon Vert, 6; Chasselas, 7; Zinfandel, 5; Riesling, 7.
Miniss, Edward	Alma	6	6	6			Yes.	18 tons, '89	
Muender, Fred.	Alma	7	7	7			Yes.	28 tons, '89	
Moody, J. C.	Alma	2	2	1	1		No.	9 tons, '89	

Santa Clara County—Continued.

Name of Owner.	Post Office and Name of Vineyard.	Total Acres in Grapes.	Acres in Bearing.	Acres in Wine Grapes.	Acres in Table Grapes.	Acres in Raisin Grapes.	Wine Maker.	Product.	Varieties.
Rankin, W. B.	Alma	40	40	57	3		Yes.	160 tons, '89	
Reihl, E.	Alma	9	9	9			Yes.	32 tons, '9	
Runnels, L. T.	Alma	2	2		2		No.	8 tons, '89	Mataro, Charbono, Sauvignon Vert.
Robens & Tuzer	Alma	6	6	6	1		No.		
Schrader, Otto	Alma	3	3	5	2		No.	20 tons, '89	
Stewart, Henry	Alma	20	20	20			No.	10 tons, '89	
Scripture, H. D.	Alma	10	10	10			Yes.	20 tons, '90	
Sauffrignon, F. J.	Alma	1	1		1		No.	30 tons, '88	
Thompson, Nellie M.	Alma	7	7	6	1		No.	5 tons, '89	
Vall, Charles	Alma	4	4	2	2		No.	25 tons, '89	
Voight, R. F.	Alma	4	4	4	3		No.	12 tons, '88	
Weaver, H. S. & John.	Alma	48	48	45	3		No.	200 tons, '88	
Welcker, W. T.	Alma	20	20	18	2		No.	80 tons, '88	
Wale, Ed.	Alma (San José)	4	4	3	1		No.	13 tons, '89	
Burrell, E.	Aviso	4	4	4			No.	15 tons, '88	
Berryessa, Josephine	Berryessa	4	4	7	3		No.		
Cross, George	Berryessa	7	7	7	4		No.	10 tons, '89	
Prussing, E., estate of.	Berryessa	3	3				No.	16 tons, '88	
Randall, A.	Berryessa	4	4	2			No.	6 tons, '88	
Walter, H.	Berryessa	2	2	2	2		Yes.	35 tons, '89	
Kennedy, W.	Campbells	9	9	9	2		No.	20 tons, '89	
Kuth, P. W.	Campbells	4	4	4			No.	20 tons, '88	
Swope, W. H.	Campbells	5	5	3			No.	20 tons, '88	
Stevens, O.	Coyote	10	10	8			No.	40 tons, '88	
Weber, Charles M.	Coyote	30	30	30			No.	120 tons, '89	
Anthony, F. M.	Cupertino	20	20	20			No.	65 tons, '90	
Baird, Percival	Cupertino	33	33	33			No.	125 tons, '90	
Byrne, G. J.	Cupertino (Glenbrook)	6	5	5			No.	25 tons, '90	
Bowden, M. C.	Cupertino	10	10			10	No.	40 tons, '90	
Cupertino Wine Co.	Cupertino	200	200	200			Yes.	800 tons, '90	Claret varieties. (University experiment block.)
Crossley, J. P.	Cupertino	40	40	40	2		No.	65 tons, '89	
Etchell, Samuel	Cupertino	40	40	38				150 tons, '81	
Graff, W. R.	Cupertino	20	20	20			No.	65 tons, '89	
Kirwin, T. K.	Cupertino	70	70	69	1		No.	315 tons, '90	

Name	Location							
Merithew, J. C.	Cupertino (San José)	40	40	40		5	Yes.	230 tons, '80
McClellan, J.	Cupertino	10	10	10		10	No.	40 tons, '89
Pringle, E. J.	Cupertino							
Raffa, O.	Cupertino							
Sellenger, L.	Cupertino	12	12	12			No.	52 tons, '88
Stelling, W. C.	Cupertino	30	30	30			No.	150 tons, '88
Stelling, John	Cupertino	10	10	10			No.	45 tons, '88
Stelling, F. E.	Cupertino	8	8	8			No.	32 tons, '89
Sworels, Peter	Cupertino	10	10	10			No.	40 tons, '88
Williams, Ira	Cupertino	6	6	6			No.	22 tons, '88
Wood, A. H.	Cupertino	28	28	28			No.	30 tons, '90
Williams, S. R.	Cupertino	25	25	25			Yes.	150 tons, '89
Williams, J. D.	Cupertino	37	37	37	6		Yes.	160 tons, '89
Bingham & Edwards	Evergreen	18	18	18			No.	75 tons, '88
Carroll, E.	Evergreen	62	62	62			No.	190 tons, '90
Chaboyer, Ramon	Evergreen	22	22	22			No.	70 tons, '89
Fuller, D. B.	Evergreen	7	7	7			No.	25 tons, '89
Fowler, A. J.	Evergreen	12	12	12	2	10	No.	60 tons, '88
Knight, W. A.	Evergreen	7	7	7			No.	25 tons, '89
Klink, Henry & John	Evergreen	10	10	10			No.	40 tons, '89
Lautz, J. W.	Evergreen	16	16	16			No.	42 tons, '88
Melcher, E. O.	Evergreen (San José)	8	8	8			Yes.	25 tons, '88
Pellier, P.	Evergreen	50	50	50			No.	250 tons, '89
Pratt, Anna M.	Evergreen (San José)	12	12	12			No.	45 tons, '88
Quimby, Irene K.	Evergreen	30	30	30			Yes.	100 tons, '88
Renaud, Leo.	Evergreen	10	10	10			No.	40 tons, '89
Smith, C. C., Jr.	Evergreen	20	20	20			No.	75 tons, '89
Snyder, Jacob	Evergreen	28	28	28		5	No.	100 tons, '89
Stevens, H. L.	Evergreen	5	5	5			No.	30 tons, '89
Vail, F. N.	Evergreen	22	22	22			Yes.	70 tons, '88
Wehner, Wm.	Highland Vineyard, Evergreen.	110	110	110			Yes.	100 tons, '90
Arnerich, Mrs. E.	Frohm	35	35	35			Yes.	110 tons, '90
Cros, Maria.	Frohm	25	25	25			No.	70 tons, '89
Robinson, Graham	Frohm	12	12	12			No.	40 tons, '89
Simonet, B. C.	Frohm	20	20	20			Yes.	75 tons, '89
Atkinson, Sarah	Gilroy	3	3	3			No.	12 tons, '90
Anson, George	Gilroy	2	2	2	1		Yes.	8 tons, '89
Cordes, P. H.	Gilroy	12	12	12	2		Yes.	50 tons, '90
Cuzard, J.	Gilroy	30	30	30			Yes.	120 tons, '89
Dowdy, John	Gilroy	20	20	20				66 tons, '89
Eckhardt, C. F.	Gilroy	7	7	7			Yes.	25 tons, '88
Francois, Mrs. A.	Gilroy	60	60	60	2			200 tons, '89
Gruwell, John G.	Gilroy	3	3	3	1		Yes.	10 tons, '80
Hagne, John	Gilroy	50	50	50			Yes.	250 tons, '89

SANTA CLARA COUNTY—Continued.

Name of Owner.	Post Office and Name of Vineyard.	Total Acres in Grapes.	Acres in Bearing.	Acres in Wine Grapes.	Acres in Table Grapes.	Acres in Raisin Grapes.	Wine Maker.	Product.	Varieties.
Hartshorn, Wm.	Gilroy	4	4	2	2		No.	20 tons, '89	
Lewis, Mrs. M. A.	Gilroy	6	6	6			No.	20 tons, '89	
O'Toole, Isabella	Gilroy	35	35	35			No.	120 tons, '89	
Specht, Fred.	Gilroy	10	10	10					
Wilson, Darsen	Gilroy	10	10	10					
Wise, John H.	Gilroy	28	26	26		2	No.	35 tons, '89	
Bubb, J. P.	Gubserville	56	56	54			Yes.	80 tons, '88	Cabernet Franc, Mataro, Charbono, Muscat.
Bucknall, W. C.	Gubserville	14	14	14			Yes.	280 tons, '89	Zinfandel, Burger, Chasselas.
Cox, William	Gubserville	4	4	2	2		No.	63 tons, '90	Zinfandel, Mataro, Muscat.
Coil, Alex.	Gubserville	4	4	4			No.	14 tons, '89	
Davidson, H.	Gubserville	20	20	20			No.	110 tons, '90	Zinfandel, Charbono, Mataro, Muscat.
Farr, Henry	Gubserville	45	45	45	4		Yes.	200 tons, '90	Zinfandel, Charbono, Malvoisie, Chasselas, Muscat.
Gruwell, M. L.	Gubserville	22	22	21	1		No.	125 tons, '89	
Groves, Jacob, estate of	Gubserville	5	5	5			No.	20 tons, '89	
Hall, Mary F.	Gubserville	15	15	15			No.	50 tons, '89	
Hanrahan, J.	Gubserville	13	13	13			No.	90 tons, '90	
Lord, T. J.	Gubserville	20	20	20			No.	80 tons, '89	
Lester, Eli, estate of	Gubserville								
Lequesne, E.	Gubserville	20	20	18	2		No.	100 tons, '89	
Mitchell, T. M.	Gubserville	17	17	17			Yes.	70 tons, '89	
Pfeffer, Wm.	Gubserville						Yes.		Cabernet Franc, Cabernet Sauvignon, Mataro, Carignan, Grenache, Sauterne varieties.
Ravenna, V.	Gubserville	30	30	30			Yes.	120 tons, '89	
Spangenberg, F.	Gubserville	6	6	6			No.	28 tons, '89	
Santos, Manuel S.	Gubserville	3	3	3			Yes.	15 tons, '89	
Sereghelli, S.	Gubserville	13	13	8	5		No.	40 tons, '89	Zinfandel, Muscat.
Scharff, J. J.	Gubserville	15	15	15			No.	50 tons, '89	
Snively, D.	Gubserville	14	14	14			No.	40 tons, '89	Mataro, Grenache, Charbono.
Vandepier, J. G.	Gubserville	14	14	14			No.	40 tons, '89	
Westlake, J. F.	Gubserville	15	15	15			No.	38 tons, '89	Zinfandel, Mataro, Charbono, Muscat.
Westlake, C.	Gubserville	26	26	18	8		No.	160 tons, '90	Mataro, Carignan, Grenache, Pinot.
Westlake & Co.	Gubserville	32	32	32			No.	97 tons, '90	
Dunn, Capt. Frank.	Lawrence	18	18	18			No.	50 tons, '89	6 acres Malbec; 12 acres Cabernet.

Name	P. O.					Cellar	Product	Varieties
Enright, James	Lawrence	8	8	8	3		30 tons, '89	
Jackson, W. E.	Lawrence	9	9	9		No.	45 tons, '89	
King & Morgans	Lawrence	9	9	9		No.	35 tons, '89	
Milliken, Samuel	Lawrence	40	40	40			160 tons, '89	
Minor, Chas. F.	Lawrence	7	7	7		Yes.	37 tons, '89	Zinfandel, Golden Chasselas.
Norcross, G. S.	Lawrence	6	6	6		Yes.	25 tons, '89	
Nichols, Chas. P.	Lawrence	12	12	12		Yes.	18 tons, '89	
Perini, Gutarde	Lawrence					No.		
Tuck, H. F.	Lawrence	21	21	21	1	No.	40 tons, '90	
Withicombe, J.	Lawrence	4	4	4	3	Yes.	15 tons, '89	
Walker, W. W.	Lone Oak Ranch	12	12	12	3	No.	42 tons, '89	Black Malvoisie, Zinfandel, Sauvignon Vert.
Austin, Mrs. C. N.	Los Gatos	2¾	2¾	2¾		No.	6 tons, '90	
Boynton, B. F.	Los Gatos	8	8	8		No.	30 tons, '90	
Black, T. K.	Los Gatos	2	2	2		No.	7 tons, '90	
Baker, Thos.	Los Gatos	6	6	6	6	No.	24 tons, '90	Muscat, Rose Peru.
Blair, J. N.	Los Gatos	6	6	6	1	No.	20 tons, '90	
Beedle, Chas.	Los Gatos	3	3	3	3	No.	12 tons, '90	
Baker, F. H.	Los Gatos	4	4	4		No.	11 tons, '90	
Belinge, F. A. A.	Los Gatos (S. F.)	3	3	3	1	No.		
Blakey, E. H.	Los Gatos	3	3	3		No.		
Brewston, John	Los Gatos	7	7	7		No.	18 tons, '89	
Baker, A. T.	Los Gatos	5	5	5	2	No.	7 tons, '90	
Benoit, Mrs. C. M.	Los Gatos	2	2	2		No.		
Brandenberg, H. H. & C. H.	Los Gatos	8	8	8	4	No.	30 tons, '90	
Cushion, E. C.	Los Gatos	4	4	4		No.	100 tons, '89	Zinfandel, Charbono, Black Pinot.
Corben, Chas.	Los Gatos	30	30	30		No.	20 tons, '89	
Carter Bros.	Los Gatos	5	5	5	2	No.	90 tons, '89	
Chittenden, Mrs. A. E.	Los Gatos	10	10	10		Yes.	95 tons, '90	
Cilker, John	Los Gatos	28	28	28		Yes.		
Coöperative Winery, Los Gatos.								
Conroy, John	Los Gatos	8	8	8		No.	28 tons, '90	
Desmarais, Louis	Los Gatos	2	2	2		Yes.	8 tons, '89	
Decker, C. M.	Los Gatos	5	5	5		No.	8 tons, '89	
Denehy, Jeremiah	Los Gatos	3	3	3		No.	18 tons, '89	
Ellis, J. E.	Los Gatos	15	15	15	10	No.	12 tons, '89	
Erickson, John	Los Gatos	8	8	8		No.	45 tons, '89	
Edwards, W. S.	Los Gatos	3	3	3	3	No.	20 tons, '89	
Ewen, W. D.	Los Gatos	2	2	2	2	No.	12 tons, '89	
Foster, J.	Los Gatos	17	17	17	7	No.	7 tons, '89	
Farley, D. J.	Los Gatos				1	No.	60 tons, '89	
Farley, E. C.	Los Gatos	3	3	3	1		12 tons, '89	Muscat, Rose Peru, Seedless Sultana, Riesling, Mataro, Malvoisie, etc.
Finley, H.	Los Gatos	4	4	4			15 tons, '89	Muscat, Tokay, Sultana, Zinfandel, Charbono.

SANTA CLARA COUNTY—Continued.

Name of Owner	Post Office and Name of Vineyard	Total Acres in Grapes	Acres in Bearing	Acres in Wine Grapes	Acres in Table Grapes	Acres in Raisin Grapes	Wine Maker	Product	Varieties
Francis, O. J.	Los Gatos	9	9	7	2		No.		Charbono, Zinfandel, Malvoisie, Chasselas, Muscat.
Grallman, C. M.	Los Gatos	3	3		3		No.	7 tons, '89	
Gist, J. A., estate of	Los Gatos	3	3		3		No.	2½ tons, '89	
Gadsil, John	Los Gatos	7	7	7			No.	8 tons, '89	
Hartman, Gustave	Los Gatos	2	2	2	2		No.	30 tons, '89	
Hill, Levi	Los Gatos	7	7	5	2		No.	40 tons, '89	
Hilton, E. F.	Los Gatos	12	12	10			No.	15 tons, '89	
Hay, W. A.	Los Gatos	4	4	4			No.	50 tons, '89	
Hulten, H.	Los Gatos	12	12	8	4		No.		
Hoffman, J. A.	Fairmount Farm, Los Gatos	8	6	8	8		No.		
Howes, Mrs. E. J.	Los Gatos	1	1		1		No.	4 tons, '89	
Jarnes, William	Los Gatos	6	6	6			No.	25 tons, '89	
Johnson, Peter	Los Gatos	10	10	10			No.	40 tons, '89	
Kennedy, E. A.	Los Gatos	6	6	5			No.	30 tons, '89	
Luckey, C. J.	Los Gatos	1½	1½		1½		No.	6 tons, '89	
Lawrence, D. M.	Los Gatos	3	3	2	1		No.		
Lewis, S.	Los Gatos	2	2	2			No.	7 tons, '89	
Lynch, G. W.	Los Gatos	6	6	4	2		No.	22 tons, '89	
Layton, P. J.	Los Gatos	3	3				No.		
Lefevre, Mrs. C.	Los Gatos	6	6	6			No.	20 tons, '89	
Lamontaigne, William	Los Gatos	30	30	25	5		No.	120 tons, '89	
Los Gatos & Saratoga Wine and Fruit Co.	Los Gatos						Yes.		
Los Gatos Cooperative Winery.	Los Gatos						**Yes.**		
Mitchell, J.	Los Gatos	4	4	2	2		No.	16 tons, '89	
Main, J. M.	Los Gatos	4	4	4			No.	16 tons, '89	
McCulloch, Mrs. F. H.	Los Gatos	3	3	3			No.	15 tons, '89	
McLellan, R. W. B.	Los Gatos	4	4		4		No.	18 tons, '89	
Miller, Mrs. M.	Los Gatos	3	3	2	1		No.	15 tons, '89	
More, W. A., estate of	Los Gatos	80	80	80			No.	350 tons, '89	
McDonald, J. W.	Los Gatos	7	7	7			No.	28 tons, '89	Ploussard, Grenache, Trousseau, Zinfandel, Pinot. Zinfandel.

Name	Location						Cellar	Product	Varieties of grapes
Morgan, C. H.	Los Gatos	4	4	4			No.	15 tons, '89	
Merriam, H. A.	Los Gatos	35	35	35	25	10	Yes.	165 tons, '89	Zinfandel, Charbono, Malvoisie, Muscat, Verdal, Rose Peru.
Nino, G.	Los Gatos								
Noble, C. W. & B. H.	Los Gatos	5	5	5	6	6	No.	25 tons, '80	Muscat, Verdal, Rose Peru.
Parsons, L. W.	Los Gatos	6	36	36	35		No.	30 tons, '80	
Pine, W. P.	Los Gatos	35	12	9		3	No.	140 tons, '89	
Riggs, Z. A.	Los Gatos	3	3	3		3	No.	50 tons, '89	
Rose, Mrs. S. M.	Los Gatos	9	9	9			Yes.	16 tons, '89	
Roberts, J. D.	Los Gatos	15	10	10		5	No.	40 tons, '89	Muscat, Rose Peru.
Rogers, Henry	Los Gatos	8	6	6		2	No.	60 tons, '89	
Roemer, C.	Los Gatos	22	22	22			No.	36 tons, '89	Charbono, Zinfandel, Mataro, Muscat, Malvoisie.
Richardson, A.	Los Gatos								Franc Pinot, Cabernet Sauvignon, Malbec, Mataro, Chauche Noir, Semillon, Sauvignon Blanc, Pinot.
Robertson, R. F.	Los Gatos	5	5	5	3	2	No.	22 tons, '89	
Strahwald, John.	Los Gatos	3	3	3			No.	11 tons, '80	
Schrepfer, Fred.	Los Gatos	4	4	2		2	No.	15 tons, '89	
Snell, D. J.	Los Gatos	3	8	3		1	No.	11 tons, '89	
Saratoga and Los Gatos Real Estate Ass'n.	Los Gatos	80	80	80	80		No.	205 tons, '89	
Sobay, A. L.	Los Gatos	15	15	15			No.	56 tons, '89	
Scott, Mrs. M.	Los Gatos	10	10	10		3	No.	35 tons, '80	
Suydam, Mrs. M. E.	Los Gatos	3					No.	11 tons, '89	
Spink, James A.	Los Gatos	10	10	10			No.	38 tons, '89	
Symonds, Mrs. B. B.	Los Gatos	23	23	23			No.	86 tons, '89	
Shannon, Thos.	Los Gatos	1	1	1		1	No.	4 tons, '89	
Saratoga and Los Gatos Winery.	Los Gatos						Yes.		
Tupper, Mrs. L. M., estate of.	Los Gatos	7	7	7	4	3	No.	26 tons, '89	
Tabacco, John.	Los Gatos	15	12	15	15	15	No.	25 tons, '89	
Tarbett, Mrs. F. B.	Los Gatos	5	5	5	3	2	No.	27 tons, '89	
Trost, A. C.	Los Gatos	7	7	7	6	1	No.	30 tons, '88	
Taylor, W. D.	Los Gatos	6	6	8	6	1	No.	22 tons, '89	
Thompson, W. H.	Los Gatos	5	5	5	5		No.	60 tons, '89	
Urquhart, R. A.	Los Gatos	18	18	14	14	2	No.	12 tons, '89	
Van Ness, H. J.	Los Gatos	4	4	4	4		No.		
Vuillemier, C. A.	Los Gatos	9	9	9			No.		
Wadaworth, H.	Los Gatos	40	40	40	40		No.	160 tons, '88	
Walker, W. W.	Los Gatos	24	24	24	24		No.	80 tons, '89	
Young, Edwin	Los Gatos	9	9	9		9	Yes.	16 tons, '89	
Yocco, C.	Los Gatos	4	4	4			No.	20 tons, '88	
Yelland, W. A.	Los Gatos	5	5	5			Yes.	50 tons, '89	
Brasch, Louis	Madrone.	16	16	16	16				

SANTA CLARA COUNTY—Continued.

Name of Owner.	Post Office and Name of Vineyard.	Total Acres in Grapes.	Acres in Bearing.	Acres in Wine Grapes.	Acres in Table Grapes.	Acres in Raisin Grapes.	Wine Maker.	Product.	Varieties.
Mabury & Co.	Madrone								See San José.
Ransome, J. W.	Madrone	170	170	170			Yes.	520 tons, '89	
Ampuero, V. W.	Mayfield	6	6	6			No.	22 tons, '90	
Bouleware, J. W.	Mayfield								
Clark, Mrs. Charlotte	Mayfield						Yes.		Leased to Charles De Toy.
Espinosa, Trinidad	Mayfield	72	72	72	2¼		Yes.	220 tons, '88	
Harrington, John A.	Mayfield	7¾	7¾	5			No.	25 tons, '88	
Hotaling, A. P.	Mayfield	6	6	6	2		Yes.	17 tons, '88	
L'Hermitte,	Mayfield (San Fran.)	60	60	58			Yes.	85 tons, '90	Zinfandel, etc.
Le Brun, Charles	Mayfield	10	10	10			Yes.	30 tons, '89	
O'Hanlon, John	Mayfield	20	20	20			Yes.	65 tons, '89	
Pringle, E. J.	Mayfield	9	9	9				36 tons, '90	
Rosenthal, J.	Mayfield (San Fran.)								See Rosenthal.
Tourmer, Mrs. H.	Mayfield	91	91	91			No.	275 tons, '88	
Yesle, V.	Mayfield	10	10	10			Yes.	38 tons, '89	
Stanford, Leland	Menlo Park (Palo Alto)	166	166	158	8		Yes.	620 tons, '90	Zinfandel, Charbono, Trousseau, Mataro, Mission, Malvoisie, Rose Peru, Isabella, Riesling, Chasselas, Verdal, Muscat.
Barber, R. S.	Milpitas	4	4	4			No.		
Bellew, M.	Milpitas					4			
Abbott, Mrs. M. F.	Mountain View	40	40	40			No.	47 tons, '90	Zinfandel, Pinot, etc.
Aubejonais, A.	Mountain View	8	8	8			Yes.	24 tons, '90	
Bergin, John	Mountain View	75	75	70	5		No.	300 tons, '90	
Briggs, George H.	Mountain View	18	18	12			No.	33 tons, '89	
Bryan, J. W.	Mountain View	30	30	30			No.	130 tons, '90	
Brown, W. W.	Mountain View	20	20	18	2		No.	70 tons, '90	Zinfandel.
Brochard, Y.	Mountain View								
Campbell, H. C.	Mt. View (San Fran.)	15	15	15			No.	60 tons, '89	
Deleutel, Charles	Mountain View								
Delmas, D. M.	Mt. View (San Fran.)	350	350	350			Yes.	1,200 tons, '89	Charbono, Zinfandel, Carignan, Chasselas, etc.
Dillen, Kate	Mountain View								
Distel, B.	Mountain View	40	40	40			Yes.	160 tons, '89	
De Toy, Charles	Mountain View								See Mrs. Charlotte Clark, Mayfield.
Emerson, S. B., est. of	Mountain View	20	20	20				60 tons, '89	

Name	Post Office					Dist.	Product	Remarks
Ehrhorn, L. M.	Mountain View	6	6	6		No.	20 tons, '89	
Gordon, A.	Mountain View	35	35	33	2	No.	130 tons, '90	
Hale, J. P. (Grant Bros., managers).	Mountain View							
Howes, C. P.	Mt. View (San Fran.)	86	85	85		Yes.	380 tons, '89	Red varieties; also Sauvignon Vert, Semillon, etc.
Heney, R., Jr.	Mountain View	84	84	84		Yes.	420 tons, '88	
Hollenbeck, Mrs. E. J.	Mountain View	2	2	1	1	No.	7 tons, '89	
Hawthorn, E.	Mountain View	8	8	8	2	No.	10 tons, '88	
Hale, Mrs. E. C.	Mountain View	30	30	30		No.	25 tons, '89	
Kifer, S. H.	Mountain View	5	5	5		No.	150 tons, '89	
Moorhead, J. M.	Mountain View	60	60	40	10	No.	25 tons, '89	
Morton Bros.	Mountain View	50	50	50		No.	200 tons, '90	
Martel, J. F.	Mountain View	1½	1½	1½	3	No.	14 tons, '88	Zinfandel, Mataro, Grenache.
Nelson, A.	Mountain View	3	3	8		Yes.	28 tons, '89	
Pichitti, V.	Mountain View	98	98	98		Yes.	400 tons, '89	
Snyder, John.	Mountain View	280	280	280		Yes.	500 tons, '89	
Scott, Mrs. E. W.	Mountain View	6	6	6		No.	25 tons, '89	
Sloat, Mrs. C. O.	Mountain View							
Swall, P.	Mountain View	8	8	5		No.	30 tons, '89	
Sherweiss, Mrs. E.	Mountain View	30	30	30	3	Yes.	120 tons, '88	
Shreve, George C.	Mt. View (San Fran.)	8	8	8		Yes.	35 tons, '89	
Smith, Mrs. Jacob.	Mountain View	4	4	4		No.	20 tons, '89	
Springer, E. F.	Mountain View	28	28	28		Yes.	120 tons, '89	
Sladky, Joseph	Mountain View	50	50	50		No.	225 tons, '89	
Truman, I. J.	Mt. View (San Fran.)	3	3	3		No.	11 tons, '89	
Weber, L.	Mountain View							
Williams, J. E.	Mountain View	6	6	6		Yes.	22 tons, '89	
Zahaldemo, A.	Mountain View	4	4	4		Yes.	20 tons, '89	
Juarez, Juan	New Almaden	4	4	4		Yes.	16 tons, '89	
Lopez, Francisco	New Almaden	2	2	2		Yes.	8 tons, '89	
Montoyo, Antonio	New Almaden	15	15	15				
Randol, J. B. (Trustee)	New Almaden	20	20		20			
Feely, D. C.	Patchen					No.	100 tons, '90	Muscat, Verdal, Cornichon, Tokay, etc.
Fowler, J. S.	Patchen	4	4		4	No.	16 tons, '90	
Norrish, J.	Patchen							
Weed, M. H.	Patchen	3	3	3	3	No.	12 tons, '90	
Wilkinson, C. C. & Bro.	Patchen	3	3	3	3	Yes.	13 tons, '89	
Auzerais, J., estate of.	San José	60	60	60		No.	225 tons, '90	
Averett, A. E.	San José	25	25	25		No.	80 tons, '90	
Alvord, H. B., & Whitton, A. K.	San José	8	8	8	2	No.	24 tons, '90	
Arques, Mrs. N. G.	San José	1	1	1	1	No.	4 tons, '90	
Allen, C. H.	San José							
Brown, J. E.	San José	2	2	2	2	No.	8 tons, '90	
Babb, F. N.	San José	3	3	3	3	No.	10 tons, '89	

SANTA CLARA COUNTY—Continued.

Name of Owner.	Post Office and Name of Vineyard.	Total Acres in Grapes.	Acres in Bearing.	Acres in Wine Grapes.	Acres in Table Grapes.	Acres in Raisin Grapes.	Wine Maker.	Product.	Varieties.
Bunnell, J. S.	San José (San Fran.)	10	10	10				28 tons, '90	
Brassy & Ahlers	San José	40	40	40				130 tons, '90	
Bitimke, H.	San José	68	45	45			No.	186 tons, '90	Cabernet Franc, Mataro, Carignan, Grenache, etc.
Bohnett, J.	San José	1½	1½		1½				
Barstow, A.	San José (San Fran.)	100	100	100			No.	400 tons, '90	
Bale, Peter	San José	41	41	41			No.	135 tons, '90	
Burns, Paul O. Wine Co.	San José	80	80	80			Yes.	270 tons, '90	
Capp, J. B.	San José	10	10		10		Yes.	30 tons, '89	
Crandall, A. W.	San José	35	35	35			No.	110 tons, '89	
Chandler, E. H.	San José	12	12	10	2		Yes.	40 tons, '89	
Caton, F. E.	San José	1	1		1		No.		
Cranz, Chas.	San José	22	22	22			No.	75 tons, '90	
Casey, L. C.	San José	2	2		2		No.	7 tons, '89	
Chapman, E. M.	San José	4	4		4		No.	14 tons, '89	
Combs, T. E.	San José (Seneca Falls, N. Y.),	30	30	30			No.	110 tons, '00	
Campbell, Mrs. L.	San José	18½	18½	18½			No.	60 tons, '89	Muscat, Rose Peru, Malvoisie.
Dudley, Dr. J. P.	San José	5	5		5		No.	20 tons, '89	
Dumont, Luis	San José	20	20	20			No.	65 tons, '89	
Durkee, Mrs. D.	San José	10	10			10	No.	35 tons, '89	Muscat.
Dixon, Isaac	San José	3	3	3			No.	10 tons, '89	
Dent, R. E.	San José	10	10	10			No.	35 tons, '89	
Estrade, Prosper	San José	70	70	70			Yes.	225 tons, '90	
Estrade, Ant.	San José	17	17	17			Yes.	60 tons, '90	
Escover, J. P.	San José	8	8	8			No.	25 tons, '90	
Easterday, F.	San José	45	45	45					
Freitag, N. A.	San José	13	13	10	3		No.	35 tons, '89	
Fisher, Mrs. J.E. (Belle)	San José	21½	21½	21½			No.	60 tons, '89	
Golinsky & Brinder-stein.	San José	4	4	4				13 tons, '89	
Gaines, W. S.	San José	35	35	35			Yes.	115 tons, '89	
Gunckel, W. F.	San José	40	40	20	20		No.	225 tons, '89	
Guppy, E. H.	San José	37	24	24					
Gutierrez, Julia.	San José	2	2	2				50 tons, '89	Zinfandel, Mataro, resistant roots.

Name	Location					Wine	Production	Varieties
Holcomb, C. F.	San José	8	8	8	2		32 tons, '89	
Heddery, A. B. (H. L. Gordon, agent).	San José	6	6	6		No.	8 tons, '89	
Harrison, A. L.	San José	20	20	20	15	No.	120 tons, '90	
Hutchins, Samuel	San José	2½	2½	2¼	1½	No.	12 tons, '89	
Hale, J. P.	San José	10	10	10		No.	35 tons, '89	
Haines, N. J.	San José	30	30	30		Yes.	180 tons, '89	Mataro, Grenache, Zinfandel, Black Pinot, Cabernet.
Hall, E. G.	San José	85	20	20			45 tons, '90	Cabernet Franc, Cabernet Sauvignon, Semillon, Verdot.
Howard, C. W.	San José	10	10	10	2	No.	45 tons, '89	Zinfandel, Mataro, Charbono, Grenache.
Hale, H. B.	San José	16	16	16		No.	65 tons, '89	
Ickes, D. W.	San José	14	14	14	10	No.	60 tons, '89	
Johnson, J. B.	San José	10	10	10	5	No.	53 tons, '80	
Johnson, J., estate of	San José	60	60	55	1	No.	220 tons, '89	
Johnson, Andrew	San José	1	1			No.	5 tons, '89	
Jarvis, G. M., & Co.	San José	50	50	50		Yes.	180 tons, '89	
Johnson, S. R.	San José	10	10	10	2	No.	35 tons, '89	
Kunz, F. W.	San José	2	2	2		No.	8 tons, '89	
Klee, John	San José	37	37	37	3	No.	150 tons, '89	
Klotz, Mrs. E.	San José	7	7	7	2	No.	32 tons, '89	
Klein, Karl	San José	2	2	2	2	No.	9 tons, '89	
Kelly, J. H.	San José	40	40	38		Yes.	160 tons, '90	
Kooser, H. H.	San José	150	160	150	4	No.	450 tons, '89	
Lefrance, Henry	San José	10	10	10	1	No.	30 tons, '88	
Lovely, Mrs. Eliza	San José	4	4	4		No.	16 tons, '89	
Levi, H.	San José	1	1	1	3	No.	5 tons, '89	
Laederich, Mrs. L.	San José	5	5	5		No.	20 tons, '89	
Melanson, Sylvas	San José	6	6	3		No.	30 tons, '89	
Main, H. H.	San José	6	8	8		No.	240 tons, '88	
Malavos, A.	San José and Madrone	60	60	60		No.	70 tons, '89	
Mabury, F. H., & Co.	San José	60	60	60		No.	25 tons, '89	
Mintie, Dr. A. E.	San José	20	20	20		No.	110 tons, '89	
McKeernan, Charles	San José	7	7	7		Yes.	165 tons, '88	
Malech, F. A.	San José	35	35	35	2	No.	182 tons, '90	
Markwick, L. A.	San José	40	40	38		No.	13 tons, '89	
Murphy, J. C.	San José	20	20	20		No.	75 tons, '89	
McCarthy, James	San José	3	3	3		No.	520 tons, '90	
McLeod, Mrs. E.	San José	17	17	12	5	No.	13 tons, '89	
Newman, C.	San José	6	6	6		No.	1100 tons, '90	
Phelps, M. D.	San José	80	80	80	2	No.	40 tons, '89	
Patterson, H. P.	San José	3	3	1		No.		
Portal, J. B. J.	San José	160	160	160		Yes.		
Pacific Winery	San José					Yes.		
Requart, William	San José	13	13	13		No.		Zinfandel, Mataro, Chasselas, Pinot, etc.

SANTA CLARA COUNTY—Continued.

Name of Owner	Post Office and Name of Vineyard	Total Acres in Grapes	Acres in Bearing	Acres in Wine Grapes	Acres in Table Grapes	Acres in Raisin Grapes	Wine Maker	Product	Varieties
Ryland, C. B.	San José	30	30	30			No.	100 tons, '89	
Richards, W. S.	San José	50	50	50			No.	300 tons, '89	
Redmond, A. J.	San José	20	20	20			No.	75 tons, '89	
Rich, Jacob, & Co.	San José	60	60	60			No.	250 tons, '89	
Rich, Jacob	San José	30	30	30			No.	110 tons, '89	
Rhodes, A. L.	San José	2	2		2		No.	10 tons, '89	
Ruel, E. P.	San José								
Rhien, C. E., & Thompson	San José	8	8	8			No.	40 tons, '89	
Richards, J. E.	San José	2	2	1	1		No.	6 tons, '89	
Schneider, F. A.	San José	33	33	33			Yes.	100 tons, '89	
Schiele, C. M.	San José	4	4	4			No.	15 tons, '89	
Schupp, Joseph	San José	10	10	10			No.	38 tons, '89	
Stiles, W.	San José	8	8	8			No.	30 tons, '89	
Silent, Childs & Johnson	San José	68	68	68			No.	270 tons, '89	Zinfandel, Burger, Blaue Elba, Charbono, etc.
Sternfield, John	San José	50	50	50			No.	150 tons, '89	
Souci, Mrs. M. F.	San José	7	7	7			No.	25 tons, '89	
Stockton, S. P.	San José	120	120	120			Yes.	400 tons, '89	
Start & Morrison	San José	4	4	3	1		No.	16 tons, '89	
Schofield, Chris.	San José	8	8	8			No.	32 tons, '89	
Sharer, S. N.	San José	8	8	8			No.	32 tons, '89	
Seybold, G. L.	San José	4	4		4		No.	20 tons, '89	
Tuck, H.	San José	17½	17½	17½			No.	70 tons, '90	
Treadwell & Bradford	San José	22	22	22			No.	60 tons, '89	
Van Syckle, Henry	San José	1	1		1		No.	5 tons, '89	
Whittan, A. K. & C. F.	San José	6	6		6		No.	23 tons, '89	
Wright, Daniel	San José	40	40	40			No.	160 tons, '89	
Wing, Edgar	San José	10	10	10			No.	25 tons, '89	
Wing & Barker	San José	20	20	20			No.	80 tons, '89	
Washburn, Henry	San José	35	35	35			Yes.	70 tons, '89	
Wright, J. B.	San José	38	38	38			Yes.	185 tons, '90	
Waite, John	San José	10	10	8	2		Yes.	35 tons, '89	
Zecovich, A.	San José						No.		
Baldwin, Chas. A.	Santa Clara	60	60	60			Yes.	200 tons, '90	

Name	County						Wine	Product	Varieties
Benson, H. E.	Santa Clara	1	1	1	1		No.	4 tons, '89	
Bridges, Frank	Santa Clara	15	15	6	9		No.	56 tons, '90	
Blabon, W. L.	Santa Clara	15	15	15			No.	85 tons, '90	
Blake, Ross & Grant	Santa Clara	20	20	10	2	4	No.	75 tons, '90	
Bowdist, M. S.	Santa Clara	8	8	6			No.	25 tons, '90	
Bocksch, W.	Santa Clara	30	30	30		9	No.	20 tons, '90	
Beaver, G. W.	Santa Clara	23	28	14			No.	183 tons, '89	Zinfandel, Riesling, Muscat, Verdal.
Brasch, Otto	Santa Clara	40	40	40			No.	120 tons, '90	Mataro, Charbono, Grenache.
Baserm, J. C., & Co.	Santa Clara	30	30	30			No.	110 tons, '90	Zinfandel, Charbono, Mataro.
Bracher, F. W.	Santa Clara								
Brown, G. M.	Santa Clara								
Copstein, N.	Santa Clara	2	2	1	1		No.	160 tons, '89	Zinfandel, Muscat.
Cochrane, E. O.	Santa Clara	60	40	50	10		Yes.	72 tons, '89	Zinfandel, Charbono, Cabernet Franc, Semillon.
Daggett, George	Santa Clara	16	16	14	2			14 tons, '89	
Eddy, William	Santa Clara	3	3		3		No.	160 tons, '89	Carignan, Zinfandel, Mataro, Charbono, Grenache, Malvoisie, Golden Chasselas, Muscat, Black Morocco.
Elder, Mrs. M.	Santa Clara	27	27	25	2				
Engel, Peter	Santa Clara	1	1	1	1		No.	4 tons, '89	Zinfandel, Mataro, Grenache, Muscat.
Freeman, D.	Santa Clara	40	40	37	3	14	No.	150 tons, '89	Muscat.
Foster, Joseph.	Santa Clara	15	15	18	1		No.	70 tons, '90	
Grimes, Mrs. Geo. F.	Santa Clara	18	18	37			No.	60 tons, '89	
Gartleman, D.	Santa Clara	40	40	20	3		No.	225 tons, '90	
Goodrich, E. E.	Santa Clara	20	20				Yes.	80 tons, '89	
Gusman, John G.	Santa Clara	8	8	10	8		No.	25 tons, '89	
Gardner, L. E.	Santa Clara	10	10	9			No.	45 tons, '90	Trousseau, Malvoisie, Charbono, Mataro.
Glendenning, Geo. W.	Santa Clara	8	8	9	2		No.	30 tons, '89	Charbono, Mataro, Trousseau.
Glendenning, Mrs. M.	Santa Clara	10	10	8	1		No.	40 tons, '89	Charbono, Malvoisie, Muscat.
Glendenning, J. G.	Santa Clara	9	9	8	1		No.	40 tons, '89	
Glendenning, J. E.	Santa Clara	8	8	8			No.	36 tons, '89	
Hancock, J. J.	Santa Clara (Cupertino)	20	20	20			No.	80 tons, '89	Zinfandel, Mataro.
Hollenbeck, G. E.	Santa Clara	5	5	5			No.	20 tons, '89	
Hale, Nathan	Santa Clara	60	60	60		20	No.	300 tons, '90	Tokay, Muscat, Black Hamburg.
Help, F. F. & H.	Santa Clara	20	20	20			No.	100 tons, '88	
Hines, J. W.	Santa Clara	5	5	5			No.	40 tons, '89	
Hersey, Philo	Santa Clara	10	10	10	5		No.	65 tons, '89	
Hersey, R.	Santa Clara	16	16	8	8		No.	25 tons, '89	
Hale, Mrs. E. L.	Santa Clara	6	6	6			No.	45 tons, '89	
Johnson, J. W.	Santa Clara (Lawrence)	12	12	12	2		No.	32 tons, '89	
Judson, H. C.	Santa Clara	8	8	6			No.	300 tons, '89	
Kenyon, J. M.	Santa Clara	60	60	60			No.	12 tons, '89	
Knowles, John	Santa Clara	3	3	3			No.	40 tons, '89	
Lydiard, Samuel	Santa Clara	8	8	8	8		No.	200 tons, '89	
Myerholz, C.	Santa Clara	35	35	32			No.		
Montgomery, Alex.	Santa Clara	40	40	40	3		Yes.	170 tons, '90	

SANTA CLARA COUNTY—Continued.

Name of Owner.	Post Office and Name of Vineyard.	Total Acres in Grapes.	Acres in Bearing.	Acres in Wine Grapes.	Acres in Table Grapes.	Acres in Raisin Grapes.	Wine Maker.	Product.	Varieties.
Myrick, M. H.	Santa Clara	30	30	18	12		No.	200 tons, '90	
Miller, W. C.	Santa Clara	22	22	22	1		No.	75 tons, '90	
Morton, Seth	Santa Clara	1	1				No.	6 tons, '89	
McCarthy, John	Santa Clara	3	3	8			No.	13 tons, '89	
Porter, W. R.	Santa Clara	10	10						
Preston, J. B.	Santa Clara	80	80	60			No.	490 tons, '89	
Pierce, R. T.	Santa Clara	100	100	100			Yes.	520 tons, '90	Zinfandel, Mataro, Carignan, Sauvignon Vert.
Pierce, James P.	Santa Clara	60	60	50	10		Yes.	300 tons, '90	Carbernet, Mataro, Charbono, Semillon, Sauvignon Vert, Rose Peru, Muscat, Chasselas.
Pollard, Mrs. C. O.	Santa Clara	74	74	64	10		Yes.	333 tons, '89	
Regnart, Robert	Santa Clara	13	13	13			No.	40 tons, '89	
Regnart, Henry	Santa Clara	24	24	24			No.	100 tons, '89	Zinfandel, Charbono, Mataro.
Santa Clara College	Santa Clara	35	35	33	2		Yes.	130 tons, '89	
Santa Clara College	Santa Clara	50	50	50			Yes.	200 tons, '89	
Saul, John	Santa Clara	2	2	2			Yes.	9 tons, '89	
Sanford, F. C.	Santa Clara	16	16	16			No.	60 tons, '89	Charbono, Trousseau.
Stewart, G. W.	Santa Clara	45	45	35	10		No.	315 tons, '90	Zinfandel, Charbono, Mataro, Grenache, Muscat.
Silva, José	Santa Clara	2½	2½	2½			Yes.	8 tons, '89	
Sutherland, D.	Santa Clara	30	30	30			Yes.	120 tons, '89	
Scott, Miss A. R.	Santa Clara	155	155	155			Yes.	680 tons, '89	
Sorosis Fruit Farm	Santa Clara	2	2	1	1		No.	8 tons, '89	
Van Dine, E., estate of	Santa Clara	14	14	14			No.	60 tons, '89	
Winchester, Mrs. L. L.	Santa Clara	18	18	14	4		Yes.	75 tons, '89	
Wolf, F.	Santa Clara	15	15	15			No.	60 tons, '89	
Wolf, A., & Co.	Santa Clara	6	6	6			Yes.	20 tons, '89	
Wolf, Anton	Santa Clara	9	9	9			No.	35 tons, '89	
Woodhams, A. R.	Santa Clara	4¾	4¾		4¾		No.	20 tons, '89	
Buchleman, F.	Saratoga	6	6	6			No.	20 tons, '89	
Bordi, B.	Saratoga	15	15	15			Yes.	40 tons, '90	
Brolley, A. B.	Saratoga	4	4	4			No.	13 tons, '90	
Boisserance, Victoria	Saratoga	3	3	3			No.		
Bougetie, G.	Saratoga	9	9	9			Yes.	32 tons, '90	
Bernard & Baille	Saratoga	20	20	20			Yes.	70 tons, '90	
Boyeson, H. A.	Saratoga	9	9	7		2	No.	47 tons, '90	Zinfandel, Mataro, Charbono, Muscat.

Name	Post office							Product	Remarks
Bonnette, A.	Saratoga	15	15	15			Yes.	52 tons, '90	
Cornish, Mark	Saratoga (San José)	14	14	14	2		No.	45 tons, '89	
Coye, Mrs. H. L.	Saratoga	30	30	28			No.	100 tons, '89	
Colpin, J.	Saratoga	10	10	10	2		No.	30 tons, '89	
Coppins, J. B.	Saratoga	7	7	7			No.	20 tons, '89	
Crowell, M. L.	Saratoga	43	40	38			No.	130 tons, '90	
Cottle, J. A.	Saratoga	36	38	36			No.	200 tons, '90	
Eberlin, C. A.	Saratoga	4	4	4	1		No.	14 tons, '89	
Ellsworth, S.	Saratoga	8	8	6	2		Yes.	20 tons, '89	
Ellsworth, J. H	Saratoga	8	8	8	3		Yes.	28 tons, '89	
Ferguson, J. C.	Saratoga	3	3	2			No.	12 tons, '89	
Gilbert, A. J. & C. E.	Saratoga Pk., Saratoga	12	12	10			No.	18 tons, '89	
Husted, F. M.	Saratoga	3	3	3			No.	15 tons, '89	
Hollenbeck, B. W.	Buckhorn Vineyard, Saratoga.	23	23	23			Yes.	100 tons, '90	Trousseau, Zinfandel, Mataro, Charbono.
Hourecan, J.	Saratoga	50	50	50			No.	240 tons, '89	
Hutchins, S. P.	Saratoga	8	8	8	2		No.	35 tons, '89	
Herrick, E. M.	Saratoga	20	20	18	5		No.	75 tons, '89	
Jarboe, H.	Saratoga	20	20	15	1		No.	80 tons, '89	
Jeffers, Martha	Saratoga	1	1		2		No.	5 tons, '89	Mataro, Zinfandel; 15 acres in resistant vines.
Johns, J. R.	Saratoga	12	12	10			No.	50 tons, '89	
Jones, J. J.	Saratoga	22	22	22			No.	100 tons, '89	
Johnson, J. W.	Saratoga	6	6	6	3		No.	22 tons, '89	
Kamp, O.	Saratoga	6	6	6			No.	28 tons, '89	
Loyst Bros.	Saratoga	25	25	25	5		No.	100 tons, '89	Zinfandel, Charbono.
Lotti, C., & Co.	Saratoga	15	15	15	5		Yes.	50 tons, '89	
Lotti, P., & Co.	Saratoga	15	15	15	2		Yes.	45 tons, '89	
Maclay, John, estate of	Saratoga	1½	1½	1½	1½		No.	7 tons, '89	
Meunier, Mrs. Anna	Saratoga	25	25	25			No.	100 tons, '80	
Miller, Jacob	Saratoga	8	8	8			No.	15 tons, '89	
Marion, M.	Saratoga	3	3	3	3		No.	85 tons, '89	
McDonald, A. D.	Saratoga	25	25	25			Yes.	235 tons, '90	
Malpas, A.	Saratoga	60	60	55	5		No.	8 tons, '89	
Mevi, Mrs. K. J.	Saratoga	2	2	2	2		Yes.	38 tons, '89	
Marence, A.	Saratoga	10	10	10			No.	22 tons, '89	
McPherson, D	Saratoga	5	5	5			No.	12 tons, '89	
Norton, J.	Saratoga	3	3	2	1		Yes.	60 tons, '89	
Narcisse, A. J.	Saratoga	12	12	12			No.	8 tons, '89	Charbono, Trousseau.
Pinder, G. E.	Saratoga	2	2	2	2		No.	110 tons, '89	
Plant, H. I.	Saratoga	25	25	25	5		No.	8 tons, '89	
Pickard, Mrs. C. V. C.	Saratoga	14	14	14			No.	60 tons, '89	
Parker, Mrs. Mary	Saratoga	15	15	15			No.	60 tons, '89	
Parker, S. S.	Saratoga	5	5	5			No.	30 tons, '89	
Parsons, S. H.	Saratoga	5	5	5			No.	30 tons, '89	
Plunket, R.	Saratoga	4	4	4	4		No.	16 tons, '80	

SANTA CLARA COUNTY—Continued.

Name of Owner.	Post Office and Name of Vineyard.	Total Acres in Grapes.	Acres in Bearing.	Acres in Wine Grapes.	Acres in Table Grapes.	Acres in Raisin Grapes.	Wine Maker.	Product.	Varieties.
Radoni, A.	Saratoga	12	12	12			Yes.	38 tons, '89	
Resparel, Joseph	Saratoga	20	20	20			Yes.	75 tons, '89	
Reynolds, Mrs. M. A.	Saratoga	11	11		1		No.	45 tons, '89	
Radovich, Bozo	Saratoga	35	35	35			No.	130 tons, '89	Zinfandel, Charbono, Mataro, Black Hamburg.
Sage, L. A.	Saratoga	33	33	33			No.	120 tons, '89	
Stevens, W. E.	Saratoga	12	12	12			No.	50 tons, '89	
Schatzle, Joseph	Saratoga	1	1		1		No.	5 tons, '89	
Spangler, M. H.	Saratoga	25	25	25			Yes.	90 tons, '89	
Sadler, Mrs. L. B.	Saratoga	2	2	1	1		No.	8 tons, '89	
Seavey, E. C.	Saratoga	12	12	12			No.	45 tons, '89	
Sheehan, B.	Saratoga	8	8	8			No.	30 tons, '89	
Specht, Anna	Saratoga	8	8	8			No.	30 tons, '89	
Spangler, J.	Saratoga	6	6	6			Yes.	30 tons, '89	
Taudt, John	Saratoga	15	15	15			Yes.	70 tons, '89	
Viera, A. J.	Saratoga	4	4	3	1		No.	18 tons, '89	Malvoisie, Black Hamburg.
Whipple & Goodrich	Saratoga	8	8	8			No.	30 tons, '89	
Wyate, Stephen	Saratoga	2	2		2		No.	8 tons, '89	
Whitney, J. R.	Saratoga	100	100	100			No.	400 tons, '89	
Wakefield, L. H.	Saratoga (Oakland)	80	80	80			No.	400 tons, '89	Mataro, Zinfandel, Sauvignon Vert, Grenache, Crabb's Black Burgundy, Charbono, Carignan, Chasselas, Cabernet, Malbec, Riesling, Semillon, Petite Bouschet.
Dixon, M. W.	Warm Springs (Alameda Co.).	27	27	27			No.	90 tons, '89	
Adams, E. F.	Wrights	2	2		2		No.		
Aikin, Mrs. H.	Wrights	3		3			No.		
Allen, Prof. C. H.	Togan Vineyard, Wrights.	5	3	3	5		No.		Cabernet.
Ash, Robert, President German Colony.	Wrights								
Averill, Volney	Wrights	1	1		1		No.		
Blake & Hersey	Wrights	30	30	30			Yes.	28 tons, '89	Zinfandel, Grenache, Sauvignon Vert, Green Hungarian, Petite Pinot, Semillon, St. Macaire, Folle Blanche.

Name	Location							Cellar	Product	Varieties
Borland, S. H.	Wrights	5	5					No.	20 tons, '89	
Burrell, J. B.	Wrights	15	5					No.	16 tons, '89	
Burrell, Mattie	Wrights	4	4					No.		
Carr, John	Wrights	24	12	12				No.	46 tons, '89	
Cattermole, John	Wrights	2	2					No.	8 tons, '89	
Catton, Z. A.	Wrights									
Chase, F. W.	Wrights									
Clough, H. M.	Wrights	5	2					No.		
Cuzins, H. C.	Wrights	5	2					No.	7 tons, '89	
Deacon, William	Wrights	2						No.		
Edelhard, Oscar	Wrights	10	5	5				No.		Sauvignon Vert, 2; Franken Riesling, 1½; Fraumier, 1½; Table, 5.
Eisenminger, C.	Wrights	3						No.	11 tons, '89	
Estoff, Baron Von	Wrights							No.		
Finnie, A. J.	Wrights	10								
Frebourne, Wm.	Wrights	5	4							
German Colony	Wrights	16	5							
Ghetaldi, E. de	Wrights	15						Yes.	12 tons, '89	
Gortz, Chas.	Wrights	5							21 tons, '89	
Grant,	Wrights									
Gray, James	Wrights	3	3					No.	10 tons, '89	
Hall, S. P.	Wrights	3						No.		
Hanger, M. M.	Wrights	7	3					No.		
Height, Henry	Wrights	5						No.		
Hester, F.	Wrights	20	10	10				Yes.	900 gals, '89	Franken Riesling, Rhine Riesling, Fraumier, Rulander, Table. Table, Zinfandel.
Humpreyville, Wm.	Wrights	5	2	1				No.		
Jeffries, R.	Wrights	2						No.	8 tons, '89	
Lane, D. W.	Wrights	7	7	8				No.	6 tons, '89	Table, Meunier.
Lessman, ——	Wrights									
Lent, ——	Wrights									
Lincoln, R. J.	Wrights	20	20					No.	4 tons, '89	
Lindey, G. W.	Wrights	1	1					No.		
Liston, Mary R.	Wrights	3	3					No.		
Loomis, S. L.	Wrights	1½	1½					No.	3 tons, '89	
McCracken, J.	Wrights	32½	23	12				No.	60 tons, '89	Charbono, Folle Blanche, Feher Szagos, Table.
Mattern, Frank	Wrights	2						No.		
Maynan, Thomas	Wrights	3						No.		
Meyer, E. E.	Mare Vista Vineyard, Wrights.	90	25	72	15	3		Yes.	16,000 gals, '89	Grenache, Meunier, Petite Pinot, St. George, Pinot Tannat, Cabernet, Mataro, Carignan, Franken Riesling, Johannisberg Riesling, Fraumier, Sauvignon Vert, Marsanne, Semillon, Muscadelle du Bordelaise, Burger, Gutedel, Rulander, Folle Blanche, Muscat, Charbono.
Miller Bros.	Wrights	17	15	15		2		No.	75 tons, '89	Muscat, Table.

SANTA CLARA COUNTY—Continued.

NAME OF OWNER.	Post Office and Name of Vineyard	Total Acres in Grapes.	Acres in Bearing.	Acres in Wine Grapes.	Acres in Table Grapes.	Acres in Raisin Grapes.	Wine Maker.	Product.	Varieties.
Mohr, ——	Wrights	4	4		4		No.	11 tons, '89	Zinfandel, Muscat, Table.
Montgomery, D. H.	Wrights	30	25	8	17	5	No.		Charbono, Table, Folle Blanche.
Morrell, H. O.	Loma Prieta Vineyard, Wrights.	20	14	7	13		Yes.	10,000 gals., '89	
Muller Bros.	Wrights.	10		5	5		No.		Green Hungarian, Franken Riesling, Tentura, Table.
Nelson, R.	Wrights	3			3		No.	30 tons, '89	
Norton, Mrs. M. G.	Wrights	30	15		15	15	No.	20 tons, '89	
O'Brien, Thomas	Wrights	14	7		7		No.		
Percival, R.	Wrights	12	7		12				
Rankin, J. C.	Wrights	2	2		2		No.	25 tons, '89	
Reese, W. L.	Wrights						No.	8 tons, '89	
Rushion, A.	Wrights	11			11				
Schrolder, J.	Wrights	9			4				
Scholle, Anton	Wrights	5		5	5		No.		Meunier, Grenache, Mataro.
Sears, Arthur	Wrights	7			7		No.		
Sears, Wm.	Wrights	39	20	15	24		No.	13 tons, '89	Meunier, Table, Gutedel, Mataro, Sauvignon Vert.
Shropstadter, Wm.	Wrights						No.		
Slaughter, Thos. S.	Wrights	8			3	5	No.		Table, Muscat.
Sorrell, F.	Wrights								
Stammer, ——	Wrights								
Taylor, D.	Wrights	12	7		7		No.	30 tons, '89	
Vincent, W.	Wrights	3	3		3		No.	15 tons, '89	
Wilcox, Mrs. H. L.	Wrights								
Wilson, M. M.	Wrights								
Windel, H.	Wrights	5	5		5		No.	10 tons, '89	
Wright Bros.	Wrights	8	8		8		No.	35 tons, '89	
Wright, E.	Wrights	4	4		4		No.	16 tons, '89	
Totals for county		11,523	11,031	10,294	1,126	103			

SANTA CRUZ COUNTY.

Name of Owner.	Post Office and Name of Vineyard.	Total Acres in Grapes.	Acres in Bearing.	Acres in Wine Grapes.	Acres in Table Grapes.	Acres in Raisin Grapes.	Wine Maker.	Product in 1889.	Varieties.
Eaton, John	Aptos	1			1				Table,
Lilliencranz, A.	Aptos	70		45	25		No.		Verdal, Zinfandel, Mondeuse, Petite Syrah, Beclan, Malvoisie, Victoria, Mataro.
Luz, Joseph S.	Aptos	5			5				Table,
Primrose, J. P.	Aptos	2			2				Table,
Ben Lomond Wine Co.	Ben Lomond	90	70	90			Yes.	30,000 gals.	Gray Riesling, Chauche Noir.
Benchamp, H. L.	Ben Lomond	20	20	17	3		No.		Gray Riesling, Charbono, Chauche Noir.
Blodgett, S.	Ben Lomond	5	5	5			No.		Zinfandel.
Bongoat, H.	Ben Lomond	6	6	6			Yes.		
Osterhaus, J. A.	Ben Lomond	10	10	10			No.	40 tons.	Chauche Noir.
Waldo, F.	Ben Lomond	20	20	20			No.	30 tons.	Gray Riesling, Chauche Noir.
Quinstorf, F.	Bonny Doon	2	2		2		No.		Table,
Briggs, J. W.	Boulder Creek	10	10	10			No.		Gray Riesling, Chauche Noir.
Burns, F.	Boulder Creek	20	20	20			No.		Gray Riesling, Chauche Noir.
Fogler, Joseph	Boulder Creek	20	17	18	2		Yes.	10,000 gals.	Sauvignon Vert, 4; Semillon, 2; Merlot, 2; Zinfandel, 4; Charbono, 1.
Fox, G. W.	Boulder Creek	2	2		2		No.		Table,
Horstmann, H.	Boulder Creek	16	16	6	10		Yes.	5,000 gals.	Zinfandel, 5; Petite Pinot, 1.
Horstmann, W. F.	Boulder Creek	12	9	4	8		Yes.	1,000 gals.	Table, 8; Zinfandel, 1; Charbono, 3.
Kauffman, John	Boulder Creek	15		7	8		No.	20 tons.	Zinfandel, 7; Table, 8.
Maitland, Wm.	Boulder Creek	46	44	38	8		Yes.	12,000 gals.	Table, 8; Sauvignon Vert, 12; Zinfandel, 15; Cabernet Sauvignon, 5; Merlot, 1; Charbono, 1; Grenache, 3.
Veatch, H. C.	Boulder Creek	14	14	14			Yes.	5,000 gals.	Zinfandel, 14.
Wilson, D.	Boulder Creek	20	20	20			No.		Zinfandel.
Ceschi, F.	Corralitos	3	2	3			Yes.	800 gals.	Zinfandel, Malvoisie, Fontainebleau, Barbera.
Comstock, L. H.	Felton	8	6	4	4		No.	24 tons.	Gray Riesling, Chauche Noir, Charbono, Mission.
Martin, L.	Felton	12	12	12			Yes.	3,000 gals.	Charbono, etc.
Josselyn, Mrs.	Felton	25		25			Yes.		Gray Riesling, 12; Chauche Noir, 13.
Peterson, Peter	Felton	20	20	20			No.		Chauche Noir, Zinfandel.
Cornwall, P. B.	Glenwood (San Fran.).	30	15	22	2	6	Yes.	2,000 gals.	Muscat, 6; Table, 2; Chauche Noir, 5; Gray Riesling, 5; Petite Pinot, 5; Zinfandel, 1.
Erdman, Wm.	Glenwood	30	30	30			Yes.		Chauche Noir, 15; Gray Riesling, 15.
Farrington, Wm.	Glenwood	14	14	14			No.	20 tons.	Charbono, 5; Zinfandel, 5; Trousseau, 4.

SANTA CRUZ COUNTY—Continued.

Name of Owner.	Post Office and Name of Vineyard.	Total Acres in Grapes.	Acres in Bearing.	Acres in Wine Grapes.	Acres in Table Grapes.	Acres in Raisin Grapes.	Wine Maker.	Product in 1889.	Varieties.
Fournier, J. H.	Glenwood	12	12	10	2		Yes.	5,500 gals.	Mataro, 4; Merlot, 2; Malbec, 1½; Sauvignon Vert, 3; Table, 1½.
Gay, Alfred	Glenwood	20	20	20			Yes.	5,000 gals.	Zinfandel, 10; Charbono, 10.
Hill, Mrs.	Glenwood	6		6			No.		Cabernet Sauvignon, Merlot, 3; Sauvignon Blanc, Semillon, 3.
Hoods, Mrs.	Glenwood	2			2		No.		Table.
Kloss, Mrs. Lena	Glenwood	63	63	48	10	5	Yes.	20,000 gals.	Sauvignon Vert, 9; Chauche Noir, 8; Petite Pinot, 6; Gray Riesling, 6; Feher Szagos, 2; White Tokay, 2; Muscat, 5; Mission, 3; Black Hamburg, 12.
Lindsey, Mrs.	Glenwood	30	20	25	5		Yes.	8,000 gals.	Chauche Noir, 10; Gray Riesling, 5; Zinfandel, 5; Meunier, 2; Malvoisie, 3.
Martin, Chas. C.	Glenwood	62	29	30	26	6	Yes.	5,000 gals.	Table, 26; Muscat, 6; Chauche Noir, 15; Charbono, 15.
Mel, Henry	Glenwood	67	67	55	9	3	Yes.	20,000 gals.	Merlot, 5; Malbec, 3; Balazetto, 3; Zinfandel, 5; Chauche Noir, 20; Meunier, 5; Gray Riesling, 5; Semillon, 5; Muscadelle du Bordelais, 3; Frontignan, 1; Muscat, 3; Table, 9.
Nelson, Thomas	Glenwood	9	9	2	7		No.	27 tons.	Table, 7; Charbono, 2.
Peoples, Charles	Glenwood	4	4				Yes.		Verdal, Muscat, Mission, Catawba.
Robb, Col. Thomas P.	Sea View Villa, Glenwood.	30		10	20		No.		Zinfandel, 10; Table, 20.
Wadsworth, William	Glenwood	4	4		4		No.		Table.
Bassett, Francis	Laurel	2			2				Table.
Bassett, James E.	Laurel	2			2				Table.
Bassett, Jerome	Laurel	1			1				Table.
Cadwell, Caleb, est. of	Laurel	1			1				Table.
Crane, A. C.	Laurel	10		10					Zinfandel, 10.
Colden, D.	Laurel	3		3					Table.
Emery, William	Laurel	4	4	4			No.	17 tons.	Charbono.
Fredel, M.	Laurel	10	10	3	7		No.	19 tons.	Grenache, 2; Table, Sauvignon Vert, 1.
Jones, Clayton	Laurel	1			1		No.		
Jones, David	Laurel (San Fran.)	4	2		4				Table.
King, J. B.	Laurel	4			4				Table.

Name	Post Office					Distillery	Capacity	Varieties
Marks, Hermann	Laurel	2			2			Table.
Springer, Dr.	Laurel	1			1			Table.
Young, ——	Laurel	5			5			Table.
Binder, H.	Santa Cruz	10		8	2	No.		Cabernet Sauvignon, 4; Merlot, Table.
Bram, Geo. A.	Santa Cruz	44	40	38	6	Yes.	8,000 gals.	Semillon, 8; Chauche Noir, 3; Gray Riesling, 15; Zinfandel, 7; Petite Pinot, 3; Johannisberg Riesling, 2; Table, 6. Verdal, 12.
Brown, B. C.	Santa Cruz	12	12	12		Yes.		Cabernet Sauvignon and Merlot, 3; Sauvignon Blanc and Semillon, 3.
Call, Henry	Santa Cruz	3		3		Yes.	Close system.	Cabernet Sauvignon and Merlot, 8½; Sauvignon Blanc and Semillon, 8½.
Eaton, John	Santa Cruz	6	6	6		No.	Close system.	Cabernet Sauv., Franc Pinot.
East View Vineyard	Santa Cruz	17		17		No.	100 tons.	Semillon, Crabb's Black Burgundy, Chauche Noir, Gray Riesling.
Fairhurst, Thos.	Santa Cruz	16	3s	16	20	No.	18 tons.	Malvoisie, Zinfandel, Chauche Noir.
Fitch, Edwin	Santa Cruz	35		15		Yes.	135 tons.	Chauche Noir, Gray Riesling, Zinfandel, Johan. Riesling, Semillon, Mataro, Colombar.
Foote, Rev. G. W.	Santa Cruz	15	15	5	10	No.	40 tons.	Malvoisie, Cabernet Franc, Chauche Noir, Gray Riesling, Zinfandel.
Galbraith, W. H.	Santa Cruz	65	65	50	15	Yes.		Cabernet Franc, Cabernet Sauvignon, Malbec, Merlot, Zinfandel.
Gankroger, J. W.	Santa Cruz	25	26	25	2	No.		Zinfandel, 14; Balaret, 12; Riesling, 17; Semillon, 12; Mataro, 4; Petite Pinot, 3; Sauvignon Blanc, 2; Malvoisie, 4.
Hihn Co., F. A.	Promontory Vineyard, Santa Cruz.	20	20	18				Cab. Sauvignon, Sauvignon Blanc, Semillon.
Jarvis, John	Santa Cruz	63	53	58	5	Yes.	30,000 gals.	Rose Peru, Muscat, Gray Dijas, Fontainebleau, Black Hamburg, Zinfandel.
Jensen, ——	Santa Cruz	1		1		No.		
Keisling, S. P.	Santa Cruz	5			5			
Kerr, Wm.	Santa Cruz	30	30	30		Yes.	6,000 gals.	Semillon, Sauvignon Blanc, Muscadelle du Bordelais, Cabernet, Riesling, Pinot, Gamay Nicolos.
Logan, J. H.	Santa Cruz	15	16	15		Yes.		Trousseau, 4; Cabernet Sauvignon Vert, 8; Sauvignon Blanc, Semillon, 8.
McKenzie, Mrs. K.	Santa Cruz	20		20		No.	40 tons.	Chauche Noir, Crabb's Burgundy, Zinfandel.
McMullen, Frank	Santa Cruz	30	30	10	20	No.		Zinfandel, Mataro, Trousseau, Cabernet Sauv., Merlot, Johan. Riesling, Sauvignon Vert, Muscadelle du Bordelais.
Merrill, Frank	Santa Cruz	5			5	No.		
Monmonier, C.	Sconbique Vineyard, Santa Cruz.	16	16	16		Yes.	3,000 gals.	
Monteverde, P.	Santa Cruz	5	5	5		Yes.	4,000 gals.	Mission, Zinfandel, Muscat, Fontainebleau, Rose Peru.
Pedimont Bros.	Santa Cruz	30	30	30		Yes.	8,000 gals.	Zinfandel, Mission, Rose Peru, Fontainebleau.
Roston, Geo.	Santa Cruz	10	10	10		No.	20 tons.	Zinfandel.

SANTA CRUZ COUNTY—Continued.

Name of Owner.	Post Office and Name of Vineyard.	Total Acres in Grapes.	Acres in Bearing.	Acres in Wine Grapes.	Acres in Table Grapes.	Acres in Raisin Grapes.	Wine Maker.	Product in 1889.	Varieties.
Santa Cruz Mountain Wine Company.	Santa Cruz						Yes.		
Saufrigner, J.	Santa Cruz	4	4	2	2		Yes.	5 tons.	Mission.
Scott, Mrs. A. E.	Santa Cruz	54	25	54			Yes.	Close system.	Cabernet Sauvignon, Cabernet Franc, Merlot, Verdot, Sauvignon Blanc, Semillon, Muscadelle du Bordelaise, Franc Pinot, Burat, Petite Syrah.
Stewart, Dr. John A.	Santa Cruz	5		5			Yes.	Close system.	Cabernet Sauvignon and Merlot, 2½; Sauvignon Blanc and Semillon, 2½.
Wilson, John	Santa Cruz						No.		
Avron, J.	Soquel	31	31	31			Yes.	7,000 gals.	Charbono, 4; Zinfandel, 3; Petite Pinot, 4; Folle Blanche, 12; Malvoisie, 12.
Bertling, B.	Soquel	20	20	20			Yes.	2,900 gals.	Zinfandel, 12; Charbono, Chauche Noir, Riesling, Semillon.
Brunet, J.	Soquel	8	8	6	1	1	Yes.	9,000 gals.	Zinfandel, Charbono, Grenache, Malvoisie, Petite Pinot, Riesling, Muscat, Black Hamburg.
Dakin, Isaac	Laurel Glen Vineyard, Soquel.	10	6		10		No.		
Gafert, Alfred	Soquel	1			1		No.		
Gardner, Henry	Soquel	1			1		No.		
Gregory, H. P., est. of.	Soquel	70	60	64	6		No.	75 tons.	Zinfandel, 30; Mataro, 2; Chauche Noir, 12; Riesling, 10.
Hall, Henry C.	Soquel	12	12	12			Yes.	25 tons.	Zinfandel.
Lumburg, S.	Soquel	2			2		No.		
O'Neil, T.	Soquel	6			6		No.		
Oliver, W.	Soquel	5			5		No.		
Peterson, P.	Soquel	5			5		No.		
Riley, T. B. W.	Soquel	33	10	22	11		No.		Zinfandel, Riesling.
Verwald, H.	Soquel	4	3	2	2		Yes.	400 gals.	Zinfandel.
Walker, W. S.	Soquel	1			1		No.		
Capelli, C.	Watsonville	7		7			Yes.	3,000 gals.	Zinfandel.
Totals for county		1,684	1,187	1,365	319	21			

SHASTA COUNTY.

Name of Owner.	Post Office and Name of Vineyard.	Total Acres in Grapes	Acres in Bearing.	Acres in Wine Grapes	Acres in Table Grapes	Acres in Raisin Grapes	Wine Maker	Product in 1889.	Varieties.
Coffman, A.	Albertson								
Woodman, L. C.	Albertson								
Alexander, Samuel	Anderson	30	15			30	No.		
Anderson, L. R.	Anderson	1				1	No.		
Anderson, Thomas	Anderson	2				2	No.		
Armstrong, Samuel	Anderson	2				2	No.		
Arnold, Mrs. M.	Anderson	1				1	No.		
Baldwin, James	Anderson								
Baldwin & Atherton	Anderson	2½	2½		1	1½	No,		
Bainbridge, J. P.	Anderson	1	1			1	No.		
Beardsley, I. W.	Anderson								
Beeves, N. A.	Anderson	1	1		1		No.		
Broadhurst, F. F.	Anderson	4				4	No.		
Buffum, Frank A.	Anderson	1	1			1	No.		
Buffum, M. P.	Anderson	20	10		20		No.		
Burtner, G. W.	Anderson	5	5			5	No.		
Buss & Abbott	Anderson	1	1		1		No.		
Casto, M. D. & M. L.	Anderson	8	8			8	No.		
Dodd, T. F.	Anderson	5				5	No.		
Dozier, A.	Anderson	6	3			6	No.		
Fickas, Adam	Anderson	2	2		1	1	No.		
Finley, Joseph	Anderson								
Frisbie, E. G. & L. C.	Anderson	5½	5½			5½	No.		
Gates, W. C.	Anderson	2			1	1	No.		
Green, G. W.	Anderson	5½	5½			5½	No.		
Hawes, William	Anderson	2½	2½		2½		No.		
Hawley, C. H.	Anderson	1	1		1		No.		
Hubbard, A. W.	Anderson	5	5	1		4	No.		
Hussey, S. P.	Anderson	1	1			1	No.		
Johnson, B. W.	Anderson								
Johnston, Wm. M.	Anderson	1½	1½		1½		No.		
Klukkert, B.	Anderson	2	2	1		1	No.		
King, Mrs. C. J.	Anderson	5½	5½			5½	No.		
Lahere, Wm. De	Anderson								

SHASTA COUNTY—Continued.

Name of Owner.	Post Office and Name of Vineyard.	Total Acres in Grapes.	Acres in Bearing.	Acres in Wine Grapes.	Acres in Table Grapes.	Acres in Raisin Grapes.	Wine Maker.	Product in 1889.	Varieties.
McDannals, H. A.	Anderson	4		2		2	No.		
Montgomery, Jas.	Anderson								
Nunnally, H. H.	Anderson								
Newton, E. E.	Anderson	10	10			10	No.		
Newton, J. F.	Anderson	4	4			4	No.		
Newton, O. L.	Anderson	2	2			2	No.		
Palmer, Chas. M.	Anderson								
Palmer, E. S.	Anderson								
Parker, S. C.	Anderson	3				3	No.		
Shanahan, T. W. H.	Anderson	5	5	3	2		No.		
Shasta County Fruit Co.	Anderson	1½	1½			1½			
Shoupe Bros.	Anderson								
Tarlton, J. D.	Anderson	7	7		3	4	No.		
Thomas & Holcom	Anderson	3			1	2	No.		
Taylor, T. G.	Anderson	4	4		4		No.		
Wise, M. F.	Anderson	2½			½	2			
Ball, ——	Ball's Ferry								
Logan, A.	Ball's Ferry								
Winsel, J. F.	Ball's Ferry								
Baldeschivieler, G.	Buckeye	1	1			1	No.		
Hagenbaugh, Wm.	Buckeye	1			1		No.		
Husser, John	Buckeye	2			1	1	No.		
Janssen, J. H.	Buckeye	1¼	1	1			No.		
Pratt, R. H.	Buckeye	2			1	¼	No.		
Potter, H. E.	Buckeye	1				2	No.		
Seaman, Porter	Buckeye	3	3	3			Yes.		
Stickley & Kenyon	Buckeye	1½	1½		½	1			
Harrison, John, est. of	Blair	6	6	6			Yes.		
Richardson, E. W.	Blair	1½	1½	1½			Yes.		
Clarke, ——	Cottonwood	1	1		1		No.		
Henning, A. P.	Cottonwood	20	20			20	No.		
Kimble, Wilhelmina	Cottonwood	5			2	3	No.		
McCabe, E. J.	Cottonwood	2			1	1	No.		
Schmeiderer, W.	Cottonwood	2	2						

Name	Post Office								Remarks
Turner, J.	Cottonwood								
White, H. D.	Cottonwood								
Brown, Wm.	French Gulch								
Morrell, M.	French Gulch								
Andrews & Carpenter	Gas Point							Yes.	
Fitz, Henry E.	Gas Point							Yes.	
Andree, Rudolph	Igo	1	1	1			2	No.	
Bull, W. D.	Igo	2¾	2⅔	½			1		
Develin, John	Igo								
Doll, Valentine	Igo							Yes.	
Forschler, Mrs. E.	Igo	1	1	1	1			No.	
Jones, E. R.	Igo	1	1	1					
Kingsbury, Chas.	Igo								
Leiter, Alex.	Igo								
Ludwig, Alex.	Igo	5	5	1				Yes.	
Loeffler, G.	Igo	5	5					Yes.	
Burgdorf, Chas.	Leighton	½	1	½	1		½	No.	
Hastings, W. R.	Leighton	5	5	6				Yes.	
Kelley, J. A.	Leighton	4	4				4	No.	
Kelley, J. J.	Leighton	2	2				2	No.	
Luscher, S. G.	Leighton	1	1	1	1			No.	
Leighton, B.	Leighton	2⅔	2⅔	2½				No.	
Osborne, D. C., estate of	Leighton	4	4				4	No.	
Shaffer, B. A.	Leighton	3	3	1	2			Yes.	
Smith, F. & S.	Leighton	15	15	15		2		No.	No record. Mission.
Asbell, J. M.	Millville	1¼	1¼	10	1½			No.	No record. Not known.
Beale, E. M.	Millville	10	10	10				Yes.	
Cutler, H. H.	Millville								
Derch, Fred.	Millville	1	1	1	1			No.	No record. Not known.
Edington, J. S.	Millville	2	2	2	2			Yes.	No record.
Garner, C. C.	Millville								
Hoffman, Frank	Millville								
Hust, Jos.	Millville								
Haws, Wm.	Millville								
Lee, Wm. C.	Millville	1	1		1			No.	No record. Not known.
March, W. F.	Millville	1¼	1¼			1¼		No.	No record. Not known.
Nichols, J. L.	Millville	1	1					No.	No record. Not known.
Reed, W. K.	Millville	⅛	⅛		⅞				
Reineke, Chris.	Millville								
Schooling, Oliver	Millville	1	1	1	1			No.	No record. Not known.
Smith, Wm. A.	Millville	1	1					Yes.	
Standford, F. W.	Millville								
Talbourne, John J.	Millville								
Thierkoff, J. Anthony	Millville								
Wilkinson & Ross	Millville								

Shasta County—Continued.

Name of Owner.	Post Office and Name of Vineyard.	Total Acres in Grapes.	Acres in Bearing.	Acres in Wine Grapes.	Acres in Table Grapes.	Acres in Raisin Grapes.	Wine Maker.	Product in 1889.	Varieties.
Cutler, H. H.	North Cow Creek								
Forrester, J.	North Cow Creek								
Lenn, I.	North Cow Creek								
Meyers, F.	North Cow Creek								
Rediker, A.	North Cow Creek	4	4	4			Yes.		
Rediker, W.	North Cow Creek								
Woodman, L. C.	North Cow-Creek								
Waldorf, S.	Oak Run	1	1		1				
Estep, Alfred	Oak Run	2	1½		½		No.	No record.	Not known.
Duncan, J. C.	Olinda	1½	1			1	No.		
Finley, H. H.	Olinda	1	1½			1	No.		
McGuinness, Henry	Olinda	1	1			1	No.		
Mewes, Robert	Olinda	4	4			4	No.		
Root, E. F.	Olinda	4	4	1	1	4	No.		
Shoup, Frank	Olinda	6	3	1		6	No.		
Smith, Peter T.	Olinda	3	2	2		1	No.		
Williamson, P. L.	Olinda	2	1	1		1	Yes.		
Quinn, Timothy	Ono	1					Yes.		
Banks, S. E.	Pinckney								
Alicamp, ——	Redding	2½			½		No.		
Bentley, George H.	Redding								
Bush, C. C.	Redding								
Brincard, James	Redding								
Chenoworth, S.	Redding	12		12		35	No.		
Darlot & Pradel	Redding	45	45		10		No.		
Dozier, L. F.	Redding	2	2		2		No.		
Edge, G. & A.	Redding								
Fisher, F. W.	Redding	1			1		No.		
Friesen, Jacob	Redding								
Frietes, Joseph	Redding	3	3		1		No.		
Houn, D. N.	Redding	2			2	2	No.		
Isaacson & Sullivan	Redding	12	6		12		No.		
Lee, W. C.	Redding								
McCoy, A. S. J.	Redding								

Name	Locality						
McMurray, ——	Redding		No.			2	2
Nunamaker & Dolde	Redding					2	
Oliver, Ben.	Redding						
Reid, E. A.	Redding						
Schneider, Louis	Redding						
Wilber, Mrs. E. P.	Redding		No.	4	3		7
Cochran, James R.	Redding		No.		1½	2½	1½
Meyer, Fred.	Roberts		Yes.			1	2½
Standford, G. N.	Roberts		No.				1¾
Warren, E. E.	Roberts		No.		3	20	3
Woodman, L. C.	Roberts		Yes.			1	20
Yank, Joseph	Roberts		Yes.		¼	1	1
Morley, W. W.	Round Mountain						¼
Miller, W. P.	Shasta						
Leschinsky, A.	Shasta						
Schroeter, G. C.	Shasta						
Wieser, Mrs. H. A.	Shasta						
Camden, Charles	Stella						
Desmond, Denis	Stella						
Harrison, John	Stella						
Williams, John	Stella		Yes.	1		1	2
Bass, J. S. P.	Stillwater		No.	¾	1		¾
Dierckson, Claus	Stillwater		Yes.	3		8	10
Fish, F. W., estate of .	Stillwater		No.	4			4
Morehead, W. A.	Stillwater		No.			3	3
Schade, C. F.	Stillwater		No.	1	1¼	1	2½
Shupe, C. F.	Stillwater		No.	2	1	3	3
Williams, J. D. H.	Stillwater		No.		¾		¾
Miller, J. F. & C. B.	Whitmore		No.	3			3
Parsons, T. H.	Whitmore						
Totals for county				242	104	122	432	468

SOLANO COUNTY.

Post Office and Name of Vineyard.	Total Acres in Grapes.	Acres in Bearing.	Acres in Wine Grapes.	Acres in Table Grapes.	Acres in Raisin Grapes.	Wine Maker.	Product in 1889.	Varieties.
Batavia	20	20	15	5		No.		Muscat.
Batavia	40	40	20		20	No.		Zinfandel, Mission.
Benicia	35	35				No.		
Benicia	35	35				No.		
Benicia	50	50				No.		
Cordelia	50	50				No.		
Cordelia	25	25				No.		
Cordelia	5	5				No.		
Cordelia	30	30				No.		
Cordelia	10	10				No.		
Cordelia	5	5				No.		
Cordelia	80	80				No.		
Cordelia	15	15				No.		
Cordelia	6	6				No.		
Cordelia	15	15				No.		
Cordelia	150	100				Yes.		
Cordelia	10	10				No.		
Cordelia	10	10				No.		
Cordelia	40	40				No.		
Cordelia	10	10				No.		
Cordelia	10	10				No.		
Cordelia	25	25				No.		
Cordelia	30	30				No.		
Cordelia	80	80				No.		
Cordelia	100	100				Yes.		
Cordelia	30	30				No.		
Cordelia	35	35				No.		
Cordelia	30	30				Yes.		
Cordelia	20	20				No.		
Davisville	40	40			40	No.		
Davisville	40	40		30	40	No.		
Davisville	140	140			110	No.		Muscat.
Dixon	50	50	34		18	No.		Muscat, Burger.

Name	Post Office	Acres bearing	Acres not bearing	Total acres	Wine made	Tons	Varieties
Currey, John	Dixon	5	40	45	No.		
Currey, M. S.	Dixon	12	58	70	No.		
Evans, G. H.	Dixon	2	13	15	No.		
Kline, J.	Dixon	5	15	20	No.		
McCune, Joe.	Dixon	4	8	12	No.		
Rockwell, M. S.	Dixon	4	14	18	No.		
Stephens, R.	Dixon	10		10	No.		
Stewart, D. S.	Dixon		20	20	No.		
Wells, W. H.	Dixon	30		30	No.		
Sackett, F. E.	Pleasant Valley						
Lamar, H.	Pleasant Valley	277		277			
Campbell, J. P.	Suisun			13	No.		
Dickie, A. A.	Suisun			10	No.		
Hench, Wm.	Suisun			10	No.		
Kimball, L. F.	Suisun			10	No.		
Lemon, J.	Suisun			35	No.		
McNulty, James.	Suisun			20	No.		
O'Kell, E. J.	Suisun			20	No.		
Gordon, Wm.	Suisun			10	No.		
O'Kell, E. J.	Suisun			30	No.		
Oliver, J. M.	Suisun			10	No.		
Reams, Col.	Suisun			3	No.	90 tons.	Zinfandel.
Roberts, Chas.	Suisun	3		10	No.	60 tons.	Malvoisie, Zinfandel.
Bassford, Frank	Vacaville	10		10	No.	20 tons.	Muscat, Tokay.
Bassford, H. A.	Vacaville	19		19	No.		Muscat, Tokay.
Bassford, J. M., Jr.	Vacaville	14		14	No.		Muscat, Tokay.
Bassford, J. M., Sr.	Vacaville	10		10	No.		Muscat, Tokay.
Blake, Jos.	Vacaville	18		18	No.		Muscat, Rose Peru, Tokay.
Blake, Mrs. E. A. C.	Vacaville	15		15			Muscat, Rose Peru, Tokay, Fontainebleau.
Brislow, S. D.	Vacaville	12		12			Muscat, Rose Peru, Tokay, Malvoisie.
Buck, F. Herbert	Vacaville	3		3			Tokay.
Buck, Frank H.	Vacaville	12		12		50 tons.	Tokay, Muscat, Emperor.
Buck, J. K.	Vacaville	3		3			Tokay.
Buck, L. W.	Vacaville	20		20		150 tons.	Tokay, Muscat, Rose Peru, Fontainebleau, Emperor.
Buck, L. W. & F. H.	Vacaville	85		85		400 tons.	Tokay, Muscat, Rose Peru, Emperor, Fontaine-bleau.
Buck, W. H.	Vacaville	16		16	No.		Tokay, Muscat, Emperor, Fontainebleau.
Buckingham, Mrs. E. P.	Vacaville	95		95	No.		Muscat, Tokay, Chasselas, Zinfandel, Sultana.
Buckingham & Watson	Vacaville	60		60	No.		Muscat, Fontainebleau, Rose Peru.
Cargill, P.	Vacaville	7		7	No.		Muscat, Fontainebleau.
Chinn, R. H.	Vacaville	100		100	No.	20 tons.	Muscat, Tokay, Rose Peru.
Christopher, B. F.	Vacaville	6		6			Muscat, Tokay, Zinfandel.
Chubb, C. M.	Vacaville	5		5			Muscat, Fontainebleau.
Collins, J. R.	Vacaville	15		15			Muscat, Tokay, Rose Peru, Malvoisie.

SOLANO COUNTY—Continued.

Post Office and Name of Vineyard.	Total Acres in Grapes.	Acres in Bearing.	Acres in Wine Grapes.	Acres in Table Grapes.	Acres in Raisin Grapes.	Wine Maker...	Product in 1889.	Varieties.
Vacaville	15	15		10	5		50 tons.	Muscat, Tokay, Rose Peru.
Vacaville	6	6		4	2	No.		Muscat, Tokay, Sultana.
Vacaville	4	4		4		No.		Muscat.
Vacaville	4	4		4				Muscat, Malvoisie, Chasselas.
Vacaville	23	23	8½	19½				Muscat, Tokay.
Vacaville	34	34		34				Muscat, Tokay, Rose Peru, Fontainebleau, Zinfandel.
Vacaville	5	5		5				Muscat, Tokay, Rose Peru, Emperor, Chasselas.
Vacaville	15	15		15				Fontainebleau, Muscat.
Vacaville	7	7		7				Muscat, Tokay, Rose Peru.
Vacaville	7	7		7				Muscat.
Vacaville	20	20		20				Muscat, Rose Peru, Fontainebleau.
Vacaville	8	8		8		No.		Muscat, Tokay, Rose Peru, Malvoisie.
Vacaville	5	5		5		No.		Muscat, Tokay.
Vacaville	30	30		30		No.		Muscat, Emperor.
Vacaville	11	11		11				Muscat, Tokay.
Vacaville	18	18		18				Tokay.
Vacaville	5	5		5				Muscat, Tokay, Rose Peru, Fontainebleau.
Vacaville	12	12		12	4			Muscat, Tokay, Emperor.
Vacaville	8	8		4				Muscat, Tokay, Malvoisie.
Vacuville	16	16		16				Muscat, Tokay, Fontainebleau, Rose Peru.
Vacaville	18	18		18				Muscat, Tokay, Fontainebleau, Rose Peru.
Vacaville	42	42		42				Muscat, Tokay, Fontainebleau, Rose Peru.
Vacaville (San Fran.)	15	12		15	20	No.		Muscat, Tokay, Emperor, Fontainebleau, Rose Peru.
Vacaville	32	32		12				Muscat, Tokay.
Vacaville	8	8		8				Rose Peru, Tokay.
Vacaville	10	10		10		Yes.		Rose Peru, Sweetwater.
Vacaville	250	250	250					Zinfandel, Riesling, Chasselas.
Vacaville	14	14		14				Zinfandel, Tokay, Rose Peru, Emperor, Muscat.
Vacaville	4	4		4			17 tons.	Muscat.
Vacaville	25	25	3	22				Muscat, Tokay, Malvoisie, Zinfandel, Fontaine-bleau.

Name of Owner	Post Office and Name of Vineyard	Total Acres in Grapes	Acres in Bearing	Acres in Wine Grapes	Acres in Table Grapes	Acres in Raisin Grapes	Wine Maker	Product in 1889	Varieties
Robinson, J. M.	Vacaville	18	18	---	18	---	---	---	Muscat, Tokay.
Rogers, J. N.	Vacaville	45	5	---	45	---	---	---	Muscat, Fontainebleau, Tokay.
Smith Ranch, W. W.	Vacaville	30	30	---	30	---	---	---	Muscat, Tokay.
Starke, J. V., estate of	Vacaville	18	18	---	18	---	---	60 tons.	Muscat, Tokay, Fontainebleau.
Steiger, A.	Vacaville	20	20	---	20	---	---	30 tons.	Muscat, Rose Peru, Malvoisie.
Sweeney, O.	Vacaville	2	2	---	2	---	---	---	Muscat, Fontainebleau.
Thayer & Bates	Vacaville	16	16	---	16	---	---	---	Emperor, Muscat.
Tucker & Tubbs	Vacaville	15	15	---	15	---	---	---	Emperor, Rose Peru, Fontainebleau, Muscat, Tokay.
Walker, S. C.	Vacaville	6	6	---	6	---	---	---	Rose Peru, Muscat, Tokay.
Wells, J. N.	Vacaville	8	8	3	5	---	---	---	Zinfandel, Muscat, Tokay.
Williams, Frank	Vacaville	8	8	---	4	4	---	---	Muscat, Tokay.
Wren, J. D.	Vacaville	10	10	---	10	---	---	---	Fontainebleau.
Brink, H.	Winters	7	7	---	7	---	---	40 tons.	Tokay, Fontainebleau, Muscat.
Pleasants, W. J.	Winters	6	6	---	---	6	---	---	Muscat.
Wire, Chas.	Winters	70	70	---	20	50	---	---	---
Totals for county (vines at Cordelia, etc., stated as wine grapes)		3,527	3,527	1,928	1,167	432			

SONOMA COUNTY.

Name of Owner	Post Office and Name of Vineyard	Total Acres in Grapes	Acres in Bearing	Acres in Wine Grapes	Acres in Table Grapes	Acres in Raisin Grapes	Wine Maker	Product in 1889	Varieties
Arnold, W. J.	America	25	25	25	---	---	No.	35 tons.	Zinfandel, Chasselas.
Butler, S. J.	America	12	12	12	---	---	No.	12 tons.	Zinfandel, Mission.
Faught, Willis	America	8	8	8	---	---	No.	4 tons.	Zinfandel.
Goodman, ———	America	10	10	10	---	---	No.	10 tons.	Chasselas, Mission.
Lauretson, G.	America	10	10	10	---	---	No.	20 tons.	Zinfandel.
McCann, Thos.	America	30	30	30	---	---	No.	31 tons.	Zinfandel, Burgundy.
Pitts, Thomas	America	10	10	10	---	---	No.	10 tons.	Zinfandel.
Sharp, Nathan	America	10	10	10	---	---	No.	10 tons.	Zinfandel.
Tarwater, M. W.	America	10	10	10	---	---	No.	6 tons.	Zinfandel, Mission.
Taylor, William	America	8	8	8	---	---	No.	8 tons.	Zinfandel.
Italian-Swiss Agricultural Colony	Asti	600	600	600	---	---	Yes.	150,000 gals.	Zinfandel and varieties.

SONOMA COUNTY—Continued.

Name of Owner.	Post Office and Name of Vineyard.	Total Acres in Grapes.	Acres in Bearing.	Acres in Wine Grapes.	Acres in Table Grapes.	Acres in Raisin Grapes.	Wine Maker.	Product in 1889.	Varieties.
Carter, C. C.	Calistoga	18	18	18			No.	60 tons.	Zinfandel.
Douselman, Joseph	Calistoga	10	10	10			No.	10 tons.	Zinfandel.
Klotz, J. P.	Calistoga	25	25	25			Yes.	75 tons.	Zinfandel and mixed.
Mee, Mrs.	Calistoga	12	12	12			No.	12 tons.	Zinfandel.
Albee, F. T.	Cloverdale	10	10	10			No.	40 tons.	Zinfandel.
Black, W. H.	Cloverdale	30	30	30			No.	80 tons.	Zinfandel and mixed.
Bowman, Mrs.	Cloverdale	6	6	6			No.	15 tons.	Zinfandel.
Burroughs Bros.	Cloverdale	5	5	5			No.	10 tons.	Mission.
Champion, John	Cloverdale	75	30	75			No.	62 tons.	Chasselas, Burger.
Chisholm, D.	Cloverdale	5	5	5			No.	5 tons.	Zinfandel.
Cooley, J. B.	Cloverdale	60	60	60			No.	100 tons.	Zinfandel and mixed.
Coombs, A. M.	Cloverdale	12	12		12		No.	25 tons.	Muscat.
De Hay, A.	Cloverdale	20	20	20			Yes.	40 tons.	Zinfandel, Chasselas.
De Hay, T.	Cloverdale	20	20	20			Yes.	35 tons.	Zinfandel.
Eberhardt, D. F.	Cloverdale	20	20	20			No.	40 tons.	Zinfandel.
Elliott, John	Cloverdale	10	10	10			No.	60 tons.	Zinfandel, Malvoisie.
Ferry, John	Cloverdale	30	30	30			No.	50 tons.	Zinfandel and varieties.
Furber, E. G.	Cloverdale	60	60	60			No.	140 tons.	Zinfandel and varieties.
Ginocchio, G.	Cloverdale	115	75	115			Yes.	150 tons.	Zinfandel.
Goetzelman, J.	Cloverdale	5	5	5			No.	10 tons.	Zinfandel, Malvoisie.
Haehl, Conrad	Cloverdale	30	30	30			Yes.	100 tons.	Zinfandel.
Hagmeyer, G.	Cloverdale	8	8	8			No.	10 tons.	Zinfandel.
Hall, David	Cloverdale	25	25	25			No.	80 tons.	Zinfandel and varieties.
Heald. J. G.	Cloverdale	40	40	40			No.	145 tons.	Zinfandel and varieties.
Hemstath, B.	Cloverdale	20	10	20	2		No.	18 tons.	Zinfandel, Muscat.
Herman, Mrs.	Cloverdale	12	12	10			No.	15 tons.	Zinfandel.
Hixon, Wm.	Cloverdale	10	10	10			No.	30 tons.	Zinfandel.
Hoadley, J. F.	Cloverdale	15	15	15			No.	40 tons.	Zinfandel.
Holloway, J. C.	Cloverdale	65	65	53	12		No.	120 tons.	Muscat, Tokay, Zinfandel, Malvoisie.
Howard, D.	Cloverdale	10	10	10			No.	30 tons.	Zinfandel.
Kneist, C.	Cloverdale	30	30	30			No.	60 tons.	Zinfandel and mixed.
Larison, Sam	Cloverdale	25	25	25			No.	50 tons.	Zinfandel and mixed.
Layman, Wm.	Cloverdale	15	15	15			No.	36 tons.	Zinfandel.
Lodger, A. C.	Cloverdale	15	15	15			No.	50 tons.	Zinfandel.

Name	Location					Resident	Production	Variety
Leroux, Jules	Cloverdale	15	15	15		No.	40 tons.	Zinfandel.
Leroux, Peter	Cloverdale	15	15	15		No.	40 tons.	Zinfandel.
Luning, N.	Cloverdale	10	10	10		No.	25 tons.	Zinfandel.
McCray, W. H.	Cloverdale	20	20	20		No.	50 tons.	Zinfandel and mixed.
McElamey & Smith	Cloverdale	40	40	40		Yes.	150 tons.	Zinfandel.
Meyerholfer, J.	Cloverdale	45	45	45		No.	100 tons.	Zinfandel.
Moulton, Mrs.	Cloverdale	75	75	75		No.	160 tons.	Zinfandel and mixed.
Mowbray, Mrs.	Cloverdale	10	10	10		No.	25 tons.	Zinfandel.
Nervo, B.	Cloverdale	10	10	10		No.	20 tons.	Zinfandel.
Parazzo, G.	Cloverdale	20	20	20		No.	50 tons.	Zinfandel.
Plaskett, Peter	Cloverdale	5	5	5		No.	20 tons.	Zinfandel, Mission.
Porterfield, J. W.	Cloverdale	60	60	60	5	No.	130 tons.	Zinfandel, Tokay, Mission.
Porterfield, Wm.	Cloverdale	32	32	32		No.	75 tons.	Zinfandel, Malvoisie.
Purcilio, C.	Cloverdale	20	20	22		No.	40 tons.	Zinfandel.
Radkey, Fred.	Cloverdale	12	12	12		No.	30 tons.	Zinfandel and mixed.
Semple, C. H.	Cloverdale	5	5	5	4	No.	10 tons.	Mission.
Sink, D.	Cloverdale	35	35	35		No.	50 tons.	Zinfandel.
Sink, W. D.	Cloverdale	32	20	20		Yes.	50 tons.	Zinfandel.
Todd, P. W.	Cloverdale	22	22	22		No.	30 tons.	Zinfandel.
Turner, John	Cloverdale	12	12	12		No.	40 tons.	Zinfandel, Muscat.
Wambold, D. M.	Cloverdale	10	10	10		No.	45 tons.	Zinfandel, Mission.
Wilson, J.	Cloverdale	15	15	15		No.	80 tons.	Zinfandel.
Winders, Mrs.	Cloverdale	40	40	40		No.	75 tons.	Zinfandel.
Winter & Son	Cloverdale	45	30	45		No.	15 tons.	Zinfandel and mixed.
Worth, C.	Cloverdale	6	0			No.	30 tons.	Zinfandel.
Yordi, F.	Cloverdale	17	17	17		No.	40 tons.	Zinfandel, Mission.
Zalfo, C.	Cloverdale	15	15	15		No.	60 tons.	Zinfandel.
Bell, G. K.	Cozzens	20	20	20		No.	35 tons.	Zinfandel.
Bell, J. S.	Cozzens	15	15	15		No.	35 tons.	Zinfandel.
Board, William	Cozzens	15	15	15		No.	60 tons.	Zinfandel and mixed.
Bonner, Robert	Cozzens	20	20	20		No.	20 tons.	Zinfandel.
Bryant Bros.	Cozzens	10	10	10		No.	15 tons.	Mixed.
Bourdens, P.	Cozzens	6	6	6		Yes.	10 tons.	Zinfandel.
Cozzens, D.	Cozzens	5	5	5	5	No.	60 tons.	Zinfandel and mixed.
Fricke & Pries	Cozzens	20	20	20		Yes.	50 tons.	Muscat.
Hartsock, Mrs.	Cozzens	5	5	5		No.	10 tons.	Zinfandel.
Hendricks, M. C.	Cozzens	20	20	20		No.	60 tons.	Zinfandel.
Hohlengrin, S. P.	Cozzens	20	20	20		Yes.	40 tons.	Zinfandel and mixed.
Parkerson, C. J.	Cozzens	10	6	10		No.	5 tons.	Zinfandel.
Patronack, F.	Cozzens	25	25	25		Yes.	60 tons.	Zinfandel and mixed.
Patten, J.	Cozzens	20	20	20		No.	50 tons.	Zinfandel and mixed.
Patton, R. R.	Cozzens	6	6	6		No.	15 tons.	Zinfandel.
Phillips, G. D.	Cozzens	10	10	10		No.	25 tons.	Zinfandel and mixed.
Price, John	Cozzens	15	15	15		No.	50 tons.	Zinfandel and mixed.
Pritchett, J. S.	Cozzens	15	15	15		No.	30 tons.	Zinfandel and mixed.

SONOMA COUNTY—Continued.

NAME OF OWNER.	Post Office and Name of Vineyard.	Total Acres in Grapes.	Acres in Bearing.	Acres in Wine Grapes.	Acres in Table Grapes.	Acres in Raisin Grapes.	Wine Maker.	Product in 1889.	Varieties.
Thompson, Chas.	Cozzens	10	10	10			No.	25 tons.	Mission.
Van Allen, John	Cozzens	20	20	20			No.	60 tons.	Zinfandel.
Wagelee, Conrad	Cozzens	20	20	20			No.	60 tons.	Zinfandel and mixed.
Ward, A. T.	Cozzens	5	5	5			No.	10 tons.	Mixed.
Wood, G. D.	Cozzens	20	20	20			No.	50 tons.	Zinfandel and mixed.
Wright, Ben F.	Cozzens	10	10	10			No.	25 tons.	Zinfandel.
Adell, Mrs. Frank	Forestville	8	8	8			No.	12 tons.	Zinfandel.
Anderson, L. S.	Forestville	8	8	8			No.	15 tons.	Zinfandel.
Archer, Mrs.	Forestville	30	30	30			No.	60 tons.	Zinfandel and mixed.
Bushnell, A.	Forestville	15	15	15			No.	15 tons.	Zinfandel.
James, C. G., estate of.	Forestville	10	10	10			No.	20 tons.	Zinfandel.
Jewett, J. E.	Forestville	15	15	15			No.	30 tons.	Zinfandel.
McAndrews, P.	Forestville	15	15	15			No.	20 tons.	Zinfandel.
Madelock, W.	Forestville	5	5				No.	10 tons.	Muscat, Tokay.
Merrett, John	Forestville	20		20			No.	Not bearing.	Zinfandel.
Norton, E. A.	Forestville	20	20	20			No.	40 tons.	Zinfandel.
Ricard, W. G.	Forestville	15	15	15			No.	30 tons.	Zinfandel.
Richlieu & True	Forestville	5	5	5			No.	10 tons.	Zinfandel.
Thomas, Isaiah	Forestville	12	12	10	2		No.	20 tons.	Zinfandel, Muscat.
Walsh, M.	Forestville	15	15	15			No.	50 tons.	Zinfandel.
Alton, John L.	Fulton	50	50	50			Yes.	7,000 gals.	Zinfandel.
Barnes, W. P.	Fulton	11	11	11			No.	14 tons.	Zinfandel, Burger.
Chaffee, John	Fulton	6	6	6			No.	2 tons.	Zinfandel.
De Wolf, Mrs.	Fulton	12	12	12			No.	5 tons.	Zinfandel.
Dwight, L.	Fulton	8	8	8			No.	20 tons.	Zinfandel, Riesling.
Gingley, A.	Fulton	7	7	7			No.	14 tons.	Zinfandel.
Harris, Henry	Fulton	36	36	36			No.	90 tons.	Zinfandel, Malvoisie.
Howe, E. A.	Fulton	11	11	11			No.	36 tons.	Zinfandel, Riesling.
Likins, J. W.	Fulton	12	12	12			No.	50 tons.	Zinfandel.
Logue, A.	Fulton	15	15	15			No.	13 tons.	Zinfandel, Mission.
Looney, William	Fulton	16	16	16			No.	16 tons.	Zinfandel and mixed.
Malone, Frank	Fulton	15	8	15			No.	10 tons.	Zinfandel.
Malone, James	Fulton	18	18	18			No.	15 tons.	Zinfandel, Mission.
Matson, Mrs.	Fulton	10	10	10			No.	20 tons.	Mission.

Name	Location							Variety
Meacham, A.	Fulton	15	15	15		No.	5 tons.	Zinfandel, Riesling.
Swafel, Walter	Fulton	48	48	48		No.	85 tons.	Mission, Riesling.
Wood, W.	Fulton	7	7	7		No.	14 tons.	Zinfandel.
Wright, Adam	Fulton	12	12	12		No.	24 tons.	Zinfandel.
Archambeau, Mrs.	Geyserville	20	20	20		No.	25 tons.	Zinfandel, Mission.
Bennett, Jacob	Geyserville	10	10	10		No.	20 tons.	Zinfandel.
Bosworth, C. M.	Geyserville	20	20	20		No.	40 tons.	Zinfandel.
Boyd, Thomas	Geyserville	5	5	5		No.	10 tons.	Mixed.
Burr, Frank	Geyserville	25	25	25		No.	60 tons.	Mission, Zinfandel.
Crocker, Henry	Geyserville	20	20	20		No.	45 tons.	Zinfandel.
Cummings, J. M.	Geyserville	10	10	10		No.	20 tons.	Zinfandel.
Denari, A.	Geyserville	40	40	40		Yes.	20 tons.	Zinfandel.
Ellis, L. G.	Geyserville	35	35	35		No.	75 tons.	Zinfandel and mixed.
Fay, John	Geyserville	30	30	30		Yes.	40 tons.	Zinfandel.
Feldmeyer & Stamer	Geyserville	20	20	20		No.	50 tons.	Zinfandel.
Gaiter, J.	Geyserville	15	15	15		No.	30 tons.	Zinfandel.
Gibney, George	Geyserville	20	20	20		No.	40 tons.	Zinfandel.
Griffith, W.	Geyserville	10	10	10		No.	20 tons.	Zinfandel.
Hamilton, Mrs.	Geyserville	6	6	6		No.	12 tons.	Zinfandel.
McDonough, M.	Geyserville	15	15	15		No.	30 tons.	Zinfandel.
Meyers, Claus	Geyserville	30	30	30		No.	60 tons.	Zinfandel.
Montague, Charles	Geyserville	15	15	15		No.	40 tons.	Zinfandel.
Moore, C. P.	Geyserville	60	60	60		No.	160 tons.	Mixed.
Morrill, Mrs.	Geyserville	20	20	20		No.	60 tons.	Zinfandel.
Ormsby, M. P.	Geyserville	10	10	10		No.	25 tons.	Zinfandel and mixed.
Petray, G. W.	Geyserville	10	10	10		No.	20 tons.	Zinfandel, Malvoisie.
Renuff, A. A.	Geyserville	8	8	8		No.	16 tons.	Zinfandel.
Schmitzer, C. H.	Geyserville	15	15	15		No.	30 tons.	Zinfandel and mixed.
Smith, Thos.	Geyserville	30	30	30		No.	60 tons.	Zinfandel.
Stites, Alex.	Geyserville	10	10	10		No.	20 tons.	Zinfandel and mixed.
Strode, John	Geyserville	50	50	50		No.	100 tons.	Zinfandel.
Strode, S. E.	Geyserville	10	10	10		No.	20 tons.	Zinfandel and mixed.
Teebe, W.	Geyserville	10	10	10		No.	20 tons.	Zinfandel.
Waldon, Ed.	Geyserville	10	10	10		Yes.	20 tons.	Zinfandel and mixed.
Weiland, John	Geyserville (San Fran)	40	40	40		Yes.	80 tons.	Zinfandel.
Winders, Mrs.	Geyserville	40	40	40		No.	80 tons.	Zinfandel and mixed.
Wisecarver, J. R.	Geyserville	50	60	50		No.	100 tons.	Zinfandel and mixed.
Allen, Reuben	Glen Ellen	12	12	12		No.	30 tons.	Zinfandel.
Bowen, John	Glen Ellen	20	20	20		No.	40 tons.	Zinfandel.
Bowen, Sarah E.	Glen Ellen	25	25	25		No.	50 tons.	Zinfandel.
Cal., State of (Home for Feeble-Minded).	Glen Ellen	40	40	5	35	No.	40 tons.	Zinfandel, Tokay, Ferrara.
Chavet, Joshua	Glen Ellen	10	10	10		Yes.	10 tons.	Gutedel.
Clark, George	Glen Ellen	10		10		---	Not bearing.	Tokay.
Clausen, Charles	Glen Ellen	30	30	30		No.	75 tons.	Zinfandel.

SONOMA COUNTY—Continued.

NAME OF OWNER.	Post Office and Name of Vineyard.	Total Acres in Grapes.	Acres in Bearing.	Acres in Wine Grapes.	Acres in Table Grapes.	Acres in Raisin Grapes.	Wine Maker.	Product in 1889.	Varieties.
Crosby, James	Glen Ellen	10	10	10			No.	20 tons.	Mixed.
Frideger, Jacob	Glen Ellen	15	15	15			Yes.	30 tons.	Zinfandel.
Gatey, Mrs.	Glen Ellen	12		12			Yes.	Not bearing.	Mixed.
Groeskopf, A.	Glen Ellen	25	26	25			Yes.	50 tons.	Zinfandel.
Hendley, John	Glen Ellen	8	8	8			No.	20 tons.	Zinfandel.
Hilton, W. H.	Glen Ellen	40	26	40			No.	50 tons.	Zinfandel.
Hurd, Rudolph	Glen Ellen	10		10			No.	Not bearing.	Zinfandel.
Johnson, Charles	Glen Ellen	10	10	10			Yes.	20 tons.	Mixed.
Justi, Mrs. M. C.	Glen Ellen	10	10	10			Yes.	20 tons.	Zinfandel, Mission.
Kohler & Frohling	Glen Ellen (San Fran.)	120	40	120			Yes.	60,000 gals.	Sauvignon.
La Motte, A. V.	Glen Ellen	35		35			Yes.	Not bearing.	Zinfandel.
McEwen, James	Glen Ellen	40	40	40			Yes.	60,000 gals.	Zinfandel, Riesling.
McGinty, James	Glen Ellen	12	12	12			No.	15 tons.	Zinfandel.
Miller, Robert	Glen Ellen	6	6	6			Yes.	12 tons.	Zinfandel.
Monahan, P.	Glen Ellen	20	5	15	5		Yes.	20 tons.	Zinfandel, Tokay.
Peter, Martin	Glen Ellen	40	15	40			No.	30 tons.	Gutedel, Riesling.
Powers, Pierce	Glen Ellen	10	10	10			Yes.	20 tons.	Zinfandel.
Scheick, J. G.	Glen Ellen	15	10	15			Yes.	25 tons.	Riesling.
Stier, G.	Glen Ellen	15	15	15			Yes.	30 tons.	Zinfandel.
Tarrant, H. F.	Glen Ellen	30	20	30			Yes.	40 tons.	Zinfandel.
Thomas, G. W.	Glen Ellen	7	7	7			No.	3 tons.	Zinfandel.
Thompson, W. A.	Glen Ellen	10		10				Not bearing.	Zinfandel and mixed.
Warfield, Mrs. Kate	Glen Ellen	25	25	25			Yes.	50 tons.	Zinfandel.
Watson, J. L.	Glen Ellen	50	50	50			No.	27 tons.	Semillon.
Weaver, Andrew	Glen Ellen	20	20	20			No.	60 tons.	Zinfandel.
Wezner, J.	Glen Ellen	10		20				Not bearing.	Zinfandel.
Weise, Christian	Glen Ellen	20	20	20			Yes.	3,000 gals.	Zinfandel, Gutedel.
Zane, Joel M.	Glen Ellen	25	25	25			No.	100 tons.	Zinfandel, Mission.
Austin, G. T.	Guerneville	10	10	10			No.	20 tons.	Mixed.
Baldwin, D.	Guerneville	15	15	15			No.	40 tons.	Zinfandel.
Carr, William	Guerneville	5	5	5			No.	10 tons.	Zinfandel.
Eckman, John	Guerneville	10	10	10			No.	25 tons.	Zinfandel.
Joost, J.	Guerneville	15	15	15			No.	25 tons.	Zinfandel.
Kese, R. R.	Guerneville	15	15	15			No.	30 tons.	Zinfandel and mixed.

Name	Location						Tons	Variety
Korbel Bros.	Guerneville	175	175	175		Yes.	400 tons.	Zinfandel and mixed.
Prosek, Dr.	Guerneville	20	20	20		No.	50 tons.	Mixed.
Ridenhour, L. W.	Guerneville	10	10	5	5	No.	25 tons.	Zinfandel, Muscat.
Sullivan, C. J.	Guerneville	20	20	20		No.	50 tons.	Zinfandel and mixed.
Wehrspon, A.	Guerneville	15	15	15		No.	30 tons.	Zinfandel, Burger.
Algren, George	Healdsburg	6	6	6		No.	15 tons.	Mission.
Allen, Wm. T.	Healdsburg	12	12	12		No.	25 tons.	Mission.
Aradien, Wm.	Healdsburg	10	10	10		No.	20 tons.	Zinfandel.
Axford, Wm.	Healdsburg	10	10	10		No.	20 tons.	Zinfandel.
Bailache, John N.	Healdsburg	65	65	66		Yes.	196 tons.	Zinfandel, Riesling.
Baker, A. M.	Healdsburg	12	12	12		No.	25 tons.	Zinfandel.
Bank of Healdsburg	Healdsburg	279	279	279		No.	568 tons.	Zinfandel and mixed.
Beeson, S.	Healdsburg	8	8	8		No.	15 tons.	Zinfandel.
B-ll, John	Healdsburg	20	20	20		No.	60 tons.	Zinfandel and mixed.
Bice, Mrs.	Healdsburg	8	8	8		No.	20 tons.	Zinfandel, Mission:
Black, W. A.	Healdsburg	8	8	6		No.	12 tons.	Zinfandel.
Bledsoe, A. J.	Healdsburg	30	30	30		No.	60 tons.	Zinfandel.
Bradford, R. A.	Healdsburg	40	40	40		No.	80 tons.	Zinfandel.
Bryant, D. S.	Healdsburg	12	12	12		No.	25 tons.	Zinfandel.
Burnham, A. E.	Healdsburg	10	10	10		No.	20 tons.	Mixed.
Callahan, J.	Healdsburg	15	15	15		No.	30 tons.	Zinfandel, Mission.
Coghill, A. J.	Healdsburg	40	40	40		No.	75 tons.	Zinfandel and mixed.
Coulson, John	Healdsburg	30	30	30		Yes.	60 tons.	Zinfandel, Mission.
De Weiderhold, A. E. S.	Healdsburg	10	10	10		No.	20 tons.	Zinfandel.
Didier,	Healdsburg	10	10	10		No.	25 tons.	Zinfandel.
Dotta, L.	Healdsburg	25	25	25		Yes.	60 tons.	Zinfandel and mixed.
Dunn, C. J.	Healdsburg	75	75	75		Yes.	200 tons.	Zinfandel.
Feely, M.	Healdsburg	8	8	8		No.	18 tons.	Zinfandel.
Ferguson, John	Healdsburg	18	18	18		No.	30 tons.	Mixed.
Ferguson, Paris	Healdsburg	18	18	18		No.	40 tons.	Zinfandel, Mission.
Ferguson, W. V.	Healdsburg	13	18	18		No.	73 tons.	Z.nfandel, Malvoisie.
Fortier, P.	Healdsburg	6	6	6		No.	15 tons.	Zinfandel.
Foster, Robert	Healdsburg	15	15	15		No.	30 tons.	Zinfandel, Mission.
Frampton, Mrs.	Healdsburg	25	25	25		No.	50 tons.	Zinfandel, Mission.
Frank, D. C.	Healdsburg	6	6	6	10	No.	15 tons.	Zinfandel.
Gallaway, A. J.	Healdsburg	60	60	40		Yes.	175 tons.	Zinfandel, Mission, Tokay.
Gardini, John	Healdsburg	50	50	50		No.	100 tons.	Z.nfandel and mixed.
Goddard, Daniel	Healdsburg	15	15	15		No.	40 tons.	Zinfandel.
Grant, Mrs. A.	Healdsburg	40	40	40		No.	80 tons.	Zin'andel, Mission.
Hale, M. N.	Healdsburg	20	20	20		No.	80 tons.	Zinfandel, Chasselas.
Hall, L., & Son	Healdsburg	25	25	25		No.	50 tons.	Zinfandel.
Hamilton, G. S.	Healdsburg	25	25	25		Yes.	50 tons.	Zinfandel and mixed.
Hammerken, H.	Healdsburg	10	10	10		No.	20 tons.	Zinfandel.
Henton, S. O.	Healdsburg	20	20	20		No.	50 tons.	Zinfandel.
Hendricks, J. M.	Healdsburg	12	12	12		No.	25 tons.	Zinfandel.

SONOMA COUNTY—Continued.

Name of Owner.	Post Office and Name of Vineyard.	Total Acres in Grapes.	Acres in Bearing.	Acres in Wine Grapes.	Acres in Table Grapes.	Acres in Raisin Grapes.	Wine Maker.	Product in 1889.	Varieties.
Hodges, A. E.	Healdsburg	13	13	13			No.	28 tons.	Zinfandel.
Holst, Peter	Healdsburg	25	25	25			Yes.	50 tons.	Zinfandel and mixed.
Hopkins, M.	Healdsburg	200	200	200			Yes.	450 tons.	Zinfandel, Riesling.
Howland, W.	Healdsburg	5	5	5			No.	10 tons.	Zinfandel.
Howland & Wheldon	Healdsburg	10	10	10			No.	28 tons.	Zinfandel.
Isaacs, A.	Healdsburg	10	10	10			No.	25 tons.	Zinfandel, Mission.
Jaffe, L.	Healdsburg	12	12	12			No.	25 tons.	Zinfandel, Mission.
Jehle, Leo	Healdsburg	15	15	15			Yes.	40 tons.	Zinfandel.
Jewett, D. G.	Healdsburg	15	15	15			No.	50 tons.	Zinfandel.
King, John	Healdsburg	58	50	58			No.	60 tons.	Zinfandel.
King, William	Healdsburg	15	15	10			No.	25 tons.	Zinfandel.
Kelly, Mrs.	Healdsburg	15	15	15			No.	90 tons.	Zinfandel, Mission.
Lane, R. J.	Healdsburg	6	6	6			No.	12 tons.	Malvoisie, Mission.
Laughlin, M.	Healdsburg	10	10	10			No.	20 tons.	Zinfandel.
Lewis, Richard	Healdsburg	65	65	65			No.	150 tons.	Mixed.
Litton, Mrs.	Healdsburg	5	5	5			No.	10 tons.	Zinfandel, Mission.
Lombard, ——	Healdsburg	15	15	15			No.	15 tons.	Zinfandel.
Lombard, Chas.	Healdsburg	5	5	5			No.	10 tons.	Zinfandel.
Luce, M. Y.	Healdsburg	60	60	60			No.	120 tons.	Zinfandel and mixed.
Luking, H.	Healdsburg	15	15	15			No.	30 tons.	Zinfandel.
McCarty, Wm.	Healdsburg	6	6	6			No.	15 tons.	Zinfandel.
McClish, John	Healdsburg	20	20	20			No.	40 tons.	Zinfandel.
McClish, Mrs.	Healdsburg	6	6	6			No.	12 tons.	Zinfandel, Mission.
McElhaney, J. M.	Healdsburg	18		18				Not bearing.	Mixed.
McKneadney, H.	Healdsburg	40	40	40			No.	160 tons.	Zinfandel, Burger.
McLaughlin, C. W.	Healdsburg	6	6	6			No.	10 tons.	Zinfandel.
Masona, ——	Healdsburg	60	60	60			Yes.	150 tons.	Zinfandel and mixed.
Merchant, T. S.	Healdsburg	160	140	160			Yes.	150 tons.	Zinfandel and mixed.
Miller, Geo. T.	Healdsburg	32	2	32			No.	60 tons.	Burgundy and mixet.
Miller, James	Healdsburg	30	30	30			No.	75 tons.	Zinfandel, Burger.
Miller, Joshua	Healdsburg	6	6	6			No.	15 tons.	Zinfandel.
Miser, H., estate of	Healdsburg	13	13	13			No.	52 tons.	Zinfandel.
Mulcahay, Mrs. J.	Healdsburg	9	9	9			No.	20 tons.	Zinfandel.
Newcome, ——	Healdsburg	10	10	10			No.	20 tons.	Zinfandel.

Name	Location							Tons	Varieties
Norton, Capt. L. A.	Healdsburg	110	110	110			No.	150 tons.	Zinfandel, Chasselas.
Ogilvie, Capt.	Healdsburg	6	6	6			No.	12 tons.	Malvoisie.
Ottmer, Dr. H. C.	Healdsburg	15	15	15			No.	35 tons.	Zinfandel.
Passalaqua, A. G.	Healdsburg	17	17	17			Yes.	60 tons.	Zinfandel, Riesling.
Passalaqua, F.	Healdsburg	20	20	20			No.	26 tons.	Zinfandel.
Paxton, Mrs. J. A.	Healdsburg	60	60	60			Yes.	150 tons.	Zinfandel and mixed.
Peck, John, Jr.	Healdsburg	5	5	5			No.	10 tons.	Mission.
Peterson, C.	Healdsburg	5	5	5			No.	12 tons.	Zinfandel.
Phillips, D. D.	Healdsburg	30	30	30			No.	60 tons.	Zinfandel.
Phillips, P. J. (heirs)	Healdsburg	25	25	25			No.	50 tons.	Zinfandel.
Plumb, Wm.	Healdsburg	11	11	11			No.	45 tons.	Zinfandel.
Powell, R.	Healdsburg	6	6	6			No.	15 tons.	Zinfandel, Mission.
Prouse, Daniel	Healdsburg	15	15	15			No.	30 tons.	Zinfandel.
Prouse, S.	Healdsburg	25	25	25			No.	50 tons.	Zinfandel, Mission.
Purser, Edward	Healdsburg	25	25	25			Yes.	60 tons.	Mixed.
Reiners, C. A.	Healdsburg	60	60	60			No.	150 tons.	Zinfandel and mixed.
Rickman, H.	Healdsburg	12	12	12			No.	25 tons.	Zinfandel.
Robinson, J.	Healdsburg	20	20	20			No.	40 tons.	Zinfandel.
Robinson, R.	Healdsburg	5	5	5			No.	10 tons.	Zinfandel.
Rodgers, John L.	Healdsburg	18	18	18			No.	50 tons.	Zinfandel, Mission.
Ross, R. B.	Healdsburg	8	8	8			No.	16 tons.	Zinfandel.
Saryisson, C.	Healdsburg	8	8	8			No.	10 tons.	Zinfandel.
Saum, George	Healdsburg	5	5	5			No.	10 tons.	Mixed.
Scatena, M.	Healdsburg	75	75	75			Yes.	160 tons.	Zinfandel and mixed.
Schwarz, H.	Healdsburg	15	15	15			No.	30 tons.	Zinfandel.
Seaman, John	Healdsburg	6	6	6			No.	10 tons.	Zinfandel, Chasselas.
Sinn, E. & G.	Healdsburg	128	128	128			Yes.	252 tons.	Zinfandel.
Smith, Samuel	Healdsburg	15	15	15			No.	35 tons.	Zinfandel.
Snider, Mrs. J.	Healdsburg	12	12	12			No.	25 tons.	Zinfandel.
Steinbach, Fred.	Healdsburg	5	5	5			No.	5 tons.	Zinfandel.
Story, George	Healdsburg	6	6	6			No.	12 tons.	Zinfandel, Muscat.
Thomann, A.	Healdsburg	36	36	36			No.	75 tons.	Zinfandel and mixed.
Trapet, J. B.	Healdsburg	15	15	15			No.	30 tons.	Zinfandel.
Treadway, D. G.	Healdsburg	8	8	8			No.	10 tons.	Zinfandel, Mission.
Trimble, Mrs. M. J.	Healdsburg	12	12	12			No.	30 tons.	Zinfandel.
Truitt, Mrs.	Healdsburg	6	6	6			No.	12 tons.	Zinfandel.
Tucker, John	Healdsburg	35	35	35			No.	75 tons.	Zinfandel, Mission.
Van Allen, Wm.	Healdsburg	30	30	30			No.	60 tons.	Zinfandel, Mission.
Walters, S.	Healdsburg	25	25	25			No.	60 tons.	Zinfandel and mixed.
Warner, A. L.	Healdsburg	22	22	22	20		No.	100 tons.	Zinfandel, Mission.
Warren, W. P.	Healdsburg	13	13	13			No.	45 tons.	Zinfandel, Riesling, Tokay.
Weaver, Dr. C. W.	Healdsburg	14	14	14			No.	20 tons.	Zinfandel, Chasselas.
Weidland, Frank	Healdsburg	20	20	20			No.	25 tons.	Zinfandel.
Wheaton, John	Healdsburg	15	15	15			No.	50 tons.	Zinfandel, Chasselas.

Sonoma County—Continued.

Name of Owner.	Post Office and Name of Vineyard.	Total Acres in Grapes.	Acres in Bearing.	Acres in Wine Grapes.	Acres in Table Grapes.	Acres in Raisin Grapes.	Wine Maker.	Product in 1889.	Varieties.
Whitcomb, J.	Healdsburg	30	30	30			No.	60 tons.	Zinfandel.
Wise, Captain E. E.	Healdsburg	70	70	70			Yes.	200 tons.	Mixed.
Young Bros.	Healdsburg	7	7	7			No.	15 tons.	Zinfandel.
Delafield, R. H.	Kellogg	35	35	25			Yes.	Mildewed.	Semillon and mixed.
Folker, J. H. A.	Kellogg	70	50	70			Yes.	20 tons.	Foreign varieties.
Hood, George	Kellogg	125	125	125			No.	375 tons.	Foreign varieties.
McDonald, Frank	Kellogg	12	12	12			No.	20 tons.	Chasselas, Mission.
Schwart, A.	Kellogg	5	5		5		No.	10 tons.	Tokay, Muscat.
Ahern, J. B.	Lakeville	13	13	13			Yes.	20 tons.	Zinfandel.
Bihler, Wm.	Lakeville	170	170	170			No.	510 tons.	Zinfandel, Malvoisie.
Eggelston, George	Lakeville	15	15	15			No.	40 tons.	Zinfandel, Malvoisie.
Fritz, John	Lakeville	40	40	40			No.	75 tons.	Zinfandel and mixed.
Hardin, Andrew	Lakeville	20	20	20			No.	35 tons.	Zinfandel.
Keenan, A.	Lakeville	20	20	20			No.	60 tons.	Mixed.
Mills, Mrs.	Lakeville	15	15	15			No.	30 tons.	Mixed.
White, J. H.	Lakeville	20	20	20			No.	50 tons.	Zinfandel, Malvoisie.
Wiswell, N.	Lakeville	7	7	7			No.	12 tons.	Mixed.
Donahue, J. M., estate of	Littons	150	160	150			No.	300 tons.	Zinfandel, Mission.
Haigh, E.	Littons	5	5	5			No.	10 tons.	Mission.
Long, G. W.	Littons	20	20	20			No.	40 tons.	Zinfandel.
Long, Isaac	Littons	20	20	20			No.	40 tons.	Zinfandel.
Marshall, Robert	Littons	15	15	15			No.	30 tons.	Zinfandel.
Perry, E. G.	Littons	40	40	40			No.	80 tons.	Zinfandel, Malvoisie.
Shriver, G.	Littons	10	10	10			No.	20 tons.	Zinfandel, Mission.
Anderson, A. J. F.	Los Guillicos	35	25	35			Yes.	50 tons.	Zinfandel, Riesling.
Box, J. A.	Los Guillicos	22	22	22			No.	68 tons.	Zinfandel, Gutedel.
Carpenter, H. B.	Los Guillicos	60	85	60			No.	60 tons.	Zinfandel.
Clark, Mrs. C.	Los Guillicos	100	75	100			No.	150 tons.	Zinfandel, Charbono.
Drummond, J. H., estate of.	Los Guillicos	160	130	150			No.	250 tons.	Zinfandel.
Hammond, Arthur	Los Guillicos	6			6		No.	Not bearing.	Tokay.
Hood, Mrs. E. A.	Los Guillicos	225	200	225			Yes.	800 tons.	Zinfandel, Mission, Chasselas.
Luttrell, J. K.	Los Guillicos	100	60	100			No.	150 tons.	Zinfandel, Chasselas.
Macartney, E. A.	Los Guillicos	100	100	100			No.	200 tons.	Zinfandel and mixed.

Name	Location							
Shaw, James A.	Los Guillicos (Wildwood).	200	160	200		Yes.	400 tons.	St. Macuire, Cabernet, Pinot, etc.
Yost, John D., estate of	Los Guillicos	10	20	20		No.	Not bearing.	Tokay.
Adam, Henry	Occidental	20	8	8	10	No.	30 tons.	Zinfandel.
Beedle, L.	Occidental	8	10	10		No.	10 tons.	Zinfandel.
Bone, Wm.	Occidental	10	5	5		No.	20 tons.	Mission.
Branr, W.	Occidental	14	14	14		No.	20 tons.	Zinfandel.
Chenoweth, J. H.	Occidental	14	14	14		No.	20 tons.	Zinfandel.
Crispi, John	Occidental	10	10	10		No.	10 tons.	Zinfandel.
Devers, E. F.	Occidental	25	25	25		No.	20 tons.	Zinfandel and mixed.
Dragoo, N.	Occidental	10	10	10		Yes.	60 tons.	Zinfandel.
Dupont, Joseph	Occidental	20	20	16		No.	20 tons.	Zinfandel.
Gallagher, John	Occidental	8	8	8	4	No.	40 tons.	Zinfandel, Muscat.
Hauseman, A.	Occidental	13	13	13		No.	15 tons.	Zinfandel and mixed.
Kloppumburg, W.	Occidental	75	75	75		No.	10 tons.	Zinfandel.
Lancel, A., & Sons	Occidental	10	10	10		Yes.	100 tons.	Zinfandel and French varieties.
Lamoni, Louis	Occidental	20	20	20		No.	10 tons.	Zinfandel.
Ludolf, H.	Occidental	10	10	10		Yes.	20 tons.	Zinfandel.
Markey, C. P.	Occidental	40	40	33	7	No.	20 tons.	Zinfandel.
Nolan, C.	Occidental	5	5	5		No.	60 tons.	Zinfandel, Mission, Tokay.
Speciter, R.	Occidental	16	16	16		No.	10 tons.	Zinfandel.
Stewart, W.	Occidental	12	12	12		No.	20 tons.	Zinfandel.
Stoote, Charles	Occidental	5	5	5		No.	30 tons.	Zinfandel.
Van Winkle, Charles	Occidental	20	20	20		No.	10 tons.	Zinfandel.
Adamson, Charles	Penn's Grove	5	5	5		No.	50 tons.	Zinfandel.
Bannon, John	Penn's Grove	6	8	6		No.	10 tons.	Zinfandel.
Formschlag, John.	Penn's Grove	10	10	10		No.	6 tons.	Mission.
Goodwin, James	Penn's Grove	5	5	5	5	Yes.	25 tons.	Sweetwater, Muscat, Tokay.
Maas, Claus	Penn's Grove	20	20	20		No.	10 tons.	Zinfandel.
Page, Wilfred	Penn's Grove	7	7	7		No.	30 tons.	Zinfandel and mixed.
Black, Mrs. J. W.	Petaluma	15	15	15		No.	15 tons.	Mixed.
Crane, Richard H.	Petaluma	10	10	10		No.	45 tons.	Zinfandel, Mission.
Drees, Mrs.	Petaluma	12	12	7		No.	25 tons.	Zinfandel, Mission.
Hoff, R. W.	Petaluma	80	80	80	5	No.	30 tons.	Zinfandel, Muscat.
Jewell, I. R.	Petaluma	80	80	80		No.	200 tons.	Zinfandel, Burgundy.
Jordan, John	Petaluma	5	5	5		Yes.	175 tons.	Zinfandel and mixed.
McConnell, Wm.	Petaluma	40	40	40		No.	10 tons.	Zinfandel.
Staedler, J. G.	Petaluma	7	7	7		No.	50 tons.	Zinfandel.
Todd, James	Petaluma	10	10	10		No.	15 tons.	Zinfandel.
Preston, Mrs. H. L.	Preston	20	20	20		No.	40 tons.	Zinfandel.
Arnold, A. W.	Santa Rosa	40	40	40		No.	20 tons.	Zinfandel.
Atterbury, W. B.	Santa Rosa	20		20		No.	120 tons.	Semillon.
Atterbury, W., Jr.	Santa Rosa	30	25	25			Not bearing.	
Austin, H. W.	Santa Rosa	30	25	25	5	No.	50 tons.	Zinfandel, Sweetwater.
Austin, James	Santa Rosa	80	80	50	30	No.	120 tons.	Zinfandel, Sweetwater, Malvoisie, Mission.

Sonoma County—Continued.

Name of Owner.	Post Office and Name of Vineyard.	Total Acres in Grapes.	Acres in Bearing.	Acres in Wine Grapes.	Acres in Table Grapes.	Acres in Raisin Grapes.	Wine Maker.	Product in 1889.	Varieties.
Austin, James H.	Santa Rosa	12	12	12			No.	20 tons.	Zinfandel, Riesling.
Badger, D.	Santa Rosa	12	12	12			No.	12 tons.	Zinfandel, Burger.
Badger, Joseph J.	Santa Rosa	40	40	40			No.	50 tons.	Zinfandel, Burger.
Bailiff, John	Santa Rosa	55	55	55			Yes.	120 tons.	Zinfandel, Mission.
Bannister, Alfred	Santa Rosa	110	110	110			Yes.	160 tons.	Zinfandel and mixed.
Barbino, Thomas	Santa Rosa	15	6	15			No.	5 tons.	Zinfandel.
Barnes, Ruth, estate of.	Santa Rosa	30	20	20			No.	40 tons.	Zinfandel, Mission.
Benjamin, A.	Santa Rosa	30	30	30			No.	60 tons.	Zinfandel.
Benson & Cralle	Santa Rosa	164	120	164			Yes.	200 tons.	Zinfandel, Chasselas, Riesling.
Bertoli, Paul	Santa Rosa	7	7	7			Yes.	14 tons.	Zinfandel.
Bolle, Henry	Santa Rosa	80	80	80			Yes.	550 tons.	Chasselas, Zinfandel, Riesling.
Bradlaugh, S.	Santa Rosa	10	10	10			No.	20 tons.	Mission.
Brewer, Henry	Santa Rosa	23	23	23			No.	10 tons.	Zinfandel.
Bruner, J. W.	Santa Rosa	25	25	25			No.	25 tons.	Zinfandel and mixed.
Bruning, C. H. W.	Santa Rosa	10	10	10			No.	10 tons.	Zinfandel.
Brush, J. H.	Santa Rosa	20	20	20			No.	40 tons.	Zinfandel.
Becchi, Henry	Santa Rosa	7	7	7			No.	15 tons.	Mission.
Buckner Bros.	Santa Rosa	70	45	70			Yes.	60 tons.	Zinfandel, Chasselas.
Campbell, C.	Santa Rosa	10	10	10			No.	20 tons.	Mixed.
Carr, Nelson	Santa Rosa	50	50	50			No.	100 tons.	Zinfandel, Mission.
Cassasoa, D.	Santa Rosa	24	24	24			No.	24 tons.	Zinfandel.
Cattron, Mrs. E.	Santa Rosa	18	8	18			No.	15 tons.	Zinfandel.
Chiles, William	Santa Rosa	65	65	63	2		No.	60 tons.	Zinfandel, Mission.
Clark, Jas., estate of	Santa Rosa	80	80	80			No.	200 tons.	Zinfandel and mixed.
Chopius, J.	Santa Rosa	40	40	40			No.	20 tons.	Zinfandel.
Coffman, John	Santa Rosa	7	7	7			No.	14 tons.	Mission.
Cook, I. F.	Santa Rosa	6	6	6			No.	5 tons.	Zinfandel.
Cooper, Lewis	Santa Rosa	18	18	18			No.	30 tons.	Zinfandel.
Coulter, S. T.	Santa Rosa	12	12	12			No.	50 tons.	Zinfandel, Mission.
Cowan, Wm.	Santa Rosa	15	15	15			No.	15 tons.	Zinfandel.
Crane, Robt.	Santa Rosa	18	18	14	4		No.	54 tons.	Zinfandel, Morocco.
Dalzell, Wm.	Santa Rosa	10	10	10			No.	20 tons.	Zinfandel.
Davis, G. W. & E. W.	Santa Rosa	140	140	140			Yes.	150,000 gals.	Zinfandel, Mission.
Denny, J. P.	Santa Rosa	30	15	30			No.	12 tons.	Zinfandel.

Name	District						Tons	French varieties.
De Turk, Isaac	Santa Rosa	100	100	100		Yes.	200 tons.	Zinfandel.
Dickenson, W. L.	Santa Rosa	20	20	20		No.	40 tons.	Mixed.
Dickenson,	Santa Rosa	80	80	80	5	No.	120 tons.	Zinfandel, Muscat.
Dillon, James	Santa Rosa	15	15	10		No.	10 tons.	Zinfandel.
Dohrman, John	Santa Rosa	28	28	28		Yes.	60 tons.	Zinfandel.
Dohm, George E.	Santa Rosa	60	60	60		Yes.		Zinfandel.
Dondero, B.	Santa Rosa	6	6	6		No.	8 tons.	Zinfandel.
Dresser, Levi	Santa Rosa	12	12	12		No.	20 tons.	Sweetwater.
Exter, John, estate of	Santa Rosa	18	18	18		No.	10 tons.	Zinfandel, Mission.
Fickes, Mrs.	Santa Rosa	50	60	60		No.	140 tons.	Zinfandel.
Fowler, Mrs. Annie	Santa Rosa	15	15	15		No.	30 tons.	Zinfandel, Burger.
Fraser, L.	Santa Rosa	25	25	25		No.	70 tons.	Zinfandel and mixed.
Fulkerson, S. T.	Santa Rosa	16	16	16		No.	20 tons.	Zinfandel.
Fulkerson, T. S.	Santa Rosa	18	16	16		No.		Zinfandel, Burger, etc.
Gamble, Capt. Geo. H.	Santa Rosa	125	90	125		Yes.	100 tons.	Zinfandel and mixed.
Gardner, Clement	Santa Rosa	12	10	12		No.	10 tons.	Zinfandel and mixed.
Garrison, Wm.	Santa Rosa	10	10	10		No.	10 tons.	Zinfandel, Burger.
Geary, T. J.	Santa Rosa	30	30	30		No.	30 tons.	Zinfandel, Riesling.
Goldfish, Wilson & Co.	Santa Rosa	40	40	40		No.	25 tons.	Zinfandel, Mission.
Good, John	Santa Rosa	15	15	15		No.	20 tons.	Zinfandel and mixed.
Gregg, G. T.	Santa Rosa	30	30	30		No.	70 tons.	Zinfandel, Riesling, Burger.
Grieves, Wm.	Santa Rosa	100	60	100		No.	100 tons.	Zinfandel and mixed.
Grasse, Guy E.	Santa Rosa	40	30	40		No.	70 tons.	Zinfandel and mixed.
Gwynn, Wm.	Santa Rosa	7	6	7		No.	3 tons.	Zinfandel.
Gupil, J. H.	Santa Rosa	19	19	19		Yes.	38 tons.	Zinfandel, Sweetwater.
Haas, John	Santa Rosa	22	12	22		No.	5 tons.	Zinfandel, Riesling.
Hafte, Fritz	Santa Rosa	10	10	10		No.	2 tons.	Zinfandel, Riesling.
Hardesty, Chas.	Santa Rosa	33	33	30	3	No.	60 tons.	Zinfandel, Mission.
Harris, Jacob	Santa Rosa	8	8	8		No.	10 tons.	Zinfandel, Burger.
Harris, R. A.	Santa Rosa	5	5	5		No.	10 tons.	Zinfandel, Malvoisie.
Harris, T. M.	Santa Rosa	13		13		No.	15 tons.	Zinfandel, Mission.
Harrison, Thos.	Santa Rosa	30	30	30		No.	25 tons.	Zinfandel.
Hastin, F. D.	Santa Rosa	130	130	130		Yes.	20 tons.	Zinfandel.
Hirshler, Ed.	Santa Rosa	25	25	25		No.	40 tons.	Mission.
Heisel, Paul, estate of	Santa Rosa	25	25	25		No.	25 tons.	Zinfandel, Mission.
Hessel, Andrew	Santa Rosa	20	15	20		No.	14 tons.	Zinfandel.
Hillman, James	Santa Rosa	7	7	7		No.	10 tons.	Zinfandel.
Hodge, A. L.	Santa Rosa	80	80	80		No.	160 tons.	Riesling, Zinfandel, Burger.
Hopper, Thomas	Santa Rosa	20	20	20		No.	20 tons.	Zinfandel, Burger.
Hudson Heirs	Santa Rosa	18	18	18		No.	30 tons.	Zinfandel, Burger.
Hunger, Felix	Santa Rosa	40	40	40		No.	35 tons.	Zinfandel, Riesling.
Hutchinson, Samuel	Santa Rosa	20	20	20		No.	30 tons.	Zinfandel.
Irwin, A.	Santa Rosa	10	10	10		No.	20 tons.	Zinfandel.
Kauffman, John	Santa Rosa	10	10	10		No.	10 tons.	Zinfandel.
Kennedy, C. A.	Santa Rosa	25	25	25		No.	50 tons.	Zinfandel.

SONOMA COUNTY—Continued.

Name of Owner.	Post Office and Name of Vineyard.	Total Acres in Grapes.	Acres in Bearing.	Acres in Wine Grapes	Acres in Table Grapes.	Acres in Raisin Grapes.	Wine Maker.	Product in 1889.	Varieties.
Knapp, W. l.	Santa Rosa (Fair View)	80	80	80	5		No.	160 tons.	Zinfandel, Burger.
Knecht, Francis	Santa Rosa	50	50	45			No.	75 tons.	Muscat, Zinfandel, Burger.
Knorr, Geo.	Santa Rosa	25	25	25			No.	20 tons.	Zinfandel.
Kurtz, Henry	Santa Rosa	50	50	50			No.	50 tons.	Zinfandel.
Lague, B.	Santa Rosa	30	30	30			Yes.	60 tons.	Zinfandel and mixed.
Lague, Frank	Santa Rosa	30	30	30			Yes.	60 tons.	Zinfandel and mixed.
Largomasino, B.	Santa Rosa	20	10	20			Yes.	5 tons.	Zinfandel.
Lawler, John	Santa Rosa	12	12	12			No.	50 tons.	Zinfandel and mixed.
Lay, Clarke & Co.	Santa Rosa	400	300	400			Yes.	600 tons.	Zinfandel, Riesling, Burger.
Lock,	Santa Rosa	30	30	30			No.	60 tons.	Zinfandel, Chasselas.
Locke, J. N.	Santa Rosa	10	10	10			No.	20 tons.	Zinfandel, Muscat.
McCormick, John	Santa Rosa	15	7	15			No.	5 tons.	Malvoisie and mixed.
McGregor, Frank	Santa Rosa	25	25	25			No.	25 tons.	Zinfandel.
McKusick, William	Santa Rosa	10	10	10			No.	20 tons.	Zinfandel.
Manion, Mrs. E. J.	Santa Rosa	20	20	20			No.	60 tons.	Zinfandel. Mission.
Man, C.	Santa Rosa	9	9	9			No.	20 tons.	Zinfandel.
Miller, George	Santa Rosa	16	16	16			No.	16 tons.	Zinfandel and mixed.
Millington, Mrs.	Santa Rosa	30	30	30			No.	60 tons.	Zinfandel.
Mina, Joe.	Santa Rosa	16	12	16	1		No.	5 tons.	Zinfandel.
Moore, H.	Santa Rosa	9	9	8			No.	9 tons.	Zinfandel, Muscat.
Moore, Mrs.	Santa Rosa	23	23	23			No.	30 tons.	Zinfandel.
Morrow, James	Santa Rosa	10		10	5		No.	Not bearing.	Mixed.
Murdock, L. A.	Santa Rosa	35	35	30			No.	75 tons.	Zinfandel, Burger.
Nagle, F. G.	Santa Rosa	30	30	30			No.	100 tons.	Zinfandel.
Near, C. D.	Santa Rosa	30	30	30			No.	60 tons.	Zinfandel, Malvoisie.
Norris, Charles G.	Santa Rosa	40	40	40	1		No.	80 tons.	Zinfandel, Malvoisie.
Ort, Julius	Santa Rosa	5	5	4			No.	2 tons.	Mission, Muscat.
Peizzi, Victor	Santa Rosa	20	13	20			Yes.	20 tons.	Zinfandel.
Peterson, Ed.	Santa Rosa	10	10	10			No.	20 tons.	Zinfandel.
Pfeinston, John	Santa Rosa	25	25	25			No.	25 tons.	Zinfandel.
Phillips, George	Santa Rosa	12	12	12			No.	25 tons.	Zinfandel.
Pflying, Walter	Santa Rosa	130	130	130			Yes.	280 tons.	Riesling, Zinfandel, Chasselas.
Poulin, Louis	Santa Rosa	8	8	8			Yes.	30 tons.	Zinfandel.
Ricksecker, L. C.	Santa Rosa	10	10	10			No.	20 tons.	Zinfandel.

Name	Post office					Resident	Product	Varieties
Requa, A. A.	Santa Rosa	28	18	28		Yes.	30 tons.	Zinfandel and mixed.
Roberts, Frank	Santa Rosa	15	15	15		No.	30 tons.	Zinfandel.
Ross, Richard	Santa Rosa	25	20	25		No.	40 tons.	Zinfandel, Burger.
Saxton, A.	Santa Rosa	5	5	5		Yes.	5 tons.	Zinfandel.
Schalich, Antone	Santa Rosa	18	18	18		No.	25 tons.	Zinfandel, Riesling.
Scheibel, Theodore	Santa Rosa	50	60	60		No.	40 tons.	Zinfandel and mixed.
Schriever, A.	Santa Rosa	18	18	18		Yes.	30 tons.	Zinfandel.
Seimer, D.	Santa Rosa	10	10	10		No.	20 tons.	Zinfandel.
Sheplar, S. H.	Santa Rosa	30	80	80		No.	60 tons.	Zinfandel, Mission.
Shibald, —	Santa Rosa	15	15	15		No.	30 tons.	Zinfandel.
Simonds & Gem.	Santa Rosa	20	20	20			20 tons.	Zinfandel, Burger.
Smithers, George F.	Santa Rosa	9	22	9		No.	Not bearing.	Tokay, Hamburg.
Sonoma Co. Poor Farm	Santa Rosa	22	22	22		No.	46 tons.	Zinfandel and mixed.
Stewart, J. H.	Santa Rosa	9	9	9		No.	18 tons.	Zinfandel, Malvoisie.
Story, S. C.	Santa Rosa	30	30	30		No.	60 tons.	Zinfandel.
Striddle, Charles	Santa Rosa	55	55	55		No.	75 tons.	Zinfandel and mixed.
Strong, John	Santa Rosa	30	30	30		No.	60 tons.	Zinfandel and mixed.
Stuart, S. A. & A. M.	Santa Rosa	60	60	60		No.	100 tons.	Zinfandel and mixed.
Sutherland, E. H.	Santa Rosa	60	60	60		No.	100 tons.	Zinfandel.
Swan, Fred.	Santa Rosa	20	20	20		No.	30 tons.	Riesling.
Swan, L.	Santa Rosa	25	25	25		No.	20 tons.	Zinfandel, Mission.
Talbot, Holma	Santa Rosa	20	20	20		No.	40 tons.	Zinfandel, Gutedel.
Talbot, Joseph	Santa Rosa	10	15	15		No.	30 tons.	Mission, Muscat.
Tallman, Joseph	Santa Rosa	28	28	28		No.	52 tons.	Zinfandel.
Taucer, Albert.	Santa Rosa	18	9	18	5	No.	10 tons.	Zinfandel, Sweetwater.
Taylor, John S.	Santa Rosa	60	60	60		No.	130 tons.	Zinfandel, Mission.
Taylor, Mrs.	Santa Rosa	30	30	30		No.	60 tons.	Zinfandel.
Thorpe, R. W.	Santa Rosa	13	11	13		No.	5 tons.	Zinfandel, Gutedel.
Trotter, R.	Santa Rosa	20	10	20		No.	20 tons.	Zinfandel and mixed.
Underhill, Charles	Santa Rosa	38	38	38		No.	52 tons.	Zinfandel.
Vallerza, John	Santa Rosa	5	5	5		No.	10 tons.	Zinfandel, Mission.
Van Winkle, Mrs. W. P.	Santa Rosa	20	20	20		No.	21 tons.	Zinfandel, Malvoisie.
Von Grafen, Charles	Santa Rosa	10	10	10		No.	25 tons.	Zinfandel.
Ward, Thomas.	Santa Rosa	50	50	50		No.	100 tons.	Zinfandel.
Ware, A. B.	Santa Rosa	70	70	70		No.	150 tons.	Zinfandel.
Ware, William	Santa Rosa	20	20	20		No.	40 tons.	Zinfandel, Mission.
Warner, James J.	Santa Rosa	75	75	75		No.	200 tons.	Zinfandel.
Wells, Clark	Santa Rosa	16	16	16		No.	23 tons.	Zinfandel, Mission.
Wells, George W.	Santa Rosa	8	8	8		No.	12 tons.	Zinfandel, Malvoisie.
Wells, Pleasant.	Santa Rosa	148	148	148		No.	390 tons.	Burger, Zinfandel, Malvoisie.
Wendt, Fred.	Santa Rosa	15	15	15		No.	40 tons.	Mixed.
Wendt, Fred.	Santa Rosa	7	7	7		Yes.	15 tons.	Zinfandel, Malvoisie.
Whittaker, G. N.	Santa Rosa	50	50	50		Yes.	100 tons.	Zinfandel and mixed.
Wilson, J. B.	Santa Rosa	5	5	5	5	No.	8 tons.	Zinfandel.
Wilson, J. E.	Santa Rosa	43	43	43		No.	120 tons.	Zinfandel, Muscat.

SONOMA COUNTY—Continued.

Name of Owner.	Post Office and Name of Vineyard.	Total Acres in Grapes.	Acres in Bearing.	Acres in Wine Grapes.	Acres in Table Grapes.	Acres in Raisin Grapes.	Wine Maker.	Product in 1889.	Varieties.
Wolfe, August	Santa Rosa	11	11	11			No.	11 tons.	Zinfandel.
Wrightson, Francis	Santa Rosa	34	34	34			No.	75 tons.	Zinfandel.
Wright, W. S. M.	Santa Rosa	5	5	5			No.	15 tons.	Zinfandel.
Wymore, C. C.	Santa Rosa	27	27	27			No.	40 tons.	Mission.
Yandle & Glynn	Santa Rosa	9	9	9			No.	18 tons.	Zinfandel and mixed.
Allen, Otis	Sebastopol	13	13	13			No.	13 tons.	Zinfandel, St. Macaire.
Atkinson, P. H.	Sebastopol	10						Not bearing.	Zinfandel and mixed.
Ayers, H. G.	Sebastopol	15	15	15			No.	30 tons.	Zinfandel and mixed.
Barnes, Henry	Sebastopol	10	10	10			No.	20 tons.	Zinfandel, Mission.
Beattie, A.	Sebastopol	12	12	12			No.	20 tons.	Zinfandel.
Bennett, J.	Sebastopol	8	8	8			No.	15 tons.	Zinfandel.
Bennett, T. N.	Sebastopol	10	10	10			No.	20 tons.	Zinfandel, Mission.
Bonnardell, P.	Sebastopol	20	20	20			Yes.	40 tons.	Zinfandel.
Briggs, Alfred	Sebastopol	28	28	28			No.	40 tons.	Zinfandel, Mission.
Brown, J.	Sebastopol	20	20	20			No.	30 tons.	Zinfandel.
Bussman, A.	Sebastopol	12	12	12			No.	5 tons.	Zinfandel.
Calder, Mrs. A.	Sebastopol	20	20	20			No.	25 tons.	Zinfandel.
Cody, L. O.	Sebastopol	30	30	20	10		No.	50 tons.	Zinfandel, St. Macaire, Black Prince.
Coon, L. O.	Sebastopol	7	7	7			No.	10 tons.	Zinfandel.
Corbin, F. B.	Sebastopol	8	8	8			No.	10 tons.	Zinfandel.
Crawford, Thomas	Sebastopol	10	10	10			No.	15 tons.	Zinfandel.
Dale, Mrs. M.	Sebastopol	5	5	5			No.	5 tons.	Zinfandel.
Davis, M.	Sebastopol	20	20	20			No.	40 tons.	Zinfandel and mixed.
Deittrich, G.	Sebastopol	30	30	30			No.	50 tons.	Zinfandel and mixed.
Devans, F. T.	Sebastopol	10	10	10			No.	20 tons.	Zinfandel and mixed.
Drosbach, A.	Sebastopol	8	8	8			No.	16 tons.	Zinfandel.
Emerson, J. W.	Sebastopol	5	5	5			No.	10 tons.	Zinfandel.
Fine, A.	Sebastopol	20	20	20			No.	15 tons.	Tokay, Zinfandel, Muscat.
Fletcher, Mrs.	Sebastopol	10	10	10			No.	15 tons.	Zinfandel.
Fredericks, Geo.	Sebastopol	35	35	35			Yes.	50 tons.	Zinfandel.
Frei, L.	Sebastopol	75	75	75			No.	150 tons.	Zinfandel, Riesling.
Gillam, Mrs.	Sebastopol	5	5	5			No.	10 tons.	Zinfandel.
Gott, A.	Sebastopol	5	5	5			No.	12 tons.	Zinfandel.
Green, J. R.	Sebastopol	40	40	40			Yes.	40 tons.	Zinfandel, Mission.

Name	Location							Tons	Variety
Grosse, Peter	Sebastopol	25	25	25		---	No.	40 tons.	Zinfandel and mixed.
Hall & Barnett	Sebastopol	5	5	5		---	No.	10 tons.	Zinfandel.
Hallberg, J. F.	Sebastopol	5	5	5		---	No.	10 tons.	Mixed.
Hamilton, Geo.	Sebastopol	50	50	50		---	No.	100 tons.	Zinfandel and mixed.
Hathway, E. L.	Sebastopol	7	7	7		---	No.	5 tons.	Zinfandel.
Hayden, E. W.	Sebastopol	20	20	20		---	No.	30 tons.	Zinfandel and mixed.
Hill, William	Sebastopol	200	200	200		---	Yes.	600 tons.	Zinfandel, Burger.
Johnson, W. M.	Sebastopol	15	15	15		---	No.	20 tons.	Zinfandel.
Kauffman, Frank	Sebastopol	7	7	7		---	No.	10 tons.	Zinfandel.
Kauffman, L.	Sebastopol	10	10	10		---	No.	20 tons.	Zinfandel.
Kelley, J. W.	Sebastopol	12	12	12		---	No.	15 tons.	Zinfandel.
Leiber, W. S.	Sebastopol	35	35	35		---	No.	8 tons.	Zinfandel.
Leiby, George	Sebastopol	7	7	7		---	No.	25 tons.	Zinfandel.
Litchfield, Durant	Sebastopol	15	15	15		---	No.	30 tons.	Zinfandel, Muscat.
Litchfield, J. M.	Sebastopol	18	17	17	3	---	No.	10 tons.	Zinfandel.
Lowery, C. C.	Sebastopol	7	7	7		---	No.	30 tons.	Zinfandel and mixed.
Lynch, D. B.	Sebastopol	30	30	30		---	No.	5 tons.	Zinfandel.
Meyers, William	Sebastopol	20	20	20		---	No.	10 tons.	Zinfandel.
Mole, J.	Sebastopol	6	6	6		---	No.	25 tons.	Zinfandel and mixed.
Morse, Wm. P.	Sebastopol	15	15	15		---	No.	20 tons.	Zinfandel.
Murge, Henry	Sebastopol	10	10	10		---	No.	20 tons.	Zinfandel.
Murphy, John	Sebastopol	14	14	14		---	No.	20 tons.	Zinfandel.
Nugent, Mrs. J.	Sebastopol	15	15	15		---	No.	8 tons.	Zinfandel.
Palmer, C. H.	Sebastopol	5	5	5		---	No.	20 tons.	Zinfandel.
Polifka, Chas.	Sebastopol	10	10	10		---	Yes.	20 tons.	Zinfandel.
Pool, Capt. J. F.	Sebastopol	12	12	12	4	---	No.	30 tons.	Mission, Muscat.
Raup, William	Sebastopol	15	15	15		---	No.	25 tons.	Zinfandel.
Roberts, J. M.	Sebastopol	20	20	20		---	No.	30 tons.	Zinfandel.
Sanborn, G. N.	Sebastopol	5	5	5		---	No.	5 tons.	Zinfandel.
Schirner, E.	Sebastopol	25	25	25		---	No.	50 tons.	Zinfandel, Pinot.
Schlake, Christian	Sebastopol	20	20	20		---	No.	20 tons.	Zinfandel.
Showalter, S.	Sebastopol	5	5	5		---	No.	10 tons.	Zinfandel.
Solomon, Charles	Sebastopol	23	23	23		---	No.	10 tons.	Zinfandel.
Stevens, William	Sebastopol	10	10	10		---	No.	12 tons.	Zinfandel.
Tasker, J.	Sebastopol	8	8	8		---	No.	15 tons.	Zinfandel, Mission.
Urton, J. U.	Sebastopol	82	82	82	3	---	No.	50 tons.	Zinfandel.
Ward, M.	Sebastopol	10	10	10		---	No.	15 tons.	Zinfandel.
Warner, J. L.	Sebastopol	30	30	30		---	No.	30 tons.	Zinfandel.
Weeks, Percy	Sebastopol	20	20	20		---	No.	20 tons.	Mixed.
Whaley, S.	Sebastopol	30	30	30		---	No.	50 tons.	Zinfandel, Mission.
Williams, John A.	Sebastopol	5	5	5		---	No.	10 tons.	Zinfandel.
Wilson & Co.	Sebastopol	40	40	40		---	No.	100 tons.	Zinfandel and mixed.
Wilsey, J. W.	Sebastopol	22	25	22		---	No.	50 tons.	Zinfandel, Muscat.
Alexander, R.	Soda Rock	10	10	10		---	No.	20 tons.	Zinfandel.
Andrews, Mrs. A. B.	Soda Rock	9	9	9		---	No.	15 tons.	Zinfandel.

SONOMA COUNTY—Continued.

NAME OF OWNER.	Post Office and Name of Vineyard.	Total Acres in Grapes.	Acres in Bearing.	Acres in Wine Grapes.	Acres in Table Grapes.	Acres in Raisin Grapes.	Wine Maker.	Product in 1889.	Varieties.
Arthur, Daniel	Soda Rock	14	14	14			No.	30 tons.	Zinfandel.
Bailey, W. H.	Soda Rock	35	35	35			No.	75 tons.	Mixed.
Bidwell, James	Soda Rock	15	15	15			No.	30 tons.	Zinfandel.
Bidwell, John	Soda Rock	10	10	10			No.	25 tons.	Zinfandel.
Collins, J. W.	Soda Rock	20	20	20			No.	50 tons.	Mixed.
Givins, R. R.	Soda Rock	18	18	18			No.	54 tons.	Zinfandel, Chasselas.
Hutchinson, J.	Soda Rock	6	6	6			No.	10 tons.	Zinfandel.
Ley, C. W.	Soda Rock	10	10	10			No.	20 tons.	Zinfandel.
Merk, B.	Soda Rock	6	6	6			No.	16 tons.	Mixed.
Michaelson, L.	Soda Rock	25	25	25			No.	50 tons.	Zinfandel.
Osborn, S. J.	Soda Rock	96	96	96			No.	200 tons.	Riesling, Zinfandel, Chasselas.
Agnew, S. J.	Sonoma	15	15	15			No.	30 tons.	Zinfandel.
Akers, M. P.	Sonoma	5	5	5			No.	2 tons.	Zinfandel.
Alexander, Wm.	Sonoma	15	15	15			No.	30 tons.	Zinfandel.
Barnard, N. S.	Sonoma	10	10	10			No.	20 tons.	Burger, Chasselas.
Bates, Mrs. T.	Sonoma	15	15	15			No.	30 tons.	Zinfandel.
Batto, John	Sonoma	20	20	20			No.	20 tons.	Mixed.
Bayes, H. E.	Sonoma	15	15	15			No.	25 tons.	Zinfandel, Chasselas.
Breitenbach, F.	Sonoma	5	5	5			No.	10 tons.	Burger, Chasselas.
Bulotti, V.	Sonoma	15	15	15			Yes.	30 tons.	Zinfandel.
Burris, Wm. estate of.	Sonoma	40	40	40			No.	80 tons.	Zinfandel and mixed.
Cady, Mrs. M. K	Sonoma	25	25	25			Yes.	25 tons.	Zinfandel.
Callaway, David	Sonoma	10	10	10			No.	20 tons.	Zinfandel.
Campbell, B. F.	Sonoma	20	20	10	10		No.	50 tons.	Tokay, Muscat, Chasselas.
Chart, Obed	Sonoma	15	15	15			No.	30 tons.	Zinfandel.
Church, D.	Sonoma	5	5	5			No.	10 tons.	Zinfandel.
Clark, J.	Sonoma	30	30	30			No.	40 tons.	Zinfandel.
Clark, Robert	Sonoma	25	25	25			No.	50 tons.	Zinfandel and mixed.
Cluve & Duhring	Sonoma	20	20	20			No.	40 tons.	Zinfandel and mixed.
Cooper, J. R. & T. S.	Sonoma	12	12	12			No.	20 tons.	Zinfandel.
Craig, O. W.	Sonoma	30	30	30			No.	100 tons.	Riesling, Semillon.
Demartini, J.	Sonoma	15	15	15			No.	30 tons.	Zinfandel.
Donlevy, J.	Sonoma	5	5	5			No.	10 tons.	Burger.
Douglas, P., estate of.	Sonoma	5	5	5			No.	10 tons.	Zinfandel.

Name	Location							Varieties
Drahms, A.	Sonoma.	20	20	20		No.	40 tons.	Zinfandel.
Dresel & Co.	Sonoma.	100	100	100		Yes.	200 tons.	Chasselas, Burger.
Dreyfus, B., & Co.	Mt. Pisgah Vineyard, Sonoma (San Fran.)	300	300	300		Yes.	220 tons.	Zinfandel, Riesling, Burger.
Dunn, T. M.	Sonoma.	40	40	40		No.	60 tons.	Zinfandel, Chasselas.
Engler, George	Sonoma.	40	15	15		Yes.	80 tons.	Zinfandel, Gutedel.
Enos, John S.	Sonoma.	25	25	25		No.	25 tons.	Mixed.
Erlich, F.	Sonoma.	20	20	20		Yes.	30 tons.	Zinfandel, Riesling.
Ewell, P. D. F.	Sonoma.	30	30	30	10	No.	60 tons.	Tokay and mixed.
Fisher, Fred.	Sonoma.	30	30	30		No.	40 tons.	Zinfandel, etc.
Fisher, G. F.	Sonoma.	30	30	30		No.	50 tons.	Zinfandel and mixed.
Frapoli, B., estate of	Sonoma.	10	10	10		Yes.	150 tons.	Zinfandel, Chasselas.
Glaister, T. S.	Sonoma.	70	70	70		No.	50 tons.	Zinfandel.
Goodman, W.	Sonoma.	25	25	25		No.	30 tons.	Zinfandel.
Gough, John	Sonoma.	60	15	60		Yes.	200 tons.	Zinfandel, Chasselas.
Gundlach, Jacob	"Rhinefarm," Sonoma	100	100	100		No.	100 tons.	Zinfandel and mixed.
Hall, Robt.	Sonoma.	60	60	60	5	No.	60 tons.	Zinfandel, Tokay.
Harper, John.	Sonoma.	25	25	25		No.	20 tons.	Zinfandel.
Harris, Granville	Sonoma.	10	10	10		No.	50 tons.	Zinfandel, Chasselas.
Hanbert, August	Sonoma.	25	25	25		No.	200 tons.	Zinfandel, Semillon, Mataro.
Hearst, Geo., estate of	Madrone Vineyard, Sonoma (San Fran.)	150	100	150		Yes.		
Heggie, Manuel	Sonoma.	8	8	8	4	No.	8 tons.	Semillon, Tokay.
Heller, M., estate of	Sobre Vista Vineyard, Sonoma.	30	10	30	30	Yes.	20 tons.	Zinfandel, Chasselas.
Hooper, George F.	Sonoma.	100	75	75	25	Yes.	125 tons.	Riesling, Gutedel, Tokay.
Howe, Robert	Sonoma.	78	76	70	6	No.	120 tons.	Zinfandel, Chasselas, Tokay.
Hyde, W. H.	Sonoma.	100	100	100		Yes.	200 tons.	Zinfandel and mixed.
Knight, L.	Sonoma.	25	20	20	5	No.	40 tons.	Zinfandel, Tokay.
Leiding, C. F.	Sonoma.	20	20	20		No.	40 tons.	Zinfandel, Chasselas.
Lonnibos, John	Sonoma.	65	55	65		Yes.	100 tons.	Zinfandel, Riesling.
Losse, J.	Sonoma.	25	25	25		No.	50 tons.	Zinfandel and mixed.
Lubeck, C. W.	Sonoma.	15	15	15		No.	25 tons.	Zinfandel.
McGill, C. W.	Sonoma.	20	20	20		No.	40 tons.	Zinfandel, Chasselas.
McLaughlin, P. L., Mrs.	Sonoma.	50	50	50	5	Yes.	100 tons.	Zinfandel, Tokay.
Madison, J. H.	Sonoma.	25	25	25		No.	40 tons.	Zinfandel.
Mattison, ———	Sonoma.	15	15	15		No.	30 tons.	Zinfandel, Burger.
Mayer, Jacob	Sonoma.	10	10	10		No.	10 tons.	Zinfandel.
Merrill, R. A.	Sonoma.	5	5	5	4	No.	5 tons.	Zinfandel.
Morris, T. D.	Sonoma.	12	8	8	5	No.	19 tons.	Zinfandel, Tokay, Gutedel.
Morris Bros.	Sonoma.	20	15	35		No.	45 tons.	Zinfandel, Tokay.
Norris, Shubeck	Sonoma.	35	35	35		No.	75 tons.	Zinfandel, Chasselas.
O'Brien, John	Sonoma.	10	10	10		No.	5 tons.	Zinfandel.
Orsi, R.	Sonoma.	10	10	10		No.	20 tons.	Zinfandel.
Parker, F.	Sonoma.	10	10	10		No.	20 tons.	Zinfandel,

Sonoma County—Continued.

Name of Owner.	Post Office and Name of Vineyard.	Total Acres in Grapes.	Acres in Bearing.	Acres in Wine Grapes.	Acres in Table Grapes.	Acres in Raisin Grapes.	Wine Maker.	Product in 1889.	Varieties.
Peterson, E.	Sonoma	18	18	18			No.	40 tons.	Zinfandel.
Pickett, H.	Sonoma	10	10	10			No.	20 tons.	Zinfandel.
Poppe, Julius	Sonoma	20	20	20			Yes.	40 tons.	Zinfandel.
Prunty, C. L.	Sonoma	40	40	40			No.	80 tons.	Zinfandel.
Ringstrom, S. R.	Sonoma	10	10	10			No.	20 tons.	Zinfandel.
Rixford, E. P.	Sonoma	20	20	20			No.	40 tons.	Zinfandel.
Rodgers, W. K.	Sonoma	30	30	30			No.	30 tons.	Zinfandel.
Rufus, Otto	Sonoma	15	15	15			Yes.	30 tons.	Zinfandel, Chasselas.
Sears, G. C. P., estate of	Sonoma	125	100	125			No.	200 tons.	Zinfandel and mixed.
Seipp, J. C.	Sonoma	15	15	15			No.	30 tons.	Zinfandel.
Sharpe, J. W.	Sonoma	15	15	5	10		No.	30 tons.	Tokay and mixed table.
Shaw, O. B.	Sonoma	10	10	5	5		No.	20 tons.	Tokay and mixed.
Shaw, S. H.	Sonoma	6	6	6			No.	12 tons.	Mixed.
Skinner, John	Sonoma	16	16	16			No.	30 tons.	Zinfandel.
Sonoma Valley Bank	Sonoma	30	30	30			No.	60 tons.	Zinfandel.
Spencer, Mrs. C.	Sonoma	100	100	100			No.	150 tons.	Zinfandel, Mission.
Steiger, E.	Sonoma	30	30	30			Yes.	60 tons.	Zinfandel.
Stevenot, E. K.	Sonoma	15	15	10	5		No.	30 tons.	Semillon, Tokay.
Terry, Mrs. M.	Sonoma	30	30	30			No.	60 tons.	Zinfandel and mixed.
Thomas, R.	Sonoma	15	15	10	5		No.	30 tons.	Zinfandel, Tokay.
Thompson, P. H.	Sonoma	20	20	20			No.	40 tons.	Zinfandel.
Thompson, W. A.	Sonoma	35	35	35			No.	60 tons.	Zinfandel, Burger.
Vallejo, M. G., estate of	Sonoma	8	8		8		No.	16 tons.	Tokay and mixed table.
Wadsworth, John	Sonoma	10	10	10			No.	20 tons.	Zinfandel, Burger.
Watriss, Frank	Sonoma	25	25	25			No.	40 tons.	Zinfandel.
Willet, F. A.	Sonoma	15	15	15			No.	40 tons.	Zinfandel.
Wilson, C. S.	Sonoma	8	7	8			No.	15 tons.	Zinfandel.
Winkle, Henry, estate of	Sonoma	110	60	110			Yes.	120 tons.	Zinfandel, Riesling.
Young, Mrs. M. E.	Sonoma	15	16	15			No.	30 tons.	Chasselas, Malvoisie.
Fisk, John	Stewart's Point.	6	6	6			No.	10 tons.	Mixed.
Haupt, Chas.	Stewart's Point.	5	5	5			No.	9 tons.	Mixed.
Montague, H.	Stewart's Point.	6	6	6			No.	12 tons.	Mixed.
Brown, George	Stony Point.	30	30	30			No.	60 tons.	Zinfandel.
Hamilton, G. W.	Stony Point.	40	40	35	5		No.	75 tons.	Zinfandel, Muscat.

Name	Post Office						Tons	Varieties
Jones, John	Stony Point	30	30	30		No.	50 tons.	Zinfandel, Mission.
Loftus, P.	Stony Point	15	15	15		No.	30 tons.	Zinfandel.
Murphy, Pat.	Stony Point	10	10	10		No.	20 tons.	Zinfandel.
Benson, John	Trenton	10	10	10		No.	15 tons.	Zinfandel.
Bernard, J.	Trenton	20	20	20		No.	5 tons.	Zinfandel.
Billings, John	Trenton	10	10	10		No.	12 tons.	Zinfandel, Mission.
Cassin, Henry	Trenton	6	6	6		Yes.	6 tons.	Mission.
Cesera, C.	Trenton	47	47	47		No.	100 tons.	Zinfandel, Madeira.
Clarke, Horace	Trenton	43	43	43		No.	80 tons.	Zinfandel, Mission.
Fleming, J. M.	Trenton	16	16	16		No.	25 tons.	Zinfandel, Mission.
Franks, Fred.	Trenton	8	8	8		No.	16 tons.	Zinfandel.
Glass, Philip	Trenton	27	27	27		No.	32 tons.	Zinfandel, Burger.
Griffith, N. A.	Trenton	18	18	18		No.	12 tons.	Zinfandel, Mission.
Grove, George	Trenton	10	10	10		No.	20 tons.	Riesling, Chasselas.
Jones Bros.	Trenton	12	12	12		No.	18 tons.	Zinfandel, Mission.
Lynch, A.	Trenton	10	10	10		No.	5 tons.	Zinfandel.
McLellan, E. S.	Trenton	14	14	14		No.	18 tons.	Zinfandel, Mission.
Meyers, L.	Trenton	12	12	12		No.	15 tons.	Zinfandel.
Ramus, Joseph	Trenton	8	8	8		No.	16 tons.	Zinfandel, Burger.
Revello, Joe	Trenton	16	16	16		No.	16 tons.	Zinfandel.
Surthyne, E.	Trenton	42	42	42		No.	65 tons.	Zinfandel.
Tucker, H. T.	Trenton	65	65	65		No.	10 tons.	French varieties.
Adler, Robert	Windsor	18	18	18		No.	45 tons.	Zinfandel, Mission.
Arata, B.	Windsor	8	2	8		No.	2 tons.	Zinfandel.
Barth, Adam	Oak Grove Vineyard, Windsor.	30	30	30		Yes.	60 tons.	Zinfandel, Gutedel.
Bechman, John	Windsor	9	9	9		No.	15 tons.	Zinfandel.
Brooks, William	Windsor	12	12	12		No.	12 tons.	Mission.
Brown, Fred.	Windsor	96	96	96		No.	200 tons.	Zinfandel, Burger.
Brumfield, S.	Windsor	18	18	18		No.	30 tons.	Zinfandel, Mission.
Burke, Mrs. J.	Windsor	18	18	18		No.	30 tons.	Zinfandel.
Calhoun, G. W.	Windsor	18	18	18		No.	20 tons.	Zinfandel.
Chisholm, John	Windsor	6	6	6		No.	18 tons.	Zinfandel.
Clark, Benjamin	Windsor	14	14	14		No.	15 tons.	Zinfandel.
Clark, James	Windsor	6	6	6		No.	25 tons.	Zinfandel, Riesling.
Clark, J. S.	Windsor	20	20	20		No.	12 tons.	Mission.
Cooper Heirs	Windsor	30	30	30		No.	10 tons.	Mission.
Cunningham, Z. H.	Windsor	40	15	40		No.	30 tons.	Zinfandel, Mission.
Dickenson, J. R.	Windsor	20	40	20		No.	60 tons.	Zinfandel, Riesling, and mixed.
Doran, J.	Windsor						Not bearing.	Zinfandel.
Fairman, T. W.	Windsor	6	6	8		No.	6 tons.	Zinfandel.
France, Andrew	Windsor	6	6	6		No.	12 tons.	Zinfandel.
Fredson, J.	Windsor	12	12	12		Yes.	25 tons.	Riesling, Mission.
Grove, David	Windsor	40	40	40		No.	60 tons.	Zinfandel, Mission.
Gunn, J. O'B.	Windsor	100	50	100		Yes.	225 tons.	Riesling, Zinfandel, Chasselas,

SONOMA COUNTY—Continued.

Name of Owner.	Post Office and Name of Vineyard.	Total Acres in Grapes.	Acres in Bearing.	Acres in Wine Grapes.	Acres in Table Grapes.	Acres in Raisin Grapes.	Wine Maker.	Product in 1889.	Varieties.
Henderson, Mary	Windsor	7	7	7			No.	15 tons.	Zinfandel, Mission.
Hendley, J. S.	Windsor	15		15			No.	Not bearing.	Mission and mixed.
Higby, L. M.	Windsor	23	23	23			No.	23 tons.	Zinfandel.
Hotchkiss, W. J.	Windsor	150	150	150			Yes.	300 tons.	Zinfandel.
Jacobson, J. H.	Windsor	14	14	14			No.	25 tons.	Zinfandel.
Keeler, John	Windsor	25	25	25			No.	25 tons.	Zinfandel, Mission.
Kise, Philip	Windsor	6	6	6			Yes.	8 tons.	Burgundy, Mission.
Kohler & Frohling	Windsor						Yes.		
Kunde, Louis	Windsor	10	10	10			No.	10 tons.	Zinfandel.
Latimer, L. D.	Windsor	46	46	46			No.	50 tons.	Zinfandel and mixed.
Laughlin, Lee	Windsor	8	8	8			No.	16 tons.	Mission.
Laughlin, James	Windsor	25	25	25			No.	50 tons.	Zinfandel.
Laughlin, John	Windsor	10	10	10			No.	20 tons.	Zinfandel.
Laveroni, John	Windsor	12		12				Not bearing.	Zinfandel.
Lehn, Charles	Windsor	38	38	38			Yes.	75 tons.	Zinfandel, Mission.
McCoy, A. E.	Riverside Farm, Windsor	25	25	25			Yes.	50 tons.	Zinfandel.
McCutcheon, W. C.	Windsor	12	12	12			No.	12 tons.	Zinfandel, Malvoisie.
Meyers, Dillon	Windsor	11	11	11			Yes.	38 tons.	Mission, Riesling.
Meyers, Mrs.	Windsor	7	7	7			No.	15 tons.	Mission, Zinfandel.
Michelson, George	Windsor	30	16	30			No.	15 tons.	Mission.
Miller, James R.	Windsor	30	30	30			No.	75 tons.	Zinfandel.
Miller, Jeannette	Windsor	12	12	12			No.	12 tons.	Zinfandel, Mission.
Morgan, Fred.	Windsor	10	10	10			No.	10 tons.	Mission.
Nally, A. B.	Windsor	10	10	10			No.	5 tons.	Mission.
Packwood, A. J.	Windsor	10	10	10			No.	20 tons.	Zinfandel.
Peterson, B. A.	Windsor	30	30	30			No.	80 tons.	Mission.
Petray, R. A.	Windsor	20	20	20			No.	40 tons.	Zinfandel.
Philpott, R. F.	Windsor	5	5	5			No.	10 tons.	Zinfandel, Chasselas.
Pohley, Margaret	Windsor	25	25	25			No.	50 tons.	Zinfandel, Mission.
Pool, H. J.	Windsor	37	37	37			No.	50 tons.	Zinfandel, Gutedel.
Reed, J. C.	Windsor	5		5				Not bearing.	Zinfandel, Mission.
Runyon, H. L.	Windsor	9	9	9			No.	10 tons.	Zinfandel, Mission.
Schlosser, Tuomas	Windsor	10	10	10			No.	10 tons.	Zinfandel.

Name of Owner.	Post Office and Name of Vineyard.	Total Acres in Grapes.	Acres in Bearing.	Acres in Wine Grapes.	Acres in Table Grapes.	Acres in Raisin Grapes.	Wine Maker.	Product in 1889.	Varieties.
Schmidt, Mrs. E.	Windsor	25	25	25	..	..	Yes.	30 tons.	Zinfandel.
Shears, Orren	Windsor	10	10	10	..	..	No.	20 tons.	Mission.
Surrhyne, E.	Windsor	8	8	8	..	..	No.	16 tons.	Zinfandel.
Ward, N.	Windsor	65	65	65	..	..	No.	130 tons.	Zinfandel.
Wetcoat, A. R.	Windsor	10	10	10	..	..	No.	15 tons.	Mission.
Wilson, Alex.	Windsor	30	30	30	..	..	No.	60 tons.	Zinfandel.
Wilson, M. A.	Windsor	46	46	46	..	..	No.	150 tons.	Zinfandel and mixed.
Wright, Frank	Windsor	10	10	10	..	..	No.	25 tons.	Zinfandel.
Totals for county		22,683	21,053	22,351	332	..			

STANISLAUS COUNTY.

Name of Owner.	Post Office and Name of Vineyard.	Total Acres in Grapes.	Acres in Bearing.	Acres in Wine Grapes.	Acres in Table Grapes.	Acres in Raisin Grapes.	Wine Maker.	Product in 1889.	Varieties.
Collins, Asa	Knight's Ferry	4	4	2	2	..	No.	..	..
Morrison Bros.	Knight's Ferry	4	4	..	4	..	No.	..	..
Prowse, J. J.	Knight's Ferry	4	4	..	4	..	..	..	..
Schell, H. R.	Red Mountain Vineyard, Knight's Ferry	80	70	80	..	4	Yes.	30,000 gals.	Mission, Zinfandel, Cabernet Sauvignon, Mataro, Trousseau, etc.
Slook, Jacob	Knight's Ferry	4	4	..	3	..	No.	..	..
Smith, Samuel, & Son	Knight's Ferry	3	3	..	..	..	No.	..	..
Henry, Ora M.	Modesto	400	..	..	..	400	..	..	..
Hill, C. S. S.	Oakdale	20	..	..	..	20	..	Not bearing.	Muscat.
Hickman, L. M.	Turlock‡	100	..	..	..	100	..	Not bearing.	..
Totals for county		619	89	82	13	524			

SUTTER COUNTY.

Name of Owner.	Post Office and Name of Vineyard.	Total Acres in Grapes	Acres in Bearing.	Acres in Wine Grapes	Acres in Table Grapes	Acres in Raisin Grapes	Wine Maker	Product in 1889.	Varieties.
Bihlman, Geo.	Live Oak	2½	2½	2½			No.		
Locke, Geo.	Live Oak	2½	2½			2½	No.		Muscatel.
Stafford, Wm.	Live Oak	1	1		1				Muscatel, Tokay.
Ashley, J.	Meridian	6	6			6	No.		Muscatel.
Jones, J. G.	Meridian	1½	1½			1½	No.		Muscatel.
Raub, S. H.	Meridian	1	1			1	No.	7 tons.	Muscatel.
Thornbrough, E. F.	Meridian	1½	1½			1½	No.		Muscatel.
Bray Bros.	Nicolaus	½	½	½			No.		
Chandler, A. L.	Nicolaus	1½	1½			1½	No.		Muscatel.
Jackson, A. T.	Nicolaus	1½	1½	1½			No.		
Jones, James	Nicolaus	¾	¾	¾			No.		
Chandon & Klockenbaum.	Oakland	12	12	12					Mission.
Smith, Mary S.	Oakland	10	10			10			Muscatel.
Wilkie, J. B.	Oakland	16	16			16			Muscatel.
Spilman, W. T.	Pennington	2	2		⅔	1⅓	No.		Muscat, Tokay.
Algeo, J. M.	Pleasant Grove	1	1			1	No.		
Holloman, J.	Sutter City	4	4	4			No.		
Moody, S.	Sutter City	3	3		3				
Saye, Geo. M.	Sutter City	1⅔	1⅔		1⅔		No.		
Thompson, Wm., Sr.	Sutter City	1½	1½			1½	No.		Muscatel, Thompson Seedless.
Wadsworth, W. M.	Sutter City	15	3		3	12	No.		Muscatel.
Berg Bros.	Yuba City	8			8		No.		
Bunce, P. L.	Yuba City	1	1		1		No.		Rose Peru, Tokay.
Carpenter, Geo.	Yuba City	25	25			25			Muscatel.
Davis, Robert	Yuba City	1	1		1		No.		
Frisbie, B. F.	Yuba City	40				40			Muscatel.
Hixon, E. W.	Yuba City	11	11			11			Muscatel.
Hull, T. B.	Yuba City	20	20			20	No.		Muscatel.
Keak, Robert	Yuba City	1⅔	1⅔	1⅔			No.		Zinfandel.
Kells, R. C.	Yuba City	46	46		20	26		276 tons.	
Kirk, C. J.	Yuba City	2				2	No.		Muscatel.
Kirk, T. L.	Yuba City	3	3		3		No.		
McCune, Phil.	Yuba City	20	20			20	No.		Muscatel.

Name of Owner	Post Office and Name of Vineyard	Total Acres in Grapes	Acres in Bearing	Acres in Wine Grapes	Acres in Table Grapes	Acres in Raisin Grapes	Wine Maker	Product in 1889.	Varieties.
Ohleyer, George	Yuba City	3	3	1	1	1	No.		Zinfandel, Muscatel, Tokay.
Onstott, J. P.	Yuba City	26	26			20	No.		Muscatel.
Pease, George	Yuba City	20	20			2½			Muscatel.
Sammis, W. E.	Yuba City	2½	1			1			Muscatel.
Stabler, B. G.	Yuba City	1	20.	8	2	10	No.		Zinfandel, Muscatel, Tokay.
Starr, Geo. F.	Yuba City	20	4	1¾		2¾	No.		
Stoker, B. F.	Yuba City	4	3			3			Muscatel.
Stoker, W. H.	Yuba City	3	4			4			Muscatel.
Stone, F. L.	Yuba City	4	5	5					Zinfandel.
Walthers, C.	Yuba City	5	40						Muscatel.
Williams, C. E.	Yuba City	40	1		1	40		240 tons.	Black Hamburg.
Mathews, J.	West Butte	1	1½						Muscatel.
Robinson, G. W.	West Butte	1½				1½	No.		
Totals for county		370	287	38	47	285			

TEHAMA COUNTY.

Name of Owner	Post Office and Name of Vineyard	Total Acres in Grapes	Acres in Bearing	Acres in Wine Grapes	Acres in Table Grapes	Acres in Raisin Grapes	Wine Maker	Product in 1889.	Varieties.
Wilson, H. C.	Corning	3	3		3		No.	9 tons.	
Glenn, H. J., estate of.	Henleyville	3	3		3		No.	6 tons.	
Dailey, L. C.	Hunters	4	4			4	No.	13 tons.	
Sanford, Ansel	Hunters	5	5			5	No.	14 tons.	
Cockburn, Thos.	Paskenta	3	5		2	3	No.	10 tons.	
Flournoy, G. H.	Paskenta	3	3			3	No.	8 tons.	
Halley, W. H.	Paskenta	4	4			4	No.	7 tons.	
Wakefield, H.	Paskenta	12	12			12	No.	24 tons.	
Ames, S. R.	Proberta	5			5		No.		
Banks, H. H.	Red Bluff	3	3			3	No.	6 tons.	
Barley, E. S.	Red Bluff	12				12	No.		
Bresler, H.	Red Bluff	3	3			3	No.		
Burrichter, H.	Red Bluff	5	5		5		No.	9 tons.	
Calkins, J. A.	Red Bluff	8	8		4	4	No.	10 tons.	
Cofer, G. W.	Red Bluff	10	10		2	8	No.	20 tons.	
Cone, J. S.	Red Bluff	10	10		4	6	No.	20 tons.	

Tehama County—Continued.

Name of Owner.	Post Office and Name of Vineyard.	Total Acres in Grapes.	Acres in Bearing.	Acres in Wine Grapes.	Acres in Table Grapes.	Acres in Raisin Grapes.	Wine Maker.	Product in 1889.	Varieties.
Cowles, I. S.	Red Bluff	10	10		4	6	No.	18 tons.	
Drane, J. F.	Red Bluff	10	10		3	7	No.	30 tons.	Muscat.
Duncan, Wm.	Red Bluff	10	10			10	No.	10 tons.	
Eby, Jackson	Red Bluff	6	6		6		No.	6 tons.	
Gallatin, Albert	Red Bluff	8	8		4	4	No.	20 tons.	
Gilmore, John	Red Bluff	10	10		10		No.	6 tons.	
Lee, B. B.	Red Bluff	3	3		3		No.	16 tons.	
Stoll, Geo.	Red Bluff	8	8		8		No.	6 tons.	
Warner, A. J.	Red Bluff	5	5		1	5	No.	7 tons.	
Butler, Isabella	Tehama	5	5		3	2	No.	9 tons.	
Finnell, John	Tehama	6	6		6	2	No.	14 tons.	
Harvey, Joseph	Tehama	6	6		4		No.	18 tons.	
Hildebrandt, R.	Vina	8	8		4	4	No.		
Stanford, Leland	Vina Vineyard, Vina	3,825	2,500	3,705		120	Yes.	6,000 tons.	Zinfandel, Trousseau, Burger, and many others.
Totals for county		4,012	2,660	3,705	80	227			

TULARE COUNTY.

Name of Owner.	Post Office and Name of Vineyard.	Total Acres in Grapes.	Total Acres in Wine Grapes.	Acres in Wine Grapes not Bearing.	Total Acres in Raisin Grapes.	Acres in Raisin Grapes Bearing.	Acres in Raisin Grapes not Bearing.	Acres in Muscats.	Acres in Malagas.	Acres in Sultanas.	Wine Maker.
Akins, ——	Armona	6			6		6	6			No.
Allen, L.	Armona	10			10		10	10			No.
Armstrong, Mrs.	Armona	3			3	3		3			No.
Battenfeldt, W.	Armona	20			20		20	20			No.
Beall, Z. D.	Armona	20			20		20	20			No.

Name	Location	No.	No.	No.	No.
Biddle, Samuel E.	Armona	15	15		15
Bozeman, J. W.	Armona	27	6	21	27
Brown, O. C.	Armona	110	80	30	110
Buckner, A. B.	Armona	20	20		20
Buckner, W. V.	Armona	20	20		20
Camp, George	Armona	80		80	80
Crow, ——	Armona	15	15		15
Doyle, C. W.	Armona	11	11		11
Gibson, E. J.	Armona	18	6	12	18
Giddings, W. R.	Armona	10		10	10
Gray, H. P.	Armona	160	80	80	160
Kern, George	Armona	14	14		14
Knapp, A. E.	Armona	12	12		12
McDonald, P.	Armona	15	12	3	15
Manter, Charles	Armona	18	6	12	18
Miller, Dr. W. H.	Armona	20	20		20
Moody, P. S.	Armona	5	5		5
Newlin, H.	Armona	8	8		8
Newton, M.	Armona	10	10		10
Ogden, W.	Armona	10		10	10
Ordway, ——	Armona	20		20	20
Ritchman, S.	Armona	23		23	23
Roberts, ——	Armona	6		6	6
Robinson, W. W.	Armona	20	20		20
Rout, J. H.	Armona	8	8		8
Shore, John H., estate of	Armona	25	15	10	25
Sims, ——	Armona	15	15		15
Trimble, J. K.	Armona	18	18		18
Vandelear, J. W.	Armona	25	25		25
Walker, Sam.	Armona	40		40	40
Antrim, H.	Dinuba	10	10		10
Barr, P.	Dinuba	5		5	5
Bingham, O.	Dinuba	20	20		20
Giddings, C. T.	Dinuba	5	5		5
Giddings, Ed.	Dinuba	5	5		5
Gilbert, D. E.	Dinuba	3		3	3
Hall, H.	Dinuba	20	20		20
McCracken Bros.	Dinuba	20	20		20
Sibley, James	Dinuba	80		80	80
Sibley, Sam.	Dinuba	20		20	20
Williams, Mrs.	Dinuba	10		10	10
Ayers, A. S.	Grangeville	10	3	7	10
Blowers, C. M.	Grangeville	22	11	11	22
Bloyd, W. W.	Grangeville	25	25		25
Brown, Jesse	Grangeville	6	6		6

TULARE COUNTY—Continued.

Name of Owner.	Post Office and Name of Vineyard.	Total Acres in Grapes	Total Acres in Wine Grapes	Acres in Wine Grapes not Bearing	Total Acres in Raisin Grapes	Acres in Raisin Grapes Bearing	Acres in Raisin Grapes not Bearing	Acres in Muscats	Acres in Malagas	Acres in Sultanas	Wine Maker
Chambers, J.	Grangeville	22			22	22		22			No.
Childress, J.	Grangeville	10			10		10	10			No.
Cody, Geo. W.	Grangeville	15			15	11	4	15			No.
Duray, M.	Grangeville	3			3	3		3			No.
Ezery, J.	Grangeville	25			25		25	25			No.
Foster Bros.	Grangeville	20			20		20	20			No.
Gerow, Ed.	Grangeville	10			10	10		10			No.
Hackett, H.	Grangeville	8			8	8		8			No.
Harlick, W.	Grangeville	5			5	5		5			No.
Harris, J. W.	Grangeville	7			7	7		7			No.
Hatch, M.	Grangeville	25			25		25	25			No.
Hays, A. B.	Grangeville	23			23	23		23			No.
Henderson, C. N.	Grangeville	16			16		16	15			No.
Kurtz, John	Grangeville	60			60	50	10	60			No.
Leavens, P.	Grangeville	2			2	2		2			No.
Lobdell, D. G.	Grangeville	25			25	25		25			No.
Long, A. W.	Grangeville	30			30		30	30			No.
Marlow, W.	Grangeville	5			5		5	5			No.
Nathan Bros.	Verona Vineyard, Grangeville	75			75	20	55	75			No.
Newport & Railsback	Grangeville	30			30		30	30			No.
Niels, John	Grangeville	12			12	12		12			No.
Patterson, Jim	Grangeville	15			15		15	15			No.
Railsback, Frank	Grangeville	15			15		15	15			No.
Railsback, George	Grangeville	20			20		20	20			No.
Reeve, George	Grangeville	70			70	70		70			No.
Ritchie, J.	Grangeville	14			14	14		14			No.
Robinson, J. S.	Grangeville	205			205		205	205			No.
Robinson, M. D.	Grangeville	7			7	1	6	7			No.
Sanborn, E.	Grangeville	45			45	15	30	45			No.
Scazighini, P.	Grangeville	11			11	11		11			No.
Sullivan, John L.	Grangeville	11			11	11		11			No.
Sullivan, J. S.	Grangeville	3			3	2	1	3			No.
Thyarks, George	Grangeville	20			20	15	5	20			No.
Tilton, J. E.	Grangeville	15			15	15		15			No.

Name	Location	No.	No.	No.	No.	No.
Tomer, John, estate of	Grangeville	8		3	8	8
Wood, G. W., estate of	Grangeville	30	20	10	30	30
Woods, W.	Grangeville	3		3	3	3
Hayes, T.						
Mallock, P.	Goshen	25	25		25	25
Swank, J. W.	Goshen	10	10		10	10
Alcorn, I. P.	Goshen	2	2		2	2
Aldrage, A.	Hanford	12	8	4	12	12
Andrews, Mrs. M.	Hanford	5	2	8	5	5
Barber, E. H.	Hanford	6		6	6	6
Barkman, F. L.	Hanford	12	12		12	12
Barton, H. D.	Hanford	8	8		8	8
Bateman, B. A.	Hanford	15	15	6	15	15
Belnap, J. W.	Hanford	20	14	6	20	20
Benedict & Walker	Hanford	16	10		16	16
Bigford, ———	Hanford	20	20		20	20
Block, W. H.	Hanford	10	10		10	10
Bock, E. S.	Hanford	8	8	8	8	8
Boker, S.	Hanford	5	5	8	5	5
Bowmer, Joe	Hanford	10	7		10	10
Brandon, I. J.	Hanford	8		4	8	8
Bruner, J.	Hanford	15	15	5	15	15
Buhler, J.	Hanford	6	2	3	6	6
Burdge, A.	Hanford	15	10		15	15
Camp & Wisebarm	Hanford	3			3	3
Camp, W. H.	Hanford	28	28	15	28	28
Camp, W. S.	Hanford	20	5	15	20	20
Chadwick, C.	Hanford	40	25		40	40
Clark, ———	Hanford	2	2		2	2
Coe, C. H.	Hanford	2		2	2	2
Coffey, Frank	Hanford	6	6		6	6
Comfort, G. B.	Hanford	2	2		2	2
Cotton, G. W.	Hanford	5	5	8	5	5
Courtney, J.	Hanford	16	8	5	16	16
Cressey, L.	Hunford	45	40		45	45
Cross, O. R.	Hanford	8	8	6	8	8
Curtis, A. B.	Hanford	8	2		8	8
Davis, Hugh	Hanford	10	10		10	10
Davis, J.	Hanford	3	3	8	3	3
Dawson, John	Hanford	8			8	8
Deardoff, J. H.	Hanford	10	10		10	10
Dillon, Bob	Hanford	7	7		7	7
Dillon, F.	Hanford	6	6		6	6
Ensign, J. C.	Hanford	5	5		5	5
Fellows, D. S.	Hanford	10	2	8	10	10

TULARE COUNTY—Continued.

Name of Owner	Post Office and Name of Vineyard	Total Acres in Grapes	Total Acres in Wine Grapes	Acres in Wine Grapes not Bearing	Total Acres in Raisin Grapes	Acres in Raisin Grapes Bearing	Acres in Raisin Grapes not Bearing	Acres in Muscats	Acres in Malagas	Acres in Sultanas	Wine Maker
Fisher, H.	Hanford	20			20		20	20			No.
Fisher, Sam	Hanford	30			30		30	30			No.
Gant, V.	Hanford	40			40		40	40			No.
Gregory, L. N.	Hanford	30			30		30	30			No.
Griswold, O. T.	Hanford	16			16		16	16			No.
Hackett, Jesse	Hanford	15			15		15	15			No.
Hambleton, J. M.	Hanford	10			10		10	10			No.
Hamilton, C. B.	Hanford	12			12	12		12			No.
Hamilton, Geo.	Hanford	10			10		10	10			No.
Harris, J.	Hanford	25			25		25	25			No.
Hawley, L. C.	Hanford	10			10		10	10			No.
Hawley, S. V.	Hanford	4			4		4	4			No.
Hayward, D. C.	Hanford	40			40		40	40			No.
Hearing, F.	Hanford	4			4	1	3	4			No.
Henderson, W.	Hanford	12			12		12	12			No.
Hicks, B.	Hanford	7			7		7	7			No.
Hill, I. V.	Hanford	10			10		10	10			No.
Hill, V. E.	Hanford	10			10		10	10			No.
Hill, William	Hanford	10			10		10	10			No.
Hooper Tract	Hanford	5			5		5	5			No.
Howard, W. H.	Hanford	5			5		5	5			No.
Isaacs, F. N.	Hanford	2			2		2	2			No.
Itni, J.	Hanford	47			47	12	35	47			No.
Ivin, E. P.	Hanford	10			10	10		10			No.
Jenkinson, Robert	Hanford	12			12	4	8	12			No.
Jenkinson, T.	Hanford	8			8	3	5	8			No.
Johnson, H. E.	Hanford	5			5	5		5			No.
Kelley, Ed.	Hanford	8			8		8	8			No.
Kerr, E. W.	Hanford	15			15		15	15			No.
King, C.	Hanford	20			20		20	20			No.
King,	Hanford	5			5	2	3	5			No.
Knough, J. H.	Hanford	12			12	12		12			No.
Lake, C.	Hanford										No.
Land, A. W.	Hanford	20			20	5	15	20			No.

Name	Location	No.	No.	No.	No.	No.	No.
Laughlin, Jesse	Hanford		10	10		10	10
Levin, Antone	Hanford		35	35		35	35
Levins, B.	Hanford		14		14	14	14
Lewellin, W.	Hanford		2	2		2	2
Ludlow, M.	Hanford		7	7		7	7
Ludlow, V. P.	Hanford		9	9		9	9
McGuire, Mrs. M.	Hanford		18	18		18	18
McJunkin, J. T.	Hanford		35	15	20	35	35
Manassee & Co.	Hanford	120	6	6		6	6
Manassee, Jim	Hanford		25	5	20	25	25
Miesenheimer, M.	Hanford		3		3	3	3
Moore, F.	Hanford		7		7	7	7
Morris, ____	Hanford		10	10		10	10
Motheral, N. W.	Hanford		40	10	30	40	40
Murray, G. W.	Hanford		5	5		5	5
Neame, E. A.	Hanford		12	12		12	12
Neame, A.	Hanford		9	5	4	9	9
Newport, John	Hanford		25	13	12	25	25
Newport, Wm.	Hanford		20	5	15	20	20
Nickolson, W. G.	Hanford		55	40	15	55	55
Noel, H. M.	Hanford		16	16		16	16
Paddock, C.	Hanford		9	6	3	9	9
Paige, Root & Chittenden	Lucerne Vineyard, Hanford		810	930		930	930
Parker, H. S.	Hanford		20	8	12	20	20
Parker, I.	Hanford		15	7	8	15	15
Park, Rev. A. G.	Hanford		20	7	13	20	20
Parish, F.	Hanford		54	42	12	54	54
Parlin, W. W.	Hanford		60	20	30	60	60
Payton, John	Hanford		2	2		2	2
Peacock, H. F.	Hanford		2	2		2	2
Peacock, Joseph	Hanford		10	10		10	10
Pepys, H. F.	Hanford		2		2	2	2
Phillips, P. C.	Hanford		8	8		8	8
Raich, John	Hanford		26	26		26	26
Rawlins, J. E.	Hanford		13	13		13	13
Read, W. H.	Hanford		10	6	4	10	10
Reding & Fraser	Hanford		15	10	5	15	15
Rice, J. O.	Hanford		2		2	2	2
Richland Colony Tract	Hanford		80	80		80	80
Riffe, James	Hanford		3	3		3	3
Robinson, J. W.	Hanford		170	130	40	170	170
Ross, Nevil	Hanford		8	8		8	8
Scribner, Ben	Hanford		10		10	10	10
Sharp, B. V.	Hanford		20	14	6	20	20
Sharp, C.	Hanford		10	10		10	10

TULARE COUNTY—Continued.

Name of Owner	Post Office and Name of Vineyard	Wine Maker	Acres in Sultanas	Acres in Malagas	Acres in Muscats	Acres in Raisin Grapes not Bearing	Acres in Raisin Grapes Bearing	Total Acres in Raisin Grapes	Acres in Wine Grapes not Bearing	Total Acres in Wine Grapes	Total Acres in Grapes
Shoemaker, ——	Hanford	No.			7	7		7			7
Shoemaker, H.	Hanford	No.			10		10	10			10
Simpson, Bob	Hanford	No.			12		12	12			12
Sinn, D.	Hanford	No.			2	2		2			2
Smith, John	Hanford	No.			5	5		5			5
Smith, Jud.	Hanford	No.			20	20		20			20
Smith, Oliver	Hanford	No.			12	12		12			12
Steinman, F.	Hanford	Yes.			5		5	5		7	12
Stokes, Mrs. James	Hanford	No.								18	18
Stone, A. M.	Hanford	No.			12	8	4	12			12
Tomes, Sam	Hanford	No.			10	10		10			10
Van Valer, P.	Hanford	No.			8		8	8			8
Van Valkenburg, J.	Hanford	No.			20	20		20			20
Van Vlear, J. W.	Hanford	No.			20	20		20			20
Viney, D. B.	Hanford	No.			20	20		20			20
Viney, William	Hanford	No.			20	12	8	20			20
Wait, R. S.	Hanford	No.			12	12		12			12
Wasson, William	Hanford	No.			15	15		15			15
Wilburn, J. W.	Hanford	No.			5	5		5			5
Willson, J. A.	Hanford	No.			80	70	10	80			80
Wilson, Jim	Hanford	No.			10	10		10			10
Wisebaum, N.	Hanford	No.			5	5		5			5
Abrams, E.	Lemoore	No.			10	10		10			10
Ayers, A. M.	Lemoore	No.			2	2		2			2
Bauer, G.	Lemoore	No.			4	4		4			4
Bricknell, H. F.	Lemoore	No.			8		8	8			8
Brownstone, D.	Lemoore	No.			10		10	10			10
Byron, W. H.	Lemoore	No.			50	30	20	50			50
Copeland, Mrs. L.	Lemoore	No.			22	16	6	22			22
Cunningham, W. S.	Lemoore	No.			4		4	4			4
Del Monte Vineyard	Lemoore	No.			40		40	40			40
Dingley, Han & Co.	Lemoore	No.			175	45	130	175			175
Douglass & Thorn	Lemoore	No.			40	30	10	40			40
Ezery, J. T.	Lemoore	No.			8		8	8			8

		No.	No.	No.	No.	No.
Fields, G.	Lemoore	10	10		10	10
Flory, J.	Lemoore	25	20	5	25	25
Foster, G. S.	Lemoore	2		2	2	2
Fox & Sweetland	Lemoore	13	13		13	13
Fox, Joel A.	Lemoore	8		8	8	8
Garrett, W. J.	Lemoore	7		7	7	7
Glass, J. P.	Lemoore	2	2		2	2
Gray, R. P.	Lemoore	17	11	6	17	17
Heinlen, John	Lemoore	35	35		35	35
Heinlen, M. A.	Lemoore	20	20		20	20
Hill, E.	Lemoore	20	10	10	20	20
Hitchcock, L. H.	Lemoore	25	19	6	25	25
Hodgekins,	Lemoore	6	5		6	6
Hutton, A.	Lemoore	11	6	5	11	11
Kidd,	Lemoore	3		3	3	3
Kline, M. J.	Lemoore	4		4	4	4
McGlashen, A.	Lemoore	10	10		10	10
McLaughlin, Fred.	Lemoore	16	10	6	16	16
McLaughlin, S. A.	Lemoore	20		20	20	20
Merz, J.	Lemoore	10	10		10	10
Moore, Dr. L. L.	Lemoore	35		35	35	35
Schilikeiser, A.	Lemoore	22		22	22	22
Shore, Dud	Lemoore	10	10		10	10
Simpson, Mrs. B.	Lemoore	5		5	5	5
Sims, J. S.	Lemoore	15		15	15	15
Southerland, James	Lemoore	40	40		40	40
Steels,	Lemoore	10	10		10	10
Taylor, A.	Lemoore	4	4		4	4
Underwood, W.	Lemoore	4	4		4	4
Whiteside,	Lemoore	8	8		8	8
Williams, Joseph	Lemoore	20		20	20	20
Berrey, G. S.	Lindsay	10	10		10	10
Bacon, J. A.	Orosi	10	10		10	10
Bob, W. H.	Orosi	20	20		20	20
Brump & Agee	Orosi	30	30		30	30
Edmiston, W. B.	Orosi	15	15		15	15
Edwards, J. H.	Orosi	20	20		20	20
Furtney, D. H.	Orosi	6	6		6	6
Goodwin, O. C.	Orosi	10	10		10	10
Pugh, James	Orosi	5	5		5	5
Ross, W.	Orosi	20	20		20	20
Schaffer, D. R.	Orosi	20	20		20	20
Whidder, D. G.	Orosi	20	20		20	20
Anderson, G. G.	Traver	8	8		8	8
Archer, J. W.	Traver	5	5		5	5

TULARE COUNTY—Continued.

Name of Owner	Post Office and Name of Vineyard	Total Acres in Grapes	Total Acres in Wine Grapes	Acres in Wine Grapes not Bearing	Total Acres in Raisin Grapes	Acres in Raisin Grapes Bearing	Acres in Raisin Grapes not Bearing	Acres in Muscats	Acres in Malagas	Acres in Sultanas	Wine Maker
Barres, E.	Traver	12			12		12	12			No.
Bellville, Rev.	Traver	10	10								No.
Boon, T. J., & Bro.	Traver	40			40	40		40			No.
Boon, T. J.	Traver	10			10	10		10			No.
Boyd, J. A.	Traver	10			10	5	5	10			No.
Clark, Jim	Traver	7			7		7	7			No.
Clough, P.	Traver	4			4	4		4			No.
Fairwether, A. J.	Traver	15			15		15	15			No.
Gregg, L. W.	Traver	2			2	2		2			No.
Gregory & Cress	Traver	35			35		35	35			No.
Gass, B.	Traver	15			15	12	3	15			No.
Griggs, John	Traver	5			5	5		5			No.
Herman & Eldred	Traver	20			20		20	20			No.
Houston, J.	Traver	7			7	7		7			No.
Logins, W. E.	Traver	2			2	2		2			No.
McCallahan, A.	Traver	21			21		21	21			No.
McCann, T. B.	Traver	5			5	2	3	5			No.
McCarthy, I. P.	Traver	5			5	3	2	5			No.
McCubbin, John C.	Traver	15			15		15	15			No.
McFarlan, G. W.	Traver	2			2	2		2			No.
Macomber, J. W.	Traver	5			5	5		5			No.
Millsop, M.	Traver	14			14	14		14			No.
Morton, Mrs.	Traver	5			5		5	5			No.
Pennybacker, W.	Traver	10	10								No.
Phelps, O. B.	Traver	12			12			12			No.
Russell, J. C.	Traver	65			65	60	5	65			No.
Russell, W. E.	Traver	8			8		8	8			No.
Sneider, E.	Traver	15			15	7	8	15			No.
Williams, C. H.	Traver	7			7		7	7			No.
Williams, W. A.	Traver	6			6	6		6			No.
Adler, Mrs. J.	Tulare	10			10		10	10			No.
Alexander, S. F.	Tulare	15			15	15		15			No.
Ambrose & Gillespie.	Tulare	11			11		11	11			No.
Anderson, G.	Tulare	10			10		10	10			No.

Name	County	No.	No.	No.	No.
Anderson, James	Tulare	10	10	10	10
Berge, E.	Tulare	16	16	16	16
Bertch, George	Tulare	5	5	5	5
Bishop, B. F.	Tulare	25	25	25	25
Blythe, S. A.	Tulare	10	10	10	10
Blythe, W. L.	Tulare	10	10	10	10
Bockwith, J. B.	Tulare	20	20	20	20
Brown, W. E.	Tulare	24	24	24	24
Burnett, M. M.	Tulare	15	15	15	15
Burnett, W. J.	Tulare	65	65	65	65
Cartmitt, W. B.	Tulare	24	24	24	24
Chandler, R.	Tulare	9	9	9	9
Chapin, C. A.	Tulare	40	40	40	40
Coggeshall, W. H.	Tulare	80	40	80	80
Coleman, H.	Tulare	10	10	10	10
Delta Vineyard	Tulare	165	165	165	165
De Witt, M.	Tulare	10	10	10	10
Dore, J.	Tulare	15	15	15	15
Dow, B. N.	Tulare	10	10	10	10
Dutcher, Dr. E. W.	Tulare	12	12	12	12
Dye, H. E.	Tulare	5	5	5	5
Dyer, H. K.	Tulare	10	10	10	10
Elder, ——	Tulare	15	15	15	15
Erwin Bros.	Tulare	18	18	18	18
Fifield, G. B.	Tulare	20	20	20	20
Fleichman, L. E.	Tulare	10	10	10	10
Flower, S.	Tulare	8	8	8	8
Fowler, F. D.	Tulare	8	8	8	8
Goble Bros.	Tulare	10	10	10	10
Gould, James	Tulare	32	32	32	32
Hall, A. P.	Tulare	20	20	20	20
Hall, C. F.	Tulare	10	10	10	10
Hamilton, J. B.	Tulare	6	6	6	6
Hammond, D. O.	Tulare	8	8	8	8
Hawkins, J. C.	Tulare	5	5	5	5
Hitchcock, J. R.	Tulare	4	4	4	4
Hoffman, S. E.	Tulare	10	10	10	10
Hough, A. M.	Tulare	20	20	20	20
Hough, R. N.	Tulare	20	20	20	20
Huff, M.	Tulare	10	10	10	10
Hunt, M. C.	Tulare	20	20	20	20
Ingam, S. S.	Tulare	10	10	10	10
Jacobs, J. J.	Tulare	80	40	80	80
James, W. A.	Tulare	12	12	12	12

TULARE COUNTY—Continued.

Name of Owner.	Post Office and Name of Vineyard.	Total Acres in Grapes	Total Acres in Wine Grapes.	Acres in Wine Grapes not Bearing	Total Acres in Raisin Grapes.	Acres in Raisin Grapes Bearing	Acres in Raisin Grapes not Bearing	Acres in Muscats	Acres in Malagas	Acres in Sultanas	Wine Maker.
Jennings, —	Tulare	2			2		2	2			No.
Johnson, W. L.	Tulare	10			10		10	10			No.
Langdon, W. J.	Tulare	10			10		10	10			No.
Langdon, W. J.	Tulare	8			8		8	8			No.
Lustfield, A.	Tulare	5			5		5	5			No.
Mackie, J. W.	Tulare	3			3		3	3			No.
McLennon, Dr.	Tulare	20			20		20	20			No.
McMillin, R. T.	Tulare	25			25		25	25			No.
Madden & Castle	Tulare	60			60		60	60			No.
Madden, Wheeler & Zartman.	Tulare	45			45		45	45			No.
Manuel, —	Tulare	10			10		10	10			No.
Merritt, A. P.	Tulare	16			16	8	8	16			No.
Moit, A. E.	Tulare	20			20		20	20			No.
Morehead, J. A.	Tulare	4			4		4	4			No.
Mosher, C. H.	Tulare	20			20		20	20			No.
Murray, J. & P. M.	Tulare	15			15		15	15			No.
Neff, A. D.	Tulare	35			35		35	35			No.
Nelson, C.	Tulare	13			13		13	13			No.
Nousiton, B.	Tulare	8			8		8	8			No.
Paige & Morton	Roble Vista Vineyard, Tulare	500			500	500		460		40	No.
Paige, Morton & Monteagle	Tulare	300			300		300	300			No.
Paul, A. A.	Tulare	20			20		20	20			No.
Premo, M.	Tulare	28			28		28	28			No.
Prescott, G. W.	Tulare	15			15		15	15			No.
Reading, George	Tulare	12			12		12	12			No.
Read, R. L.	Tulare	20			20		20	20			No.
Rhoderfer, Ed.	Tulare	8			8		8	8			No.
Riffls, Dr. E. K.	Tulare	5			5		5	5			No.
Rogers, H. C.	Tulare	10			10		10	10			No.
Rosenthal, F.	Tulare	20			20		20	20			No.
Schoeneman & Zumwalt.	Tulare	40			40		40	40			No.
Shackelford, James	Tulare	10			10		10	10			No.
Shreve, A. M.	Tulare	10			10		10	10			No.
Solomon, I. E.	Tulare	5			5		5	5			No.

		No.	No.	No.	No.
Steinanger, E. A.	Tulare	10	10	10	10
Tagget, Dr. C.	Tulare	10	10	10	10
Talbot, C.	Tulare	20	20	20	20
Tandy, H. F.	Tulare	14	14	14	14
Tayler, O. B.	Tulare	5	5	5	5
Townsend & Myrehen	Tulare	20	20	20	20
Truitt, Geo.	Tulare	18	18	18	18
Turner, A.	Tulare	15	15	15	15
Turner, J. T.	Tulare	20	20	20	20
Turner, T.	Tulare	20	20	20	20
Twaddle, Jim	Tulare	25	25	25	25
Twaddle, Tom	Tulare	18	18	18	18
Waggie, Jim	Tulare	10	10	10	10
Wagon, J. I.	Tulare	10	10	10	10
Wallace, A. J.	Tulare	20	20	20	20
Wallace, H.	Tulare	25	25	25	25
Warner, J. H.	Tulare	20	20	20	20
Weigle, ——	Tulare	10	10	10	10
White, ——	Tulare	10	10	10	10
Wiles, A.	Tulare	20	20	20	20
Williams, Jesse	Tulare	3	3	3	3
Wilson, E. M.	Tulare	6	6	6	6
Wisham Bros.	Tulare	20	20	20	20
Wikowski, S.	Tulare	10	10	10	10
Woodard, A. G.	Tulare	10	10	10	10
Worms, A.	Tulare	12	12	12	12
Wright, I. W.	Tulare	42	42	42	42
Zumwalt, J. B.	Tulare	20	20	20	20
Zumwalt, J. B.	Tulare	10	10	10	10
Anderson Bros.	Visalia	10	10	10	10
Anderson, D. O.	Visalia	8	8	8	8
Averill, C.	Visalia	5	5	5	5
Brown, S. C.	Visalia	25	25	25	25
Cutler, A. B.	Visalia	20	20	20	20
Davis, S. F.	Visalia	20	20	20	20
Dean, G. C.	Visalia	10	10	10	10
Dodge, R. L.	Visalia	7	7	7	7
Dudley, M.	Visalia	5	5	5	5
Evans, S.	Visalia	2	2	2	2
Fisher, J.	Visalia	2	2	2	2
Fowler, F	Visalia	8	8	8	8
Gidding, C. J.	Visalia	2	2	2	2
Hayes, Jack	Visalia	20	20	20	20
Hughlen, T. A.	Visalia	20	20	20	20
Jacobs, T., & Bro.	Visalia	9	9	9	9

TULARE COUNTY—Continued.

Name of Owner.	Post Office and Name of Vineyard.	Wine Maker.	Acres in Sultanas	Acres in Malagas	Acres in Muscats	Acres in Raisin Grapes not Bearing	Acres in Raisin Grapes Bearing	Total Acres in Raisin Grapes.	Acres in Wine Grapes not Bearing	Total Acres in Wine Grapes	Total Acres in Grapes
Kelsey, W. F.	Visalia.	No.			200	200		200			200
Lankins, E. O.	Visalia.	No.			3	3		3			3
McIntyre, ——	Visalia.	No.			10	10		10			10
McKinley, G. C.	Visalia.	No.			20	20		20			20
Manock, O. F.	Visalia.	No.			2	2		2			2
Miles, Ed.	Visalia.	No.			3	3		3			3
Miller, E. O.	Visalia.	No.			10	10		10			10
Mosier, J. C.	Visalia.	No.			20	20		20			20
Murry, A. H., Jr.	Visalia.	No.			15	12	3	15			15
Parker & Rich	Visalia.	No.			2	2		2			2
Parr, J. R.	Visalia.	No.			10	10		10			10
Parrish, R. H.	Visalia.	No.			10	10		10			10
Reed, R. L.	Visalia.	No.			20	20		20			20
Sharp, George	Visalia.	No.			15	15		15			15
Smith, S.	Visalia.	No.			10	10		10			10
Steinman, F.	Visalia.	Yes.			5		5	5		7	12
Stokes, Mrs. James	Visalia.	No.								18	18
Van Valer, E. L.	Visalia.	No.			3	3		3			3
Ward, J. C.	Visalia.	No.			3	3		3			3
White Bros.	Visalia.	No.			10	10		10			10
Zumwalt, D. K.	Visalia.	No.			8	8		8			8
Totals for county					9,849	7,327	2,592	9,849		70	9,919

TUOLUMNE COUNTY.

Name of Owner.	Post Office and Name of Vineyard.	Total Acres in Grapes.	Acres in Bearing.	Acres in Wine Grapes.	Acres in Table Grapes.	Acres in Raisin Grapes.	Wine Maker.	Product in 1889.	Varieties.
Culbertson, G. F.	Big Oak Flat								
Goodwin, J. A.	Chinese Camp								
Meneke, Wm.	Chinese Camp								
Quinn, H.	Chinese Camp								
Cavron, Mrs. M.	Columbia								
Jarvis, ——	Columbia								
Milan, J.	Columbia								
Nichol, J.	Columbia								
Pedistre, John	Columbia								
Schilling, A.	Columbia								
Trask, P. M.	Columbia								
Winchester, Gen. J.	Columbia								
Blackburn, James	Jamestown								
Loney, James	Jamestown								
Peireira, John	Jamestown								
Brignordella, G.	Sonora								
Bacigalupi, A.	Sonora								
Carveron, Mrs.	Sonora								
Champney, A. D.	Sonora								
Engler, ——	Sonora								
Merringo, A.	Sonora								
Mundorff, J.	Sonora								
MacPherson, G. F.	Sonora								
Podesto, A.	Sonora								
Rosasco, J.	Sonora								
Restanno, G.	Sonora								
Trask, M.	Sonora								
Wight, Geo.	Sonora								

VENTURA COUNTY.

Name of Owner.	Post Office and Name of Vineyard.	Total Acres in Grapes.	Acres in Bearing.	Acres in Wine Grapes.	Acres in Table Grapes.	Acres in Raisin Grapes.	Wine Maker.	Product in 1889.	Varieties.
Del Valle, Ysabel	Camulos	35	35	35			Yes.	10,000 gals.	Mission.
Atmore, M.	Fillmore	5	5	5			No.		Muscat.
Burson, E.	Fillmore	3	3		3		No.		Rose Peru, Black Hamburg.
Conaway, J. A.	Fillmore	2	2		2		No.		Rose Peru, Muscat.
Cook, H.	Fillmore	10	10			10	No.		Muscat.
Decker, C. A.	Fillmore	5	5	5			No.		Muscat.
Harris, Charles	Fillmore	10	10			10	No.		Muscat.
Keane, J.	Fillmore	30	30			30	No.		Muscat.
Kenney, Benj.	Fillmore	5	5			5	No.		Muscat.
Kenney, Cyrus	Fillmore	5	5			5	No.		Muscat.
Klages, H. F.	Fillmore	3	3		3		No.		Rose Peru, Muscat.
Riley, W.	Fillmore	2	2		2		No.		Zinfandel, Black Burgundy, Mataro, Burger, and many others.
Bracken, James	Nordhoff	16	16	16			Yes.		Black Prince, Muscat.
Clark, Thomas	Nordhoff	6	6	5		1	Yes.		Muscat.
Denison, H. J.	Nordhoff	6	6			6	No.		Muscat.
Pinkerton, John	Nordhoff	12	12			12	No.		Zinfandel, Black Prince.
Robinson, Capt.	Nordhoff	4	4			4	No.		Black Prince.
Thompson, Thomas	Nordhoff	12	12	12			Yes.		Muscat.
Walnut, Nick	Nordhoff	16	16	16			Yes.		Black Morocco, Muscat, Tokay.
Cook, D. C.	Piru	100				100	No.		Muscat.
Waring, B. F.	Piru	3	3		3		No.		
Carr, John B.	Santa Paula	4				4	No.		Muscat.
Eaton, C.	Santa Paula	10	10		10		No.		Muscat.
Kent, W. F.	Santa Paula	10	10			10	No.		Muscat.
Einstein & Bernheim	Ventura	6	6	6					Mission.
Totals for county		320	216	100	23	197			

YOLO COUNTY.

Name of Owner.	Post Office and Name of Vineyard.	Total Acres in Grapes.	Acres in Bearing.	Acres in Wine Grapes.	Acres in Table Grapes.	Acres in Raisin Grapes.	Wine Maker.	Product in 1889.	Varieties.
Hushey, D. N.	Black's Station	60	60			60	No.		
Chiles, J. F. & W. D.	Davisville	100	100	40	30	30	No.		
Gould, May I.	Davisville	100	100		90		No.		Muscatel, chiefly.
LaRue, H. M.	Davisville	30	30	30			No.		
Swingle, G. H.	Davisville	30	30		30		No.		
Epstein, Henry (Arpad Harasthy & Co.)	Orleans Vineyard, Madison	340	340	340			Yes.		Sundry.
Devilbiss, J. A.	Winters	30	30		30		No.		Sundry.
Griffin, J. B.	Winters	160	100		160		No.		Sundry.
Hill, F. S.	Winters	35	35	35			No.		Sundry.
Hill, H. A.	Winters	30	30		30		No.		Sundry.
Hill, J. H.	Winters	40	40	20	20		No.		Sundry.
Reid, W. B.	Winters	30	30		30		No.		Sundry.
Robinson, W. H. & Bros.	Winters	100	100		100		No.		Sundry.
Slade, V.	Winters	40	40		40		No.		Sundry.
Armstrong & Alge	Woodland	75	75	45	30		No.		Sundry.
Bitzer, U.	Woodland	15	15	10	5		No.		Sundry.
Blowers, R. B.	Woodland	20	20		20		No.		Emperor and Sultana, chiefly.
Bowen Bros.	Woodland	100	100		20	80	No.		Sundry.
Briggs, Mrs. E.	Woodland	160	160	160		160	No.		Muscatel.
Bullard, F.	Woodland	200	200	160	40		No.		Sundry.
Clanton, E. J.	Woodland	30	30			30	No.		Muscatel.
Clark, E.	Woodland	10	10		10		No.		Sundry.
Deaner, H. S.	Woodland	100	100	100			No.		Sundry.
Deinfonne, A.	Woodland	15	15	15			No.		Sundry.
Dillon, J. Y.	Woodland	10	10	10			No.		Sundry.
Fisher, Henry	Woodland	40	40	26		40	No.		Sundry.
Fiske, George D.	Woodland	25	25	25			No.		
Fitz, R.	Woodland	80	80	80			No.		Sundry.
Fuchs. J.	Woodland	30	30	20	10		No.		Sundry.
Gillup, Ed.	Woodland	30	30	10	10	20	No.		
Hall, A. M.	Woodland	10	10		10		No.		
Harris, W. J., estate of	Woodland	10	10	10			No.		Sundry.
Harlan, J. H.	Woodland	160	160	100		60	No.		Sundry.

YOLO COUNTY—Continued.

Name of Owner.	Post Office and Name of Vineyard.	Total Acres in Grapes.	Acres in Bearing.	Acres in Wine Grapes.	Acres in Table Grapes.	Acres in Raisin Grapes.	Wine Maker.	Product in 1889.	Varieties.
Henel, Jacob, estate of.	Woodland	30	30		10	20	No.		Sundry.
Holmes, L. B.	Woodland	20	20		10	10	No.		Sundry.
Hugh, Mrs. S. E.	Woodland	15	15		15		No.		Sundry.
Jackson, B.	Woodland (San Fran.)	100	100		50	50	No.		
Jackson, Mrs. C. C.	Woodland	20	20		10	10	No.		Sundry.
Kincheloe Bros.	Woodland	30	30	30			No.		
McGuff, Wm.	Woodland	40	40	25		15	No.		Sundry.
McWilliams, J. S.	Woodland	10	10		10		No.		Sundry.
Merritt, H. P.	Woodland	40	40		40		No.		Sundry.
Noe, J. R.	Woodland	15	15		15		No.		Muscatel, chiefly.
Reed, Geo. B.	Woodland	160	160			160	No.		
Redden, John A.	Woodland	40	40		20	20	No.		
Rich, S. D.	Woodland	25	25		15	10	No.		Sundry.
Ross, Thos.	Woodland	65	65		25	40	No.		
Ryder, T. H.	Woodland	60	60		40	20	No.		Zinfandel.
Schuesley, John	Woodland	160	160	160			No.		Sundry.
Strong, A., estate of	Woodland	60	60	30	30		No.		
Thomas, S. D., estate of	Woodland	40	40		20	20	No.		Muscatel, Sultana.
Vansie, Dick	Woodland	20	20		10		No.		Sundry.
Willoughby, J. N.	Woodland	10	10		15		No.		Sundry.
Witham, A. M.	Woodland	15	15				No.		Muscatel, chiefly.
Woodland, Mrs. A. B.	Woodland	160	160			160	No.		Sundry.
Wyckoff, N., estate of	Woodland	320	320	300	10	10	Yes.		
Yolo Winery	Woodland						Yes.		
Totals for county		3,700	3,700	1,575	1,000	1,125			

YUBA COUNTY.

Name of Owner.	Post Office and Name of Vineyard.	Total Acres in Grapes.	Acres in Bearing.	Acres in Wine Grapes.	Acres in Table Grapes.	Acres in Raisin Grapes.	Wine Maker.	Product in 1889.	Varieties.
Frei, Henry	Brown's Valley	10	10	10			No.	30 tons.	
Hendricks, M. V.	Brown's Valley								
Kupser, Bayott.	Brown's Valley								
McDowell, R.	Brown's Valley								
Pelletier, J.	Brown's Valley								
Ricard, F.	Brown's Valley								
Ramm, John	Camptonville	60	60	60			Yes.	180 tons.	
McDowell, C.	Cigar Flat	40	40	40			No.	120 tons.	
Brown, J.		3	3		3		No.	9 tons.	
Chandon, A.	Marysville								
Colema Colony	Marysville	50			50				
Friedel, Chris.	Marysville								
Gray, A. C.	Marysville	40	40	20	20		No.	120 tons.	
Greeley, F. H.	Marysville	20	20	20			No.	60 tons.	
Harter, J.	Marysville	20	20	20			No.	60 tons.	
Houg, Jo	Marysville	20	20	20			No.	60 tons.	
Mathews, E.	Marysville	20	20	20			No.	60 tons.	
McMillen, R. O.	Marysville	40	40	40			No.	120 tons.	
Miller Bros.	Marysville								
Rideout, N. D.	Marysville	30	30		30		Yes.	90 tons.	
Schimpf, J.	Marysville	20	20	10	10		No.	60 tons.	
Shendon,	Marysville	60	60	60			Yes.	180 tons.	
Sieber, G.	Marysville	10	10	10			No.	30 tons.	
Simpson,	Marysville	20	20	20			No.	60 tons.	
Smith, Herman	Marysville	10	10	10			No.	30 tons.	
Thompson, M.	Marysville								
Tomb, J., estate of.	Marysville	20	20	20			No.	60 tons.	
Waldron,	Marysville	40	40	40			No.	120 tons.	
Lane, Riley	Newbert's	100	100	100			No.	300 tons.	
O'Brien, J.	Smartsville	30	30	30			No.	90 tons.	
Durst, Dr. M. H.	Wheatland	20	20	20			No.	60 tons.	
Grass, Frank	Wheatland	10	10		10		No.	30 tons.	
New England Vineyard									
Totals for county		693	643	570	123				

A PARTIAL DIRECTORY

OF THE

GRAPE GROWERS AND WINE MAKERS

EAST OF THE ROCKY MOUNTAINS.

COMPILED BY

WINFIELD SCOTT,

Secretary of the Board of State Viticultural Commissioners.

DIRECTORY OF EASTERN GRAPE GROWERS AND WINE MAKERS.

ALABAMA.

NAME.	Post Office.	Acres in Vines.	Wine Maker.
Merritt, D. W.	Abbeville, Henry County		
Silver, W. H.	Bay Minette, Baldwin County		
Kean, Dan D.	Birmingham		
Schell, Joseph	Brierfield, Bibb County		
Saunders, Hon. James E.	Courtland, Lawrence County	10	Yes.
Blato, Charles	Cullman		
Cullman Wine Company	Cullman		Yes.
Klien, John G.	Cullman		
Underwood, J. C.	Huntsville		
Steele, Prof. J. S.	Mobile		
Steele, J. P.	Mobile		
Price, T. W.	Rehoboth, Wilcox County		
Roper, Nelson	Trinity, Morgan County	5	Yes.
Sewell, W. Q., & Sons	Trinity, Morgan County	10	Yes.
Franklin, C. H.	Union Springs	2½	Yes.
Moore, A. A.	Union Springs	½	No.
Moultrie, J. L.	Union Springs	1	Yes.
Paulk, D. J.	Union Springs	2	Yes.
Rosenstihl, ——	Union Springs	½	No.

ARKANSAS.

NAME.	Post Office.	Acres in Vines.	Wine Maker.
Norwood, C. M.	Bluff City, Nevada County		
Mattock, Amos	Champagnolle	1	Yes.
Askew, Mrs. L.	El Dorado	4	Yes.
Askew, Mrs. J. H.	El Dorado		Yes.
McMurrain, M. B.	El Dorado	2	Yes.
Shuler, J. F.	El Dorado		
Arehios, L.	Fayetteville	2	Yes.
Gildersleeve, F. I.	Fayetteville	2	No.
Inobnit, Christ.	Fayetteville	⅓	No.
Kesslar, Phil.	Fayetteville	5	Yes.
Roeher, I. F.	Fayetteville	3	No.
Trahin, J. E.	Fayetteville	6	Yes.
Forman, D. D.	Hackett City		
Thweatt, N. B.	Hickory Plains		Yes.
McHenry, C. P.	Hillsboro	5	Yes.
Dengler, F.	Hot Springs	21	
Laurence, G. W.	Hot Springs		
Luetsher, John U.	Hot Springs		
Veasey, G. I. B.	Lacey		Yes.
Krieg, G.	Lamar	1	Yes.
Krieg, M.	Lamar	2	Yes.
Buehring, E.	Lutherville	1½	Yes.
Drittler Bros.	Lutherville	2	Yes.
Doerr, C.	Lutherville	1¾	Yes.
Hahn, F. A.	Lutherville	1¼	Yes.
Hentschell, G.	Lutherville	½	No.
Pommerenke, J.	Lutherville	½	Yes.
Schatz, J. E.	Lutherville	1	Yes.
Schneider, F.	Lutherville	¼	Yes.
Westphal, L.	Lutherville	2	Yes.
Woltman, H.	Lutherville	1	Yes.

NAME.	Post Office.	Acres in Vines.	Wine Maker.
Matthews, S. J.	Lutherville	9	Yes.
Curry, —	Pine Bluff		Yes.
Gill, J. B.	Springdale		
Martin, Dr. J. W.	Warren		
Jester, S. D.	Wiggs		

COLORADO.

NAME.	Post Office.	Acres in Vines.	Wine Maker.
Weston, Eugene	Cañon City		
Newcomb, J. H.	Denver		
Mitchell, E. F.	Trinidad	1½	No.
Murry Bros.	Trinidad	1	No.

DAKOTA.

NAME.	Post Office.	Acres in Vines.	Wine Maker.
Andrews, H. D. E.	Greenwood		
Flick, J. D.	Rockport		
Zienert, A.	Bon Homme		

DISTRICT OF COLUMBIA.

NAME.	Post Office.	Acres in Vines.	Wine Maker.
Xander, C.	Washington		

FLORIDA.

NAME.	Post Office.	Acres in Vines.	Wine Maker.
Moulton, H. D.	Arredonda (Taunton, Mass.)	15	No.
Tuttle, R. S.	Beaucler's Bluff		
Florida Wine Company	Clay Springs		
Bates, M.	Hermitage	5	No.
Howe, B. J.	Hermitage	1	No.
Martin, Mrs. M.	Hermitage	33	Yes.
Ward, H. D.	Hermitage	3	No.
Davis, George W.	Jacksonville		
Stewart, Henry I.	Jasper		
Lock, James W.	Key West		
White, Frank	Live Oak		
Bidwell, A. J.	Maitland		
Hostetter & Lehman } South Lake Wine Company }	Marion	25	Yes.
Eischelberger, A. L.	Ocala		
Boykin, J. C.	Orange Hill		
Ball, W. D.	Orange Park		
Barbier, Ed.	Tallahassee	8	Yes.
Craig, John	Tallahassee	3	Yes.
Dubois, E.	Tallahassee	49	Yes.
Hare, Capt.	Tallahassee	1	Yes.
Lankey, Charles	Tallahassee	7	Yes.
Pichard, H.	Tallahassee	1	Yes.

Florida—Continued.

NAME.	Post Office.	Acres in Vines.	Wine Maker.
Rippert, J.	Tallahassee	3	Yes.
Ronald, ——	Tallahassee	20	Yes.
Sague, ——	Tallahassee	5	Yes.
Lehmon, Jacques	Whitesville		

GEORGIA.

NAME.	Post Office.	Acres in Vines.	Wine Maker.
Burke, F. E.	Americus		
Berckmans, P. J.	Augusta	10	No.
Bunch, J. W.	Augusta	4	No.
Gibson, B. G.	Augusta	15	No.
Nelson, Wm. K.	Augusta	8	No.
Bowers, Byron	Bainbridge	10	Yes.
Stafford, W. C.	Barnsville	1	No.
Bivins, J. H.	Barnard		
Bowie, Wm. C.	Buck Creek		
Belk, Hollis	Buena Vista	4	
Prather, J. O.	Cenwell	4	
Hay, James A.	Cuthbert	14	Yes.
Hay, W. C.	Cuthbert		
Hood, A.	Cuthbert	15	Yes.
Martin, J. C.	Cuthbert	7	Yes.
Saxon, R. B.	Cuthbert	5	Yes.
Toombs, J. P.	Cuthbert	12	Yes.
Biney, Thomas	Dalton	$\frac{1}{2}$	
Haig, Wm.	Dalton	3	Yes.
Henderson, Frank	Dalton	2	
Jones, B. F.	Dalton	4	Yes.
Krisher, Peter	Dalton	2	Yes.
Richardson, W. C.	Dalton	2	Yes.
Saxon, Bunk	Dalton	2	
Heyward, ——	Darien	20	Yes.
Brian, Mrs. J. W.	Dillon		
Keller, Bartow	Eden		Yes.
Rainy, D. W.	Ellaville		
Anderson, W. W.	Forsyth		
Anderson, W. J.	Fort Valley		
Bentley, O. S.	Gainsville		
Bishop, J. M.	Griffin	3	
Brooks, A.	Griffin	2	
Daniel, R. T.	Griffin	5	
Flint, T. W.	Griffin	5	
Goddard, L. W.	Griffin	5	
Hallady, Mrs.	Griffin	2	
Hasselkus, H.	Griffin	10	Yes.
Hasselkus, H. W.	Griffin	20	Yes.
Keller, John	Griffin		
Lauren, J. M.	Griffin	6	
Mallory, R. D.	Griffin	4	
Manley, M.	Griffin	4	
Mathews, T. G.	Griffin	4	
Middle Georgia Wine Company	Griffin		
Mitchell, T. J.	Griffin	10	
Patrick, A.	Griffin	10	
Peden, P. D.	Griffin	4	
Ray, R.	Griffin	2	
Roberts, U. C.	Griffin	2	
Schuerman & Hasselkus	Griffin	15	
Stewart & Hasselkus	Griffin	4	
Stewart, G. C.	Griffin	10	
Stewart, G.	Griffin	8	
Waddell, W.	Griffin	4	
Warder, Wm.	Griffin	10	Yes.
White, G. B.	Griffin	4	
Woodruff, W. W.	Griffin		
Hape & Bucher	Hapeville		
Goss, Wm. J.	Harmony Grove		

GEORGIA—Continued.

NAME.	Post Office.	Acres in Vines.	Wine Maker.
Seidell, C. W.	Hartwell		
Smith, J. E.	Hatcher Station		
Mitchell, J. B.	Hawkinsville	6	Yes.
Ryan, L. C.	Hawkinsville	6	Yes.
Schneider, J. H.	Hawkinsville	12	Yes.
Parker, Wm. H.	Johnston Station	1	Yes.
Anthony, E. R.	Macon	6	Yes.
Milne, David	Macon		
Fletcher, A. A.	Marietta		
	Around Marshallville	20	
Brooks, A.	Pomona	5	
Crocker, S. S.	Pomona	6	
Gray, S. F.	Pomona	8	
Jones, J.	Pomona	2	
Manley, R.	Pomona	4	
Patterson, H.	Pomona	3	
Smith, P.	Pomona	10	
Spangler, R. T.	Pomona	8	
Sutherland, A. & J.	Pomona	15	
Wayman, S. W.	Pomona	15	
Bourquin, G.	Savannah		No.
Howe, Wm.	Savannah		
Taylor, Jno. C., estate of.	Savannah	5	Yes.
Bedier, H.	Sunnyside	7	Yes.
Keel, Capt. J. McIntosh	Sunnyside	5	
Miller, J. A. O.	Sunnyside	3	
Vandyke, A. G.	Sunnyside	30	
Sanford, H. H.	Thomasville	2	No.
Clark, I. G.	Tusculum		
Beatty, Jas.	Vineyard	15	No.
Freeman, J.	Vineyard	3	
Freeman, W. T.	Vineyard	5	
Galhouse, H.	Vineyard	18	
Genell, G.	Vineyard	2	
Goetz, A.	Vineyard	12	No.
Hughes, V.	Vineyard	30	No.
Hunt, J. J.	Vineyard	10	No.
Husted, J. D.	Vineyard	20	No.
Oetter, Rudolph	Vineyard	25	
Stapleton, J.	Vineyard	5	
Taylor, A.	Vineyard	4	
Wanten, Macon	Warthen		

ILLINOIS.

NAME.	Post Office.	Acres in Vines.	Wine Maker.
Aul, George	Albany	½	No.
Hanks, S. B.	Albany	5	No.
Olds, G. W.	Albany	¼	No.
Paddock, C. B.	Albany		
Whitcomb, —	Albany	1	No.
Coles, Frank	Albion	2	No.
Dawes, James	Albion	2	No.
Dawes, Josiah	Albion	1	No.
Painter, Wash.	Albion	1	Yes.
West, Charles	Albion	4	Yes.
McWhorter, Tyler	Aledo		
Brown, J. S.	Alton	2	No.
Hayden, F.	Alton	10	No.
McPike, H. G.	Alton	1	No.
Riehl, E. A.	Alton	4	No.
Roberts, Mrs. Dr. H. N.	Alton	8	No.
Starr, James E.	Alton		
Wesenberg, H.	Alton	12	Yes.
Wesenberg, Charles	America	30	Yes.
Burnam, John	Batavia		
Lake, L. L., M.D.	Belvidere		

ILLINOIS—Continued.

NAME.	Post Office.	Acres in Vines.	Wine Maker.
Bloomington Nursery Company.	Bloomington	10	No.
Eisenberger, George	Bloomington	1	Yes.
Schmidt, Wm.	Bloomington	4	Yes.
Schroeder, Dr. Herman	Bloomington (50,000 vines)		Yes.
Bueckman, Wm.	Bremen	2	No.
Siekemyer, E. F.	Bremen		
Welge, C.	Bremen	2	No.
Dietzel, Henry A.	Carlyle		
Wilson, James	Centralia		
Johnson, B. F.	Champaign		
Aszman, William	Chester	4	No.
Bode, Henry	Chester	2	No.
Bueckman, F.	Chester	3	Yes.
Haeck, Mrs.	Chester	2	No.
Mueller, Edward	Chester	3	Yes.
Steuben Wine Company	Chicago, 246 Madison Street		
Warner, Charles	Clearlake (P. O., Springfield)		Yes.
Moore, C. H.	Clinton	½	Yes.
Linnell, L. T.	Cobden		
Albright, Samuel	Damascus	1½	Yes.
Buckman, B.	Farmingdale		No.
Bentley, C. N.	Freeport	½	No.
Hunt, R. W.	Galesburg		
Ambuehl, Nicholas	Highland	4	Yes.
Balsiger, John	Highland		
Kuhnen, C. F.	Highland	1	Yes.
Labhardt, M.	Highland	4	Yes.
Lorenz, Frank	Highland	1	Yes.
Pagan, August J.	Highland	7	Yes.
Doan, Frank	Jacksonville	1	Yes.
Gordon, John	Jacksonville	1	Yes.
Miller, E. T.	Jacksonville		
Cunningham, Mr.	Kankakee	¼	No.
Grimm, Mr.	Kankakee	1¼	Yes.
Pottenger, Wilson	Kankakee	3	No.
Cotta, J. V.	Lanark		
Ostrander, Dr. C. B.	Lodemia		
Gibbs, John	Lynnville	½	Yes.
Johnson, Robt.	Makanda	4	No.
Eisenmeger, Geo. C.	Mascoutah		
Steritz, Louis	Melville	2	Yes.
Galusha, O. B.	Morris		
Dausch, F.	Mound City	6	Yes.
Porterfield, W. H.	Mount Erie		
Rey, J. M.	Mount Sterling		
Anton, Rudolph	Nauvoo	2	No.
Argast, Henry	Nauvoo	4	No.
Argast, Jno. F.	Nauvoo	5	Yes.
Baumert, Mrs. Geo.	Nauvoo	4	No.
Baxter, E., & Sons	Nauvoo	25	Yes.
Beger, A.	Nauvoo	15	Yes.
Berger, Henry	Nauvoo	4	No.
Berger, Herman	Nauvoo	4	No.
Blake, Thos.	Nauvoo	8	No.
Boedecker, F.	Nauvoo	8	No.
Bohne, Carl	Nauvoo	10	Yes.
Bossler, Joseph	Nauvoo	6	Yes.
Boxhoefer, M.	Nauvoo	4	Yes.
Burmeister, C.	Nauvoo	9	Yes.
Cambre, E., & Son	Nauvoo	12	Yes.
Dachroth, George	Nauvoo	4	No.
Diemer, H., Sr.	Nauvoo	3	Yes.
Diemer, John	Nauvoo	8	No.
Disse, Dr. Henry	Nauvoo	6	No.
Fisher, Antone	Nauvoo	3	Yes.
Gross, John	Nauvoo	6	Yes.
Gross, J. M.	Nauvoo	8	Yes.
Haas, Herman	Nauvoo	6	Yes.
Haas, Joseph	Nauvoo	19	Yes.
Harmon, Peter	Nauvoo	3	Yes.

Illinois—Continued.

NAME.	Post Office.	Acres In Vines.	Wine Maker.
Hauptman, George	Nauvoo	3	No.
Hauptman, Mike	Nauvoo	3	No.
Hauptman, Mrs. John	Nauvoo	3	No.
Hertenstein, Mike and William	Nauvoo	9	Yes.
Hombrechet, Alois	Nauvoo	4	Yes.
Krueger, Emil, & Son	Nauvoo	3	Yes.
Leininger, Jacob	Nauvoo	3	No.
Machenheimer, J.	Nauvoo	4	Yes.
Martzholf, John	Nauvoo	6	No.
Meinberg, Joseph	Nauvoo	4	Yes.
Mulch, C.	Nauvoo	7	Yes.
Mulch & Schoell	Nauvoo	10	No.
Paul, William	Nauvoo	6	No.
Peikard, Frank	Nauvoo	3	No.
Reimbold, Rev. H. J.	Nauvoo	5	No.
Rheinberger, A.	Nauvoo	10	Yes.
Rheinberger, John J.	Nauvoo	6	Yes.
Ritter, Geo.	Nauvoo	12	Yes.
Rohne, H.	Nauvoo	4	Yes.
Rudolph, Anton	Nauvoo	2	No.
Schneider, Mrs. (widow)	Nauvoo	6	No.
Schoell, F.	Nauvoo	3	No.
Schroeter, C.	Nauvoo	3	Yes.
Schupp, Laurence	Nauvoo	7	No.
Stahl, Wm.	Nauvoo	16	No.
Stutz, George	Nauvoo	3	Yes.
Stutz, John	Nauvoo	3	Yes.
Tanner, John, Sr.	Nauvoo	7	Yes.
Tanner, John, Jr.	Nauvoo	5	Yes.
Augustine & Co.	Normal	$\frac{3}{4}$	No.
Eyestone, Mr.	Normal	1	No.
Gaston, J. R.	Normal	$\frac{1}{2}$	No.
Home Nursery Co.	Normal	1	No.
Phœnix Nursery Co.	Normal	2	No.
Watson, W. A.	Normal	$\frac{1}{2}$	No.
Clark, J. B.	Onarga		
Hatheway, E. C.	Ottaway		
Eberspaecher, Christian	Pana	1	Yes.
Heberlein, John	Pana	$\frac{1}{2}$	Yes.
Mantz, William	Pana	1	Yes.
Metzger, Adam	Pana	$\frac{1}{3}$	Yes.
Weber, Geo.	Pana	1	Yes.
Bancroft, L. R.	Pontiac		
Bonvallet, P. A.	St. Anne	25	Yes.
Crosby, J. N.	St. Anne	10	No.
Schneiter, Fred.	St. Elmo	12	Yes.
Maurer, Jacob	Shelbyville	$\frac{1}{2}$	Yes.
Mittendorf, Louis	Shelbyville	1	Yes.
Mochel, Fred.	Shelbyville	$\frac{1}{8}$	No.
Mochel, Michael	Shelbyville	$\frac{1}{8}$	No.
Roessler, Edward	Shelbyville	1	Yes.
Roessler, Philip	Shelbyville	$\frac{1}{4}$	No.
Ruch, Michael	Shelbyville	1	Yes.
Ruff, George	Shelbyville	$\frac{1}{8}$	No.
Stilgebauer, Henry	Shelbyville	1	Yes.
Hood, Thomas	Springfield		
Neef, Emil	Springfield		
Kircher, John	Strasburg	$\frac{3}{8}$	No.
Kull, James	Strasburg	$\frac{3}{8}$	No.
Thomas, George A.	Toulon		
Grisso, George W.	Tower Hill	$\frac{3}{4}$	Yes.
Sigfried, Henry	Tower Hill	$\frac{1}{2}$	Yes.
Aldrich, H. J.	Villa Ridge	12	No.
Ayers, E. T.	Villa Ridge	20	No.
Clancy, M.	Villa Ridge	10	No.
Davidson, C. C.	Villa Ridge	6	No.
Dille, James	Villa Ridge	10	No.
Ehartan, John	Villa Ridge	10	No.
Ehartan, W.	Villa Ridge	10	No.
Endicott, George W.	Villa Ridge	16	Yes.

ILLINOIS—Continued.

NAME.	Post Office.	Acres in Vines.	Wine Maker.
Gould, George	Villa Ridge	10	No.
Hogandobler, Henry	Villa Ridge	10	No.
Hogandobler, Horace	Villa Ridge	10	No.
Johnson, H.	Villa Ridge	12	No.
Kinker, J. H.	Villa Ridge	10	No.
Lutkin, H. G.	Villa Ridge	25	No.
McBride, M. J.	Villa Ridge	10	No.
Miller, J.	Villa Ridge	5	No.
Minnich, George	Villa Ridge	6	No.
Minnich, W. P.	Villa Ridge	6	No.
Prindle, D.	Villa Ridge	10	No.
Redan, L.	Villa Ridge	10	No.
Robinson, A. B.	Villa Ridge	6	No.
Roche Bros.	Villa Ridge	75	No.
Royall, Dr.	Villa Ridge	10	No.
Sheirick, B. H.	Villa Ridge	8	No.
Tobin, James	Villa Ridge	10	No.
Winens, D.	Villa Ridge	10	No.
Worthen, A. H. & G. B.	Warsaw		Yes.
Frost, Ralph	Winchester	1	No.
Gibbs, Wm.	Winchester	1	Yes.
Gordon, Wm.	Winchester	½	Yes.

INDIANA.

NAME.	Post Office.	Acres in Vines.	Wine Maker.
Chriestman, F.	Bluffton		
Eaton, T. A. R.	Bluffton		
Horton, Theo.	Bluffton		
Cox, R. M. J.	Brownston	1⁄16	No.
Falk, Frank	Brownston	1	Yes.
Rodman, Mrs. Kate	Brownston	⅜	Yes.
Scott, Mrs. Mary	Brownston	¼	Yes.
Vaslage, Geo.	Brownston	¼	Yes.
Woodmansee, W. G.	Brownston	1⁄16	No.
Ragan, W. H.	Clayton		
Martin, A. F., & Sons	Delphi		
Armantrout, J. N.	Frankfort		
Kite, David	Freetown	1	Yes.
Furnas, Jno. W.	Indianapolis		
Schueller, Julius A.	Indianapolis (81 E. Court Street)		
Johnson, Sylvester	Irvington		
Slater, Nelson	Lagrange		⅛
Alexander, Sterling	Leavenworth	8	No.
Hilgart, ——	Leavenworth	6	Yes.
Sacksteder, Chas.	Leavenworth	2	Yes.
Sacksteder, J.	Leavenworth	30	Yes.
Morris, Geo.	Lewisville		
Stewart, Wm. M.	Marengo	3	Yes.
Vanmeter, John	Marengo	7	Yes.
Hamman, Valentine	Millwood		
Anderson, S. J.	Morgantown		
Green, John O.	New Albany		
Kanzie, Victor	New Albany		
Mitchell, G. D.	Petersburg		
McNamara, J. G.	Pierceton		
Jones, Elisha	Princeton		
James, Horace E.	Rensselaer		
Fox, H. C.	Richmond		
Pierce, Ashie	Ridgeville	½	
Rone, Abel	Ridgeville	¼	
Beil, Daniel	Rolling Prairie		
Ward, Thomas J.	Saint Mary's		
Shirley, Christian	Salem, Washington County		
Dannatell, Halleck	Seymour	1	Yes.

INDIANA—Continued.

NAME.	Post Office.	Acres in Vines.	Wine Maker.
Spencer, Calvin	Spencer		
Ostabrook, A. F.	Sullivan		
Beacham, E.	Terre Haute	4	No.
Bremer, J.	Terre Haute	2	No.
Byrner, A.	Terre Haute	4	No.
Curtis, C.	Terre Haute	3	No.
Dreher, C.	Terre Haute	3	Yes.
Haas, E.	Terre Haute	5	Yes.
Monninger, Philip H.	Terre Haute	25	Yes.
Shazer, Joe	Terre Haute	4	No.
McCarthy, J. F.	Valparaiso		
Brindly, Gasper	Vevay	1½	Yes.
Morerod, Aime	Vevay	½	Yes.
Norrissez, Charles	Vevay	½	Yes.
Stucy, Henry	Vevay	½	Yes.
Trafelet, Daniel	Vevay	1½	Yes.
Burnet, Stephen	Vincennes		
McDermott, Patrick	West Fork	5	Yes.
Arter, M.	Winchester	1	
Claton, James	Winchester	½	
Fields, Obedia	Winchester	½	
Foofman, Daniel	Winchester	2	Yes.
Guthel, Charles	Winchester	½	Yes.
Luely, John	Winchester	¼	
Shetterly, Mrs.	Winchester	¼	
Snedker, —	Winchester	¼	
Summers, John D.	Winchester		
Wyseng, Frank	Winchester	½	

IOWA.

NAME.	Post Office.	Acres in Vines.	Wine Maker.
Gregory, J.	Ames		Yes.
Lane, Miss Carrie C.	Charles City		
Orwig, R. G.	Des Moines		
Arnold, G. P.	Garden Grove		
Moore, W. W.	Gillett's Grove		
Williams, L. A.	Glenwood	4	
Amana Society	Homestead		
Maas, D.	Homestead		
Eggert, C. N.	Iowa City		
Fertig, William	Keokuk	½	No.
Milton, George O.	Keokuk	½	No.
Jacox, G. B.	White Elk Vineyard, Keokuk	75	Yes.
Jeager, Edmund	Keokuk	40	Yes.
Meister, —	Keokuk	6	Yes.
Oertell, I.	Keokuk	¼	Yes.
Rabor, —	Keokuk	¼	No.
Shappach, —	Keokuk	¼	Yes.
Snyder, John	Keokuk	¼	No.
Wilson, L. A.	Keokuk	10	No.
Conrad, C.	Marengo		
Dansler, J.	Marengo		
Feller, L.	Marengo		
Fitzer, M.	Marengo		
Gearing, J.	Marengo		
Kruse, Peter	Marengo	2	No.
Langlas, G.	Marengo		
Lortz, G.	Marengo		
Rathgen, H.	Marengo		
Smith, Charles	Marengo		
Specht, Charles J.	Marengo		
Stevens, J.	Marengo		
Swaney, J.	Marengo		
Tanner, J. U.	Marengo		

Iowa—Continued.

NAME.	Post Office.	Acres in Vines.	Wine Maker.
Flint, Edwin	Mason City		
Littler, Nathan	Washington	¼	
Harrington, T.	Williamsburg		
Holden, M. W.	Williamsburg		

KANSAS.

NAME.	Post Office.	Acres in Vines.	Wine Maker.
Euler, A.	Centralia	¼	No.
Hodgins, J.	Centralia		
Holtzlander, E.	Centralia	½	No.
Knott, D.	Centralia	½	No.
Lynn, A. W.	Centralia	¼	No.
Meyer, 1.	Centralia	¼	No.
Stickney, I. W.	Centralia	2	No.
Van Patten, D.	Centralia	¼	No.
Ashby, Geo. W.	Chanute		
Williams, O. N.	Columbus		
Brown, J. P.	Council Grove		
Doniphan Vineyard	Doniphan		
Stark, Chas.	Elk City		
Richey, John	Galva		
Mosteller, G. W.	Girard		
Sanderson, B. D.	Girard		
Hund, Wendel	Hund Station		
Lawrenson, R. E.	Junction City		
Haag, A.	Leavenworth	6	Yes.
Harloux, John and Jake	Leavenworth	4	No.
Langworthy, Dr. B.	Leavenworth (Kansas City, Mo.)	4	No.
Rodenburg, John	Leavenworth	4	Yes.
Stayman & Black	Leavenworth	4	Yes.
Stayman, Dr. J.	Leavenworth		
Swagler, Jacob	Leavenworth	3	Yes.
Insley, J. N.	Oskaloosa		
Poff, J. A.	Russell		
Baldwin, S.	Seneca	½	No.
Fuller, I.	Seneca	¼	No.
Gaston, L. H.	Seneca	¼	No.
Hobbs, R. L.	Seneca	½	No.
McBride, A.	Seneca	½	No.
Peckham, J. H.	Seneca	½	No.
Tutt, L. M.	South Cedar		

KENTUCKY.

NAME.	Post Office.	Acres in Vines.	Wine Maker.
Townsend, P. E.	Adairville		Yes.
Culbertson, W. W.	Ashland		
Dawson, Jerry	Bacon Creek		
Heverline, John	Bedford	½	Yes.
Parker, W. J.	Bedford	1	Yes.
Welty, John	Bedford	½	No.
Highbaugh, Mrs. M.	Bonnieville		
Jameson, W. K.	Bonnieville		No.
Stamp, J. M.	Bonnieville		
Whitman, Wm. A.	Bonnieville		
Wright, Mrs. Fannie	Bonnieville		
Brashear, W. C.	Bowling Green	2	Yes.
Briggs & Edwards	Bowling Green	10	Yes.
Cook, Wm.	Bowling Green	1	Yes.
Edwards, C. R.	Bowling Green	1	Yes.

KENTUCKY—Continued.

NAME.	Post Office.	Acres in Vines.	Wine Maker.
Ewing, James F.	Bowling Green	1	Yes.
Sears, Thomas.	Bowling Green	1	Yes.
Schneider, Joseph.	Bowling Green	4	Yes.
Younglove, Joseph I.	Bowling Green	8	Yes.
Hale, Charles P.	Calhoun		
Marriott, J. B.	Cecelia		
Zincus, Julius	Cloverport	10	Yes.
Craddock, Col. Jerry	Cumnor		
Laferty, Henry	Cumnor		
Clark, J. A.	Earlington	4	No.
Coenen, Mrs. A. M.	Earlington	5	No.
Earlington Wine Co.	Earlington	26	Yes.
O'Brien, L. H.	Earlington	3	No.
Gardiner, Judge W. H.	Elizabethtown		
Miller, Mrs. Sallie	Elizabethtown		
Decker, J.	Fern Creek		
Taylor, E. H., & Sons	Frankfort		
Wethercutt, Stephen	Grayson	1½	No.
Williams, J. W.	Greensburg		
Owens, Jordan	Hardyville		
Elliott, John R.	Harrodsburg	5	Yes.
Geibel, K., Sr.	Henderson	¾	Yes.
Hubbard, Jake	Hodgensville		
Twyman, J. W.	Hodgensville		
Hodgen, Mrs. Matt.	Horse Cave		
Katz, ——	Horse Cave		
Mustain, John	Horse Cave		
Mustain, Tom	Horse Cave		
Nolin, Sam	Horse Cave		
McKee, J. A., & Co.	Kingsville		
Chapman, J. B.	Lebanon		Yes.
Knott & Chapman	Lebanon		Yes.
Gardiner, Geo. H.	Litchfield		
Kennedy, Thomas S.	Louisville		
Bowls, James	Mackville	4	Yes.
Carrier, J. W.	Mackville	5	Yes.
Eason, William	Mackville	3	Yes.
Toomey, Avon	Mackville	2	Yes.
Bourland, J.	Madisonville		Yes.
Coffin, Mark	Melton		Yes.
Craddock, W. B.	Munfordville		
Cumpton, James	Munfordville		
Eps, Charlie	Munfordville		
Fitzallen, Charlie	Munfordville		
Gibson, Wm.	Munfordville		
Hubbard, John	Munfordville		
Hubbard, Mrs. Kate.	Munfordville		
Logson, Van Buren	Munfordville		
Martin, Capt. H. C.	Munfordville		
Payton, S. M.	Munfordville		
Walton, C. J.	Munfordville		
Wood, Dave	Munfordville		
Bent, J. M.	Mount Sterling		
Richards, John	Nolin		
Menard, Stephen	Paducah		Yes.
Coakley, B. F.	Powder Mills		
Lane, Harvey	Rio		
Carden, Mrs. Genie	Rowlett's Station		
Coats, W. S.	Rowlett's Station		
Curle, Stephen	Rowlett's Station		
Gardener, John	Rowlett's Station		
Maxey, P. L.	Rowlett's Station		
Harbison, John	Russellville		
Bent, J. M.	Saulsberry	1	Yes.
Logsdon, William	Thompsonville	5	Yes.
Upton, Hardin	Uptonville		
Angel, E. M.	Woodsonville		
Garvin, James	Woodsonville		
Woodson, A. L.	Woodsonville		

LOUISIANA.

Name.	Post Office.	Acres in Vines.	Wine Maker.
Burn, Milton	Covington	½	No.
Cahier, Jules	Covington	⅓	Yes.
Dutruch, Alphonse	Covington	3	Yes.
Ellerman, H.	Covington	1	Yes.
Gotti, Louis	Covington	½	Yes.
Labat, J. M.	Covington	½	No.
Lossette, Francois	Covington	1½	Yes.
Mathies, Fritz	Covington	½	No.
Mathiew, Louis E.	Covington	2½	Yes.
Munch, John T.	Covington	2	Yes.
Perreand, A., Sr.	Covington	½	Yes.
Schultz, Christian	Covington	½	No.
Fuhrmann, Mrs. J.	Madisonville	¾	Yes.
Aveilhé, Rev. Eugene	Mandeville	½	Yes.
Mignot, Rev. Canon	Mandeville	¾	Yes.
Erath, Albert	New Orleans		
Gehlbach, Charles	New Orleans		
Wila, Casper	New Orleans		
Cousin, Maxine	Slidell	½	No.
Jennings, J. M.	Winnfield		

MARYLAND.

Name.	Post Office.	Acres in Vines.	Wine Maker.
Giddins, L.	Annapolis		
Wallace, Col. James	Cambridge		Yes.
Stevens, Charles	Denton		
Maxwell, John J.	East Newmarket		
Waters, L. L.	Princess Anne		Yes.
Woolford, Royer	Princess Anne	20	Yes.
Spence, Irving	Snow Hill		

MASSACHUSETTS.

Name.	Post Office.	Acres in Vines.	Wine Maker.
State Agricultural College	Amherst	3	No.
Crocker, Alfred	Barnstable		
O'Brien, John	Bradford		
Woodman, C.	Cambridge		
Bull, Ephraim W.	Concord	1	No.
Coughlin, John	Concord	1	No.
Coughlin, Nicholas	Concord	1	No.
Garty, James	Concord	½	No.
Hunt, Wm. H.	Concord	5	No.
Hurd, Wm. F.	Concord	5	No.
Hutchins, Charles	Concord	2	No.
Keyes, John S.	Concord	1	No.
Litchfield, Paul	Concord	2	No.
Merwin, H. C.	Concord	2	No.
Messer, George H.	Concord	¼	No.
Moore, John H.	Concord	5	No.
Pratt, F. G.	Concord	1	No.
Wheeler, Alvah E.	Concord	1	No.
Wheeler, Anson	Concord	2	No.
Wheeler, Frank	Concord	4	No.
Wheeler, George F.	Concord	3	No.
Wood, James B.	Concord	8	No.
Wright, Geo. H.	Concord	4	No.
Churbuck, Wm. E.	East Wareham	3	Yes.
Gibbs, Benj. F.	East Wareham	4	Yes.

MASSACHUSETTS—Continued.

NAME.	Post Office.	Acres in Vines.	Wine Maker.
Pease, Richard L.	Edgartown		
Nichols, Dr. J. R.	Haverhill		
France, James	Holyoke		
Pineo, Peter	Hyannis		
Hoxie, D. E.	Leeds	3	No.
Clement, Asa	Lowell		
Paige, Joseph W.	Medfield	½	
Strong, Wm. C.	Newton Highlands		
Talbot, J. W.	Norwood		
Rogers, E. S.	Salem		
Smith, E. J.	Smith's Ferry	5	Yes.
Moulton, H. D.	Taunton		
Everett, O. E.	Williamsburg	2	No.
Kinney, F. J.	Worcester		

MICHIGAN.

NAME.	Post Office.	Acres in Vines.	Wine Maker.
Bradfield, Edward	Ada		Yes.
Baldwin, J. D.	Ann Arbor		
Woodworth, S. E.	Battle Creek		
Withey, W. T.	Benton Harbor		
Jaqueth, S. P.	Benzonia		
Munson & Knapp	Grand Rapids		No.
Pearsall, S. M.	Grand Rapids		
Perkins, Mr.	Grand Rapids		No.
Weatherby, W. W.	Grand Rapids		
Roberts, R. Z.	Harrisville		
Higbee, John	Ionia	3	No.
Hosford, George	Ionia	15	Yes.
Kellogg, R. M.	Ionia	4	No.
Le Valley, L. Holden	Ionia	7	No.
Rust, C. E.	Ionia		
Smith, Nelson	Ionia	8	No.
Shoemaker, Michael	Jackson		Yes.
Stearns, I. N.	Kalamazoo		No.
Newcombe, H. M.	Ludington		
Blome, Wm. H.	Monroe	10	No.
Boyer, G.	Monroe	6	No.
Dalber, Mrs. A.	Monroe	2	No.
Dental, —	Monroe	6	No.
Dewey, J. B.	Monroe	2	No.
Dewey, J. W.	Monroe	3	No.
Diedrich & Breisacher	Monroe (Detroit)		No.
Dubois, Louis	Monroe	15	No.
Entemann, E.	Monroe	6	Yes.
Gittler, John	Monroe	7	No.
Gittler, Mike	Monroe	5	No.
Greening, J. C.	Monroe	8	No.
Kawzier, Chas.	Monroe	6	No.
Kirchengoessner, Chas.	Monroe	5	No.
Kirchmaier, Theo.	Monroe	3	No.
Nelson, John	Monroe	3	No.
Obermaier, Geo.	Monroe	3	No.
Paulding, M.	Monroe	4	No.
Peppler, Louis	Monroe	4	No.
Rauch, John R.	Monroe	2	No.
Reisig, Gustave	Monroe	8	
Reisig, Fred.	Monroe	7	
Reisig, Leonard	Monroe	4	
Robert, James I.	Monroe	3	No.
Sedlaczek, Joseph	Monroe	4	Yes.
Smith, J. R.	Monroe	5	No.
Sterling, J. M.	Monroe	10	No.
Sturn, B.	Monroe	2	No.

MICHIGAN—Continued.

NAME.	Post Office.	Acres in Vines.	Wine Maker.
Toll, Chas.	Monroe	4	No.
Verhoeven, B.	Monroe	2	No.
Weier, Anton	Monroe	15	Yes.
Cummins, Mr.	Sparta		No.
Swartz, Mr.	Sparta		No.
Ramsdell, J. G.	Traverse City		
Graham, Elwood	Walker		No.

MINNESOTA.

NAME.	Post Office.	Acres in Vines.	Wine Maker.
Luedloff, Charles	Carver	$\frac{1}{2}$	Yes.
Ruediger, ——	Carver	$\frac{3}{4}$	Yes.
Adam, D. A.	Hutchinson	$\frac{1}{4}$	Yes.
Davis, L. R.	Lac-qui-parle		
Clarke, Charles H.	Minneapolis		
Pettit, C. H.	Minneapolis		
Lord, O. M.	Minnesota City		
Ohland, F.	Norwood	$\frac{1}{2}$	Yes.
Carter, T. G.	St. Peter		
Ford, L. M.	St. Paul		
Smith, Truman M.	St. Paul		
Dieterle, Herman	Wabasha		
Peterson, ——	Waroma	$\frac{1}{2}$	No.
Bicker, J.	Winona	2	Yes.
Knopp, M.	Winona	7	No.
Ackerman, J. H.	Young America	$\frac{1}{2}$	Yes.
Ackerman, W.	Young America	$\frac{1}{4}$	Yes.
Buesther, Ernst	Young America	$\frac{1}{2}$	Yes.

MISSISSIPPI.

NAME.	Post Office.	Acres in Vines.	Wine Maker.
Howard, H. H.	Carthage		
Holden, G. W.	Enterprise		
Graham, T. B.	Forest		
Anderson, John E.	Holly Springs	2	No.
Bishop, J.	Holly Springs	4	Yes.
Buckhaman, George M.	Holly Springs	1	No.
Davis, Orlando	Holly Springs	$\frac{1}{2}$	No.
Jones, W. A.	Holly Springs	$\frac{1}{2}$	No.
Shuford, Dr. F. B.	Holly Springs	$\frac{1}{2}$	No.
West, A. M.	Holly Springs	1	No.
Miller, J. M. D.	Iuka		
Shanom, J. J.	Meridian	$\frac{1}{2}$	Yes.
Bolton, R.	Pontotoc		
Cullen, Dr.	Oxford		
Skipwith, T. H.	Oxford		
Turner, William	Oxford		
Gains, Cole & Co.	State Line		Yes.
Seabrook, John P.	State Line		Yes.
Hardy, C.	Victoria	$\frac{1}{2}$	No.
Withers, A. Q.	Victoria	1	Yes.
Arrington, Burrell	Waynesboro		Yes.
Davis, W. S.	Waynesboro		
Gray, H.	Waynesboro		Yes.
Gray, J. L.	Waynesboro		Yes.
Hopper, J. C.	Waynesboro		
McRae, M. L.	Waynesboro		
Russell, A. G.	Waynesboro		

MISSOURI.

Name.	Post Office.	Acres in Vines.	Wine Maker.
Bachmann, Christ.	Amazonia	1/2	Yes.
Egger, Samuel	Amazonia	1/4	Yes.
Harvey, Wash.	Amazonia	1/2	Yes.
King, Wm.	Amazonia	1/2	Yes.
Knechtenhofer, Wm.	Amazonia	1/4	Yes.
Miller, John	Amazonia	1/4	Yes.
Riesenmey, Fred.	Amazonia	1/4	Yes.
Segessemann, Gottleib	Amazonia	1 1/2	Yes.
Strasser, Alfred	Amazonia	3/4	Yes.
Vetter, John	Amazonia	1	Yes.
Wenger, John	Amazonia	1/2	Yes.
Zimmermann, John	Amazonia	13	Yes.
Grimes, R. P.	Astoria		
Mansfield, John W.	Astoria		
Schneider, Nicholas	Avenue City	1/2	Yes.
Gast Wine Co.	Baden (St. Louis)	30	Yes.
Carpenter, Daniel	Barry		
Dailey, W. W.	Beaver		
Allemann, Sam	Berger	20	No.
Dilthy, Peter	Berger	10	No.
Finke, Mrs.	Berger	10	No.
Geiger, L.	Booneville		
Wertheimer, M. J.	Booneville	20	Yes.
Brown, Geo.	Brookfield	1	Yes.
Brown, S. H.	Brookfield	3	Yes.
Gamble, Joseph	Brookfield	1	No.
Bush, Gidor	Bushberg		
Bush, Raphael	Bushberg		
Bush & Son & Messner	Bushberg		Yes.
Zoog, Florian	Carterville		
Conrad, C.	Carthage		
Kübler, C.	Carthage		
Lohmar, Henry	Cassville	10	Yes.
Kehn, Dr. A.	Castor	1/3	Yes.
Jackson, John T.	Chillicothe		
Blankenship, J.	Corsicana		
Muench, Frederick	Dutzow		
Agnew, S. H.	Edina		
Harmon, Daniel	Erie	1/4	No.
Brown, J. J.	Forsyth		
Mueller, Lois	Glen Allen	1/2	Yes.
Reilly, John A.	Glen Allen	2	Yes.
Steiner, Louise	Granby	2	Yes.
Zoellner, Louis	Granby	1	Yes.
Scroggs, W. S.	Greenville		
Carver, James	Guilford		
Bell, N. B.	Hamilton	1	Yes.
Bauer, Mrs.	Hermann	10	No.
Bomfare, John	Hermann	10	No.
Buddemeyer, F.	Hermann	25	No.
Bürbel, Fred.	Hermann	30	Yes.
Burchhardt, Emil	Hermann	25	No.
Burchhardt, Fred.	Hermann	20	No.
Burchhardt, Wm.	Hermann	20	No.
Dilthey, Mrs. Barbara	Hermann	10	No.
Eberlin, Albert	Hermann	20	Yes.
Eberlin, Louis	Hermann	30	Yes.
Feil, Carl	Hermann	10	No.
Fleisch, Christ.	Hermann	20	No.
Foerber, Adam	Hermann	20	No.
Foerber, Valentine	Hermann	30	No.
Frank, Fritz	Hermann	15	No.
Glaser, Mrs.	Hermann	40	No.
Glaser, Richard	Hermann	20	No.
Glott, G.	Hermann	10	No.
Good, Anton	Hermann	10	No.
Gross, Charles	Hermann	10	No.
Grossman, G.	Hermann	20	No.
Haagen, A.	Hermann	10	Yes.

MISSOURI—Continued.

NAME.	Post Office.	Acres in Vines.	Wine Maker.
Hemme, Christ.	Hermann	30	No.
Henze, Henry	Hermann	30	No.
Hickman, Capt. W. L.	Hermann	20	No.
Hoeberle, Mathias	Hermann	10	No.
Hoeberle, Mrs.	Hermann	10	No.
Hundhausen, Julius	Hermann	30	Yes.
Kuhn, Mrs. Mary	Hermann	30	No.
Loehnig, Rich.	Hermann	20	No.
Loehnig, O., & Co.	Hermann	50	Yes.
Ludwig, F.	Hermann	10	No.
Luigenfelder, Louis	Hermann	10	No.
Maagelin, C.	Hermann	10	No.
Martin, Ernst	Hermann	10	No.
Mueller, Beruh	Hermann	10	Yes.
Mueller, J. G.	Hermann	50	Yes.
Mueller, Mrs.	Hermann	20	Yes.
Mueller, Havier	Hermann	30	Yes.
Neidbudt, John	Hermann	40	Yes.
Noe, Mrs.	Hermann	30	No.
Petrus, Beruh	Hermann	40	Yes.
Petrus, Fritz	Hermann	40	Yes.
Poeschel, Michael	Hermann	15	Yes.
Poeschel, Mrs. Dora	Hermann	50	No.
Puchta, Adam	Hermann	35	Yes.
Puchta, Chris.	Hermann	25	Yes.
Rhodius, Mrs. E.	Hermann	40	No.
Roemer, Christ.	Hermann	15	No.
Ruediger, Louis	Hermann	20	No.
Schmidt, —	Hermann	25	No.
Sperry, Wm.	Hermann	20	Yes.
Stein, Franz.	Hermann	20	No.
Stone Hill Wine Co.	Hermann	100	Yes.
Strassner, Beruh	Hermann	15	No.
Strassner, Joe.	Hermann	10	No.
Strecher, Wm.	Hermann	25	No.
Strehly, Hugo.	Hermann	10	No.
Suedmeyer, Christ.	Hermann	10	No.
Uffelmann, John	Hermann	15	No.
Vallet, Fred.	Hermann	20	No.
Vogt, Mrs.	Hermann	20	Yes.
Voigt, Otto	Hermann		
Walch, Henry	Hermann	10	No.
Walker, Otto	Hermann	20	No.
Weber, Martin	Hermann	10	No.
West, John	Hermann	10	No.
Werner, Christ.	Hermann	20	No.
Will, John	Hermann	10	No.
Willie, John	Hermann	10	No.
Wittmann, David	Hermann	20	No.
Wittmann, Louis	Hermann	10	No.
Wittmann, Robert	Hermann	10	No.
Zeller, John	Hermann	20	Yes.
Krell, N.	Hornet		
Rousch, J.	Joplin		
Schefferdecker, C.	Joplin		
Northup, Wm.	Kingston	1	Yes.
Northup, M. D.	Kingston		
Grove, F. A., M.D.	Kirksville.		
Brandohl, Ludwig	Laclede	3	Yes.
Brown, S. H.	Laclede	3	Yes.
Sprechelmeyer, Dr. J. C.	Lange's Store.	25	No.
Boardman, C.	Linneus.		Yes.
Engehart, Christopher	Lutesville.	1	No.
Slaybaugh, Samuel	Lutesville.	1	No.
Stenm, A. C.	Lutesville.	1	No.
Schrock, Anton	Marble Hill.	½	Yes.
Gaunt, Thos. W.	Marysville		
Maynard, Dr.	May	½	No.
Wilson, Q. M. K.	Moberly		
Rommel & Sobbe	Morrison	50	Yes.

Missouri—Continued.

NAME.	Post Office.	Acres in Vines.	Wine Maker.
Kirchhoff, Gust.	Morrison	10	No.
Landrum, R. H.	Mount Vernon.		
Jaeger, Hermann	Neosho	15	Yes.
Jaeger, John	Neosho	5	Yes.
Schoenborn, Ernest	Neosho	3	Yes.
Zimmermann, J.	Neosho		
Marcusson, Geo.	New Boston	½	Yes.
Stone, G. H.	New Boston	1	No.
Zoellner, L.	Newtonia		
Thudium, John G.	North Salem	6	Yes.
Kempt, F. A.	Norwood		
Baumgartner, S.	Pierce City	½	Yes.
Graef, L.	Pierce City		
Herman, Martin	Pierce City	1	Yes.
Mettlach, John P.	Pierce City	1	Yes.
Shaffer, G. M.	Pierce City	½	Yes.
Berten, D.	Pineville	½	No.
Lawrence, J. P.	Pineville	½	No.
Lagron, Arthur	Rhineland		
Wild, Herman	Sarcopic		
Caldwell, Wm.	Savannah		
Ent, William	Savannah	1	Yes.
Thudium, John G.	Sedgwick	2	Yes.
Schiffbaur, Jos.	Seneca		
Brock, W. A.	Split Log	½	No.
Garnette, J. L.	Split Log	½	No.
Gavin, J. M.	Split Log	½	No.
McConnell, G. B.	Split Log	1	No.
Kirchgraeber, Jos.	Springfield		
American Wine Company	St. Louis.		
Gast Wine Company	St. Louis.		
Beck, Domineck.	St. Joseph	5	Yes.
Digel, Christ.	St. Joseph	3	Yes.
Goff, N. D.	St. Joseph	6	Yes.
Haffner, Christ.	St. Joseph		
Ridgway, Nathaniel M.	Trenton		
Fulkerson, Abram	Tuscumbia		
Liston, E.	Virgil City		
Ames, William B.	Warrensburg		
Speiss, H.	Warrensburg		
Monks & Green	West Plains		
Risley, Sama	West Plains		
Pamperl, John	Winigan	1	Yes.

NEW MEXICO.

NAME.	Post Office.	Acres in Vines.	Wine Maker.
Rosenfeld, B.	Georgetown		
Casad, T.	Mesilla		
Thomson, John H.	Santa Fe		
Hubbard, E. J.	Socorro		

NEBRASKA.

NAME.	Post Office.	Acres in Vines.	Wine Maker.
Allen, James T.	Omaha		
Chaney, S. G.	Wahoo		

NEW JERSEY.

NAME.	Post Office.	Acres in Vines.	Wine Maker.
Bishop, Howard	Beverly	5	No.
Boyd, William H.	Beverly	5	No.
Krim, William	Beverly	10	Yes.
Marter, Edward	Beverly	5	No.
Parry, Oliver	Beverly	15	No.
Vansciver, Charles	Beverly	5	No.
Vansciver, E. R.	Beverly	5	No.
Townsend, F. Sidney	Cape May	1	No.
Jessup, George W.	Cinnaminson	5	No.
Collings, Richard T.	Collingswood		
Horner, Joel	Delair	10	No.
Baniehr, J. H.	Egg Harbor City	3	No.
Bauge, Henry	Egg Harbor City		
Baum, Henry	Egg Harbor City	15	Yes.
Behns, William	Egg Harbor City		
Bergmann, Philip	Egg Harbor City		
Bolte, H.	Egg Harbor City	3	No.
Bolte, William	Egg Harbor City	3	Yes.
Borm, Charles	Egg Harbor City		Yes.
Bower, Joe	Egg Harbor City	1	Yes.
Braunbeck, William	Egg Harbor City		
Brendal, Joseph	Egg Harbor City	1	No.
Butterhof, John	Egg Harbor City	6	Yes.
Dihlmann, John	Egg Harbor City		
Doell, Amandus	Egg Harbor City	2	No.
Dryer, Ernest	Egg Harbor City	1	Yes.
Emmendorf, Mrs.	Egg Harbor City	4	Yes.
Ertel, Louis	Egg Harbor City		
Fiedler, Herman	Egg Harbor City		
Freitag, Geo.	Egg Harbor City	5	Yes.
Friedler, Frederick	Egg Harbor City	1	Yes.
Gissel, Jacob	Egg Harbor City	1	No.
Glatthorn, Louis	Egg Harbor City	1	Yes.
Grunler & Bahnne	Egg Harbor City		
Gunther, Gustavus	Egg Harbor City		
Hanselman, Geo.	Egg Harbor City	5	Yes.
Hanselman, John	Egg Harbor City	10	Yes.
Hanselman, Michael	Egg Harbor City		
Hartmaier, Peter	Egg Harbor City		Yes.
Hassentenfel, Mrs.	Egg Harbor City	1	Yes.
Heil, Augustus	Egg Harbor City	8	Yes.
Hincke, G., heirs of	Egg Harbor City	4	No.
Hincke, Julius	Egg Harbor City	15	Yes.
Hoebel, Hugo	Egg Harbor City		Yes.
Hoenes, John	Egg Harbor City	2	Yes.
Hoffman, Valentine P.	Egg Harbor City		No.
Karrer, Wm.	Egg Harbor City	8	No.
Kertz, Jacob	Egg Harbor City		
Keyser, Herman	Egg Harbor City	6	Yes.
Kiebat, Mrs.	Egg Harbor City		
Kimmick, I.	Egg Harbor City	6	Yes.
Kurnig, Jacob	Egg Harbor City		
Leipe, William	Egg Harbor City	3	Yes.
Meyer, H.	Egg Harbor City	3	Yes.
Mewes, Eugene	Egg Harbor City		No.
Michel, ——	Egg Harbor City	3	No.
Mueller, B. H.	Egg Harbor City	2	No.
Nehr, Joseph	Egg Harbor City		
Oberst & Sons	Egg Harbor City		
Oberst, S.	Egg Harbor City		Yes.
Oberst, Stephen	Egg Harbor City		Yes.
Oeltjenbruns, D.	Egg Harbor City	2	No.
Oeser, William	Egg Harbor City	1	
Orfall, Henry	Egg Harbor City	3	Yes.
Pfeiffer, Henry	Egg Harbor City	3	Yes.
Ranscher, Ed.	Egg Harbor City	8	Yes.
Reimann, Dr. Robert	Egg Harbor City	5	Yes.
Renault, L. N.	Egg Harbor City		
Ribat, Mrs.	Egg Harbor City	2	Yes.

NEW JERSEY—Continued.

NAME.	Post Office.	Acres in Vines.	Wine Maker.
Roesch, Joseph	Egg Harbor City		
Saalmann, Charles	Egg Harbor City	12	Yes.
Schirmer, L. T.	Egg Harbor City	6	Yes.
Schroeder, ——	Egg Harbor City	6	Yes.
Schroeder, ——	Egg Harbor City	2	No.
Schmidt, E. A.	Egg Harbor City		Yes.
Schuster, John	Egg Harbor City		
Simmers, William	Egg Harbor City	4	Yes.
Specht, Jacob	Egg Harbor City	2	No.
Sludtler, Casimir	Egg Harbor City		
Steigauf, Philip	Egg Harbor City	1	No.
Stroedtmann, William	Egg Harbor City		
Stortz, Fritz	Egg Harbor City		
Tapken, ——	Egg Harbor City	2	No.
Tapken, ——	Egg Harbor City	3	No.
Teal, William	Egg Harbor City	2	Yes.
Undernehrer, Joseph	Egg Harbor City	3	No.
Van Riel, Rev.	Egg Harbor City		
Wagner, ——	Egg Harbor City	1	Yes.
Waschow, Ferdinand	Egg Harbor City		
Wichelmann, Wm.	Egg Harbor City		
Williams, Wm.	Egg Harbor City	2	No.
Wolf, George	Egg Harbor City		
Wolsieler, Wm. & J. H.	Egg Harbor City	5	Yes.
Young, Louis	Egg Harbor City	3	No.
Hill, William	Flemington		
Olmstead, H. C.	Flemington	1	Yes.
Harris, Thos. W.	Forest Grove		
North, Dr. J. H.	Hammonton	2	Yes.
Parkhurst, L. H.	Hammonton	8	Yes.
Ransom, J. O.	Hammonton	10	Yes.
Sproulle, E. R.	Hammonton	1	
Van Ness, John H.	Hilton		
Duroe, Daniel	Landisville	13	Yes.
De Bauge, Chas.	Maine Avenue	4	Yes.
Dumas, Francois	Maine Avenue	8	Yes.
Zacco, Apolinare	Maine Avenue		
Hovner, Daniel	Merchantville	5	No.
Potts, John	Merchantville	10	No.
Collins, John G.	Moorestown	10	No.
Runyon, John R.	Morristown		
Demarest, J. M.	Mountain View		
Goldsmith, W. H.	Newark	6	No.
McDowell, Wm.	Newark		
Guinn, P. T.	Newark		
Ward, Wm. B.	Newark	3	No.
Blish, Samuel	New Brunswick		
Doolittle, W. M.	Ocean View		
Evaul, Isaac	Palmyra	5	No.
Hylton, Dr. J. D.	Palmyra	5	No.
Parry, Charles	Parry	5	No.
Parry, Wm.	Parry	10	No.
Speer Wine Co. (Alfred Speer, President)	Passaic	66	Yes.
Bonner, Mr.	Pomerania	1	Yes.
Champion, Mr.	Pomerania	1	Yes.
Filling, H.	Pomerania	1	Yes.
Filling, Lewis	Pomerania	$\frac{1}{2}$	Yes.
Fink, William	Pomerania	1	Yes.
Grunow, Albert	Pomerania	3	Yes.
Henchel, George	Pomerania	3	Yes.
Henman, John C.	Pomerania	2	Yes.
Kreig, Wm.	Pomerania	8	Yes.
Swickerath, Joseph	Pomerania	10	Yes.
Thirow, Frank	Pomerania	2	Yes.
Fuller, A. S.	Ridgewood		
Lippincott, Edward	Riverton	5	No.
Logan, Wm. J.	Somerville		
Anderson, John	Vineland	10	Yes.
Baker, P.	Vineland		

NEW JERSEY—Continued.

NAME.	Post Office.	Acres in Vines.	Wine Maker.
Beck, Chas...	Vineland	1	Yes.
Beck, Philip	Vineland	8	Yes.
Bidwell, Dr. E. C.	Vineland		
Bosio, C.	Vineland		
Brown, Henry	Vineland		
Cavagnaro, F.	Vineland	10	Yes.
Dean, M. L.	Vineland		
Dexter, L. W.	Vineland		
Green, James	Vineland	1	Yes.
Hoffmyer, H.	Vineland	8	Yes.
Jones, E. G.	Vineland		
Laubsch, Louis	Vineland	12	Yes.
Meech, W. W.	Vineland		
Muhleisen, Geo. B.	Vineland	2	Yes.
Pearson, A. W.	Vineland	10	Yes.
Raische, Chas.	Vineland		
Raisch, Henry	Vineland	1	Yes.
Reustle, David	Vineland	2	Yes.
Reustle, F.	Vineland	10	Yes.
Rice, Phil.	Vineland		
Sauer, F.	Vineland	10	Yes.
Scheer, Augustus	Vineland	8	Yes.
Snell, Chas.	Vineland	1	Yes.
Vernino, Jim	Vineland		
Welch, Dr. C. E.	Vineland		

NEW YORK.

NAME.	Post Office.	Acres in Vines.	Wine Maker.
Blackford, Joseph	Adam's Basin	6	
Fetter, J. E.	Adam's Basin		
Hosford, David R.	Adam's Basin		
Schiess, Augustus	Adam's Basin		
Bogue, Virgil	Albion		
Dibble, John A.	Albion	6	
Gates, Charles P.	Albion		
McNall, Watson C.	Albion		
Parker, Mary	Albion		
Payne, Carlton A.	Albion		
Peterson, John H.	Albion		
Tanner, W. A.	Albion		
Sleight, Carlton W.	Allen's Hill	25	
Van Dusen, John H.	Arcadia	4	
Van Dusen, Richard	Arcadia	3	
Cox, James R.	Auburn		
Snyder, R. M.	Auburn	2	
Giddings, D. Burr	Baldwinsville	18	
Bogue, Nelson	Batavia		
Brundage, A. C.	Bath	8	No.
Brundage, Ad.	Bath	6	No.
Brundage, George A.	Bath	8	No.
Brundage, J. W.	Bath	7	No.
Bronson, George	Bath	10	No.
Bronson, Isaac	Bath	10	No.
Casson, Dr.	Bath	12	No.
Eastwood & Wolf.	Bath	80	Yes.
Howell, D. C., & Co.	Bath	40	No.
Longwell, Charles	Bath	4	No.
Longwell, John	Bath	5	No.
Stenton Co. Vineyard Associa'n.	Bath		
Tobias, H. M.	Bath	4	No.
Mead, Joshua	Bellona		
Becker, A. S.	Benton Center		
Gage, S. B.	Benton Center		
Gage, S. Granger	Benton Center		
Hewes, M. B.	Bergen		

NAME.	Post Office.	Acres in Vines.	Wine Maker.
Brown, Everett	Bluff Point		
Brown, George H.	Bluff Point	20	No.
Coleman, E. T.	Bluff Point	10	No.
Fitzwater, Charles W.	Bluff Point	20	No.
Frimmingham, James	Bluff Point	25	No.
Gilder, John	Bluff Point	15	No.
Long, Eli	Bluff Point	10	No.
Moore, George D.	Bluff Point		
Parker, George H.	Bluff Point	30	No.
Pepper, James	Bluff Point	15	No.
Purdy, Frank H.	Bluff Point	25	No.
Sill, H. R.	Bluff Point	12	No.
Wilson, J. S. & E. B.	Bluff Point	14	No.
Barton, E. C.	Branchport	50	No.
Belknap, James A.	Branchport		
Davis, Melvin J.	Branchport		
Millspaugh, Charles	Branchport	20	No.
Rose Bros.	Branchport	20	Yes.
Rose, Edmund	Branchport	12	No.
Wright, David	Branchport	10	Yes.
Reed, Thomas H.	Brewster's Station		
Beedle, J. W.	Brockport		
Bentley, Almond	Brockport		
Bentley, Manly T.	Brockport		
Brainard, Geo. J.	Brockport	12	
Bulkley, H. L.	Brockport		
Chamberlain, H. T.	Brockport	25	
Cooley, Willard A.	Brockport		
Doty, Alva	Brockport		
Hammond, Geo. T.	Brockport		
King, Nelson A.	Brockport		
Mershon, James	Brockport		
Quinn, Hugh	Brockport		
Taylor, Adin B.	Brockport		
Barker, Deville	Brocton		
Becker, A.	Brocton		
Becker, Philip	Brocton		
Becker, W. H.	Brocton	40	No.
Brainard, Fay	Brocton		
Brainard, Orin O.	Brocton		
Breen, James	Brocton	65	No.
Breen, Mrs.	Brocton		
Breen, Wm.	Brocton	20	No.
Buckner, E.	Brocton	75	No.
Burr, Ovett	Brocton		
Butler, Capt. Jas.	Brocton		
Chamberlain, O. J.	Brocton		
Clark, Sherman	Brocton		
Crandall, J. E.	Brocton		
Dean Bros.	Brocton	75	
Dean, Mary S.	Brocton		
Farnhaus, Carl	Brocton		
Farnhaus, Jonas	Brocton		
Fay, A. A.	Brocton		
Fay, Franklin, & Son	Brocton	50	No.
Fay, Otis N.	Brocton		
Grant, G.	Brocton		
Haight, Geo.	Brocton	38	No.
Haight, Mark	Brocton		
Haight, Mark & Ransom	Brocton		
Hall, R. A.	Brocton		
Harlenburg, Denty	Brocton	20	No.
Hatch, John L.	Brocton		
Hull, C. W.	Brocton		
Hull, D. W.	Brocton		
Johnson, Bruce	Brocton		
Johnson, Cornelia	Brocton		
Johnson, N. D.	Brocton	60	No.
Judson, C. K.	Brocton	60	No.
Judson & Lyman	Brocton		

NEW YORK—Continued.

NAME.	Post Office.	Acres in Vines.	Wine Maker.
Kelley Bros.	Brocton	50	No.
Kelley, Leslie	Brocton		
Manton, P. M.	Brocton	4	
Martin, Jonas, & Sons	Brocton	200	Yes.
Martin, William	Brocton	20	No.
Monfort, G. L., & Son	Brocton	80	No.
Monhall, Bridget	Brocton		
Moss, T. S.	Brocton	75	No.
Pettitt, W. W., & Sons	Brocton	20	No.
Powell, Cressie	Brocton	100	
Ryckman, G. E.	Brocton	135	Yes.
Schoenfield, Gustavus	Brocton		
Skinner, A. A.	Brocton	25	
Skinner, E. W.	Brocton	46	No.
Skinner, George L.	Brocton	33	No.
Sullivan, L. D.	Brocton		
Taylor, E. B.	Brocton		
Tucker, E. B.	Brocton		
Walden & Son	Brocton		
Warner, Charles	Brocton		
Weld, Willard H.	Brocton		
Wenborn, C. A.	Brocton		
Westerling, Samuel	Brocton		
Zahonk, Joseph	Calicoon		
Gould, E. Dwight	Cambria		
Phillips, E. Burt	Cambridgeport		
Andruss, C. J.	Canandaigua	40	
Bush, Osband T.	Canandaigua	25	
Green, Miles H.	Canandaigua	30	
Ross, M. L.	Candor	11	
Chapel, Stephen	Carleton		
Roberts, John B.	Carleton		
Jordan, L. J.	Carleton Station		
Jordan, Theda V.	Carleton Station		
Porter, J. H.	Carleton Station		
Lacy, M. C.	Carlyon	5	
Bliss, Guilford D.	Castile		
Tabor, H. E.	Castile		
Tallman, G. B.	Castile		
Wynkoop, E. H.	Catskill		
Mack, H. Q.	Catskill Station		
Ashley, Charles W.	Chatham		
Porter, Abram C.	Chittenange		
Adams, George	Churchville		
Bailey, William	Churchville		
Taylor, Royal W.	Clarendon		
Allen, Henry	Clarkson		
Nellis, George B.	Clarkson		
Seneca Chief Vineyard Company	Clifton Springs		
Dwight, Benjamin W.	Clinton		
Donaldson, Daniel J.	Clintondale		
Heaton, Reuben B.	Clintondale		
Barton, A. & A. K.	Clyde	2	No.
Buell, J.	Clyde	6	No.
Crawford, C.	Clyde	2	No.
Devereaux, A. F.	Clyde	2	Yes.
Porter, E.	Clyde	2	No.
Weed, B.	Clyde	13	No.
Purdy, Leo W.	Cold Springs		No.
Harmon, A. W.	Corfu		
Cartwright, Minor T.	County Line		
Porter, S. J. & T. M.	County Line		
Carr, W. I.	Crosby		
Clark, Margaret E.	Dansville		
Cole, Geo. S. & E.	Dansville	25	
Patchin, E. S. & Chas. V.	Dansville	10	
Bartlett, W. C.	Demster	5	
Hathorn, E. L.	Dey's Landing	11	
Sayre, Caleb	Dey's Landing	20	
Skinner, Aaron B.	Dey's Landing	18	

NAME.	Post Office.	Acres in Vines.	Wine Maker.
Almy, Chas. W. & W. C.	Dundee	30	
Fitzsimmons, Walter	Dundee	23	
Pierce, H. W. & L. S.	Dundee	12	
Reynolds, Louis H.	Dundee	11	
Day, Ralph	Dunkirk	80	Yes.
Paul, W. W.	East Bloomfield	25	
Stebbins, Isaac N.	East Carleton		
Warner, James H.	East Groveland		
Lusk, Jacob	East Palmyra	2	
Wheeler, C. P.	East Wilton		
Burnap, Martha A.	Eddytown	10	
Broque Bros.	Elba		
Pettit, Dorastus	Fair Haven	25	
Phillips, Geo. W.	Fair Haven		
Turner, Isaac	Fair Haven		
De Nise, Garrett	Fairport	16	
Warner, Fred.	Fairport	6	
Austin, E. G.	Fairville	3	
Gillett, N. M.	Fayetteville		
Heuber, Louis	Fayetteville		
Putnam, Geo. H.	Fayetteville		
Wells, Samuel J.	Fayetteville	25	
Worden, Palmer	Fayetteville	12	
Allen, C. C.	Ferguson's Corners	6	
Allen, Valentine	Ferguson's Corners		
Benson, Orson	Fishers		
Burrows, J. G.	Fishkill	20	Yes.
Cary, Wm. M.	Fishkill	25	Yes.
Parsons Sons	Flushing, Long Island		
Le Fever, Josiah	Forest Glen		
Dunn, Thomas	Forest Lawn		
Torrey, John	Fowlerville		
Crissey, S. S.	Fredonia		
Gardner, R. W.	Fredonia	20	Yes.
Goodell, B. J.	Fredonia	32	No.
Hubbard, T. S., & Co.	Fredonia	35	No.
Josselyn, Geo. S.	Fredonia		
Roesch, Louis	Fredonia		
Stevens, W. H.	Fredonia		
Stone, S. E.	Fredonia	55	No.
Webster, L. B.	Fredonia	40	Yes.
Young, Leonard J.	Fredonia		
Pratt, Jonathan S.	Furnaceville	5	
Sanders, Eugene	Furnaceville	6	
Thompson, Edward	Furnaceville		
Reed, W. W.	Gaines		
Sanford, L. A.	Gaines		
Wadhams, S. W.	Garland		
Smith, E. J.	Gasport	4	
Cleveland, O. C.	Geneseo		
Jones, R. M.	Geneseo		
Marsh, A. L.	Geneseo		
Cook, Henry J.	Geneva	6	
Tompkins, William	Germantown		
French, Myron L.	Gibsonville		
Mason, C. C. & F. E.	Gilbert's Mills	3	
Hopkins, E. A.	Glen Cove		
Peche, —	Glenora		
Parker, George	Gouverneur		
Clarke, John D.	Griggsville		
Williams, H.	Groton		
Gleason, Alfred	Grove Springs	10	Yes.
Abbott, Frank	Hammondsport	7	No.
Abbott, Theodore H.	Hammondsport	12	No.
Babcock Bros., Drs.	Hammondsport	40	Yes.
Babcock, M. & O. H.	Hammondsport	16	No.
Baucher & Masson	Hammondsport	40	Yes.
Beers, Ed. & Fred.	Hammondsport	5	No.
Benham, Charles	Hammondsport	3	No.
Benham, Henry	Hammondsport	4	No.

NEW YORK—Continued.

NAME.	Post Office.	Acres in Vines.	Wine Maker.
Benner, William	Hammondsport	3	No.
Boothe, A. E.	Hammondsport	6	No.
Booth, M.	Hammondsport	11	Yes.
Brundage, George	Hammondsport	8	Yes.
Brundage, J. W.	Hammondsport	12	No.
Brush, George	Hammondsport	4	No.
Cameron, D.	Hammondsport	14	No.
Campbell, H. H.	Hammondsport		
Casteline, D.	Hammondsport	5	No.
Champlin, C. A.	Hammondsport	35	Yes.
Champlin, H. M.	Hammondsport	30	Yes.
Columbia Wine Company	Hammondsport	20	Yes.
Conley, Anthony	Hammondsport	2	Yes.
Coryell, F. H.	Hammondsport	4	No.
Coryell, Frank	Hammondsport	5	No.
Covert, F. M.	Hammondsport	5	No.
Danes, Geo.	Hammondsport	7	No.
Darrowe, E. B.	Hammondsport	35	No.
Dildene, Wm.	Hammondsport	8	No.
Drew, Jepth	Hammondsport	5	No.
Eaton, Geo.	Hammondsport	5	No.
Edgett, Jos.	Hammondsport	8	No.
Egelstone, David	Hammondsport	5	No.
Fairchild, H. P.	Hammondsport	50	Yes.
Fairchild, O. H.	Hammondsport	40	Yes.
Fairland, W.	Hammondsport	2	Yes.
Frey, Jacob, & Sons	Hammondsport	20	Yes.
Gardner, Major	Hammondsport	8	No.
Germania Wine Company	Hammondsport	10	Yes.
Haase, Mrs. M.	Hammondsport	20	Yes.
Haggadon, T. J.	Hammondsport	5	No.
Haight, S. E.	Hammondsport	7	No.
Hammondsport Wine Company	Hammondsport	4	Yes.
Howell, D. C., & Co.	Hammondsport	35	Yes.
Hultenschmidt, Augustus	Hammondsport	15	No.
Hunt, F.	Hammondsport	15	No.
Jump, G. V.	Hammondsport	20	No.
Kingsley, L. & F.	Hammondsport	2	No.
Longwell, Moosbrugger & Co.	Hammondsport	6	Yes.
Longwell, Randall	Hammondsport	20	No.
Mason, Lyn	Hammondsport	60	No.
McFie, Thomas	Hammondsport	23	No.
Mills, J. C.	Hammondsport	6	No.
Monarch Grape and Wine Company(T. M. & O. H. Younglove)	Hammondsport	50	Yes.
Moore, Trevor & Hubert	Hammondsport	25	No.
Myrtle, B. F.	Hammondsport	4	No.
Nichols, W. H.	Hammondsport	25	No.
Nichols, G. W.	Hammondsport		
O'Loughlin, James	Hammondsport	10	Yes.
Parker, J. R.	Hammondsport	5	No.
Parker, Wm.	Hammondsport	6	No.
Pattison, Walter	Hammondsport	6	No.
Randel, W. S.	Hammondsport	8	Yes.
Ray, Joseph	Hammondsport	3	No.
Ray, Richard	Hammondsport	1½	No.
Retan, N.	Hammondsport	15	Yes.
Retan, S. L.	Hammondsport	15	No.
Rose, D.	Hammondsport	20	No.
Sargent, A. J.	Hammondsport	20	No.
Saun, T.	Hammondsport	10	Yes.
Scofield, Jas.	Hammondsport	10	No.
Simpson, W.	Hammondsport	2	Yes.
Smith & McCorn	Hammondsport	25	No.
Smith, Jos. L.	Hammondsport	16	Yes.
Sprague, David	Hammondsport	4	No.
Sprague, Joseph	Hammondsport	6	No.
Taltz, F.	Hammondsport	8	No.
Thelen, N.	Hammondsport	6	Yes.
Thorp, James	Hammondsport	10	No.

New York—Continued.

NAME.	Post Office.	Acres in Vines.	Wine Maker.
Urbana Wine Cellar	Hammondsport	75	Yes.
Wheeler, Graham	Hammondsport	20	Yes.
Wheeler, Monroe	Hammondsport	10	Yes.
Hinman, Benj. & E. P.	Hannibal	12	
Lund, E. A. & A. H.	Hannibal	11	
Rice, A.	Hannibal	11	
Shutts, G. J.	Hannibal		
Henderson, J. D.	Herkimer		
Baker, John M. & E. J.	Hickory Corners		
Condren Bros.	Hickory Corners		
Levan, S. S.	Hickory Corners		
Martin, Aaron	Hickory Corners		
Van Dusen, A. E.	Hickory Corners		
Deyo, Mrs. Zorada	Highland		
Elting, C. W.	Highland		
Hasbrouck, Angelo	Highland		
Leroy, David	Highland		
Rhodes, Aaron	Highland		
Rogers, Samuel	Highland	80	
Taylor, John F.	Highland		
Terpenning, A.	Highland		
Thorn, Salmon P.	Highland		
Williams, Nathan	Highland		
Seneca Lake Wine Co.	Himrods		
Fowler, Thomas N.	Holley		
Fuller, John B.	Holley		
Hurd, Ellen A.	Holley		
Tuttle, Geo. E.			
Blackmer, M. H. & H. P.	Honeoye	25	
Rennoldson, Thomas R.	Honeoye	25	
Hakes, H.	Honeoye		
Rapeljec, L. C.	Hopewell Junction		
Shull, Josiah	Ilion		
Pierce, Chas. O.	Ira		
Roe, N. S.	Ira		
Sprague, C. B.	Ira	12	
Irondequoit Wine Co.	Irondequoit		
Crandall, P. B.	Ithaca		
Carry, Wm.	Johnsville		
Johnson, Robt.	Johnsville		
Ladue, Jno. M.	Johnsville		
Pierce, L. V.	Johnsville	20	Yes.
Waldo, J. B.	Johnsville	20	No.
Bridgeman, C. S.	Kendall		
Snow, James G.	Kenyonville		
Bradbury, Daniel	Kingston		
Barrett, E. H. & Alice S.	Knowlesville		
Fitch, Willard R.	Knowlesville		
Shaw, Richard	Knowlesville	20	
Smith, G. A.	Knowlesville		
Trow, William	Knowlesville	6	
Webster, Henry	Knowlesville		
Burley, William	Lakeville		
Roe, L. P. & L. M.	Lakeville		
West, L. P.	Lakeville		
Hotchkiss, George A.	Lewiston		
Nichols, L. M.	Lewiston		
Clum, Ferdinand	Lincoln		
Esley, Alfred	Lincoln	4	
Oyston, Charles	Little Falls		
Ames, Ellsworth E.	Lockport		
Bowen, George W.	Lockport	25	
Clark, B. Wheaton	Lockport	25	
Cushman, S. Frost	Lockport		
Emerson, G. E.	Lockport		
Fritton, Silas	Lockport		
Gould, John B.	Lockport		
Hoag, C. S.	Lockport		
Hyman, J. S.	Lockport		
Moore, Henry	Lockport		

NEW YORK—Continued.

NAME.	Post Office.	Acres in Vines.	Wine Maker.
Niagara White Grape Company	Lockport		
Ringueberg, N. S.	Lockport		
Taylor, A. L.	Lockport		
Urtel, Henry	Lockport		
Van Shuler, D.	Lockport	12	
Wakeman, J. E.	Lockport	12	
Warterbury, W. D.	Lyndonville		
McPherson, J. C.	Lyons	18	No.
Van Dusen, H. P.	Lyons	10	
Osborn, Ozias.	Manlin's Station		
Stratton, Geo. W.	Marion		
Van Duzen, William	Marion	8	
Caywood, A. J., & Sons	Marlboro		
Albone, John	Medina		
Balch, William J.	Medina		
Hess, J. H.	Medina		
Howell, H. B.	Medina		
Sandhovel, Peter	Mexico		
Barnes, W. D.	Middlehope	35	No.
Barlow, A. G. & E. D.	Middleport		
Gardner, L. A.	Middleport		
Wait, H. L.	Millville		
Abbott, Franklin	Mitchelville	7	No.
Abbott, Theodore	Mitchelville	6	No.
Barrett, A.	Mitchelville	5	No.
Bronson, C. H.	Mitchelville	10	No.
Carman, Joseph	Mitchelville	5	No.
Dildine, Uriah	Mitchelville	12	No.
Randle, Wm.	Mitchelville	5	No.
Bell, George W.	Montezuma		
Crosby, N. H.	Moscow		
Bills, Nancy & N. B.	Mount Morris		
George, William	Mount Morris		
McPherson, J. C.	Mumford	18	
Maxfield, D. H.	Naples		
Sagar, J.	Naples		
Budd, S. E.	Newark	2	
Goldsmith, W. H.	Newark		
Ridley, William	Newark	5	
Roberts, H. Nelson	Newark	5	
Soverhill, G. M.	Newark	6	
Van Dusen, Dr.	Newark		
Van Benschotten, H.	Newark		
Barnes, Nath.	Newburg		
Carmer, A. T.	Newfane		
Corwin, P. H.	Newfane		
Barker, D. A.	North Bergen		
Dean, Thomas J.	North Bergen		
Holbrook, S. H.	North Bergen		
Reed, Charles N.	North Bergen		
Lamereaux, Geo.	North Hector	2	
Mekeel, A. M.	North Hector	40	
Coleman, R. W.	North Ridgeway		
Stannard, Ransom	Norton Hill		
Cook, E. J. & S. A.	Oaks Corners	6	
Emerson, Geo. C.	Oaks Corners		
Mickelson, J. K.	Oaks Corners	2	
New, H. D. & Mary E.	Ogden		
Albright, John H.	Ontario	25	
Howe, O. M.	Ontario	2	
Niles, Mrs. Mary	Ontario	1	
Pintler & Van Der Veer	Ontario	12	
Pratt, J. Demar	Ontario	10	
Ricker, E. L.	Ontario	40	
Thompson, A. J.	Ontario	6	
Turner, J. B.	Ontario	2	
Whitcomb, F.	Ontario	5	
Hooker, William	Ontario Center	6	
Anderson, Mary A. & D. S.	Orleans	11	
Wheat, V. B., & Son	Orleans	22	

New York—Continued.

NAME.	Post Office.	Acres in Vines.	Wine Maker.
Whitney, Almon C.	Orleans		
Whitney, C. P.	Orleans	25	
Jenkins, Robert	Oswego Center	3	
Cleveland, Sophia B.	Ovid Center	12	
Russell, H. W.	Owego		
Hylton, John D.	Palmyra		
Stafford, E. G.	Palmyra		
Tilden, Christopher	Palmyra		
Rouse, Lorenzo	Paris		
Trescott, B. T.	Pavilion		
Kittridge & Sons	Peekskill		
Saddleson, R.	Pekin		
Clark, Franklin E.	Penfield		
Thomas, A. P.	Penfield	8	
Bordwell, Ernest	Penn Yan	19	No.
Brown, M. Gulick	Penn Yan	25	No.
Butler, John H.	Penn Yan	150	Yes.
Fenton, George	Penn Yan	25	Yes.
Hart & Scott	Penn Yan	12	No.
Hammondsport Vintage Co.	Penn Yan		
Miller, James	Penn Yan	6	No.
Mills, Horace F.	Penn Yan	20	No.
Purdy, Frank H.	Penn Yan		
Purdy, John	Penn Yan		
Purdy, Joseph	Penn Yan	20	No.
Schofield, R. F.	Penn Yan		
Seneca Lake Grape and Wine Co.	Penn Yan		
Shannon & Eastman	Penn Yan	17	No.
Sheppard, Geo. S.	Penn Yan	21	No.
Snow, Geo. C.	Penn Yan	75	No.
Stever, J. A.	Penn Yan	70	Yes.
Wixon, Norman	Penn Yan		
Andrews, Parris	Perry		
Benedict, Charles J.	Perry		
Fitch, Cyrus W.	Perry		
Gillette, Isaac	Perry		
Hathaway, M.	Perry		
O'Connor, P.	Perry		
Simmons, Chas. F.	Perry		
Tabor, A. M.	Perry		
Cosad, D.	Phelps	25	
Leake, Delia M.	Phelps	11	
Newell, Mrs. F. K.	Phelps	2	
Norris, T.	Phelps	5	
Pardee, E. J.	Phelps	6	
Pardee, Howard & F. M.	Phelps	2	
Richmond, James	Phelps	20	
Rockefeller, A. B.	Phelps	11	
Rogers, P. S.	Phelps	6	
Stryker, W. S.	Phelps	25	
Vrooman, Henry S.	Phelps	2	
Whitbeck, George V. H.	Phelps	25	
Young, Elkanah	Phelps		
Bailey, John W.	Plattsburg	½	
Hall, S. P.	Pomfret		
Hayden, Lucy T.	Port Byron	11	
Myers, J. & G. A.	Port Byron	13	
Myers, William	Port Byron	13	
Paddack, C. A.	Port Byron	6	
Paddack, C. B.	Port Byron	2	
Rhodes, W. R.	Port Byron		
Root, Helen and William H.	Port Byron	4	
Arnold, G. M.	Portland		
Arnold, Sam	Portland		
Barhite, T.	Portland		
Camel, Patrick	Portland		
Case, Cass	Portland		
Coon, M. S.	Portland		
Corell, Joseph, & Son	Portland		
Crandall, Ed.	Portland		

NEW YORK—Continued.

NAME.	Post Office.	Acres in Vines.	Wine Maker.
Crosby, C. R.	Portland		
Crosby, T.	Portland		
Dean Bros.	Portland		
Dudley, E. E.	Portland		
Fay, E. H.	Portland	25	No.
Flint Bros.	Portland		
Fuller, G. W.	Portland	25	No.
Fuller, M. P.	Portland		
Hiller Bros.	Portland		
Hipwell, Jacob	Portland		
Hobrook, Josiah	Portland		
Hull, D.	Portland		
Keet, Henry	Portland		
McFadden & Sons	Portland		
McGarrell, Hugh	Portland		
McGinnis, Frank	Portland		
Marsh, G. W., & Taylor	Portland		
Merrick, F. P.	Portland		
Monfort, Frank	Portland		
Monfort, W. J.	Portland		
Morse, Samuel	Portland		
Munger, G. W.	Portland		
Outhank, B.	Portland		
Pecor, Chas.	Portland		
Pecor, Frank	Portland		
Powell, O. W.	Portland	100	No.
Powers, J. A.	Portland		
Skinner, E. W.	Portland	20	
Skinner, Frank	Portland		
Skinner, Homer	Portland		
Taylor, Henry	Portland		
Titus, N. J.	Portland		
Tyler, Cass	Portland		
Walker, Alley	Portland		
Walker, Jas.	Portland		
Weigle, Bridget	Portland		
Wolobey, J. M.	Portland		
Wood, S. B.	Portland		
Van Deventer, H. B.	Port Washington	2	Yes.
Tappan, Chas. O.	Potsdam		
Hyatt, N. R.	Pulteney		
Wagener, Jacob	Pulteney		
Burmaster, Chas.	Ransomville		
Burmaster, Henry	Ransomville		
Andrus, Rollin	Red Creek		
Abbott, F.	Rheims	10	No.
Abbott, T. H.	Rheims	15	No.
Arlany, Wm.	Rheims	25	No.
Boothe, A.	Rheims	6	Yes.
Booth, M. U.	Rheims	12	No.
Brundage, John	Rheims	4	Yes.
Brundage, Mrs. Ed.	Rheims	4	No.
Champlin, Chas.	Rheims	40	No.
Champlin, Harry	Rheims	35	No.
Columbia Wine Co.	Rheims	20	Yes.
Connolly, Anthony	Rheims	1	Yes.
Dildine, Miss Delia	Rheims	6	No.
Eastwood & Wolf	Rheims	35	Yes.
Eaton, Geo.	Rheims	5	No.
Edgett, Jos.	Rheims	12	Yes.
Evans, Frank	Rheims	10	No.
Frey, H., & Hobbs	Rheims	20	Yes.
Haase, Chas. P.	Rheims	4	Yes.
Haase, Mrs.	Rheims	25	Yes.
Haggadorn, T. J.	Rheims	8	No.
Henderson, R. J.	Rheims	8	No.
Lobeck, H. E.	Rheims	11	No.
Longwell, Randall	Rheims	25	Yes.
Mason & Bauder	Rheims	40	Yes.
Nichols, Wm. A.	Rheims	40	No.

NEW YORK—Continued.

NAME.	Post Office.	Acres in Vines.	Wine Maker.
Parker, J. R.	Rheims	5	No.
Parker, W. T.	Rheims	4	No.
Pleasant Valley Wine Co.	Rheims	60	Yes.
Randall, Wm. S.	Rheims	8	No.
Sauer, Mrs. J.	Rheims	15	No.
Sergant, Joe	Rheims	15	No.
Simpson, Wm.	Rheims	1½	Yes.
Smith, Joseph	Rheims	20	No.
Sprague, David	Rheims	4	No.
Thelen, Nic.	Rheims	5	No.
Thompson, G. H.	Rheims	4	No.
Green, R. M.	Rhinebeck		
Jones, P. D.	Ridge		
Tenant, C. W.	Ripley	40	No.
Cayuga Lake Niagara Vyd. Co.	Rochester	200	
Ellwanger & Barry	Rochester		
Seneca Lake Niagara Vineyard Co.	Rochester	240	
Hunt, Julius F.	Romulus	11	
King Niagara Grape Co.	Romulus	150	
Newman, W. Jared	Romulus	6	
Steele, H. Frederick	Romulus	35	
Hasbrouck, James S. & E.	Rosendale		
Bogart, Elbert	Roslyn	3	Yes.
Kern, John	Rossville	1	Yes.
La Vand, F.	Rossville		
Theal, Louis	Rossville		
Ellis, Don C.	Royalton		
Mackey, James	Royalton		
Gannet, E. B.	Sackett's Harbor	2	No.
Lee, Mrs. E. E.	Savona	9	No.
Lacy, Edward T.	Scottsville	5	
Severance, H. R. & J. D.	Scottsville		
Stewart, Wm. & M. J.	Scottsville		
Johnson, L. P.	Seneca Castle	25	
Peck, Henry J.	Seneca Castle	11	
Edwards, Wm. H.	Setauket, Long Island		
Butler, Rufus	Sheridan	7	Yes.
Carey, L. M.	Sheridan	12	Yes.
De Land, J.	Sheridan	4	Yes.
Garlock, N. H.	Sheridan	8	No.
Griswold, E. J.	Sheridan	5	No.
Hanlet, E. E.	Sheridan	10	Yes.
Huyck, F. B.	Sheridan	5	Yes.
Johnson, W. R.	Sheridan	5	Yes.
Kruger, F.	Sheridan	3	No.
Lucas, Alva	Sheridan	17	No.
Manton, P. M.	Sheridan		
Merrett, N. G.	Sheridan	6	No.
Meyer, Jacob	Sheridan	12	Yes.
Miller, Robt.	Sheridan	10	Yes.
Morey, Wm. M.	Sheridan	4	Yes.
Morrison, P.	Sheridan	10	No.
Morse, J. H.	Sheridan	5	No.
Morse, R.	Sheridan	6	No.
Morton, H. S.	Sheridan	10	No.
Newell, O. W.	Sheridan	15	Yes.
Sweet, W. J.	Sheridan	8	No.
Tarbox, Chas.	Sheridan	4	Yes.
Tolles, E. B.	Sheridan	6	No.
Tooke, H. S.	Sheridan	4	No.
Tooke, Manley J.	Sheridan		
Aigner, F.	Silver Creek	10	No.
Crissey, S. S.	Silver Creek		
Frone, W. W.	Silver Creek	5	No.
Ide, Irwin N.	Smithboro		
Rathburn, A. T.	Smith's Mills		
Arnold, W. T.	Sodus		
Case, B. J.	Sodus	10	No.
Halcus, A. H.	Sodus		
Payne, J. E.	Sodus		

NEW YORK—Continued.

NAME.	Post Office.	Acres in Vines.	Wine Maker.
Flemming, K. M.	Sodus Point	6	
Putman, Henry.	Somerset		
Gardner, F. D.	Somerset		
Swick, H. E.	South Wilson		
Goodrich, E. W.	Spencerport		
Copley, Chas. J.	Stapleton, Long Island		
Hunter, Thomas	Sterling	20	
Kirk, James A.	Sterling	7	
Oliver, S. H.	Sterling		
Russet, Mr.	St. James, Long Island	10	Yes.
Darling, Chas. T.	Stony Brook, Long Island	6	Yes.
Westervelt, H. R.	Taughannock Falls	2	
Wilcox, John	Three-Mile Bay	1	No.
Anderson, H. S.	Union Springs		
New Urbana Wine Co.	Urbana		
Bowerman, E. C.	Victor	6	
Hastings, S. C.	Vine Valley		
Hixon, F. A.	Vine Valley		
Knapp, Albert G.	Vine Valley		
Emmerson, J. M., & Son	Washingtonville		
Harrington, E. E.	Watertown	2	No.
Marvin, Daniel S.	Watertown	1	No.
Gano, L. M.	Watkins		
Woodhull, Benj.	Webster	6	
Erwin, Wm. J.	Webster's Crossing		
Bennett, W. M.	Weedsport		
Durston, E. W. & L. A.	Weedsport		
Ewins, W. P.	Weedsport		
Lamphere, James H.	Weedsport		
Brown, John W.	West Batavia		
Allen, Mrs. Wm. N.	Westfield		
Barney, D.	Westfield	12	No.
Bartholomew, E. S.	Westfield		
Bemis, H.	Westfield	12	No.
Colburn, C.	Westfield	30	No.
Densmore, W.	Westfield	32	No.
Dixon & Faloy	Westfield	10	No.
Farel, John	Westfield	275	No.
Fay, J. R.	Westfield	10	No.
Fitch, Joseph	Westfield	12	No.
Gleason, M. B.	Westfield	7	No.
Hardenburg, J.	Westfield	25	No.
Holley, F.	Westfield	9	No.
Jillson, D. G.	Westfield	18	No.
Lamb, F.	Westfield	10	No.
Loop, J. H.	Westfield	18	No.
Mateer, R. M.	Westfield	23	No.
Minton, J. V.	Westfield	30	No.
Rumsay Bros.	Westfield	50	No.
Schofield, E. J.	Westfield		
Skinner, S.	Westfield	30	No.
Taylor, David	Westfield	18	No.
Taylor, T. B. C.	Westfield	30	No.
Thompson, H.	Westfield	30	No.
Watson, A. S.	Westfield	75	No.
Wright, R. G.	Westfield	70	No.
Fish, Chas. H.	West Kendall		
Hardenbrook, W. O.	West Kendall		
Welker, Jacob J.	West Walworth		
Bowenblust, James	West Webster	3	
Church, W. O.	Wolcott		
Jenkins, E. E. & W. U.	Wolcott		
Talcott, Joseph	Wolcott		
Van Hausen, Catherine	Wolcott		
Wise, J. W. & H. M.	Wolcott		
Pomeroy, Frederick B.	York		
Wilkinson, Wm. A.	Youngstown		

NORTH CAROLINA.

NAME.	Post Office.	Acres in Vines.	Wine Maker.
Coffey, W. C.	Boone		
Harrill, L.	Brier Creek		
Phifer, Robert F.	Concord		
Bruce, John	Fayetteville	6	No.
Broadfoot, John B.	Fayetteville	2	No.
Green, W. J.	Fayetteville	100	Yes.
Lawrence, G. W.	Fayetteville	15	Yes.
McLean, J. P.	Fayetteville	10	No.
Pearce, J. M.	Fayetteville	10	No.
Tillinghast, W. N.	Fayetteville	1	No.
Thomson, John P.	Fayetteville	10	No.
Bennett, Washington	Gibson's Mills	6	Yes.
Benbow, D.	Greensborough		
Pearsall, E. D.	Kenansville		
Hunt, S. R., & Co.	Kittrell	30	
Schenck, D.	Lincolnton		
Garrett & Co.	Littleton		Yes.
McAboy, Dr. L. R.	Lynn		
Evans, John W.	Manteo		
Garrett, C. W., & Co.	Medoc	100	
Oestel, J. F.	Morganton		
Beal, William	Murphy		
Ricks, A. H.	Nashville	20	
Gray, J. W.	Peachland	5	No.
Patrick, J. T.	Pine Bluff		No.
Van Lindley, J.	Pomona	5	No.
Andrews, P. H.	Raleigh	8	No.
Bilyew, F.	Raleigh	5	Yes.
Burwell, J. B.	Raleigh	12	No.
Cole, J. W.	Raleigh		No.
Davis, J. H.	Raleigh	10	No.
Goodwin, W. H. J.	Raleigh		No.
Edwards, C. B.	Raleigh	10	No.
Harris, R. J.	Raleigh		
Heck, J. M.	Raleigh	40	No.
Jones & Powell	Raleigh	20	No.
Lewis, Dr. R. H.	Raleigh	10	No.
Mahler, H.	Raleigh	20	Yes.
Moore, Jas.	Raleigh	10	No.
Montague, B. F.	Raleigh		No.
Royster, V. C.	Raleigh	6	No.
Satta & Wyatt	Raleigh		No.
Shellem, Geo.	Raleigh	8	Yes.
Upchurch, B. J.	Raleigh	10	No.
Watson, F. A.	Raleigh	5	No.
Whitfield, N. G.	Raleigh		No.
Williamson, B. P.	Raleigh	17	No.
Whiting, B. W.	Raleigh		No.
Wilson, O.	Raleigh	10	No.
Womble & Batchelor	Raleigh	10	No.
Woodward, Moses	Raleigh		No.
Ridgeway Wine Co.	Ridgeway		
Baxter, W. L.	Ridgeway	15	Yes.
Moore, R. G.	Ridgeway	15	Yes.
Porter, Chas.	Ridgeway	15	Yes.
Scott Bros.	Ridgeway	15	Yes.
Garrett, C. W., & Co.	Ringwood		
Bolton, Abner	Rockingham	4	Yes.
Steele, T. J.	Rockingham	10	No.
Bringle, David L.	Salisbury		
Beane, J. C.	Shelby	20	Yes.
Cleveland Vineyard Co.	Shelby	10	Yes.
Durham, C. C.	Shelby	1	No.
Fromm, C.	Shelby	¼	No.
Gillny & Webb	Shelby		
Croft, N. W.	Shore		Yes.

NORTH CAROLINA—Continued.

NAME.	Post Office.	Acres in Vines.	Wine Maker.
Bilger, H. E.	Southern Pines		No.
Bonner, John	Southern Pines		No.
Boynton, O. H.	Southern Pines		No.
Buchon, J. E.	Southern Pines		No.
Clark, A. M.	Southern Pines		No.
Douglass, B. J., Jr.	Southern Pines		No.
Eylesfield, C. J.	Southern Pines		No.
Grant, C. B.	Southern Pines		No,
Keck & Co.	Southern Pines		No.
Kemp, G. H.	Southern Pines	Average of 25 acres each.	No.
McCracken, J. B.	Southern Pines		No.
Marks, R. S., & Co.	Southern Pines		No.
Obenhauser, Fred.	Southern Pines		No.
Raymond, W. R.	Southern Pines		No.
Rockwell & Co.	Southern Pines		No.
Shaw, C. W.	Southern Pines		No.
Thompson, Chas.	Southern Pines		No.
Torbell & Co.	Southern Pines		No.
Thurston & Co.	Southern Pines		No.
Weaver, C. W.	Southern Pines		No.
Wilson, J. T.	Southern Pines		No.
Swindell, Geo. W.	Swan Quarter		
Stringfield, Geo. W.	Waynesville		
Battle, M. J.	Whitakers		
Burnett, J. H.	Whitakers	20	
Cook, A. C., & Son	Whiteville		Yes.
Lehmon, Jacques	Whiteville		
Rockwell, U. R.	Whiteville		Yes.
Whiteville Wine Co.	Whiteville	25	
Bowden, C. E.	Wilmington		No.
Noble, S. W.	Wilmington	125	Yes.
Thomas, C. G.	Wilmington		No.
Walker, Gerrett	Wilmington	5	No,
Willcard, M. S.	Wilmington		No.

OHIO.

NAME.	Post Office.	Acres in Vines.	Wine Maker.
Cunningham, John	Ada		
Sherbondy, Mrs.	Akron		
Scott, Mrs.	Akron		
Ekey, Andrew	Ashland		
Beard, C.	Avon Lake	5	No.
Beard, E.	Avon Lake	10	No.
Beard, N.	Avon Lake	15	No.
Beck, L.	Avon Lake	20	Yes.
Braman, H.	Avon Lake	12	No.
Cuyler, Capt. R.	Avon Lake		
Cuyler & Son	Avon Lake	25	No.
Dagen, Geo.	Avon Lake	5	No.
Doller, A.	Avon Lake	10	No,
Folger, Thomas	Avon Lake	40	No.
Folger & Son	Avon Lake		
Gedeohn, J.	Avon Lake	15	No.
Gierman, H.	Avon Lake	10	No.
Green, D.	Avon Lake	10	No.
Moon, Henry	Avon Lake	15	No.
Padley, F.	Avon Lake	18	No.
Scheoll, A.	Avon Lake	8	No.
Shertondy, A. W.	Avon Lake	18	No.
Titus, John	Avon Lake	25	No.
Willis, A.	Avon Lake	15	No.
Winley, A.	Avon Lake	10	No.
Crawford, Richard	Bridgeport		
Book, Ben	Catawba Island	5	No.

Ohio—Continued.

NAME.	Post Office.	Acres in Vines.	Wine Maker.
Cagney, John	Catawba Island	4	No.
Catawba Island Wine Co.	Catawba Island		Yes.
Foost, Garret	Catawba Island		
Friedman, S.	Catawba Island	10	Yes.
Furrer, B. F.	Catawba Island	14	Yes.
Kegley, Geo.	Catawba Island	8	No.
Landy, Henry	Catawba Island		
Lemmerman, Geo.	Catawba Island	8	No.
Owens Bros.	Catawba Island	6	No.
Parson, Casper	Catawba Island		
Rofker, Henry	Catawba Island	10	Yes.
Rofker, Geo.	Catawba Island	2	No.
Steffens, Conrad	Catawba Island		
Weyhe, F. W.	Catawba Island	4	No.
Smith, Rev. E. J.	Chagrin Falls	1	No.
Marzluff, Paul	Chillicothe	5	Yes.
Seney, Joshua	Chillicothe	6	No.
Smith, John	Chillicothe	5	No.
West, W. H.	Chillicothe	2	No.
Mihalovitch, Fletcher & Co.	Cincinnati		
Rheinstrom Bros.	Cincinnati		
Gidley, W.	Claribell	6	No.
Klipec, J.	Claribell	15	No.
Leslie, F.	Claribell	5	No.
Riedel, M.	Claribell	5	No.
Robbins, Geo.	Claribell	7	No.
Schmidt, J.	Claribell	7	No.
Stein, H.	Claribell	10	No.
Stenson, S.	Claribell	5	No.
Stevenson, D. M.	Claribell	8	No.
Childs, H. B.	Cleveland	55	No.
Frick, Dr. George F.	Cleveland	40	Yes.
Kendal, A. C.	Cleveland	18	
Moses, N., & Bros.	Cleveland	150	No.
Schmidt, Paul	Cleveland	16	Yes.
Walterson, M. G.	Cleveland	15	
French, A. B.	Clyde		
Beach, Joseph D.	Coal Run		
Doane, J. W.	Collamer		
Aldrich, O. W.	Columbus		Yes.
Innis, G. S.	Columbus		
Post, B. E.	Columbus		
Streeper, J. P.	Columbus		No.
Synold, A.	Columbus		Yes.
Westwater, J. M.	Columbus		No.
Wilson, Horace	Columbus		No.
Witt, M.	Columbus		No.
Albaugh, B. F.	Covington		
Bates, Horace	Cuba		
Crawford, M.	Cuyahoga Falls		
Bredbeck, Henry	Danbury	18	No.
Bush, Henry	Danbury	8	No.
Going, H.	Danbury	15	No.
Koch, William	Danbury	10	No.
Miller, Will	Danbury	12	No.
Zaller, John	Danbury	12	No.
Zollman, H.	Danbury	12	No.
Guenther, Frank	Dayton	3	
Harkes Nursery Co.	Dayton		
Herby, John J.	Dayton	1	
Knecht, Jacob	Dayton	3	
Kratochwill, Jos.	Dayton		
Kramer, Wm.	Dayton	20	Yes.
Kurtz, Frank	Dayton	2	
Linxweiler, Jacob, Sr.	Dayton	3	
Longenecker, Theo. F.	Dayton	1	
Mumma, E. B.	Dayton		
Ohmer, N.	Dayton		
Pot, August	Dayton		
Rost, Ernest	Dayton	1	

Ohio—Continued.

NAME.	Post Office.	Acres in Vines.	Wine Maker.
Siebenthaler, Jacob	Dayton	3	
Siebenthaler, John	Dayton	2	
Steinmetz, Lawrence	Dayton	3	
Stockstill, J.	Dayton		
Campbell, George W.	Delaware		
Pfiffer, John	Delaware		
Calhoon, Marshall	Dover		
Behler, Charles, Sr.	East Cleveland	18	No.
Behler, F. A.	East Cleveland	12	No.
Behler, Herman	East Cleveland	6	No.
Behler, ——	East Cleveland	35	Yes.
Chapman, H. M.	East Cleveland	35	No.
Fisher, John	East Cleveland	8	No.
Frank, Carl	East Cleveland	9	No.
Frank, Daniel	East Cleveland	8	No.
Fries, Wm.	East Cleveland	3	No.
Glenn, W.	East Cleveland	20	No.
Henderson, Mr.	East Cleveland	10	No.
Higgins, Charles	East Cleveland	3	No.
Hollister, George	East Cleveland	10	No.
Ingersol, Rev. Mr.	East Cleveland	14	No.
Jensen, Claus	East Cleveland	10	No.
Kraus, Hans	East Cleveland	8	No.
Lee, E.	East Cleveland	8	No.
Meeker, R. C.	East Cleveland	5	No.
Meyer, Henry	East Cleveland	5	No.
Morgan, H.	East Cleveland	3	No.
Nebahn, John	East Cleveland	40	No.
Palmer, L.	East Cleveland	8	No.
Quilliams, Wm. T.	East Cleveland	8	No.
Rolf, Fred.	East Cleveland	5	No.
Rush, Charles	East Cleveland	5	No.
Rush, Orlando	East Cleveland	2	No.
Rush, Sanford	East Cleveland	8	No.
Sheldon, C. N.	East Cleveland	·30	No.
Sommer, Fred.	East Cleveland	10	No.
Stahl, Frank	East Cleveland	9	No.
Taylor, Charles	East Cleveland	20	No.
Thompson, M. T.	East Rockport		
Barber, Robert	East Toledo	6	No.
Caswell, Corbin	East Toledo	3	No.
Chamberlin, Robert	East Toledo	5	No.
Harris, William	East Toledo	5	No.
Holst, L.	East Toledo		
Kenna, Frank	East Toledo	3	No.
Lerdig, William	East Toledo	3	No.
Schrier, John	East Toledo	3	No.
Tracy, William	East Toledo	3	No.
Warner, Elliott	East Toledo	4	No.
Whetmore, Luther	East Toledo	4	No.
Bullock, A. W.	Elyria	16	No.
Fay, W. L., & Co.	Elyria	18	No.
Johnston, C. W.	Elyria	18	No.
Adams, Frank	Euclid	8	No.
Ager, Geo.	Euclid	12	No.
Akins, Ralph	Euclid	22	No.
Avery, H., & Son	Euclid	14	No.
Berkhardt, J.	Euclid	10	No.
Bliss, Eugene	Euclid	18	No.
Brainard, Arthur	Euclid	35	Yes.
Brush, Col.	Euclid	16	No.
Cavanaugh, Chas.	Euclid	5	No.
Cavanaugh, John	Euclid	25	No.
Crosier, M.	Euclid	8	No.
Cushman, E. H.	Euclid		
Cushman, H., & Son	Euclid	10	No.
Davis, E.	Euclid	10	No.
Davis, John	Euclid	7	No.
Dille, W. H.	Euclid	20	No.
Durham, Mrs. Dr.	Euclid		No.

Ohio—Continued.

NAME.	Post Office.	Acres in Vines.	Wine Maker.
Gorham Bros.	Euclid	25	No.
Haskell, Mrs. J. K.	Euclid	14	No.
Harms Bros.	Euclid	60	Yes.
Hazen Bros.	Euclid	25	No.
Hermle, S.	Euclid	15	No.
Hunt, R. A.	Euclid	15	No.
Ghy, Geo.	Euclid	15	No.
Keyerleber Bros.	Euclid	17	Yes.
Manty, A.	Euclid	18	No.
Mertzel, John	Euclid	33	Yes.
Nash, Geo.	Euclid	40	No.
Nolan, Joe.	Euclid	6	No.
Oliver, Wm.	Euclid	15	No.
Oswald, John	Euclid	12	No.
Palmer, Wm.	Euclid	10	No.
Payne Bros.	Euclid	15	No.
Pelton, M. S.	Euclid	10	No.
Peters, J.	Euclid	15	No.
Powers, O. T.	Euclid	23	Yes.
Priday, Alfred.	Euclid	30	No.
Priday, Fred.	Euclid	10	No.
Priday, Henry	Euclid	30	No.
Reidel, Philip	Euclid	10	No.
Richmond, Wm.	Euclid	10	No.
Schriber, J.	Euclid	7	No.
Schuster, E.	Euclid	15	No.
Sherkey, John.	Euclid	7	No.
Sherman, John	Euclid	8	No.
Slade Bros.	Euclid	20	No.
Smoltz, John.	Euclid	9	No.
Stray Bros.	Euclid	25	No.
Stray, O. A.	Euclid	15	Yes.
Tracy Bros.	Euclid	65	No.
Verbsky Bros.	Euclid	100	Yes.
Vorce, H. G.	Euclid	26	No.
Welch, O. B.	Euclid	7	No.
Whetmore, H. S.	Euclid	55	No.
White, G.	Euclid	10	No.
White, H.	Euclid	7	No.
Blodget, Mr.	Fairmount	5	No.
Buckley, J.	Fairmount	10	No.
Chryst Bros.	Fairmount	10	No.
Hellwig, Albert F.	Fairmount	5	No.
Keane, Henry	Fairmount	10	No.
Middleton, George C.	Fairmount	8	No.
Phare, William	Fairmount	8	No.
Preyer, Charles	Fairmount	4	No.
Preyer, Emil	Fairmount	14	No.
Preyer, Robert	Fairmount	4	No.
Sambrook, George	Fairmount	4	No.
Spence, William	Fairmount	5	No.
Trowbridge, G. W.	Glendale	---------	---------
Sohn, John W. Z.	Hamilton	---------	---------
Norton, Clark	Hiram	---------	---------
Abbott, E. T.	Kelley's Island	10	No.
Beatty, Lewis	Kelley's Island	45	Yes.
Becker, Wm.	Kelley's Island	30	Yes.
Bowman, Sam	Kelley's Island	10	No.
Brown, Otto	Kelley's Island	10	No.
Cameron, A.	Kelley's Island	20	No.
Carpenter, C. C.	Kelley's Island	20	No.
Cattanach, H.	Kelley's Island	10	No.
Cogswall, F. W.	Kelley's Island	6	No.
Dodge, Otto	Kelley's Island	15	Yes.
Duvall, S. S.	Kelley's Island	25	No.
Eefers, H.	Kelley's Island	5	No.
Estes, James	Kelley's Island	40	No.
Fisher, Chas.	Kelley's Island	---------	Yes.
Hamilton Estate	Kelley's Island	100	No.
Hamilton, Robert	Kelley's Island	40	No.

Ohio—Continued.

NAME.	Post Office.	Acres in Vines.	Wine Maker.
Hauser, John	Kelley's Island	15	No.
Hess, Herman	Kelley's Island	10	No.
Huntington, Mrs. E. K.	Kelley's Island	15	No.
Irishman, H.	Kelley's Island	15	No.
Kastruck, J.	Kelley's Island	15	Yes.
Kelley, Addison	Kelley's Island	45	No.
Kelley, F. M.	Kelley's Island	8	No.
Kelley, G. A.	Kelley's Island	10	No.
Kelley, N.	Kelley's Island	12	No.
Kelley, W. D.	Kelley's Island	35	No.
Kelley's Island Wine Co.	Kelley's Island		Yes.
Koster, Mrs. H.	Kelley's Island	20	No.
Lang, Henry	Kelley's Island	8	No.
Lang, J. H.	Kelley's Island	12	No.
Lincoln, Joseph	Kelley's Island	12	No.
Meyer, Fred.	Kelley's Island	15	No.
Miller, Adam	Kelley's Island	15	No.
Maysey, R.	Kelley's Island	60	No.
Prignitz, H.	Kelley's Island	10	No.
Rauft, John	Kelley's Island	20	Yes.
Riedy, P.	Kelley's Island	25	No.
Schardler, Aug.	Kelley's Island	50	Yes.
Schardler, John	Kelley's Island	30	Yes.
Schardt, Adam	Kelley's Island	15	Yes.
Schlesselman, William	Kelley's Island	15	No.
Schorelt, Henry	Kelley's Island		Yes.
Seaton, James	Kelley's Island	12	No.
Seelholtzer, Charles	Kelley's Island	25	Yes.
Stokes, John	Kelley's Island	30	Yes.
Sweet Valley Wine Company	Kelley's Island		
Ward, E.	Kelley's Island	20	No.
Yuker, R.	Kelley's Island	7	No.
Allen, F.	Kirtland	10	No.
Carpenter, S. C.	Kirtland	20	No.
Clapp, Payson	Kirtland	6	No.
Hoose, George	Kirtland	15	No.
Hoose, Warren	Kirtland	10	No.
Hooper, Mr.	Kirtland	10	No.
Maskell, Geo.	Kirtland	8	No.
Randall Bros.	Kirtland	30	No.
Sanborn, Alden	Kirtland	10	No.
Traver, David	Kirtland	18	No.
Tryon, J. H.	Kirtland	18	No.
Upham, B. S.	Kirtland	8	No.
Wellman, M.	Kirtland	10	No.
Williams, A.	Kirtland	10	No.
Woodard, E. M.	Kirtland	20	No.
Coffin, Henry	Lakeside		Yes.
Duroy Wine Co.	Lakeside	10	
Graves, H. A.	Lakeside	14	No.
Johnson, C. D.	Lakeside	18	No.
Kelley, Robert	Lakeside	10	No.
Miller, H. H.	Lakeside	5	Yes.
Andrews, Mrs. E.	Lakewood	40	No.
Bayes, Harry	Lakewood	8	No.
Hall, Albert	Lakewood	10	No.
Hall, John C.	Lakewood	16	No.
Hall, M. C.	Lakewood	12	No.
Hall, T. C.	Lakewood	10	No.
Hotchkiss, Nobie	Lakewood	10	No.
Mail, Wm.	Lakewood	20	No.
Martinetsy, R. B.	Lakewood	12	Yes.
Mullalley, Thos.	Lakewood	10	No.
Nicolson, Ezra	Lakewood	75	No.
Peterson, Thos.	Lakewood	12	No.
Southern, Christ.	Lakewood	10	No.
Thompson, M. T.	Lakewood	8	No.
Townsend, Charles	Lakewood	8	No.
Wagar, F. H.	Lakewood	10	No.
Webb, Daniel	Lakewood	20	No.

Ohio—Continued.

NAME.	Post Office.	Acres in Vines.	Wine Maker.
Boving, Mrs. F. J.	Lancaster	3	No.
Schneider, John S.	Lancaster	30	Yes.
Van Burtons, Mr.	Lancaster		
Carver, A. M.	Little Mountain	10	No.
Hoose, Ezra.	Little Mountain	10	No.
Hoffman, George W.	Leipsic		
Nechter, John B.	Mansfield		
Palmer, F. R.	Mansfield	10	
Molitor, Casper.	Marblehead	20	Yes.
Schneiderer, C. G.	Marysville	1	Yes.
Woodruff, Theron	Mentor	10	No.
High, George M.	Middle Bass	15	Yes.
Lang, Peter	Middle Bass	10	Yes.
Rehberg, A.	Middle Bass	10	Yes.
Schardt, C.	Middle Bass	18	No.
Vogel, C.	Middle Bass	15	Yes.
Wehrle & Son	Middle Bass	50	Yes.
Wehrle, M.	Middle Bass	30	Yes.
Newton, G. F.	Millersburgh		
Johnson, F. H.	Musselman		
Vanderwort, John M.	New Antioch		
Miller, F. C.	New Philadelphia		
Axtell, Wm.	North Bass Island	29	Yes.
Boslaw, Mrs.	North Bass Island	10	No.
Combes, W. S.	North Bass Island	6	No.
Fox, A. J.	North Bass Island	10	No.
Fox, E. E.	North Bass Island	24	No.
Fox, Geo.	North Bass Island	12	No.
Herring, Geo.	North Bass Island	10	No.
Kellogg, H. S.	North Bass Island	25	Yes.
Kinney, E. L.	North Bass Island	20	No.
Cummings, Peter		18	Yes.
Fox, Peter	North Bass Island Wine Co.,	45	Yes.
Fox, Simon	North Bass Island	40	Yes.
Snide, Jasper		23	Yes.
Reichete, C.	North Bass Island	10	No.
Rinderly, Aug.	North Bass Island	8	No.
Smith, G. C.	North Bass Island	18	
Smith, Geo.	North Bass Island	24	
Smith, W. D.	North Bass Island	23	
Trehan, J.	North Bass Island	12	
Townsend, O. D.	North Bass Island	14	
Wines, Geo.	North Bass Island	23	
Dille, O. A.	Nottingham	10	
Eddy, Hays	Nottingham	10	
Gardner, A. C.	Nottingham	5	
Gardner, Perry	Nottingham	7	
Gawne, Frank	Nottingham		
Kniffin, Mrs.	Nottingham	5	
Lamb Bros.	Nottingham	20	
Lilly, Emline	Nottingham	15	
McClymonds, John	Nottingham	10	
Miller, James	Nottingham	5	
Smith, L. W.	Nottingham	10	
Stevens, A. P.	Nottingham	9	
Voorhees Bros.	Nottingham	8	
Dolaishe, Francis	Peachton	2½	Yes.
Ellithorp, Geo.	Peachton	6	No.
Henson, Charles	Peachton	4	No.
Kanker, Henry	Peachton	4	Yes.
Landy, G.	Peachton	6	No.
Landy, Henry	Peachton	6	Yes.
Landy, J.	Peachton	2	No.
Muggy, C.	Peachton	4	No.
Muggy, J. C.	Peachton	6	No.
Noeltner, A.	Peachton	4	Yes.
Pierce, F.	Peachton	3	No.
Stiffens, C. C.	Peachton	4	No.
Vogts, G.	Peachton	3	No.
Vogts, Henry	Peachton	2	No.

Ohio—Continued.

NAME.	Post Office.	Acres in Vines.	Wine Maker.
Brossia, Geo.	Perrysburg	1	No.
Brossia, John	Perrysburg	4	No.
Cook, Asher J.	Perrysburg	8	No.
Crain, Wm.	Perrysburg	3	No.
Dunipace, James	Perrysburg	18	Yes.
Horen, Casper	Perrysburg	4	No.
Hufman, John J.	Perrysburg	4	Yes.
Oliver, Paul	Perrysburg		
Penniwell, Perry	Perrysburg	4	No.
Eberswine, Fred.	Piccolo	10	No.
Bauer, Adam	Pipe Creek	5	Yes.
Ernst, C.	Pipe Creek	3	Yes.
Giesen, Fred.	Pipe Creek	3	Yes.
Lorch, Thaddeus	Pipe Creek	15	Yes.
Lorch, Theodore	Pipe Creek	15	Yes.
Ricenmulle, R.	Pipe Creek	15	Yes.
Textor, A.	Pipe Creek	1	Yes.
Windish, George	Pipe Creek	10	Yes.
Broughton, Mr.	Portage	1	
Muggy, John P.	Port Clinton		
Burggraff, F. W.	Put-in Bay	12	Yes.
Burggraff, Henry	Put-in Bay	13	Yes.
Burggraff, Mathias	Put-in Bay	70	Yes.
Doller, V.	Put-in Bay	15	Yes.
Engel, L., & Co.	Put-in Bay	10	Yes.
Fox, Nicholas	Put-in Bay	7	Yes.
Ingold, M.	Put-in Bay	12	Yes.
Kuner, Ed.	Put-in Bay	10	Yes.
Lungren & Rotert	Put-in Bay	17	Yes.
Miller, George F.	Put-in Bay	18	Yes.
Parker, A.	Put-in Bay	30	Yes.
Pfeifter, Henry	Put-in Bay	10	Yes.
Rehebesy, Wm.	Put-in Bay		
Reible, H.	Put-in Bay	10	Yes.
Riedling, Wm. O.	Put-in Bay	10	Yes.
Rotert, G. F.	Put-in Bay	9	Yes.
Ruh, Anton	Put-in Bay	13	Yes.
Ruh, Carl	Put-in Bay	18	Yes.
Stone, J.	Put-in Bay	10	Yes.
Vrooman, Philip	Put-in Bay	15	Yes.
Webster, Dr.	Put-in Bay	10	No.
Wigand, W.	Put-in Bay	12	Yes.
Beebe, Horace Y.	Ravenna		
Freeman, Isaac	Rex		
Stump, Levi	Richville		
Lord, Henry C.	Riverside		
Aspen, Isaac	Rocky River	10	No.
Bates, Ed.	Rocky River	5	No.
Gates, Chas.	Rocky River	5	No.
Alstaetter, Louis	Sandusky		
Alstaetter, William	Sandusky		Yes.
Bauer, John	Sandusky	5	Yes.
Blank, Chas.	Sandusky		
Becker, Wm.	Sandusky		Yes.
Cook & Co.	Sandusky		Yes.
Dorn, H.	Sandusky		
Engles & Krudwig	Sandusky		Yes.
Feick, Ph.	Sandusky	15	Yes.
Gensch, Louis	Sandusky		
Gunther, Aug.	Sandusky		
Hartsorn, Mrs. A.	Sandusky	22	No.
Hommel, M.	Sandusky		Yes.
Mills, Wm. H.	Sandusky		Yes.
Moos, Edward R.	Sandusky	10	Yes.
Ohly Bros.	Sandusky		
Schmidt, A., Jr., Wine Co.	Sandusky		Yes.
Schmidt, Peter	Sandusky		Yes.
Smith, George	Sandusky		
Stahle, George	Sandusky		
Stenk, Edward	Sandusky		

OHIO—Continued.

NAME.	Post Office.	Acres in Vines.	Wine Maker.
Stang, Frank	Sandusky	10	Yes.
Strobel, George	Sandusky		Yes.
Textor, A.	Sandusky		Yes.
Windish, F.	Sandusky	15	Yes.
Monroe & Wolcot	Sheffield Lake	20	No.
Smith, Peter	Sheffield Lake	15	No.
Rhoads, E. V.	St. Paris		
Albaugh, N. H.	Tadmor		
Howland, I. P.	Tallmadge	3	No.
Pierce, L. B.	Tallmadge		
Ashworth Bros.	Tippecanoe		
Brand, Henry, Wine Co.	Toledo	40	Yes.
Grasser, J.	Toledo	5	Yes.
Harris, W. C.	Toledo		
Koch, E. W. E.	Toledo	8	Yes.
Lenk Wine Co.	Toledo		Yes.
Rumeis, J.	Toledo	10	Yes.
Winsonred, L.	Toledo	7	Yes.
Berlisch, Fred.	Venice	20	Yes.
Cullen, N.	Venice	10	Yes.
Dorn, John G.	Venice	40	Yes.
Dreher, L.	Venice	20	Yes.
Heimlich, G.	Venice	13	Yes.
Klotz & Kromer	Venice	18	Yes.
Obergefall, J.	Venice		Yes.
Smith, G.	Venice	15	Yes.
Stauth, Mrs. J. C.	Venice	15	Yes.
Toole, B.	Venice	10	No.
Farnsworth, W. W.	Waterville	1	Yes.
Lower, Henry	West Cleveland	12	Yes.
Fields, E.	Wickliffe	8	
Fields, G.	Wickliffe	6	
Henisk, C.	Wickliffe	10	
Langshaw, D.	Wickliffe	10	
McArdle, M.	Wickliffe	25	
Prescott, Dr.	Wickliffe	16	
Provo, Mr.	Wickliffe	40	No.
Smart, S. W.	Willoughby	10	No.
Ward, John	Willoughby	20	No.
Boyd, Dr. S.	Wilmington		
Skimming, Robert	Wilmington		
Stoddard, Henry	Wilmington		
Taylor, Harvey	Wilmington		
Vantress, C. H.	Wilmington		
Weltz, Leo.	Wilmington		
Wolf, W. P.	Wilmington		
Jenkins, J.	Winona		

PENNSYLVANIA.

NAME.	Post Office.	Acres in Vines.	Wine Maker.
Straub, John N.	Allegheny City		
Metzgar, Levan	Altoona	11	Yes.
Gerbig, A. V.	Archibald		
Flick, Wm.	Bealsville	2	Yes.
Hoffman, J. L.	Bentleysville	15	Yes.
Strickler, Mr.	Dawson		Yes.
Carr Bros.	Erie		
Eaton, Johnston	Fairview		
Jaekel, Frederick	Hollidaysburg	13	No.
Strasser, John	Martinsburg	10	Yes.
Preston, Robt.	Monongahela		
Blaine, G. W.	North East	35	No.
Butt, A. W.	North East	30	Yes.
Butt, George	North East	12	No.

PENNSYLVANIA—Continued.

NAME.	Post Office.	Acres in Vines.	Wine Maker.
Carr, E. E.	North East	35	No.
Crawford Bros.	North East	40	No.
Davis, Fred.	North East	22	No.
Davis, O. W.	North East	20	No.
Dill, Robert	North East	30	No.
Elsworth, C. F.	North East	75	Yes.
Flemming, J. E.	North East	70	No.
Flemming, J. W.	North East	30	No.
Gay, Ira	North East	20	No.
Griffith, J. W.	North East	15	No.
Hammond, J. S.	North East	20	No.
Hard, Dr. A. B.	North East	20	No.
Higgins, John	North East	30	No.
Hillman, Rev. Mr.	North East	40	No.
Leet, Alfred	North East	30	No.
Leet, Calvin	North East	30	No.
Loop & Stettson	North East	25	No.
Morse, C. H.	North East	30	No.
Mottier, C. H.	North East	30	Yes.
Phillips, J. H.	North East	40	No.
Pierce, A. Y., & Son	North East	15	No.
Pierce Bros.	North East	60	No.
Scouller, E.	North East	20	No.
Scouller, J. B.	North East	10	No.
Seeley, Frank	North East	20	No.
Selkregg, George	North East	15	No.
Selkregg, L. D.	North East	15	No.
Selkregg, W. O.	North East	15	No.
South Shore Vineyard Co.	North East		
Stettson, A. C., & Co.	North East	25	No.
Stettson, John H.	North East	25	No.
Stinson, John	North East	40	No.
Taylor & Stockton	North East	20	No.
Whitehill, S. P.	North East	15	No.
Wing, A. K. & W. O.	North East	25	No.
Norton, Randall	Pittsburg		
Oler, Jonathan	Scenery Hill		
Shearn, Chris.	Tuckerton		
Nutt, A. C.	Uniontown		
Cleeland, J. J.	Washington	2	Yes.
Smith, Wm., & Son	Washington	2	No.
Schmidt, Chas.	Washington		
Bottomfield, Sam'l	Williamsburg	9	Yes.
Evans, Edw. J., & Co.	York		

RHODE ISLAND.

NAME.	Post Office.	Acres in Vines.	Wine Maker.
Rhodes, H. F.	East Greenwich	$\frac{1}{2}$	Yes.
Lewis, Sam.	Olneyville	$\frac{2}{3}$	
Cushman, Robt.	Pawtucket	$\frac{1}{2}$	No.
Haskell, W. H.	Pawtucket	$\frac{1}{4}$	No.
Nisbet, James	Pawtucket	$\frac{1}{2}$	No.
Channing, Dr. Wm. F.	Providence		
Manchetser, Silas	Providence	$\frac{1}{4}$	Yes.
Lawton, B. H.	Wickford		

SOUTH CAROLINA.

NAME.	Post Office.	Acres in Vines.	Wine Maker.
Satterwaite, S. C.	Aiken	15	No.
White, Tom	Anderson		
McCrary, Sam	Autun		
Bunch, Dr. G. A.	Clark's Hill	10	Yes.
Butt, Dr.	Clark's Hill	5	Yes.
Butler, Capt. J.	Clark's Hill	5	Yes.
Middleton, Col. R. H.	Clark's Hill	12	Yes.
Scott, R. H.	Clark's Hill	2	No.
Kirk & Reed	Cokesburg	2	Yes.
Reed, C. C.	Cokesburg	5	No.
Richland Wine Co.	Columbia	60	Yes.
Tillman, B. R.	Columbia	15	Yes.
Law, C. C.	Coronaca	4	Yes.
O'Neal, G. P.	Coronaca	8	Yes.
O'Neal, J. H.	Coronaca	7½	Yes.
Toushe, J. D.	Coronaca	½	Yes.
Hood, Prof.	Due West	1	Yes.
Mims, R. H.	Edgefield		
Land, C. S.	Foreston		Yes.
Beasley, C. C.	Greenville	12	No.
Beattie, W. E. & H. C.	Greenville	75	Yes.
Beattie, Mrs. J. E.	Greenville	3	No.
Buist, H. B.	Greenville	16	No.
David, J. E.	Greenville	60	Yes.
Donaldson, M. L.	Greenville		
Earle, Dr. William	Greenville	4	No.
Earle, T.	Greenville	1	Yes.
Euloe & Kemble	Greenville	10	Yes.
Gaffeur, August	Greenville	10	Yes.
Gearreaux, Mrs. F.	Greenville	5	No.
Gilreath, H. C.	Greenville	40	Yes.
Howel, A. M.	Greenville	2	Yes.
Hunt, Col. J. F.	Greenville	8	Yes.
Nelson & Rosseller	Greenville	30	Yes.
Putman, Mrs.	Greenville	5	No.
Stearns, Mr.	Greenville	5	Yes.
Weldon, Dr. R. T.	Greenville	5	Yes.
Coole, Tom	Greenwood	½	Yes.
Keller, J. Frank	Greenwood	¼	Yes.
Marshall, Dr. J. A.	Greenwood	1	Yes.
Marshall, S. B.	Greenwood	½	Yes.
Wells, W. J.	Greenwood	¼	Yes.
Zimmerman, M.	Greers	6	No.
Bunch, J. W.	Hamburg	7	No.
McGee, W. J.	Hodges	½	Yes.
Hughes, Dick	Jones	¼	Yes.
Sprott, Jos.	Jordan		Yes.
Barron, B. Pressley	Manning		Yes.
Conyers, W. I.	Manning		Yes.
Davis, T. James	Manning		Yes.
Emanuel, C. L.	Manning		Yes.
Anderson, J. C.	Moore	15	No.
Crenshaw, Matt.	Pendleton		
Patterson, A. E.	Pendleton		
Shanklin, E. H.	Pendleton		
Trescott, Henry	Pendleton	2	Yes.
Cochran, John W.	Pickens		
Day, Elias	Pickens		
Tillman, R. B.	Ropers		
Carey, John C.	Seneca	5	No.
Gignilliatt, G. W.	Seneca	5	Yes.
Lewis, Hasewell	Seneca	6	Yes.
Thompson, A. T.	Seneca		
Anderson, Gen. J. C.	Spartanburg		
Anderson, Col. Robert	Traveler's Rest	1	Yes.
Goodlet, Dr.	Traveler's Rest	1	Yes.
Brown, C. R. & P. H.	Waco		
Buerklino, George	Walhalla	5	Yes.
Gerber, Alvis	Walhalla	4	Yes.

SOUTH CAROLINA—Continued.

NAME.	Post Office.	Acres in Vines.	Wine Maker.
Harley, A. A. B.	Walhalla	2	Yes.
Kaufmann, John	Walhalla	4	Yes.
Kummerer, John	Walhalla	5	Yes.
Nelson, James	Walhalla	5	Yes.
Nield, Thomas	Walhalla	5	Yes.
Stapel Bros.	Walhalla	6	Yes.
Thaidigsmann Bros.	Walhalla	6	Yes.
Wanner, G.	Walhalla	20	Yes.
Winking, T. W.	Walhalla	25	Yes.
Pearson, J. Frank	Woodruff	1	Yes.

SOUTH DAKOTA.

NAME.	Post Office.	Acres in Vines.	Wine Maker.
Andrus, W. D. E.	Andrus	$\frac{1}{2}$	Yes.
Hutrische Society	Andrus	3	Yes.
De Linde, P.	Running Water		
McCrea, Thos.	Tyndall		Yes.
Fienert, A.	Tyndall	$\frac{1}{2}$	No.
Radway, E. M.	Wanire		Yes.

TENNESSEE.

NAME.	Post Office.	Acres in Vines.	Wine Maker.
Bennett, F. J.	Chattanooga		
Randall, M. O.	Drake	2	
Hughes, Louis	Dyersburg		
Vanderford, Chas. F.	Florence Station		
Range, J. M.	Gap Run		
Marugg, Chas., & Sons	Gruetli		
Barkley, J. M.	Jonesborough		
Mester, Geo.	Lawrenceburgh		
Conden, Wat.	Lewisburgh		
Barnes, B. B.	Memphis		
Converse, Rev. J. B.	Morristown	$\frac{1}{2}$	No.
Fuller, Dr. C. E.	Morristown	2	No.
Hickey, Rev. R. M.	Morristown	$\frac{1}{2}$	No.
Hodges, J. C.	Morristown	2	No.
Jones, Daniel	Morristown	1	No.
McCrary, G. B.	Morristown	1	No.
Sanders, Henry	Morristown	3	No.
Spoon, Jos.	Morristown	$\frac{1}{2}$	No.
Crass, M.	Murfreesborough		
Munson, J. E.	Murfreesborough		
Hofstetter, ——	Nashville	6	Yes.
Swiss, German, & Italian Colony.	Paradise Ridge		
Irvin, Dr. J. T.	Paris		
Delffs, Arnold	Shelbyville		
Meek, John M.	Strawberry Plains		
Harmley, Silas	Tracy City		

TEXAS.

NAME.	Post Office.	Acres in Vines.	Wine Maker.
Ziegler, Dr.	Alleyton	8	Yes.
Hayes, W. R.	Aransas		
Clark, Amasa	Bandera		
Erhard, C.	Bastrop		
Parvin, W. H.	Belle Plain		
Berger, H.	Bernardo	4	Yes.
Bretschneider, E.	Bernardo	4	Yes.
Trouchard, —	Bernardo	30	Yes.
Ruthven, Edwin V.	Blue Branch		
Shapard, J. H.	Brazoria		
Warren, Jerry	Brazoria		
Garrett, O. H. P.	Brenham		
Kessler, A. J.	Breslau	20	Yes.
Hopkins, Joseph	Brownsville		
Mayo, J. L.	Bryan		
Morrow, Dr. W. B.	Calvert		
Howard, Frank M.	Cameron		
Johnson, Jesse	Camp Colorado		
Schmidt, Dr. T. A.	Cat Spring		
Deats, W. S.	Clear Creek		
Hines, M. D.	Cleburne		
Wirth, Mrs.	Columbus	6	Yes.
Bupp, Mr.	Dallas		
Clark, W. J.	Dallas		
Cole, W. R.	Dallas		
Ross, W. W.	Dallas		
Braun, George	Denison	2	Yes.
Brown, Dan	Denison	1	No.
Fairbanks, I. I.	Denison	2	No.
Larkin, S.	Denison	2	No.
Munson, T. V.	Denison	12	No.
Perry, Edward	Denison	8	Yes.
Schoeff, André	Denison	2	Yes.
Schultz, F.	Denison	2	No.
Marr, James	El Paso		
Friedlander, J.	Fort Stockton		
Laake, F. A.	Frelsburg	10	Yes.
Leyendecker, J. F.	Frelsburg	5	Yes.
Miller, Charles	Frelsburg	10	Yes.
Mills, A. G.	Galveston		
Summers, Emery	Gatesville		
Talbot, R. E.	Georgetown		
Green, A. B.	Giddings		
Bower, L. J.	Graham		
Johnson, E. B.	Hallettsville		
Clarke, P. S.	Hempstead		
Perl, Dr. N.	Houston		
Stude, Alphonse	Houston		
Ford, H. H.	Jasper		
White, L. C.	Jasper		
McFarland, A.	Kerrville		
Robson, W. S.	La Grange		
Beaty, Lee	Luling		
Ward, Albert J.	Marshall		
Worswick, B. G.	Matador	20	Yes.
Krancher, J. H.	Millheim		
Hagemann, Wm.	New Ulm	15	Yes.
Unger, Philip	Palestine		
Moorhouse, T. M.	Prairieville		
Blodgett, Wm. A.	Refugio		
Fentress, Dr. D. W.	San Saba		
Logan, Geo. W.	Taylor		
Lantz, Benton	Veal's Station		
Billings, William	Victoria		
Durrett, Larkin	Weatherford		
Kelkrosh, M.	Weatherford	10	Yes.
MacKenzie, Dr. John R.	Weatherford		
Martin, John	Weatherford	5	No.
Sparks & Dawson	Weatherford	20	Yes.

TEXAS—Continued.

NAME.	Post Office.	Acres in Vines.	Wine Maker.
Thompson, S. D.	Weatherford	5	No.
Yates, William	Weatherford	15	Yes.
Van Vleck, Geo. W.	Woodville		
Kerber, Charles	Ysleta		

VIRGINIA.

NAME.	Post Office.	Acers in Vines.	Wine Maker.
Byers, Fred.	Afton	20	Yes.
Syers, Fred.	Bentivoglio	16	No.
Mosely, A. T.	Buckingham Court House		
Withwill, Wm.	Carter Bridge	5	No.
Abille, J. E.	Charlottesville	7	No.
Andrew, J. B.	Charlottesville	20	No.
Bowsork, W. H.	Charlottesville	15	No.
Bryan, J. R., Jr.	Charlottesville	40	No.
Barnley, W. R.	Charlottesville	25	No.
Caldbeck, S. W.	Charlottesville	15	No.
Chesbro, A. S.	Charlottesville	15	No.
Crockford, S. H.	Charlottesville	14	No.
Crockford, S. M.	Charlottesville	5	No.
Dabney, Dr. W. C.	Charlottesville	15	No.
Doringh, C. H. R.	Charlottesville	20	No.
Flannagan, B. C.	Charlottesville	14	No.
Friehr, Ed.	Charlottesville	14	No.
Gale, S. M.	Charlottesville		
Gentry, A. H.	Charlottesville	13	No.
Gentry, A. E.	Charlottesville	9	No.
Given & Helbish	Charlottesville	30	No.
Gordon, Marion	Charlottesville	16	No.
Harris, Capt. J. A.	Charlottesville	20	No.
Hoeberle, Jacob	Charlottesville	18	No.
Hoeberle, Louis	Charlottesville	14	No.
Hidger, Dr. C. H.	Charlottesville	11	
Holliday, A. L.	Charlottesville	30	No.
Holladay, W. A.	Charlottesville	22	No.
Hotopp, William	Charlottesville	75	Yes.
Jones, Joseph D.	Charlottesville	11	No.
Koebler, Val.	Charlottesville	10	No.
Levy, J. M.	Charlottesville	16	No.
Lyman, H. L.	Charlottesville	35	No.
Lyman, H. M.	Charlottesville	8	No.
McMurdo, C. E.	Charlottesville	22	No.
Marchant, H. C.	Charlottesville	13	No.
Mason, R. F.	Charlottesville	30	No.
Minor, W. W.	Charlottesville	9	No.
Mohning, Charles	Charlottesville	10	No.
Monticello Wine Co.	Charlottesville	60	Yes.
Moon, I. B.	Charlottesville	5	No.
Moore, John B.	Charlottesville	10	No.
Northrop, F. X.	Charlottesville	15	No.
Nullycombe, William	Charlottesville	16	No.
Porter, J. W.	Charlottesville	60	Yes.
Redmond, R. C.	Charlottesville	20	No.
Reireson, Oscar	Charlottesville	6	No.
Rossor, Gen. T. L.	Charlottesville	20	No.
Russow, A.	Charlottesville	11	No.
Townsend, J. C.	Charlottesville	13	No.
Watson, John D.	Charlottesville	10	No.
White, John M.	Charlottesville	13	No.
Williams, H. H.	Charlottesville	19	No.
Williams, T. W.	Charlottesville	15	No.
Wingfield, J. J.	Charlottesville	11	No.
Bird, Dr. R.	Cobham	40	No.
Mann, Wm.	Cobham	45	No.

VIRGINIA—Continued.

NAME.	Post Office.	Acres in Vines.	Wine Maker.
Vawter, C. E.	Crozet	9	No.
Durant, J. G.	Culpeper	18	No.
Gillam, J. A.	Eastham	16	No.
Holladay, A. L.	Eastham	50	No.
Magnider. Col. H. M.	Eastham	25	No.
Schackleford, D. O.	Eastham	25	No.
Thurman, T. L.	Eastham	35	No.
Gray, J. H.	Falls Church		
Arnaud, G.	Fredericksburg	20	Yes.
Hunter, C. E.	Fredericksburg	15	Yes.
Bazile, J. M.	French Hay	12	Yes.
Ashby & McKay	Front Royal		
Arthrell, Wm.	Glendower		
Marsh, W. Gordon	Glendower	10	No.
Baker, H. C.	Gordonsville	10	No.
Barbour, P. P.	Gordonsville	20	No.
Bausmann & Knox	Gordonsville	20	No.
Boston, H. L.	Gordonsville	9	No.
Cadmus, C. V.	Gordonsville	40	No.
Davis, F. B.	Gordonsville	13	No.
Field, Gen. Jas. G.	Gordonsville	25	No.
Frash & Co.	Gordonsville	110	Yes.
Godwin, I.	Gordonsville	10	No.
Goodman, H.	Gordonsville	10	No.
Goss, E.	Gordonsville	11	No.
Hopkinson, I.	Gordonsville	14	No.
Jones, T. S.	Gordonsville	12	No.
Knox, C.	Gordonsville	15	No.
Linney, C.	Gordonsville	22	No.
Lovelock, I.	Gordonsville	12	No.
Newman, Dr.	Gordonsville	10	No.
Newman, Reuben	Gordonsville	14	No.
Schiverchart, Chas.	Gordonsville	15	Yes.
Scott, E. W.	Gordonsville	14	No.
Stratton, R. H.	Gordonsville	10	No.
Wilkie, M.	Gordonsville	16	Yes.
Higginbotham, S. T. B.	Grantland	5	Yes.
Baier, F.	Greenfield	80	Yes.
Smith & Englehard	Greenfield		Yes.
Hilbers, Wm.	Greenwood	12	No.
Smith, Geo. C.	Hanover	5	No.
Wickhanis, Wm. C.	Hanover	15	No.
Heicken, C. A.	Hay Market		
Johnson, A. H.	Hay Market		
Hanley, C.	Heswick	18	No.
Payne, John L.	Heswick	17	No.
Randolph, W. R.	Heswick	18	No.
Bird, Wm. B.	King and Queen Court House		
Turnbull, R.	Lawrenceville		
Anderson, Joseph R., Jr.	Lee Station	10	No.
Schuricht, H. G.	Lindsay	14	No.
Watkins, George	Lindsay	15	No.
Lentz, T., & Co.	Livingston	20	Yes.
Walker, S. G.	Lynchburg		Yes.
Harnish, H. E.	Manchester	6	No.
Woolnough, C.	Mechum's River		
Lentz, F.	Montreal	50	Yes.
Dodge, Albert	Norfolk		
Jeffress, W. C.	Nottoway Court House		
Newman, J. Q.	Orange	15	No.
Hotopp, Wm. H.	Proffit	35	Yes.
Miner, W. W.	Proffit	17	No.
Russow, Adolph	Proffit	10	Yes.
Smith, Tho. I.	Proffit	10	No.
Holladay, W. L.	Rapidan	3	No.
Taylor, C. W.	Rappahannock	20	No.
Bowcock, W. H.	Ravenna	15	No.
Farish, W. G.	Ravenna	11	No.
Carnaga, J. B.	Richmond	17	Yes.
Crenshaw, O. A.	Richmond	20	No.

VIRGINIA—Continued.

NAME.	Post Office.	Acres in Vines.	Wine Maker.
Dudley, James	Richmond	10	No.
Ferrandini, R., & Son	Richmond	35	Yes.
Gilmore, M.	Richmond	20	No.
Heckler, S.	Richmond	6	No.
Jeter, L. H.	Richmond	3	No.
Kratz, John A.	Richmond	30	No.
Swinford, Howard	Richmond	8	No.
Mosby, J. D. & A. F.	Richmond	8	No.
Miller, M. A.	Richmond	40	Yes.
Pulliam, A. T.	Richmond	6	No.
Puscci, Michael	Richmond	5	No.
Smith, Col. Norman	Richmond	9	No.
Tignar, J. C.	Richmond	4	No.
Farish, William	Rio	10	No.
Nuttecombe, William	Rio	10	No.
Stockton, Mrs.	Rio	5	No.
Taylor, B.	Rio	5	No.
Prior, George W.	Ruckersville	10	No.
Rives, Thomas F.	San Marino		
Flowers, Ed.	Shadwell	18	No.
Holden, A.	Shadwell	13	No.
Smith, J. Massie	Shadwell	16	No.
Taylor, H.	Shadwell	9	No.
Montrose Wine Co.	Smithfield	4	Yes.
Goss, E. L.	Somerset	20	No.
Goss, John W.	Somerset	10	No.
Newman, R. M.	Somerset	20	No.
Christenberger, W. A.	Stony Point	10	No.
Ferguson, J. R.	Stony Point	21	No.
Goss, J. A.	Stony Point	15	No.
Nelson, P. W.	Stony Point	40	No.
Salmon, W. H.	Stony Point	16	No.
Peters, W., & Co.	Woodstock		
Wheateley, Walter	Yancy's Mills	10	No.

WEST VIRGINIA.

NAME.	Post Office.	Acres in Vines.	Wine Maker.
Chapman, T. S.	Holliday's Cove		
Ryman, A.	Wheeling	2	Yes.
Walter, Frank	Wheeling	4	Yes.
Wilhem, Mr.	Wheeling	5	Yes.
Linders, J.	Winfield		

WISCONSIN.

NAME.	Post Office.	Acres in Vines.	Wine Maker.
Kellogg, Geo. J.	Janeville		
Plumb, J. C.	Milton		
Greulich, A., & Sons	Milwaukee.		

INDEX.

www.ingramcontent.com/pod-product-compliance
Lightning Source LLC
Chambersburg PA
CBHW030358270326
41926CB00009B/1170

* 9 7 8 3 3 3 7 3 3 1 6 2 7 *